'Reveal[s] the breathtaking gamble that _____ of the era of sail. Tim Cla_____ Phil Craig . . . have _____ of participants' vivid le_____ a revisionist approach to the Trafalgar legend whi_____ _____ght the enemy to bay with a hurricane _____ _____ detach____nt, seeking fres_____

_____ey Times

'Drawing on new archive material, this bloody account of the carnage that was Trafalgar reveals why Nelson was truly Britain's God of War.'

Daily Mail

'Excellent . . . comprehensively researched, vividly written and judiciously argued. Wonderfully detailed pen portraits . . . Much new material from French and Spanish sources gives a rounded picture . . . and it is this perspective from both sides of the battle that makes the book so compelling . . . Clayton and Craig have written about conflict before and it shows.'

Saul David, *Daily Telegraph*

'If you want just one book that will show how this flood of new material can transform a story you thought you knew, while at the same time keeping you gripped like a page-turner novel, buy *Trafalgar: the Men, the Battle, the Storm* by Tim Clayton and Phil Craig. A landmark book.'

Colin White, *Observer*

'A balanced account. Clayton and Craig painstakingly point out that the legendary Nelson and the men of his fleet were not the only heroes of Trafalgar . . . One of the book's greatest strengths is the attention paid to the "perfect storm" that began only hours after the fighting had stopped and gave rise to incredible acts of heroism and self-sacrifice.'

Glasgow Herald

'Vivid and compelling . . . an account of significant importance.'

Naval Review

'Excellent . . . Clayton and Craig score with their almost minute-by-minute detail of the fighting on 21 October.'

Independent

'It reads like a novel and is the most fluent account of Trafalgar for a generation.'

Ships Telegraph

'There are many detailed personal stories here that are not well known and the authors have done a good job in telling their story. This searing, visceral, giant of a book will surely be regarded as a classic of naval literature.'

Peter Hore, *Warships International Fleet Review Literary Supplement*

Also by Tim Clayton and Phil Craig

Finest Hour
End of the Beginning

TRAFALGAR

the men, the battle, the storm
TIM CLAYTON & PHIL CRAIG

HODDER

First published in Great Britain in 2004 by Hodder and Stoughton
A division of Hodder Headline
This edition published in 2005

A Hodder paperback

1

A CIP catalogue record for this title
is available from the British Library

Maps and diagrams by Sandra Oakin

ISBN 0 340 83028 X

Typeset in Garamond by
Hewer Text Ltd, Edinburgh
Printed and bound by
Clays Ltd, St Ives plc

Hodder Headline's policy is to use papers that are natural,
renewable and recyclable products and made from wood
grown in sustainable forests. The logging and manufacturing
processes are expected to conform to the environmental
regulations of the country of origin

Hodder and Stoughton Ltd
A division of Hodder Headline
338 Euston Road
London NW1 3BH

To Lily Rose

Contents

Battle Plans

Chapter Illustrations

The illustrations at the beginning of each chapter and the captions below originate from the *Liber Nauticus* by Dominic and John Thomas Serres, first published in 1805:

'The numerous applications for rudiments to acquire a knowledge of the Drawing of shipping or ships, will, I should hope, be sufficient excuse for introducing this work to the notice of the public.'

CHAPTER ONE: 'Represents a ship of the line preparing to sail, with the men on the yards unfurling the sails.'

CHAPTER TWO: 'Capsterns, used for heaving up the cables, or to wind-up any weighty body such as masts, artillery, &c.'

CHAPTER THREE: 'A ship of the line going before the wind, with scudding sails set.'

CHAPTER FOUR: 'Rope made into what is called a coil.'

CHAPTER FIVE: 'A ship of the line *close-hauled.*'

CHAPTER SIX: 'The stern of a frigate. The stern of a ship is terminated by the taffarel above, and by the counters below; it is limited on the sides by the quarter pieces, and the intermediate space comprises the galleries and windows of the cabins.'

CHAPTER SEVEN: 'A frigate taken *all aback.* Aback is the situation of the sails when their surfaces are flatted against the mast by the force of the wind.'

CHAPTER EIGHT: 'A cutlass and hatchet for boarding.'

CHAPTER NINE: 'A frigate *going about*. About means the situation of a ship immediately after she has tacked, or changed her course by going about, and standing on the other tack.'

CHAPTER TEN: 'A gun, carriage and tackle.'

CHAPTER ELEVEN: 'Is a frigate lying-to, or *lying-by*, which means the situation of a ship when she is retarded in her course, by arranging the sails in such a manner as to counteract each other with nearly an equal effort, and render the ship almost immoveable with respect to her progressive motion or *headway*.'

CHAPTER TWELVE: 'Is called a grapple.'

CHAPTER THIRTEEN: 'The representation of a ship in stays, in the manoeuvre of tacking, at the moment the word is given to rise *tacks* and *sheets*.'

CHAPTER FOURTEEN: 'Cannister shot, chain-shot and bar-shot.'

CHAPTER FIFTEEN: 'A ship *casting*. Casting, in navigation, is the motion of falling off, so as to bring the direction of the wind on either side of the ship, after it has blown for some time right a-head.'

CHAPTER SIXTEEN: 'Represents an anchor.'

CHAPTER SEVENTEEN: 'Is a ship scudding under her foresail. The principal hazards to scudding are difficulty of steering, while for want of sea room she is in danger of being wrecked on a lea shore, a circumstance too dreadful and too well understood to require explanation.'

CHAPTER EIGHTEEN: 'Are a sort of close casks, called buoys, which are made fast by a rope to the anchor, to determine the place where the anchor is situated. Those in the form of a cone are generally used to point out dangerous banks and shallows.'

CHAPTER NINETEEN: 'Is a ship lying to under try-sail and storm stay-sail. *Trying* is the situation in which a ship lies nearly in the *trough* or hollow of the sea in tempest, particularly when it blows contrary to her course.'

CHAPTER TWENTY: 'An anchor.'

CHAPTER TWENTY-ONE: 'Is a ship under a jury fore-mast. A jury fore-mast is a temporary or occasional mast erected in a ship to supply the place of one which has been carried away by a tempest, in battle, or by the labouring of a ship in turbulent sea.'

CHAPTER TWENTY-TWO: 'Represents a cleat.'

CHAPTER TWENTY-THREE: 'Represents a ship veering.'

CHAPTER TWENTY-FOUR: 'Crest from author's Address To The Amateurs of Marine Drawing.'

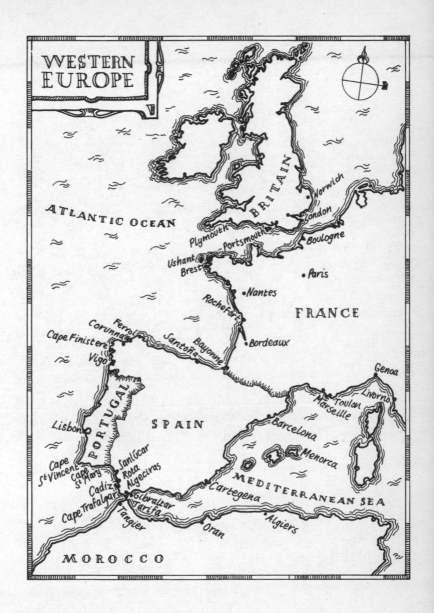

British and Combined Fleets
October 1805

British Fleet

Weather Division

Victory Vice Admiral Horatio, Viscount Nelson; Captain Thomas
 Hardy
Téméraire Captain Eliab Harvey
Neptune Captain Thomas Fremantle
Leviathan Captain Henry Bayntun
Conqueror Captain Israel Pellew
Agamemnon Captain Sir Edward Berry
Britannia Rear Admiral William Carnegie, Earl of Northesk; Captain
 Charles Bullen
Africa Captain Henry Digby
Ajax Lieutenant John Pilfold (in absence of Captain William
 Brown)
Orion Captain Edward Codrington
Minotaur Captain Charles Mansfield
Spartiate Captain Sir Francis Laforey

Lee Division

Royal Sovereign Vice Admiral Cuthbert Collingwood; Captain Edward
 Rotheram
Belleisle Captain William Hargood
Mars Captain George Duff
Tonnant Captain Charles Tyler

Bellerophon Captain John Cooke
Colossus Captain James Morris
Achille Captain Richard King
Revenge Captain Robert Moorsom
Defiance Captain Philip Durham
Dreadnought Captain John Conn
Swiftsure Captain William Rutherford
Polyphemus Captain Robert Redmill
Defence Captain George Hope
Thunderer Lieutenant John Stockham (in absence of Captain William
    Lechmere)
Prince Captain Richard Grindall

Frigates and Smaller Vessels
Euryalus Captain Henry Blackwood
Naiad Captain Thomas Dundas
Phoebe Captain Thomas Capel
Sirius Captain William Prowse
Pickle Lieutenant John Lapenotière
Entreprenante Lieutenant Robert Young

The Combined Fleet

Rearguard
Neptuno Commodore Cayetano Valdés
Scipion Captain Charles Bérenger
Intrépide Captain Louis Infernet
Formidable Rear Admiral Pierre Dumanoir; Captain Jean-Marie
    Letellier
Mont-Blanc Captain Guillaume Lavillegris
Duguay-Trouin Captain Claude Touffet
Rayo Commodore Enrique Macdonnell
San Francisco de Asís Captain Luis Flores

Centre

San Agustín Commodore Felipe Cajigal

Héros Captain Jean-Baptiste Poulain

Santísima Trinidad Rear Admiral Báltasar de Cisneros; Commodore Xavier de Uriarte

Bucentaure Vice Admiral Pierre Villeneuve; Captain Jean-Jacques Magendie

Neptune Captain Esprit-Tranquille Maistral

San Leandro Captain José Quevedo

Redoutable Captain Jean-Jacques Lucas

Vanguard

San Justo Captain Miguel Gastón

Indomptable Captain Jean-Joseph Hubert

Santa Ana Vice Admiral Ignacio de Álava; Captain José Gardoquí

Fougueux Captain Louis-Alexis Baudouin

Monarca Captain Teódoro de Argumosa

Pluton Commodore Julien Cosmao-Kerjulien

Squadron of Observation

Algésiras Rear Admiral Charles Magon; Commander Laurent Le Tourneur (acting captain)

Bahama Commodore Dionisio Alcalá Galiano

Aigle Captain Pierre Gourrège

Montañés Captain Francisco Alcedo

Swiftsure Captain Charles-Eusèbe L'Hospitalier-Villemadrin

Argonaute Captain Jacques Epron

Argonauta Captain Antonio Pareja

San Ildefonso Commodore José de Vargas

Achille Captain Louis Deniéport

Principe de Asturias Admiral Federico Gravina; Commodore Rafael de Hore

Berwick Jean Filhol-Camas

San Juan Nepomuceno Commodore Cosme de Churruca

Frigates and Brigs

Rhin Captain Michel Chesneau
Hortense Captain Louis La Marre La Meillerie
Cornélie Captain Jules-François de Martinenq
Thémis Captain Nicolas Jugan
Hermione Commander Jean-Michel Mahé
Furet Lieutenant Pierre Demay
Argus Lieutenant Yves-François Taillard

Authors' Note

To avoid confusion the ranks of French and Spanish officers have been translated to the nearest British equivalent. Accordingly, the Spanish *brigadier* or French *chef de division* has become commodore. There was no direct British equivalent for the French *enseigne* or Spanish *alférez*, so we have used the term sub-lieutenant. *Guardias Marinas*, *gardes de la marine* and *aspirants* have all been translated as midshipmen. We have avoided continuous reiteration of grades of admiral. Vice Admiral Nelson is usually referred to for convenience as Admiral Nelson. The only full admiral in either fleet was Gravina.

We have followed the practice of their respective biographers in using the shortened forms Latouche and Churruca for Louis-René Levassor, comte de Latouche-Tréville and Don Cosme Damián de Churruca y Elorza. Spanish names have been simplified: the Spanish historian Pelayo Alcalá Galiano contracted the name of his forebear Dionisio Alcalá Galiano to Galiano and we have imitated his usage for Dionisio and his son Antonio. After the revolution French officers generally dropped all signs of aristocracy in their names so that Pierre-Charles de Villeneuve became Villeneuve and Auguste-Marie Gicquel des Touches was Gicquel.

Where commonly understood British versions of foreign place names exist we have used them. So Cádiz is Cadiz and La Coruña is Corunna. Manuscripts have been transcribed exactly, as far as possible, without use of *sic*. Within quotations the names of ships have been italicised only where they were italicised in the source.

1

The Miradors of Cadiz

Cadiz stands on an island, just off the end of a long, narrow spit of land, surrounded by the Atlantic. From the Tavira Tower, the tallest mirador in the city, you can just see where the battle took place. Looking to the south, long, sandy beaches stretch down towards Cape Trafalgar. The ships fought on the horizon, nearer to Cape Roche than Trafalgar itself, a few miles from the shore. In that direction you can watch the waves breaking on the rocky shoals that still put mariners on their guard. Behind you, to the north and east, is the wide expanse of sparkling, sheltered water in Cadiz Bay, while to the south-east the main navigable channel sweeps round past the salt pans of the marshy Isla de León (still Spain's principal naval base) to the dockyard of La Carraca where the King of Spain's ships were built and repaired.

On a sunny day – and most days here are sunny – the streets of the old town radiate in black lines of deep shadow from around the base of the Tower. They have changed little since 1805: they are too narrow to take much traffic so most people walk, as they did then. The exception is the Alameda, a broad avenue overlooking the entrance to the bay. There, the elegant ladies of Cadiz still seek the shade of the exotic American trees planted along its sides. At its western end stands the glorious baroque Iglesia del Carmen where the officers of the Combined Fleet heard mass before putting to sea. From the windows of the Parador Hotel Atlantico you can watch the sun set over the fort and lighthouse of San Sebastian, look out over the stretch of water that was patrolled by Admiral Collingwood's blockading squadron and see the rocks, a few hundred yards away, that ripped the bottom out of Admiral Villeneuve's flagship during the great storm that followed the battle.

In 1805 Cadiz was the most elegant and opulent city in Spain, less grand than haughty Madrid, with its court and its aristocracy, but far more cosmopolitan. Other Spanish towns were painted white but none shone like Cadiz where the houses were faced in white marble. One writer compared it to 'a great alabaster ship floating in the midst of the seas'. The railings of the many balconies and the grilles over ground-floor windows were painted sea green. Great wooden doors, studded with brass, opened on to blue-tiled patios, luxuriant with tropical plants. Rooms were furnished with mahogany, gilt and fine glass, and with fashionable luxuries imported from France, Italy and England. The graceful façades of its harmonious, four-storey buildings concealed the roofs so that the whiteness rose into the blue sky, interrupted only by the tiled steeples and cupolas of the churches. And above all this floated the 160 miradors from which the merchants of Cadiz scoured the horizon for their homeward-bound vessels. The Tavira was the official watchtower and from here, during the summer of 1805, the city's watchmen focused their long brass telescopes on the ships of the Royal Navy.

In his fifty-seven years Vice Admiral Cuthbert Collingwood had travelled widely, and his informed opinion was that warm and windy Cadiz had 'the advantage of the finest climate in the world'. At seven in the morning on Tuesday 20 August 1805 he was on board his flagship *Dreadnought*, cruising as usual a few miles off Cadiz with his dog, Bounce, at his side. Collingwood only had three battleships, or ships-of-the-line, as they were known, because the main Spanish fleet was not in Cadiz. One, the *Colossus*, was currently inspecting a brig flying the Swedish flag, as many Spanish merchants did when trying to run his blockade.

Through his telescope, the admiral fixed his eye briefly on the harbour and made a routine count of the eight tall masts to be seen there. Four other ships were stationed near the entrance to the bay. Collingwood knew Cadiz well. He had blockaded it before in wartime and had visited it during peace. On the way home from the Mediterranean British warship often paused there to pick up a cargo of silver coins for safe carriage to England. The commission offered a valuable supplementary income for British captains. There were few such perks on blockade duty.

Self-sacrifice and duty were the watchwords of the modern navy, immensely powerful yet overstretched, so crammed with ambitious talent that it no longer promised the highroad from ability to fortune as it had fifty years earlier. Success could still bring affluence, though. Collingwood was the son of a failed Newcastle merchant but, thanks to his flourishing naval career, he had married the Lord Mayor's daughter in 1791. Since then his time with Sarah had been brief. Long years spent watching the French fleet in Brest had led him to teach his captains to be as self-denyingly stoic and disciplined as he was. He was cultured and sensitive, with a dry sense of humour. At moments his letters are wickedly funny. But he was stern: he hated drunkenness and distrusted novels, especially for girls, and this was an issue close to his heart since his eldest daughter, also Sarah, had just turned thirteen. He wanted very much to go home.

As a ship's captain he was a compassionate humanitarian, fair-minded, reluctant to flog. He loved his ships' companies, and they regarded him with affectionate respect. But the views of his brother officers were mixed. Many never penetrated his reserve. One junior later wrote that he considered him 'a selfish old bear. That he was a brave, stubborn, persevering and determined officer everyone acknowledged, but he had few, if any, friends and no admirers. In body and mind he was iron, and very cold iron.'

Whatever his faults, Collingwood was undoubtedly intelligent and cool-headed, and these qualities came to the fore when, later on the

3

morning of 20 August, unfamiliar sails were sighted on the horizon – first six, then twenty-six, then thirty-six. Collingwood was not expecting friends: there was only one explanation for such a large force. This was the French and Spanish Combined Fleet, known to be at sea under the command of Vice Admiral Pierre Villeneuve. The Royal Navy had been chasing these ships for six months, and although Collingwood had been warned that they had left Ferrol in northern Spain he had not expected them to come south. Yet, undeniably, they were now at Cadiz, and fast approaching Collingwood's own tiny squadron. His five ships – *Dreadnought*, *Colossus* and *Achille*, with the *Niger* frigate and the *Thunder* bomb-vessel in attendance – were in great danger, caught half-way between the leading vessels of the Combined Fleet and the smaller Spanish squadron in Cadiz Bay.

Dreadnought's officers swept Cadiz with their telescopes again. As yet there was no activity. Nor were Villeneuve's ships crowding on sail. They might not have realised that Collingwood's ships were British. Collingwood's chief problem was that the slow *Thunder* was nearest to the oncoming enemy, so he had to buy time to help it get away. By moving away very slowly, as if there was no danger, he tried to deceive the enemy long enough for *Thunder* to escape. The ruse worked for two hours, but then a squadron broke away from the Combined Fleet and the chase was on. *Thunder* would have been caught if her captain had not had the wit to hide in the shallow water of the Trafalgar shoals where the enemy's larger vessels dared not follow. Collingwood's other four ships had enough of a lead to beat their pursuers to the Strait of Gibraltar. With his retreat into the Mediterranean secure, Collingwood sent back his fastest ship, *Colossus*, to reconnoitre. When some ships made a push at her, Collingwood tacked to support her. The French and Spanish withdrew to Cadiz.

Next day a frigate arrived to warn Collingwood that Villeneuve was coming. He sent it to London with the news that the Frenchman was already in Cadiz.

A caricature by George Woodward, published early in 1805, summed up Spain's dilemma succinctly. *Spanish Comfort* depicted Napoleon Bonaparte threatening a Spaniard and exclaiming, 'By my imperial dignity, I'll thrash you if you don't fight', while a belligerent John Bull dressed as a sailor retorted, 'And by my blue jacket and trousers I'll drub you if you do.' Spain was sandwiched between bullies, afraid of both. Her land border made her vulnerable to Napoleon's army, the largest in the world, while her sea trade lay at the mercy of the mighty Royal Navy. Cadiz felt these pressures more than any other city in Spain.

The population was about 72,000, of which more than one in ten were foreigners, selling goods to South America and buying Andalucían and American products to send home. Three-quarters of all trade with Spain's enormous empire passed through this port. It was to Cadiz that Spanish treasure fleets had always come, and nearly all New World silver was still landed there. Every European country trading with Asia had an office in the city, because Oriental trade was done with hard cash and silver money was obtained from Cadiz. There were close links with France, which exported cloth and other manufactured goods through Cadiz to Latin America, but Great Britain was by far Spain's largest national export market.

London's representative in Cadiz was James Duff, a sherry merchant, who had lived in Andalucía so long that even Englishmen knew him as Don Diego Duff. He had moved to Spain in 1765 when he was twenty-nine. Now, still unmarried, he was growing old, but his mind was still acute. His business was big – the British bought more wine from Spain than they bought from France – and his London agent was George Sandeman, whose company still thrives. Duff had presided over the ups and downs of Britain's relationship with Spain, and tried to smooth the ride.

Between wars, invasions and blockades, Spain was trying to modernise and exploit her South American provinces. The silver mines of New Spain, Peru and La Plata were restored, and Cuba had become a rival to the British and French sugar islands in the Caribbean. To defend these possessions and guard the route home, Spain had invested heavily in her navy; by 1790 she possessed as many warships as France. The most promising young officers were instructed in advanced mathematics, astronomy, navigation and cartography as the Armada Española, the Spanish navy, led an effort to discover, map and publish the resources of the Empire.

Dionisio Alcalá Galiano was one of the heroes of Spain's new scientific navy, a gifted mathematician, a renowned navigator and an experienced explorer. He was anglophile through science, not politics, believing British mathematicians superior to French. He admired the Royal Navy for its professionalism and even spoke a little English. Knowledge of the English language was then rare in Europe (merchants or sea officers from different nations generally communicated in French) and he was proud of his skill.

Galiano helped to survey the coast of the Iberian peninsula for the first accurate *Atlas Maritimo de España*, then joined an expedition to survey the Magellan Strait and another to map the Azores. He set out with the celebrated explorer Alejandro Malaspina to survey the Spanish Empire. In 1792 King Carlos IV demanded, and Galiano undertook, a search in the Vancouver Strait for a North-west Passage from the west to the east coast of North America and proved that no such passage existed.

In 1794, when Galiano returned to Spain, his country was at war. The atheist republic of France had executed Louis XVI and Catholic Spain fought the French republicans alongside Britain. But defeats on the French border forced the King to sue for peace in 1795. A year later the French made Spain fight again, this time as their allies against Britain. This war brought a Royal Navy blockade to Cadiz: Galiano was ordered to break it and risk a voyage to Veracruz in modern Mexico to bring back much-needed silver to Spain. At the end of 1798 he left Cadiz, evading the watching eyes of the blockading squadron. He returned the following spring with two ships and three frigates loaded with treasure, the sort of target British captains dreamed of. In sailing by an unexpected route out of sight of land, relying on his instruments and calculations, he outwitted the ships sent to intercept him and brought his flotilla of treasure ships into Santoña. The government was so impressed that he was sent off a second time. On this occasion the return journey was safer: the war had ended before he got back.

Somehow James Duff contrived to remain in Cadiz throughout the war, sending out occasional letters, even as the Royal Navy ambushed Cadiz-bound treasure ships, seized the island of Trinidad and won a major sea battle over the Spanish fleet at Cape St Vincent. At this time Cadiz suffered terribly: the constant British presence outside the port annihilated her foreign trade. During these five years the British captured goods to the value of one year's normal business. The misery ended when hostilities ceased in 1801. Duff and his many Spanish friends celebrated a sudden resurgence of prosperity. But peace did not last long. A new Anglo-French war, declared on 18 May 1803, threatened even graver harm.

Napoleon had forced King Carlos IV into treaties that obliged Spain to fight alongside the French. Desperate to avoid another conflict with Britain, Spain sought to remain neutral. As an alternative to joining the war, the government in Madrid secretly offered a massive subsidy and began a long, tortuous negotiation with Napoleon's government.

Vice Admiral Horatio Nelson, put in charge of the Mediterranean Fleet, was anxious to discover Spain's true intentions so renewed an old correspondence with James Duff. The admiral reminded the Consul, whose business life depended on long-established trust, that 'next January it is twenty-seven years since our first acquaintance'. Nelson had first visited Cadiz in 1777, as an eighteen-year-old acting lieutenant, and had struck up a rapport with the wine merchant. He asked Duff for reports on Spanish naval preparations. But there was little to report in the naval base: the Spanish were genuinely trying to remain neutral and their ships were disarmed. In summer 1803 Duff affirmed that 'in their arsenals nothing is doing; they are paying off all their Seamen, who are suffered to go to their Homes'. They were making no effort to equip ships and 'there is a total want of timber in the arsenal, where there is hardly any, but the Country Pine, & in other respects it is but very poorly provided'. Duff conveyed the admiral's good wishes to his friends among the Spanish officers at Cadiz to try to keep them friendly. In October 1803 he wrote, 'I am positively assured that the neutrality of Spain is <u>certainly definitively arranged</u>.'

Nelson was convinced. He wrote to one of his own officers: 'I am clearly of opinion that Spain has no wish to go to War with England, nor can I think that England has any wish to go to War unnecessarily with Spain.' But other British naval officers liked wars with Spain for the private profit they might bring, and within a year one had brought on a crisis. In September 1804 the Spanish put troops on to their ships in Ferrol to crush a revolt in the inaccessible Basque country. Alexander Cochrane, commanding the British squadron off Ferrol, reported to London that in his opinion the Basque revolt was a pretext for arming the ships 'too flimsy to go down'. Cochrane was wrong: after his warning the Spanish immediately took their troops off. But on the basis of his mistaken assessment the Admiralty sent orders to detain four Spanish frigates bringing coin from South America to Cadiz.

Admirals William Cornwallis at Brest and Nelson in the Mediterranean were each ordered to dispatch two frigates to do the job. Nelson had the intelligence to imagine how the Spanish captains would react to such a demand. He realised that the only way to avoid bloodshed was to send such an overwhelming force that the Spanish frigates could surrender with no loss of honour. Accordingly, he detached the capable Sir Richard Strachan, in the battleship *Donegal* with four frigates, to undertake the task. But Nelson's orders reached him a week too late and the battle had already taken place.

Two frigates from Britain joined two that were already on guard off Cadiz. The Spanish appeared unexpectedly early on 5 October 1804. The result was a disastrous, bloody mess. The Spanish frigates were crowded with the wives, families and belongings of diplomats and naval officers returning home from Montevideo, and were in no condition to fight a battle. But facing an equal number of enemy frigates the Spanish commander refused to surrender. He ran for Cadiz. Their zeal animated by the extraordinary amount of prize money on offer, the British attacked. The Spanish frigate *Mercedes* caught fire and blew up. The captain, his wife and seven children, with nineteen other Spanish ladies and their families, died. One officer, Diego Alvear, watched with his eldest son from one of the other frigates as his wife and the rest of their children died. Other women and children were killed by British gunfire.

The British government's behaviour was denounced throughout Europe. And yet, astonishingly, according to the report of Pierre Gourrège, a French captain stranded in Cadiz, the people there still 'tried to justify the conduct of the English . . . hoping that this attack will not destroy the harmony between the two nations'. One astute young observer, Antonio Alcalá Galiano, son of Dionisio, also saw how the population of Cadiz was torn. 'The act of piracy . . . filled the Spanish with sorrow and rage,' he wrote, and yet there were still plenty of people in Cadiz who thought that French ambition, and especially the personal ambition of the man who had recently declared himself Emperor, 'posed a menacing threat to the independence of Spain'. The pro-French faction in Cadiz called such people Mamelukes.

Both Antonio Galiano's mother and his uncle Juan were passionate, determined Mamelukes and they loathed Napoleon. They were as shocked by the British attack on the frigates as anyone else, but they also considered the reasons why the British government had complained of the Spanish government's behaviour and the way its neutrality appeared to aid the French. While they agreed that honour demanded they must fight, they blamed the French for dragging them towards a war that nobody wanted and that they regarded as a calamity. Dionisio Galiano was neither a Mameluke nor a supporter of France. He was too deeply concerned with his scientific studies and his professional life to take much interest in politics. Even so, he was horrified by the attack on the frigates and immediately volunteered for active duty.

In Madrid the balance was tipped and Spain declared war on Britain on 12 December 1804. Two months later James Duff informed Nelson of his impending departure: 'The War with this Country, has again rendered my continuing in it rather precarious . . . & I believe it will be but for a short time.' Having contrived to obtain freedom for Nelson's best intelligence officer, who had collided with a rock off Cadiz during a storm, he asked Nelson to allow some ships belonging to anglophiles in Cadiz to enjoy an undisturbed homeward voyage from Livorno. He expected to have to leave for England in the summer, but he was wrong. It is a sign of how unwilling the Andalucíans were to sever their relations with Britain and of the extent to which he was 'well loved and highly respected' in Cadiz that Don Diego Duff remained there and continued to be known to all as the British Consul.

Spain set strict limits on support for her French ally. The Spanish Admiral Federico Gravina, acting as ambassador to France, was forbidden to allow the Spanish fleet to be taken to Brest as it had been in the last war. Gravina's secret orders stated: 'It not being in the interests of Spain that her forces should go to Brest, this must be avoided with the double object of not leaving our coasts unprotected and of preventing our allies from succeeding in their much desired landing in England.' Throughout the campaign leading to the battle of Trafalgar, the Spanish passively opposed any plans to invade Britain. Madrid wished to maintain a balance of power between Spain's two powerful neighbours, and judged that total victory for Napoleon would be as appalling for Spain as a total defeat.

His Imperial and Royal Highness Napoleon Bonaparte, Emperor of France and King of Italy, suffered no such confusion of feeling and hoped that 1805 would be the year in which he settled the destiny of the world. To this end he had devised a strategy for the invasion and conquest of Britain. It was breathtaking in its sweep and ambition: he would move fleets around the world with the same aggressive confidence that he moved brigades around a battlefield. But it relied on the Admiralty in London falling for a trick.

Napoleon aimed to draw off a large proportion of the Royal Navy with a powerful feint towards the West Indies before suddenly gathering his resources in the English Channel for an invasion of the south coast of England. In March he had ordered Admiral Villeneuve to put to sea with eleven ships-of-the-line from the French Mediterranean base at Toulon, join up with the Spanish fleet at Cadiz, cross the Atlantic and wait for the arrival of other French squadrons. Nelson had pursued Villeneuve with ten battleships.

In late May Villeneuve's orders were modified. He was to attack British Caribbean possessions, wait in the islands, then return to Europe, joining up with more ships at Ferrol in northern Spain and at Rochefort and Brest in western France. He was then to sweep into the English Channel with sixty or more ships-of-the-line, enough to give the French army sufficient protection for it to mount a bold Channel crossing before the Royal Navy had time to reposition its forces. Delayed by bad weather and an obstinate British garrison off Martinique, Villeneuve sailed to seize the British islands on 4 June and had the luck to run into a convoy of British merchantmen on the eighth. They told him that Nelson had arrived and was scouring the West Indies for him. Hearing this, Villeneuve decided to head at once for the Channel.

Fortunately for the British, a fast dispatch boat sent by Nelson observed Villeneuve's fleet as it crossed the Atlantic and reached home in time to warn the Admiralty of the French course late on 8 July. Fearful of waking the irascible First Lord of the Admiralty, his assistants did not give the message to Sir Charles Middleton, Lord Barham, until next morning. He was furious at the delay. Still in his nightshirt, the octogenarian rapidly penned new orders to frustrate the French design. Villeneuve would not, as Napoleon had hoped, get through unopposed.

On 22 July a British force of fifteen ships-of-the-line, under Vice Admiral Sir Robert Calder, intercepted Villeneuve's twenty off Cape Finisterre at the north-western tip of Spain. In thick fog the ships fought an inconclusive battle, followed by a two-day stand-off in very light winds before they lost sight of each other. Short of provisions, with damaged ships and many sick men, Villeneuve put in to the nearest friendly port, Vigo, just north of the Portuguese border. After a few days he sailed a few miles north to the twin harbours of Corunna and Ferrol, where he joined up with other French and Spanish squadrons.

Villeneuve now had twenty-eight ships in reasonable order. All that remained, in Napoleon's view, was to sail to Brest, picking up along the way five more ships that had already put to sea from Rochefort, free the twenty-one battleships that were waiting at Brest under British blockade, and head for Boulogne. But, to Napoleon's fury, Villeneuve remained in Corunna.

In Britain and in the British fleet this was felt to be a moment of great danger. Against the twenty-one enemy ships in Brest, Villeneuve's twenty-eight, and five more from Rochefort, the British at that moment could gather together only twenty-six. 'The junction of the Hostile fleet semed to theretan the Endependance of Great Britain,' wrote Able Seaman James Martin of the *Neptune*, which had just returned to Plymouth for repairs and provisions. He worried that 'the British fleet was Dispersed into Diferant Eliments', reckoning that 'what few we could Muster at Home was Altogether Incompetent'.

Martin's next experience cannot have been reassuring. *Neptune* was ordered to join Sir Robert Calder and blockade Ferrol. But on finding Villeneuve there in force, Calder judged that his eight ships could not keep him penned in, and he decided to join up with Cornwallis's larger force off Brest. He reached the French port on 13 August. Two days later, to the immense relief of Martin and his shipmates, Nelson arrived from the West Indies with twelve more ships.

Neptune's captain, Thomas Fremantle, was an old friend of Nelson, having served under him in command of a frigate in the Mediterranean: 'I put a boat in the water and was the only ship that had communication with him, Proby [Lieutenant Granville Proby] carried him all the newspapers I had and saw him for two minutes, he says lord Nelson looked very ill and his message to me was that he was half dead.' Nelson sailed for England for a brief rest cure, but he left behind ten ships to help guard the approaches to the Channel.

Calder was then sent back towards Ferrol with eighteen ships, Thomas Fremantle's *Neptune* among them, to track down Villeneuve once more. His fleet was almost within sight of the Spanish naval base when on Tuesday, 20 August, 'a Stainge Sail hove in Sight under a press of Canviss and fired Signal Guns upon witch the fleet Hove two'. It was the frigate *Naiad*, bringing news. A few days earlier, off Ferrol, she had had a narrow escape from a French fleet that had pretended to be British, using the correct British signal to ask her to identify herself. As she fled, shot from the French frigates had passed overhead. It had to have been Villeneuve. But where had he gone? In fact he had arrived at Cadiz that same morning, 20 August, surprising Collingwood, but no one in Calder's fleet yet knew this. On board *Neptune*, Captain Thomas Fremantle, Able Seaman James Martin and their shipmates prepared for action, knowing that if their eighteen ships found Villeneuve's twenty-eight, the British people expected them to destroy the hostile fleet or die in the attempt.

Napoleon spent 20 August inspecting his troops in Boulogne and cursing Villeneuve. Everything was ready. The Imperial Guard and the cavalry were with him. In the first wave 1700 specially constructed boats would lift 113,000 men and 5600 horses. A second wave of 590 transports for 48,000 men and 3400 horses would follow. Napoleon was a man who got things done. He believed in the possible. England would be overwhelmed. All that was needed was sufficient battleships to give his barges a few days' protection. From the coastal hills the Emperor could plainly see England, and the élite of his Armée d'Angleterre was as impatient as he was for the arrival of his fleet. Napoleon had joined his army at the beginning of the month and each day for the last week he had expected to see Villeneuve's sails on the horizon.

As the Emperor bubbled with anger, Villeneuve sailed into Cadiz. He was at once ashamed that he had not fought his way through to Boulogne and convinced that he had done the right thing. He did not believe that his ships could win an even battle against the British, and he was fearful of what might happen to his seamen in the English Channel. His crews from Provence, Aquitaine, Andalucía and Galicia had little acquaintance with those hazardous waters. Above all, rational calculation told Villeneuve that, with the British now evidently forewarned, it was pointless to persevere with Napoleon's plan.

At Corunna and Ferrol his anxieties had been quietly reinforced by his Spanish colleague Admiral Federico Gravina, whose secret orders from the Spanish government forbade him to go to Brest or take part in any landing in Great Britain. The Spanish admiral was probably never pushed to the point where he had to reveal his hand and refuse to sail further north, since he was able to present his unwillingness to do so as common sense. Gravina had written to Denis Decrès, Napoleon's minister of marine, on 3 August, informing him in the most polite and cogent terms that, in his view, the attempt to invade had already been defeated.

That day Villeneuve told Decrès, his old and trusted friend, that if all else failed he would go to Cadiz and join up with the Spanish squadron there. Safe within its fortified harbour he could get his ships repaired and obtain more supplies. On 7 August he wrote to Decrès, 'I am about to sail, but I don't know what I shall do.' He was worried about the eight ships that had appeared off Ferrol. It might be Nelson. 'They will follow us,' he told Decrès. 'I should be sorry to meet twenty of them. Our naval tactics are antiquated. We know nothing but how to place ourselves in line, and that is just what the enemy wants.'

Villeneuve came of ancient chivalric stock – by family right he was a Knight of Malta. He did not relish the ignominy of avoiding combat and he was apprehensive of how the Emperor would react to his behaviour. He was in no way reassured by the presence in his ship of the Emperor's aide-de-camp, General Jacques-Alexandre Lauriston, who was commanding the expeditionary force of soldiers that Villeneuve had ferried to Martinique and back. Whereas Villeneuve reported to his friend Decrès on the deficiencies of his men, ships and port facilities, Lauriston wrote weekly letters direct to Bonaparte detailing Villeneuve's excessive caution and lack of enterprise. Lauriston liked to give Villeneuve advice, and Villeneuve, in the true spirit of inter-service collaboration, liked to refuse it with what Lauriston considered a 'proud bearing and sarcastic aloofness'.

A passing merchant had told them there were only three British ships outside Cadiz, and Napoleon's aide suggested that Admiral

Charles Magon should race ahead with six ships under cover of darkness to surprise them at dawn. But Villeneuve was worried by another report that he was being tailed and he ignored the opportunity. Lauriston told Napoleon that because they had arrived in daylight the English were able to escape. Some fishermen said that had the French arrived earlier in the morning when the wind was southerly the English would not have been able to get away. But Villeneuve had been too cautious to take a risk. 'In short, Sire, the fear of Nelson prevailed,' wrote Lauriston. The bolder officers in the fleet were also disgruntled. The pugnacious and enterprising Magon, further provoked by the insolent behaviour of Collingwood's ships as they outsailed him, was furious at the missed opportunity.

Flags were hoisted in welcome above the miradors of shining white Cadiz, and crowds cheered from the Alameda and the balconies – but the fleet that swept magnificently into the bay was by no means combined, united or happy.

2

The Plum Pudding in Danger

Vice Admiral Horatio, Lord Nelson had only been back in London for a few days when a foreign tourist accosted him in the street. Andreas Andersen Feldborg was a Danish author who was visiting England to research a travel book. He wanted to show Nelson his previous work, an account of the battle of Copenhagen. In 1801 Nelson had attacked the Danish fleet at anchor in their capital to remove Denmark from the 'Armed Neutrality of the North'. It was a dangerous enterprise and the battle had been fierce. Through a timely truce, Nelson's diplomatic abilities had squeezed a victory out of what continued fighting might have turned into a defeat. Fortunately for the British, Nelson could talk as well as he could fight. Cogent, dynamic and persuasive, on paper and in person, Nelson was by far the most charismatic leader that the Royal Navy had ever had. As a result he was world famous, 'looked up to in all countries', as Thomas Fremantle put it, 'a Terror to all Maritime Powers' in the words of a letter from a would-be servant that awaited him at home.

Nelson invited Feldborg to present him with the book at his home in Merton, then a village a short distance to the south-west of London. The Dane left a vivid account of his visit on 26 August 1805. He arrived by coach, passed the lodge and drove up the thickly planted gravel drive of Merton Place, the impressive red-brick house that Nelson had bought for himself and his mistress Emma, Lady Hamilton, in 1801. As he waited in the lobby Feldborg admired a marble bust of the admiral, paintings and other curiosities, including the lightning conductor from the French flagship Nelson had blown up at the battle of the Nile. Then he was led into a 'magnificent apartment' where his eye was drawn to Lady Hamilton in the window-seat, before he located the admiral sitting quietly in full dress uniform immediately beside him at the door. Nelson had made an effort to impress – typical of a man who liked to draw full theatrical effect from everything he did.

As they talked, Feldborg noticed how 'the penetration of his eye threw a kind of light upon his countenance, which tempered its severity, and rendered his harsh features in some measure agreeable'. Nelson was a slight five foot seven with a prominent nose. He was not handsome, even before his right eye was scarred and his right arm amputated, but he was impressive: 'His aspect commanded the utmost veneration, especially when he looked upwards. Lord Nelson had not the least pride of rank; he combined with that degree of dignity which a man of quality should have, the most engaging address in his air and appearance.'

Feldborg toured the house to discover that Merton Place itself was a theatre. One of Nelson's friends, Gilbert Elliot, Lord Minto, had earlier complained that 'not only the rooms but the whole house, staircase and all, are covered with nothing but pictures of him and her, of all sizes and sorts, and representations of his naval actions, coats of arms, pieces of plate in his honour, the flagstaff of *L'Orient*, &c'. Minto thought this 'an excess of vanity which counteracts its own purpose'. Vanity there was, no doubt, but the decoration was appropriate to a house that was more often visited by tourists than by its owner. While Nelson was away, as he usually was, Merton became a national shrine, the home of the country's leading warrior, its one sure shield against the terrifying Bonaparte.

Nelson was the son of an unremarkable country clergyman from north Norfolk. He was educated at Norwich School and at North Walsham, then joined a warship commanded by his uncle, Maurice Suckling, when he was twelve. In 1777, he passed for lieutenant, illegally young at eighteen, but by then he had already sailed to the Arctic Circle, India, America and the West Indies. He became what was called a 'post captain' at twenty, which meant that he might be a rear admiral before he was forty, because promotion to that rank came through seniority rather than distinction.

As was customary, Nelson's well-placed uncle advanced his early career, but Nelson also quickly distinguished himself. During the French Revolutionary War he impressed first Lord Hood and then Sir John Jervis, the admirals commanding in the Mediterranean, and Jervis made him a commodore, acting independently with a squadron of ships though still only a captain by rank. Nelson's initial reputation as a warrior hero stemmed from a racy account of the battle of St Vincent in 1797 that he and his friend Edward Berry wrote and published. He then led two daring, though unsuccessful, attacks on Cadiz and Tenerife, reinforcing a reputation for aggression. But it was his destruction of the French fleet in the battle of the Nile in 1798 that made his name. Earl Spencer, then First Lord of the Admiralty, fainted with relief when he heard the news.

After this triumph, which temporarily marooned Napoleon in Egypt and prevented him marching east towards India, Nelson became the foremost celebrity of the age. There were Nelson ribbons, Nelson snuffboxes, Nelson fans, Nelson mugs and jugs. People wore pendants with the motto 'Nelson For Ever'. A steady stream of prints and colourful coverage in newspapers and magazines further boosted his status as national hero. Emma Hamilton did not have to buy the pots and prints that decorated the sideboards and walls of Merton Place: grateful manufacturers and publishers gave them to her to display, and relieved West and East India merchants presented her with silver plate. The King of England made Nelson Viscount Nelson; the King of Naples made him Duke of Bronte. A thankful Sultan of Turkey gave him the ridiculously oversize *chelengk*, designed for a turban, that he wore in his hat. It was the highest Turkish award for valour.

Until he read the London newspapers Nelson had thought that he would be reviled for failing to catch Villeneuve. Instead he was described as the saviour of the West Indies. The city had earlier been thrown into panic by the news that Villeneuve had joined with Admiral Gravina and was heading across the Atlantic. Nelson also learned that the country, or at least the London press, was furious with Sir Robert Calder for not sacrificing his ships to bring on a decisive engagement with Villeneuve and newspapers said that if Nelson had been in command things would have been different.

Meanwhile, the newspapers announced, 'The movements on the French coast have given rise to the belief that the invasion of England will be attempted immediately.' According to information received from Paris, 'immense numbers of troops were marching from all parts of the interior to the ports of the Channel. A formidable army of reserve is collecting at a short distance from the coast. All the General officers who are appointed to command in the intended expedition against England had set out for their respective destinations.'

Invasion fever had been running at a high pitch for months. Bonaparte had threatened to cross the English Channel ever since war broke out in 1803, and by the summer of 1805 everyone in Britain knew that he was poised and ready. The armies of France and her Bavarian and Dutch allies were camped all along the coast from Boulogne to the Scheldt, and each day brought further indications of imminent attack. Napoleon's men had beaten every force that had ever been sent against them. And if they reached England, who was to know which way local democrats and dissenters might jump, not to mention the Irish? The government had already orchestrated a frantic propaganda effort to keep John Bull behind Church and state and averse to bloodthirsty French revolutionaries. The caricaturist James Gillray was closely briefed by ministers and in May 1803 had created an unforgettable image of a ferocious, unstable Napoleon in *Maniac Ravings*. Other prints, showing nightmare visions of giant, fortified paddleboats, tunnels under the Channel and fleets of huge balloons, contributed to waves of panic. (In fact, the French had considered and abandoned such outlandish ideas. In September 1803, an American,

Robert Fulton, had even offered to build sufficient submarines for Napoleon to blockade the Thames.)

The naval bases at Chatham, Sheerness, Portsmouth and Plymouth were linked to the Admiralty by shutter telegraph, and a chain of beacons was prepared to provide instant alert against invasion. Coastal batteries were placed at strategic sites along the south coast; old castles were manned. A string of 'Martello towers' to delay landing forces was approved in August 1805. Romney Marsh was prepared for flooding and plans drawn up for a military canal behind it.

In southern England 385,000 badly armed volunteers were drilling. The London regiments had orders to be ready to march immediately. Eight hundred fishing-boats and river craft of the 'Sea Fencibles' guarded the coast, armed with cannon and manned by a further 25,000 volunteers. Newspapers reported that the admiral commanding in the Channel, Lord Keith, 'has sent away his family from the coast from his belief in the probability of immediate invasion'.

The press, denied any real knowledge of the military situation, spat invective at the 'Regicide Usurper' across the Channel. British journalists had no doubt of his intention to invade and expected him to be careless of the cost in French lives of 'an enterprize that if successful would enable France to defeat every Power in Europe':

> Our prosperity and glory and our opposition to his schemes of universal conquest rankle in his mind and prey upon his heart exciting that deadly enmity which would drown our island in blood! Whenever the day of conflict may come, we hope and trust that it will prove the period of his vanity, fame and power; and that the shores of Britain, bristling with the bayonets of her gallant defenders will gleam, like lightning, destruction on the heads of her presumptuous invaders.

Bluster as newspaper editors might about bristling bayonets, level-headed people knew that the enemy had to be stopped at sea. The best of Britain's tiny professional army had been wiped out by disease after it had invaded Saint-Domingue (now Haiti) in 1795. What was left would not stop Napoleon's battle-hardened legions if they got as far as the beaches. Cutting off supplies was no guarantee of success either. Napoleon's men were notorious for the way they lived off the land. This was why so many were furious that Calder had not fought Villeneuve harder and why, when Calder's fleet got wind of the Combined Fleet a second time, they prepared themselves for a sacrificial bloodbath.

News that Villeneuve had put to sea from Ferrol and might be approaching the Channel reached the Admiralty on 21 August, the day that Nelson first reported to Lord Barham. He realised that his stay at Merton would be short. Later that day he went from the Admiralty to the Navy Office. Then he tried to do some shopping but 'the public appearance in the streets of Lord Nelson, who in the short space of five weeks has viewed the four quarters of the Globe, attracted a concourse'.

A nervous population needed a hero and, that week, Nelson was mobbed wherever he went. An American tourist who saw him in the Strand noted that 'when he enters a shop the door is thronged till he comes out, when the air rings with huzzas and the dark cloud of the populace again moves on and hangs upon his skirts. He is a great favourite with all descriptions of people.' Lord Minto 'met Nelson to-day in a mob in Piccadilly, and got hold of his arm, so that I was mobbed too. It is really quite affecting to see the wonder and admiration, and love and respect, of the whole world; and the genuine expression of all these sentiments at once, from gentle and simple, the moment he is seen. It is beyond anything represented in a play or a poem of fame.'

It is not the most impressive exercise in numerology, but the calculations contained in William Rivers's commonplace book reveal what many ordinary British sailors thought of Napoleon: that he was the devil – or, if not, then at least one of his closest relations.

Rivers was the master gunner on board Nelson's flagship *Victory*, currently docked at Portsmouth while the admiral was being fêted in

London. The book that Rivers compiled during these months, still in beautiful condition, is kept at the Royal Naval Museum library in Portsmouth, about two hundred yards from the preserved *Victory*. It is a jumble of personal reflections, lines of doggerel verse, technical calculations and tables crammed into every available space. Given that Rivers was in charge of all the guns and ammunition on board a flagship, it is not surprising that he filled much of his book with lists of stores, details of the ranges of his guns at different elevations and the penetrative power of shot when combined with varying quantities of gunpowder. Less expected are the pages in which he proves Napoleon's diabolic nature by mathematics. Rivers awarded a number to each letter of the alphabet, one for A, two for B, conflating I and J as contemporary alphabets often did, then shifting to units of ten once he reached K, so that L counted as twenty, M as thirty, and so on. By this somewhat inelegant method the combined numerical count of the letters in the name 'Napoleon Buonaparte' came out at 666, the number of the beast.

Nelson shared his gunner's view of Napoleon. Very much the son of a conservative clergyman in his view of Church and state, he was an instinctive opponent of rebels, traitors and regicides. He burned to lead the Royal Navy to what he called an 'annihilating victory' over the French, thereby destroying any hope that the usurper Napoleon could ever depose a British king.

Nelson's last appointment on 21 August was with a man of similar opinions, Britain's prime minister, William Pitt, and two days later the admiral spent several hours closeted again with him and his principal ministers. Since he had come to power in May 1804, Pitt had been trying to persuade the Austrians and Russians to join in a new alliance against France, but he also sponsored less orthodox solutions to the country's problem. During 1804 French ships had captured a British naval officer called John Wesley Wright who had just landed two royalist agents on a mission to assassinate Bonaparte.

Since such missions invariably failed, Pitt's main effort went into coaxing Austria into the war. With a threat to his eastern borders, Pitt reasoned, Napoleon would not be able to keep his best troops poised on the Channel coast. However, the latest news of Villeneuve meant that, unless Calder could stop the French admiral, it remained possible that Napoleon might yet be able to launch his invasion before Pitt's Austro-Russian distractions could take effect. Pitt was anxious for Lord Nelson's opinion. 'I am now set up for a <u>Conjuror</u>,' Nelson wrote to his friend Captain Richard Keats, 'and God knows they will very soon find out I am far from being one, I was asked my opinion, against my inclination, for if I make one wrong guess the charm will be broken; but this I ventured without any fear, that if Calder got fairly close alongside their twenty-seven or twenty-eight Sail, that by the time the Enemy had beat our Fleet soundly, they would do us no harm this year.' Nelson expressed every confidence that his colleague would not let Villeneuve get away with his fleet intact a second time, whatever it cost.

When he had business in town Nelson stayed at Gordon's Hotel in Albemarle Street about a hundred yards from Hannah Humphrey's print shop in St James's Street where James Gillray's latest work was displayed in the windows. Nelson enjoyed caricature, especially when he or his friends were the subjects: he had once asked his wife to send out to the Mediterranean some of the caricatures made of him after the Nile. One of the prints in the shop window that August 1805 was a masterpiece entitled *The Plumb-Pudding in Danger*, published earlier in the year. Gillray depicted Pitt and Napoleon seated at table either side of a large plum pudding representing the world. Pitt's beady eyes watch Napoleon warily, as the Frenchman stabs his fork into George III's beloved Hanover, and greedily carves off Europe, while he starts to slice off the half of the pudding furthest away from the Frenchman labelled 'ocean' with 'West Indies' prominent. Great Britain remains on the plate, yet to be carved up. But now it seemed that the Emperor's fork was poised for another thrust. Gillray's dispassionate epigraph, '"the great Globe itself and all which it inherit", is too small to satisfy such insatiable appetites', resonates with the judgement of a recent French economic historian that the Anglo-French conflict parodied by

Gillray 'was the clash of two wills for power and mastery, both almost unlimited'.

Nelson's victory at Trafalgar has customarily been presented as a battle that saved Britain from invasion and classed with the two other great moments of national salvation: Drake's defeat of the Spanish Armada in 1588 and the Royal Air Force's frustration of the Luftwaffe in 1940. But the issue at Trafalgar was broader than that. It was not really a defensive battle but the aggressive climax to the rivalry so vividly portrayed in *The Plumb-Pudding*. It confirmed the Royal Navy's unassailable supremacy at sea, allowing Pitt and those who followed him into power to complete the carving of that huge chunk of pudding and put it on Britain's plate.

For a century Britain and France had been fighting what French historians have called the 'Second Hundred Years' War' and is also known as the 'Battle of the Atlantic'. Its cause was commercial: competition for trade with North and South America and for the most valuable part of America, the West Indian Islands.

Britain kept a tiny army and a vast navy. In rivalry over trade routes and colonies, this gave her an advantage over France, whose long land borders required a large regular army. As Britannia gradually extended her rule over the waves, it seemed to the French – and also the Spanish – that she was arrogating control of all maritime trade, squeezing out the competition. They tried to protect their existing share, and their strengthened navies gave the British a terrible fright during the American War of Independence (1776–83) when many of the officers who fought at Trafalgar gained their formative experience. The challenge made the British even more determined to assert their dominance and the American war was followed by an arms race as all three nations built up their fleets.

The prize at stake, Atlantic trade, formed Europe's most vibrant and expansive economic sector. France's foreign trade increased tenfold between 1716 and 1787, and by the time of her revolution she was doing three-quarters of it with the colony of Saint-Domingue, which was just a part of one West Indian island. The wealth that flowed from the vast West Indian plantations was almost unimaginable. The luxury products of the age grew there: coffee, sugar, cocoa, ginger, cotton, and indigo dye, all tended by African slaves, who were themselves a valuable commodity. In the 1780s the value of Saint-Domingue's trade – chiefly in sugar and coffee – was equal to that of all the trade of the recently named United States of America. Saint-Domingue traded mainly with Bordeaux, which, like Nantes (France's rival to Liverpool and Bristol as a slaving port), had booming industrial sectors linked with the colonial trade: sugar refineries, distilleries, tobacco factories, sailmakers, ropemakers and foundries. The Atlantic maritime provinces were soon the most industrialised in France.

The bond between commerce and naval strength was the 'prime seaman'. Men who earned their living in peacetime sailing big ships long distances to America and back sustained the navies in wartime. The West India trade accounted for two-thirds of large French ocean-going ships and the best 15,000 of France's 82,000 registered seamen. Lord Rodney argued that the West Indian trade had enabled France to dispute 'the empire of the ocean' in the American war, and France's National Assembly was told in 1790 that if the French lost this trade they could not contest a naval war in the future.

The British rightly identified French success in the West Indies as the main cause of the resurgence of their enemy's maritime and commercial power. And they were determined to undermine it. When war broke out in 1793, John Bull was already eyeing up the plum pudding, as *The Times* explained on 8 February:

France is the only power whose maritime force has hitherto been a balance to that of Great Britain and whose commerce has rivalled ours in the two worlds . . . Could England succeed in destroying the naval strength of her rival; could she turn the tide of that rich commerce, which has so often excited her jealousy, in favour of her own country . . . the degree of commercial prosperity to which the three kingdoms [of Great Britain] would then be elevated, would exceed all calculation.

It proved all too easy because after the Revolution the French navy self-destructed. *Liberté, fraternité* and especially *égalité* destroyed discipline in the fleet: nobody would take orders. Almost all officers were aristocrats and many were denounced and imprisoned. Some were guillotined; some resigned and retired to private life; some emigrated. Political chaos wrought havoc with naval planning and building programmes.

Britain took advantage of her enemy's weakness. From seventy line-of-battle ships in 1790, France's naval strength had declined to forty-seven in 1802. French trade also declined, owing to chaos in the colonies (notably civil war and slave revolts in Saint-Domingue) as well as British domination of the seas. Then Napoleon took power. Order was restored in the navy and morale soared. As soon as the preliminaries of the Peace of Amiens had been signed in October 1801 he began to organise an expedition to stabilise the chaos in Saint-Domingue. It sailed in December. In Napoleon's expansive imagination this was the first step towards the creation of a new American empire based in Louisiana, the vast province that Spain had just ceded to him. But the French expedition was decimated by disease, and by black rebels covertly aided by Britain and the United States. With a frustrated cry of 'Damn sugar, damn coffee, damn colonies!' Napoleon sold Louisiana to the Americans and used the money to finance a different approach to the Atlantic problem: a direct invasion of England.

For the British the equation was still simple. Destroy the French and Spanish navies and Britain could destroy their trade and take it over. Destroy their trade and their navies would never have enough seamen to challenge Britain again. By 1805 they had few ships left. One 'annihilating victory' would effectively complete the business.

As Admiral Nelson showed Feldborg round his house they paused on the staircase 'the walls of which were adorned with prints of his Lordship's battles, and other naval engagements; he pointed out to me the Battle of Copenhagen, which was a tolerably correct engraving'. Hanging nearby was a print in which Nelson had taken a personal interest, perhaps because the artist, Thomas Buttersworth, was a former seaman who had been invalided out of the navy. The subject was congenial to the admiral: it showed the twenty-six enemy line-of-battle ships that Nelson had helped to take between 1793 and 1801, and views of the fleet actions in which Nelson had taken part at Genoa, Cape St Vincent, the Nile and Copenhagen.

Nelson himself had supplied Buttersworth with details of the ships and with instructions like 'The Name of each ship to be wrote between the main & foremast'. He had demanded a different portrait of himself from the one that the artist and publisher had proposed. It is symptomatic of the interest that Nelson took in cultivating his own image and of his determination that people should be made aware of his achievement. But it was also a graphic depiction of how great that achievement had been. The capture of twenty-six battleships was an unprecedented personal contribution to the change in the balance of naval power. If it was necessary to annihilate the enemy's navies, Nelson was the man to do it.

3

Our Incomparable Navy

An admiral's work did not end when he reached his home. In his study at Merton Place, Nelson had to deal with correspondence on all subjects. Peers and other great men wrote to congratulate him, to recommend someone for a job, or to ask him to say a word in the right quarter that would advance a favoured person. Those with no peer to recommend them sent begging letters of varying degrees of obsequiousness. Lieutenant Thomas Cole, formerly of *Foudroyant*, had lost a leg on shore at Martinique: could Nelson recommend him for any employment? James Buffin, carpenter, was stuck on the *Medway* hulk: could he please be put on an active ship? Charles Dobson of the *Barfleur* in Cawsand Bay wanted to serve under Nelson anywhere in the world. William Compton of Weymouth, and his wife, Anne, sympathised with the way that Nelson had been foiled in the West Indies by the lies of an American merchant: 'I fear all Americans are spies for France. I know when abroad I saw all were hostile to this Country, of course all their people would designedly & treachery mislead our fleets by false intelligence!'

A minor painter named Blackberd wrote to ask if Nelson would sit for an oil. William Osborn wondered whether Nelson would help him get his son into Charterhouse School. George Owen, a seaman of Carmarthen, 'well knowing the great attention your Lordship always paid to the happiness and interest of British seamen', requested Nelson's help in getting the share of prize money due to him for service on Nelson's previous ship, *Captain*: he did not know the names of the prize agents and had only been paid a small proportion of what was due to him. Elizabeth Clod of Chelsea, widow, whose husband had once served under Nelson, recommended her son William Clod of the *Excellent*.

P. H. Clay of Aldermanbury sought Nelson's backing for a new product and sent samples: 'Since I had the honor of seeing Your Lordship at Merton Messrs. Duke & Co have made waterproof one of our patent jackets & M^o. Stanton one of the Partners in that House will have the honor to lay it before your Lordship & also a Seamans Coat done in the same way.' Clay knew that if Nelson approved he would make sure his fleet adopted the jackets. The enterprising, if opportunistic, American inventor Robert Fulton had a similar mission: having offered his submarines to Napoleon, he now suggested a secret meeting to demonstrate them as a means of blowing up the enemy fleet in Cadiz.

Between assessing widows' pleas and the merits of waterproof jackets, Nelson attended meetings in London on fourteen of his twenty-five days at home. It was hardly a holiday, but he did his best to spend some time with his family and friends.

Although he had the love and loyalty of most of those who sailed and fought alongside him, Nelson was not perfect. When he was agitated he would waggle the stump of his missing arm and his officers had learned to keep their heads down when they saw the admiral's 'fin' in motion. His relations with the Admiralty were often turbulent, and some of his senior colleagues detested him: they found him arrogant and vain, dogged in disputes over credit and prize money, and embarrassing in his private life. Many naval wives disapproved strongly of Nelson's passionate relationship with Lady Hamilton, and of his unkindness to his abandoned wife, Frances.

He had met and married Frances Nisbet in 1787 on the West Indian island of Nevis while he was serving as a captain policing trade with the islands after the American war. Frances was a widow with one son and received a modest income from an uncle. Her fortune turned out to be even smaller than they had hoped, but the real disappointment for Nelson was that she was unable to bear any more children. Fanny was a faithful and dutiful wife, but in the heady atmosphere of war-torn Naples the newly famous Nelson fell passionately in love with another woman, who, in 1801, gave him a daughter; she was christened Horatia.

His lover, Lady Hamilton or Amy Lyon, as she signed the marriage register, or Emma Hart, as she had been known in the art world, was a complex character. Like a number of prominent contemporary women (of whom several were currently rearing children with princes, dukes and politicians), she had come from nowhere on her looks, personality and sexuality.

Born in Cheshire, Emma worked first as a servant and then came to London, possibly to work for the theatrical Linley family. It is likely that she was soon drawn into prostitution or something close to it. By the time she was seventeen she had been taken up then abandoned, pregnant, by Sir Harry Fetherstonhaugh, a profligate aristocrat. Charles Greville, a young man from a noble family, rescued her, and in 1782 introduced her as a promising model to the artist George Romney and also to Sir Joshua Reynolds. Their paintings of Emma as *Nature* and as *A Bacchante* were engraved and published by John Raphael Smith, the top mezzotinter, creating an eye-catching comparison that grabbed public attention. Art critics informed the public that the breathtakingly beautiful sitter was Miss Emma Hart. She continued to appear in prints made from Romney's paintings and was soon the most celebrated female face and figure of her generation.

In 1786 the newspapers revealed that Miss Hart had left for Naples. What had happened says much about the status of low-born attractive women in Georgian society, but also about how far they could rise if they could play the game. Charles Greville had effectively given Emma to his uncle as a present. The uncle, Sir William Hamilton, already celebrated for his collections of classical antiquities, was Britain's ambassador in Naples. He was sixty, his new mistress only twenty-six, but he fell under her spell and brought her back to London in 1791 to marry her.

On that visit Emma again attracted lively publicity and speculation about her origins. 'All the world is following her and talking of her,' wrote Romney, of his former model, while the younger Thomas Lawrence sought a sitting to paint 'this wonderful woman' as *La Penserosa* for the Royal Academy exhibition of 1792. By now she had learned to sing well. Romney reported that at his house Giovanni Gallini, manager of the London opera house, 'offered her two thousand pounds a year, and two benefits, if she would engage with him, on which Sir William said pleasantly, that he had engaged her for life'. But she was chiefly 'celebrated for her readiness in assuming the attitudes peculiar to the remains of ancient sculpture, and this imitation she contrives to render highly pleasing in point of grace and expression'. A newspaper announced that she had rejected an offer of £1500 to perform for a season at Covent Garden theatre. Lady Elizabeth Foster marvelled that 'no Grecian nor Trojan princess could have had a more perfect or more commanding form', although at dinner Betty Foster was as condescending as other ladies who shared her upbringing: 'Her conversation, though perfectly good natured and unaffected, was uninteresting, and her pronunciation very vulgar.'

Society satirist 'Peter Pindar' (John Wolcot) mocked Sir William in his idiosyncratic style:

> O Knight of Naples is it come to pass,
> That thou hast left the gods of stone and brass,
> To wed a deity of *flesh* and *blood*?*
> O lock the temple with thy strongest key,
> For fear thy deity, a comely she,
> Should one day ramble, in a frolic mood.

*It is really true – the Knight *is married* to a most beautiful *virgin*, whom he styles his *Grecian*. Her attitudes are the most *desirable* models for *young* artists.

He concluded his 'Lyric Epistle to Sir William Hamilton' with an ominous reminder that Emma might revert to former ways:

Yet *should* thy Grecian Goddess fly the fane
I think that we may catch her in Hedge-Lane.†

†The resort of the Cyprian corps [ladies of pleasure], an avenue that
opens into Cockspur-street.

Sir William, however, was staunchly confident that he had judged
Emma's character correctly. George III let him know that his marriage
would not cost him his job, although Queen Charlotte, with the
snobbery of a minor German princess, refused to receive Emma at
court.

Nelson first met Emma in Naples two years later, in 1793. It must
have been like an encounter with a movie star – by then every famous
artist in Europe had painted her. When he got to know her better, in
1798, he was still impressed. 'I am writing opposite Lady Hamilton,
therefore you will not be surprised at the glorious jumble of this letter,'
he wrote to Earl St Vincent. 'Were your Lordship in my place, I much
doubt if you could write so well.' Both Hamiltons became his close
friends and Emma was breathlessly attentive to the new British Hero.
Soon they were lovers, with the tacit approval – or, at least, tolerance –
of her husband.

Emma was more than just decorative. Nelson believed that it was
through her charm and influence over Queen Caroline of Naples that
he had obtained secret permission to water his fleet in Syracuse
harbour, a vital contribution to his victory at the Nile. After that
victory, when George III declined to make Nelson an earl on the
ground that he did not have the money to support the dignity, Emma
responded, 'If I was King of England, I would make you the most
noble, puissant Duke Nelson, Marquis Nile, Earl Alexandria, Viscount
Pyramid, Baron Crocodile, and Prince Victory.'

Emma's friendship with Queen Caroline and his infatuation with
Emma led Nelson to make the darkest decision of his career. In 1799 he
allowed the King and Queen of Naples to execute those responsible for
a failed revolution in Naples, breaking the promise of a British officer
who had accepted their surrender in exchange for safe conduct to

France. He was strongly criticised in Parliament for this dishonourable act, and censured in the navy for lingering for a year with the Hamiltons at the Neapolitan court. A young artist called Henry Barker met them at Naples and saw Emma cutting up Nelson's meat for him: 'I cannot forget her appearance in the evening – her fine, commanding form dressed in a kind of robe trimmed with roses from her neck to her feet – her beautiful countenance with lovely dark eyes.' Nelson took the Hamiltons on a long Mediterranean cruise during which his admiral's quarters were transformed into a floating boudoir. Horatia was conceived on that cruise in 1800.

Once established at Merton Place, Emma's social status was ambiguous. Some members of high society received her; others preferred not to. However the prim and proper might frown, though, adulterous liaisons were far from unusual: the leader of the Whig Opposition, Charles James Fox, lived openly with a retired lady-of-pleasure, and the Duke of Clarence (later William IV) shared a home at Richmond with his mistress, the former actress Dorothy Jordan, and their children. And, anyway, Emma was not particularly interested in polite society: she was happier with the theatrical set and patrons of art, like the fabulously wealthy bisexual William Beckford, a relation of Hamilton, who was building a Gothic fantasy abbey at Fonthill in Wiltshire.

Emma had been steadily improving Merton, designing a walk that Nelson called 'the quarterdeck' leading to a summerhouse known as 'the poop'. Nelson played up to her sense of the dramatic: 'You are to be, recollect, Lady Paramount of all the territories and waters of Merton and we are all to be your guests and to obey all lawful commands.' When she dredged a canal he laughed at the idea of 'the beautiful Emma rowing a one-armed Admiral in a boat! It will certainly be caricatured.'

Off Cadiz, Admiral Collingwood tried to summon help before Villeneuve realised that the Royal Navy's blockade consisted of only three ships-of-the-line, *Dreadnought*, *Colossus* and *Achille*. His only frigate found *Mars* buying food in Tangiers. Her captain George Duff set off immediately and joined Collingwood next morning. 'I had luckily got plenty of bullocks for ourselves and the squadron, and as much vegetables as I wanted for myself,' he wrote to his wife, Sophia, at home in Edinburgh. Then Rear Admiral John Knight arrived in *Queen*, with other ships from Collingwood's squadron that he had borrowed for other duties: Charles Tyler's *Tonnant*, John Cooke's *Bellerophon* and Charles Mansfield's *Minotaur*. Collingwood's little squadron of eight battleships now stood guard over Villeneuve's forty-odd. In the pretence that they were an advance squadron, they signalled to an imaginary fleet over the horizon to conceal their weakness.

Among this small group, Collingwood seems to have unbent with his captains, all of whom were at least a dozen years younger than himself. He wrote to Charles Tyler to tease him for having been away at the crucial moment of Villeneuve's arrival: 'where have you been with your Admiral? . . . I thought you were gone to survey Torency Bay.' George Duff's first impression when he met Collingwood in May 1805 was that he was 'a fine steady good officer', and on 27 August they dined together in *Dreadnought* on a turtle that Duff had shot earlier in the day.

Duff was delighted that one of the other captains at Cadiz was John Cooke, an old and close friend. Cooke had enjoyed a successful period as a frigate captain, winning some famous actions against French frigates. Duff had been unlucky in frigates and was hoping for a change of fortune. Before Villeneuve had appeared he had written only half in jest to his wife, 'I have heard that the Spaniards expect a line-of-battle ship and a frigate home with money; so we must keep a good look out for them. I hope therefore to be able to desire you to look out for a country house, and to order a carriage to be built for us.'

James Morris of *Colossus* and Charles Tyler were also good friends. In 1798 they had been companions in adversity when each had been separately court martialled off Cadiz for the loss of his ship. Morris had reason to remember the local rocks and weather since his frigate had gone aground under the gun batteries of Rota Point across the bay from the city. Collingwood had been one of the judges at both courts-martial and had seen them both honourably acquitted. Morris was congratulated for getting his crew out and setting fire to his ship while under attack from Spanish batteries and gunboats. Tyler had led a squadron of frigates under Nelson, before commanding a battleship at Copenhagen. Captains liked to hunt in pairs, with someone to watch their back, and old friendships, like those between Tyler and Morris, Duff and Cooke, bred trust.

These captains, all in their forties, were hardened by long experience of fighting at sea. All had taken part as midshipmen or lieutenants in the frustrating battles of the American Revolutionary War and then as young captains in the more successful campaigns since 1793. Richard King, captain of *Achille*, was only thirty, too young to have taken part in the American war, but he had made several captures as a frigate captain. Command of frigates encouraged independent thought and initiative, qualities that Nelson regarded as desirable in the captain of a line-of-battle ship.

They were not merely fighting men. British officers, like the Spanish, saw themselves as men of the Enlightenment, skilled in mathematics and geometry. They regarded themselves, and were regarded by many contemporaries, as an intellectual elite. They used the best and most up-to-date scientific instruments, in whose manufacture Britain led the world – even Spanish explorers ordered their instruments from London. Not only did they know how to use their instruments, but they tested them and suggested improvements. Collingwood was lucky to have officers as good as these four, but 'such a very distinguish'd sett of fine fellows', as Nelson called his officers at Copenhagen, were by no means unusual in what he referred to as 'our incomparable navy'.

Socially, the officers were of the middle classes. Tyler was the son of an army officer, Morris of a naval captain, Cooke of an admiralty cashier and Duff of a solicitor. Elsewhere in the fleet there were aristocratic captains, and a few, like William Prowse of the frigate *Sirius*, who had started as able seamen. Entry into the British officer corps did not depend on birth, but progress was accelerated by influential patronage, although conspicuous ability and determined application helped.

Many, if not most, seamen entered the King's ships unwillingly. Recent research has shown that conditions on board were nothing like as bad as Victorian reformers liked to portay, and the old mythology of starvation, penury, buggery and the lash needs sharp modification. The Royal Navy was by far the biggest and most efficient industry of its day. Superior food, medicine and hygiene were three of its principal advantages over its rivals, and by the standards of the day its logistical support was first class. But it still had difficulty in attracting enough skilled seamen.

It is true, as is often said, that seamen's wages did not rise between 1653 and 1797, but between 1665 and 1760 there was practically no inflation. However, by 1805 things had changed: rampant inflation combined with other difficulties to make naval service less attractive than it had been formerly.

The total number of seamen in Britain, including those in the merchant service, was estimated at 136,000: in 1804 Parliament voted for a navy of 100,000 men; and in 1805 120,000. Not all would be seamen and plenty of volunteers were to be found among the adventurous young and the desperate unemployed. But naval captains needed a core crew of prime seamen with ten years' experience in big ships. There was an inevitable clash with the interests of trade. Unfortunately, the navy could only offer prime seamen a third of the pay they would get in a merchant ship. Moreover, once one was in a King's ship it was notoriously difficult to get out. The last war had endured for nine years.

Captain James Morris's ship *Colossus* was new, launched in April 1803 at Deptford on the Thames. She was not ready for manning until late in the great 'Hot Press' of March 1803 when the navy tried to raise 10,000 seamen all at once to add to the 50,000 already serving. Just before Britain declared war, warrants to press men into the navy were

issued in great secrecy and so desperate was the need that most of the
normal protections and exemptions were suspended. While the
population thought it was at peace, armed seamen and marines
descended on every ship and tavern in Portsmouth, Plymouth and
the London docks. Other ports had been struck before the news spread.
It was easily the biggest operation of its kind, unprecedentedly
ruthless and unpopular. Around Portsmouth, 'Every merchant ship
in the harbour and at Spithead was stripped of its hands, and all
the watermen deemed for His Majesty's service were carried off.
Upwards of six hundred seamen were collected in consequence of
the promptitude of the measures adopted.' The press-gangs tended to
seize everyone they could find, then release the non-seamen after
examination.

On the Thames the round-up was especially thorough. The American ambassador protested about the number of his country's citizens
who had been taken up by the gangs. Here, there was a problem: men
born in America before 1776 or even 1783 might be considered British.
But the navy was not choosy about whom it pressed, so long as they
were seamen. American seamen sometimes carried papers to prove that
they were American, but these were often forged for British seamen
who were attempting to avoid service in the Royal Navy, and were not
always respected by British captains.

One of the Americans taken was Benjamin Turner, a twenty-one-
year-old able seaman from Philadelphia, who was grabbed in Deptford
in June 1803. He refused to volunteer, no doubt objecting that he was
an American citizen, but the gang rowed him out into the river and
put him aboard the *Enterprise* tender. Another seaman described the
experience: 'Upon getting on board this vessel, we were ordered down
in the hold, and the grating was put over us; as well as a guard of
marines placed round the hatchway, with their muskets loaded and
fixed bayonets, as though we had been culprits of the first degree, or
capital convicts. In this place we spent the day and the following night
huddled together, for there was not room to sit or stand separate.'

When the hold was full the men were taken to the newly launched
Colossus at Woolwich. At that time only a few essential officers,

warrant officers and a handful of volunteers were on board. One of the first volunteers was 'a little black boy' aged nine, named George Brown – presumably by the first lieutenant since the boy 'speaks no English'. When the men entered the ship the first lieutenant rated them. Brown was rated 'boy third class', but the first lieutenant divided those over eighteen according to appearance and past experience into three kinds: 'petty and able', 'ordinary' and 'landsmen'. Each of the petty officers and able seamen was 'well acquainted with his duty as a seaman'. An ordinary seaman was 'one who can make himself useful on board, but is not an expert or skilful sailor'. Landsmen usually had no sea experience, but many jobs merely required brute strength to haul on a rope or turn a capstan and some learned enough to become seamen. The minimum requirement for safety and competence was for one-third to be able and petty, one-third ordinary and one-third landsmen.

The ship's surgeon, Edwin Jones, then inspected the men. He was not impressed by what he saw:

> Among these were a few good seamen and some stout healthy young men, chiefly watermen, but the greater part had been picked up by the Police in London. They were in general ill clothed, dirty, emaciated & squalid, consequences to be expected from their habits of life, and their various confinements, both on shore & in the tender, the venereal disease was remarkably prevalent among them . . .

He probably exaggerated: *Colossus*'s muster book lists only about a dozen convicts delivered to the navy by the 'civil powers'. They included twenty-one-year-old Frederick Fitzgerald from London and James Crowning from Cork, who was one of the venereal disease cases. There was also James Christing, a thirty-year-old Indian from Bengal, who was eventually invalided out because he couldn't stand the climate off Brittany. But muster books tended to paint the best picture of their recruits and perhaps some of those labelled 'prest' or 'volunteer' were vagrant or drunken undesirables taken off the streets by the police. The Hot Press had been at work since 9 March and by

June *Colossus* was getting the dregs. Pressed seamen often sought the first means of escape: John Hunt drowned 'in attempting to swim from the ship' as *Colossus* left Woolwich.

With the ship's company half complete, *Colossus* sailed to the Nore. There, the proper complement of 640 men was almost fulfilled when a large number of men were supplied from the receiving ship *Zealand*. The surgeon commented that 'we got some very excellent Seamen in this Draft, but a part of it resembled those we had got in the River. I picked out 7 Men who appeared to me to be totally unfit for His Majesty's service, they were sent to the Hospital ships, surveyed, and immediately invalided.' Some men tried to feign incapacity in order to be turned away. Jones accepted 'several Consumptive and infirm Patients whom it had been better to have sent away also, but the Investigation of their Complaints required some time & observation to prevent Imposition – this is the reason why so many were sent to the Hospital on our first arrival at Plymouth'.

Colossus sailed first to neutral Ferrol, to work the men up to reasonable efficiency. Once at sea, the ship proved a healthy one. This was a major concern for the navy since a serious outbreak of disease could disable a ship. For Jones the venereal complaints proved troublesome: 'a great part of them were with secondary symptoms – many of them of long standing – and hence very inveterate'. He also cured 'above a hundred slighter cases . . . principally gonorrhoea they required no confinement or excuse from duty'. Scurvy had been a terrible scourge of seamen, but by 1803 the navy had the answer: lemons in the Mediterranean and limes in the West Indies – so long as they could be acquired. On *Colossus* scurvy 'appeared pretty commonly during our first cruize, when there was no lemon juice on board to serve out to the whole Ship's Company – but it was easily subdued and during the last two cruises not a case has appeared, lemon juice having been regularly given'.

An outbreak of fever, when 161 men were listed sick and five died was the single major problem: it broke out after *Colossus* had taken in the crew of the *Magnificent* which had hit an uncharted rock and sunk. Jones traced the disease to the overcrowded conditions in damp weather when the lower decks could not be aired. *Magnificent*'s men had lost their clothes and hammocks and were obliged to sleep on the deck and it was with them that the disease started. It was contained, though, and *Colossus* remained a healthy ship. By August 1805 Captain James Morris and his officers had transformed its unpromising crew into a fine fighting unit worthy of a powerful vessel that Collingwood regarded as 'an excellent sailer'.

Charles Tyler's *Tonnant* was one of a number of ships that experienced difficulty in getting and retaining enough skilled seamen, even though it was manned at the beginning of the Hot Press. *Tonnant* was a French eighty-gun ship built at Toulon from Adriatic oak and launched in 1792. She was captured, badly damaged after a fierce defence, at the battle of the Nile. Repairs to her in Plymouth dock were completed in December 1802, and new copper sheathing was fitted to her hull by gangs of punchers and nailers 'even working in their dinner hours to complete her for commission'. When her new captain, Sir Edward Pellew, saw her, she had 'a neat stern elegantly finished in light carved work, with G.R. and a crown in the centre of the stern railing under the middle lanthorn, and her head is a bust of Jupiter hurling his thunder, all beautifully executed by Mr. Dickinson and his son, Master Carver to the Dockyard'.

Pellew was a famous Cornish frigate captain whose squadron had taken numerous valuable prizes in the last war. He brought with him to the ship a core of followers who always sailed with him, moving from ship to ship as he did. Other valuable seamen, who might have joined the ship as Pellew's followers, remained with *Tonnant* after he left. Three of the lieutenants still in the ship in 1805, Benjamin Clement, Charles Bennett and William Millett, had joined when she was commissioned. The marines, from the Plymouth Division, also joined in March 1803. Many had been born locally and reinforced the West Country character of the crew.

Towards the end of April, with the help of borrowed seamen, *Tonnant* moved to Cawsand Bay. There, more drafts of seamen, pressed or volunteer, joined her from the receiving ship, the captured *Salvador del Mundo*. They came in groups from the localities where they had been recruited. Those who were pressed together remained together. Of 272 English seamen whose place of birth was clearly stated in *Tonnant*'s muster books, fifty-nine came from Devon (many from Plymouth or Plymouth dock) and fifty-two from Cornwall. Twenty-nine came from Lancashire and nine from Cumberland, with groups from Whitehaven and Lancaster. There were forty-four Scots and thirty-three Welshmen.

Between a quarter and a third of the crews of British ships at Trafalgar were Irish, and their contribution to the battle deserves to be highlighted. Tyler himself was one of many British officers who had been born in Ireland, and Ireland also produced skilled seamen. However, the majority of the Irishmen at Trafalgar were unskilled volunteers who preferred the navy to rural poverty, political oppression – in the wake of the 1798 rising – and the degradation of the Dublin slums. There were 128 Irishmen in *Tonnant*, of whom only seventeen were rated able.

Some of those whom *Tonnant* acquired in the Hot Press of 1803, like John MacKay, aged thirty-six from Carron, Scotland, immediately became core members of the crew. Mackay was rated quartermaster, a man capable of directing the ship's steering. But there were too few experienced seamen. Also, *Tonnant*'s pressed men proved resourceful: having been taken unwillingly, many left at the first opportunity. The turnover, especially of Americans, was striking. Every time the ship went near land a few men disappeared. Four ran at Plymouth, eight in Betanzos Bay near Ferrol, six when she returned to Plymouth. It was a constant struggle to retain enough men who knew what they were doing.

Sir Edward Pellew was obliged to find more able seamen at sea and he did so with rapacious efficiency. On 1 June 1803 he intercepted the merchant ship *Rusdale* of Hull, and three men, including James Anderson, volunteered. Doubtless he was offered the choice of taking the five-pound bounty for volunteering or of being pressed anyway. Next day the *Coromandel*, returning from China, was stopped and nine men, mostly prime seamen, 'volunteered'. On 1 July *Recovery* and *Ramble*, both of London, and *Walker*, a Spanish ship, yielded seven indifferent hands. On 12 July three men were taken from the *Speculation* privateer. On 22 August the battleship *Spencer* generously provided four excellent men.

On 27 August, after a brush with *Duguay-Trouin* and *Guerrière*, Pellew recaptured the *Lord Nelson* East Indiaman with her prize crew of forty-two Frenchmen. From her original crew he took two Americans, a Swede, a Norwegian and a German; two of his French prisoners also volunteered. This process continued on every cruise in a constant attempt to replenish and improve the stock of experienced ocean-going sailors. The most enterprising coup was four seamen, one Scottish, one from Curaçao and two French, who were persuaded to leave a French corvette sheltering in the then neutral port of Ferrol.

In May 1804 Pellew left and was replaced by William Jervis. From then on the crew was relatively steady until January 1805 when Jervis drowned while visiting the admiral. His replacement, Charles Tyler, came with a new master, Edward Soper, lieutenants John Bedford, John Salmon and Frederick Hoffman and a new captain of marines, Arthur Ball. Tyler brought with him his coxswain, Thomas Phelp, and a handful of followers, including midshipmen Thomas Bourne and William Peregrine from Wales.

By the summer of 1805 *Tonnant* had roughly 35 per cent petty officers and able seamen, 25 per cent ordinary and 40 per cent landsmen and boys. Many of the landsmen might have become proficient seamen, and it may be that *Tonnant*'s first lieutenants were mean in rating their abilities, but on the face of it she had too many landsmen (208) and too few rated able and over (148) for comfort. It was a young crew, too: the landsmen were nearly all in their early twenties. The average age of ordinary seamen was twenty-six, of able seamen thirty and petty officers thirty-three. Six petty officers were in their forties and the oldest was fifty-five.

A great deal depended on the petty officers and their ability to weld experienced sailors into a team. Most of the prime seamen who remained in *Tonnant* had nominally volunteered, although some of the pressed men proved reliable. The nine able seamen pressed in Whitehaven on 12 March 1803 were still with *Tonnant* in summer 1805. By then three had been promoted to quarter gunner and one to quartermaster, and they were settled members of the ship's élite. The miracle is that, after two years in their ships, the crews of both *Tonnant* and *Colossus* had bedded in, and when it came to the crunch – as it did for *Colossus* when Villeneuve appeared off Cadiz – they performed with consummate skill.

4

Latouche's Monument

Nine months before he led the Combined Fleet into Cadiz, Pierre Villeneuve had stood on the summit of Cap Cépet, high above Toulon harbour, and delivered the funeral oration for Vice Admiral Louis-René de Latouche-Tréville:

> Indefatigable zeal, courage, prudence balanced with intrepidity, love of glory and of his native land, these qualities we shall eternally esteem and regret. They should also be the object of our constant emulation: sailors, they will ceaselessly be the object of mine! Latouche's successor promises you that: promise him by the same token that he will be sure of the same loyalty and devotion.

Villeneuve was addressing a body of French officers to whom the dead admiral had given hope and confidence and who had given him their devotion in return. Latouche had been France's Nelson – or, at least, the nearest France had had to a Nelson in recent decades. 'I had already seen a great number of officers in my career,' wrote Auguste Gicquel, a junior officer in the *Intrépide*, 'but I had never come across a true leader like the one that we had just lost, who gave the impression of possessing a superior will, capable of transforming men and dominating events.' His subordinates were determined to build a monument to him that would overlook the harbour for all time. Had he lived, he would have been the man in Cadiz preparing for battle against the British.

Latouche maintained two families and his bigamy was one proof of his charisma. After distinguishing himself in the American war he had become business manager to the executed French king's egalitarian brother, the Duc d'Orléans, which caused his ejection from the republican navy in 1793. Recalled after Napoleon's coup in November 1799, he was given command of the Combined Fleet at Brest, where he made friends with the Spanish admiral Gravina and his officers, and invited Spanish advisers on to his own staff to benefit from their experience in defending ports against the Royal Navy. In 1801 those same Spaniards helped Latouche to repel Nelson's assault on Boulogne, a small but significant victory that was much celebrated in France. Napoleon, convinced that Latouche had the energy and ability he wanted, gave him command at Toulon and a key role in planning the invasion of Britain.

At Toulon, Latouche infuriated Nelson by claiming in the spring of 1804 that he had put to flight a small British squadron commanded by the famous admiral himself. 'You will have seen Monsieur la Touche's letter of how he chased me and how I _ran_,' wrote Nelson in disgust. 'I keep it; and, by God, if I take him, he shall _Eat_ it!'

Through such touches of bravado as his 'victories' over Nelson, Latouche had transformed the morale of the men that Villeneuve now commanded. While Latouche was in charge, his sailors were paid regularly for the first time in years. He made sure that they received their new shore-going uniform of red waistcoat, blue jacket and trousers, and he introduced different-coloured cap pompoms and pennants for different ships to encourage the *esprit de corps* of the companies. The red pompom worn by the crew of his flagship, *Bucentaure*, was eventually adopted for the whole French navy.

Self-esteem was nothing without practical skill, however. Latouche instituted competitive live firing exercises, conducting one between *Bucentaure* and *Formidable*, the flagship of his junior admiral, Pierre Dumanoir. The experienced crew of *Formidable* fired seven broadsides in sixteen minutes to beat *Bucentaure*'s five in fifteen. Both were high rates of fire by French standards, and competitive by British, and Latouche soon improved the performance of his own crew. *Bucentaure*'s infantry had already triumphed over her training rival, achieving thirty musket shots each in fifteen minutes, against *Formidable*'s twenty.

Gradually, Latouche introduced inexperienced crews to sailing at sea, sending them out for little skirmishes with the British blockaders. As Auguste Gicquel recalled:

> We were anchored in the great roadstead and two of our ships took turns to be on watch at the entrance to reply to English insults. As soon as these approached, as they had got used to doing unpunished, the watchers slipped their cables; in eight minutes they were under sail and in chase of the enemy. If these were supported, other ships of our side came into the line. These were continuous manoeuvres followed by combats that formed both crews and captains. The admiral, established on top of cap Cépet, which dominates the entrance to Toulon, surveyed everything outside and inside preparing adversaries for Nelson who would be worthy of him.

Nelson, who had the manoeuvres closely watched, acknowledged that Latouche's squadron was 'full manned and by the handling of the ships apparently well manned'.

Then, in August 1804, Latouche died unexpectedly. Nelson, who had been burning to fight him, felt almost cheated. 'La Touche has given me the slip,' he wrote. 'The French papers say he died in consequence of walking so often up to the Signal-post, upon Sepet [Cap Cépet], to watch us', he discovered soon afterwards. 'I always pronounced that that would be his death.'

In December 1804 Villeneuve succeeded Latouche. He was of Provençal origin, as were the men of the Toulon squadron, and he made no important changes to Latouche's methods. But the manner in which he commanded lowered morale. 'He was an officer of merit, knowledgeable and distinguished in his manner, but he was one of the last people who should have borne such a heavy burden,' wrote Gicquel. 'Uncertain and reserved by nature, in the eyes of the fleet he struggled with the memory of the Battle of the Nile where his conduct remained unjustifiable to all men of heart.' At the Nile Nelson had been expected to attack Villeneuve's vanguard division, but instead he struck the rear of the French fleet. With the wind against him and uncertain of what to do for the best, Villeneuve failed to come to the support of his commander-in-chief. He managed to extricate two battleships and two frigates from the disaster, but some complained that he had shown a lack of zeal, or even courage.

While Latouche had seen Napoleon's idea of an invasion of Britain as a glorious challenge and tried to prepare his men for success, Villeneuve did not think that the fleet was remotely capable of carrying out such an ambitious plan, and although his doubts were probably well founded, his evident pessimism soon communicated itself to his officers. He had tried to put to sea almost as soon as he had taken over, but after he had seen the way that the Toulon masts broke in bad weather and how the sailors struggled with the storm, he wrote to the minister of marine, his old friend Denis Decrès, in a bid to postpone action:

> It is my most ardent wish that the Emperor decide not to commit any of his squadrons to the hazards of these events, for if he does the French flag will be seriously compromised. In reality it is utterly impossible for us to defeat the enemy when both sides are equal, indeed, they will beat us even when they are a third weaker than we are . . . under no circumstances do I intend to become the laughing stock of Europe by being involved in further disasters.

Here, as he knew, he was preaching to the converted. He owed his appointment at Toulon to Decrès's recommendation and was there to lend support to Decrès's own views. Denis Decrès was forty-four, two years older than Villeneuve. He had seen the ups and downs of the French navy, with victory at Chesapeake Bay and defeat at the battle of the Nile. There, he had judged it too dangerous to expose his frigate to the larger British ships by lending support to his admiral's endangered flagship and had stayed out of the fighting. He had escaped along with Villeneuve and the two had taken refuge in Malta. Although he was a gifted administrator, Decrès proved on more than one occasion that he was more keen to cling to power than to improve the French navy. In particular he avoided promoting people who might be a threat to him, and he met the Emperor's request for a list of young officers who looked like future admirals with inertia.

Both Villeneuve and Decrès genuinely believed that the French navy needed more time, more money spent on it and a great deal of practice before it was pitted against the British fleet. They felt that Latouche had given Napoleon a falsely optimistic view of the navy's chances, and their joint strategy for 1805 was to persuade the Emperor of the wisdom of their more cautious approach. Without absolutely disobeying orders, they intended to do their best not to commit the fleet to battle and especially not to throw it away in a suicidal attempt to invade Britain. Villeneuve wrote pessimistic letters to Decrès for his friend to use in dissuading the Emperor from the rash course of action upon which he seemed bent.

The view that the best way to deal with the British was to avoid a fleet action was shared wholeheartedly by Spanish captains such as Dionisio Alcalá Galiano. In June 1805 he had taken two ships out to sea to train their inexperienced crews in manoeuvre. They took an age to get under way and then, to Galiano's mortification, made terrible mistakes while tacking out of the harbour in front of people watching from the city and the British frigates observing them from out at sea. Galiano reported to Vice Admiral Ignacio de Álava, who had taken command of the fleet at Cadiz in Gravina's absence, that, owing to the present state of its crew, his ship was a laughing-stock and the men needed further training in basic seamanship before they were capable of leaving the bay. The only promising sign was their eagerness to fight. Antonio Galiano reported that his father was so disgusted that he was considering resigning from the navy at the next peace.

While the crews were belligerent, most Spanish officers were cautious about their prospects in a fleet action. Cosme de Churruca was revered in Spain to an even greater degree than his friend Dionisio Galiano. Churruca was a forty-three-year-old Basque, just under a year younger than Galiano. During the siege of Gibraltar (1779–82) he had helped to save the crews of the floating batteries set on fire by the British. Like Galiano, he had helped to chart the Strait of Magellan. Then, in 1792, he had sailed to Trinidad to map the Antilles with instruments specially ordered from London.

On his return to Spain he had worked with Antonio de Escaño on a *Diccionario de Marina* and stood in for him as chief of staff at Cadiz during Nelson's blockade of 1797–8 while he was ill. Subsequently he took his ship the *Conquistador* to Brest where he served under Latouche. In France he wrote manuals on naval discipline and training, and ship engineering.

Despite his fame, Churruca was not a wealthy man: he had not been paid for years and, in fact, was reduced to embarrassing poverty. He swept into Cadiz with the faster ships of the Combined Fleet on 20 August, wearing a tattered coat and anxious about his newly married wife Dolores, left in Ferrol with his unpaid debts. His crew had not been paid either and the next day the marines on his ship *San Juan Nepomuceno* mutinied. Churruca contrived to save the ringleaders from the death penalty and the two companies involved were disbanded and distributed among other ships. Given the abject failure of the Spanish government to look after its men, the wonder is that this was the only mutiny.

Spain's attempt at neutrality left her at a disadvantage when she decided to fight. The ships were not prepared, the crews were not in place and, having paid Napoleon for the right to remain neutral, there was no money left. When Villeneuve had appeared off Cadiz in April *en route* for the West Indies, Gravina had taken six more or less seaworthy ships to sea, but of the 2220 experienced seamen who should have been on board, 606 were missing. Villeneuve was impressed that Gravina had sailed at all. Between March and September the naval authorities in Cadiz managed to arm twenty-nine ships, but they were stretching to the limit their resources in money, materials and especially men.

Spain trained good officers but she never had enough seamen. 'The Dons may make fine ships – they cannot, however, make men,' Nelson had commented when he was once shown round Cadiz. Spain's navy was an artificial construct without a base of manpower to sustain it. The men would have arrived if trade with Latin America had been allowed to flourish. In 1783 Spain's merchant fleet was a fifth the size of that of France and an eighth of Britain's. An expanded merchant fleet would have produced more seamen, but in 1801 Spain had only 6000 employed in ocean-going vessels. That entire body would have been just enough to give the ships currently at Cadiz good crews, but few were available. An epidemic of yellow fever in 1800 had killed 5810 men and 1577 women in Cadiz, chiefly in the seafaring community where it had started. A second outbreak in 1804 caused further casualties in Cadiz, Málaga and Cartagena.

However, the Spanish had an alternative strategy to a fleet action: they were confident of their ability to defend the home base of Cadiz against any assault by the British. During the previous blockade they had devised an impressive system of defensive tactics that had been admired and copied by the French. They had repulsed Nelson in 1797 and the British had not dared to attack again.

By the time Villeneuve reached Cadiz, Álava and the governor of Cadiz, Francisco Solano, Marqués de la Solana, had already renewed and reorganised the port defences. Solano was a man of martial bearing and immense energy, more like a French soldier than a Spanish one, markedly theatrical in his self-presentation. Indeed, he had fought with the French republican army in the late 1790s in one of the regiments – the 67th – that Villeneuve had brought to Cadiz. He established four gunboat outposts, two to the north of the city at Sanlúcar and Rota, one in the little harbour on the point of Cadiz between the forts, and one to the south at the mouth of the Sancti Petri river. Strong coastal batteries were placed strategically to cover anchorages, entrances to harbours and to support the gunboats.

As soon as it reached Cadiz, the Combined Fleet began to reorganise.

The infantry disembarked and set up a camp at the far end of the harbour six miles from Cadiz 'in a very healthy place within reach of fresh water', ready to embark in two hours. Having left behind some sick men, there remained 1400 from two battalions of the 16th Regiment and about a thousand from a strong battalion of the 67th, with detachments from the 1st Swiss and the 6th Dépôt Coloniale. The 67th had a proud tradition of service at sea, tracing their history to the regiment raised by Cardinal Richelieu as 'La Marine'. The Spanish also had regiments that had long specialised in naval service, some of which had fought with the Armada in 1588. They had men from the Regimiento de Cordoba, the Regimiento de Soria, the Regimiento de Africa, the Regimiento del Corona and the Regimiento de Burgos.

The acquisition of provisions and spares for the ships was more of a problem. Fitting out fifteen ships in record time earlier that year had exhausted the resources of the Carraca, the arsenal in the Isla de León outside Cadiz. Food was in similarly short supply and it was difficult to comply with Villeneuve's demand for two months' victuals for 17,000 men. But the main problem was money. The French consul at Cadiz, Le Roy, had none and experience had taught Cadiz merchants not to accept bills drawn on the French Ministry of Marine. As for the Spanish government, that had 'not the flimsiest credit'. As a result even the agent victualler at the Isla de León wanted cash for ship's biscuit. Fortunately, the Spanish ships had been stocked for six months and transferred some provisions to the French.

Villeneuve's first full report from Cadiz to Decrès was written in his habitual gloomy style. He appreciated the Spanish point of view, which coincided with his own cool-headed assessment of their joint prospects. At present, he reported that the Tavira Tower had identified eleven British ships outside Cadiz and that another twenty-three had been seen from Lisbon, steering south.

At Boulogne, Napoleon was losing patience. He had ordered Admiral Honoré Ganteaume, in command of the twenty-one French ships-of-the-line blockaded in Brest, to be ready to leave at once. Ganteaume took the whole of his squadron to the outer roads, and when the seventeen blockading Royal Navy ships reacted by making to attack, there was a brief skirmish involving the shore batteries. Ganteaume withdrew behind the headlands, evidently no more determined to fight his way to Boulogne than Villeneuve. Later that day, 22 August, Napoleon learned that Villeneuve had left Ferrol. The Emperor was sceptical enough about this timid admiral's likely behaviour to send orders for him to Cadiz. He was to return forthwith to the Channel with as many ships as he could muster. Decrès protested, and urged the Emperor to abandon the invasion attempt.

He had not needed to waste his ink: aware that Pitt's attempts to turn the Austrians and Russians against him were bearing fruit, Napoleon was already making new plans. 'The more I reflect on the situation of Europe the more I see it is urgent to take a decisive line,' he wrote to his foreign minister, Talleyrand, on 23 August. 'I have, in reality, nothing to expect from Austria's explanation. She will only reply with fair phrases, and gain time to prevent my doing anything this winter . . . and in April I shall find 100,000 Russians in Poland, supplied by England with equipment, horses, artillery, &c., and 15,000 to 20,000 English at Malta, and 15,000 Russians at Corfu. I shall then find myself in a critical situation. My decision is made.'

On 25 August Napoleon told Talleyrand that, for the present, he had abandoned the invasion of England. He would bring his reserve units to Boulogne while his fighting battalions marched eastwards. He began to work out the routes that the renamed Grande Armée would take in its march on Vienna. For the present the troops did not move, so nobody yet knew that, during 1805 at least, the direct threat to Britain's shores had been lifted. The war was about to enter a new phase in which Napoleon's army would attack on France's eastern front, while his fleet would operate in the Mediterranean. Perhaps Villeneuve's decision to retire to Cadiz could be turned to advantage after all.

To many people in France, Napoleon was a godsend: he seemed to have realised the original goals of the Revolution without its excesses. In the navy, he allowed experienced aristocratic officers to command but kept in place the reforms that enabled talented commoners to become senior officers. There was still some dross, thanks to political extremism, but a number of talented and determined officers owed to the Revolution and then the new Emperor their opportunity to lead.

Latouche himself had supported the Revolution and his subsequent incarceration and ejection from the navy had not prejudiced him against men of quality from lowly origins. In the old Marine Royale he had encouraged such men. One of the first he had rewarded for distinction in action was Jean-Jacques Lucas, now commanding *Redoutable*. Latouche had gathered several such men about him in his flagship *Bucentaure*, and Villeneuve willingly inherited them. As adjutant, Latouche had chosen Mathieu Prigny, a charming, intelligent, civilised officer, previously in command of a frigate. His flag-captain, Jean-Jacques Magendie, had been captured three times by the British. On the last occasion in 1801, as second captain of the frigate *Africaine*, which was crowded with troops, he had been one of three hundred casualties in an especially bloody action against the British frigate *Phoebe*. *Bucentaure*'s second in command was acting Commander Joseph-Gabriel Daudignon. He was forty-four, five years older than Magendie and, like Magendie, came from Bordeaux. Before the war he had owned his own merchant ship, but when hostilities began he had been conscripted and forced to sell it for treasury bills that proved to be without value. He proved himself to Latouche through various missions in Saint-Domingue and in a skirmish with the British at Toulon. He had led the little boats in Villeneuve's attack on the Diamond Rock off Martinique earlier in the summer and he was still limping from having taken a British musket ball in his left knee.

Thirty-nine-year-old Lieutenant Fulcran Fournier, from Agde in Languedoc, had also been forced out of his family's merchant ship and into the navy. He had a broken kneecap and a scar on his left cheek from his many fights with the British, who had also captured him twice. As a veteran of the battle of the Nile his presence must have been a reminder to Villeneuve of his own less than glorious role in that defeat. Indeed, in 1803 Fournier's commander at the Nile, Admiral

Blanquet, had publicly criticised the conduct of Villeneuve and Decrès during the battle before he resigned from the navy. Both Daudignon and Fournier had recently experienced victory as well as defeat and both had distinguished themselves in independent commands. They were tough, efficient fighters and commanded a crew of which Villeneuve was proud.

The other officers of the Toulon squadron were a similar mix of aristocratic officers trained in the Marine Royale and petty officers promoted with the help of the Revolution. Louis Infernet was captain of *Intrépide*, one of the ships ceded by the Spanish, a man who was 'as big as a drum-major and as fat as a *ci-devant* Benedictine Prior'. He was of merchant-seaman stock, and by 1786 was captaining a ship when he married the daughter of a schoolteacher. The Revolution helped him, too, become a naval captain, and he did well in frigates during the 1790s. In 1804 he distinguished himself at Toulon in the same action as Daudignon, and was placed in line for the next vacancy in a battleship. When *Intrépide*'s captain was killed fighting Calder in July 1805, Infernet had been promoted.

Sub-lieutenant Auguste Gicquel had a low regard for officers promoted from the lower ranks, but he warmed to his new captain. Gicquel came from an aristocratic Breton family who had fallen on hard times. During the Revolution their home had been sacked and Gicquel had run away to sea, serving as a boy during the French fleet's lowest period. Eventually he became an officer and was made a foundation member of Napoleon's Légion d'Honneur for his bravery during the battle of Algeciras. Gicquel had also won the regard of the *Intrépide*'s crew by jumping into the sea to save a man who had fallen overboard. He had further distinguished himself when he commanded an exposed outpost in Saint-Domingue where 70 per cent of his colleagues had died from disease or been assassinated by black slaves they had thought loyal to them. He was still only twenty.

Five of the ships now at Cadiz, *Formidable*, *Scipion*, *Mont-Blanc*, *Swiftsure* and *Intrépide*, had crews who had been through some part of the 1802–3 campaign in Saint-Domingue, an exceptionally brutal affair in which atrocity had matched atrocity. In 1803 the French army had brought in slave-hunting bloodhounds borrowed from Cuba. They had fed them on slaves' flesh, starved them, then gone looking for 'brigands'.

The other five ships from Toulon were newly built or newly repaired. It had been a struggle to find crews for them. In theory the French had a system of conscription by which seamen served in relays on their warships; it required half of the young men of selected communities to go to sea together. The system had never worked properly in wartime and had broken down completely over recent years so that the Ministry of Marine was reduced to pressing in the British style. Officers of the press began with lists of those liable for service, but such men quickly learned how to avoid them. In late autumn 1803 Honoré Ganteaume, then maritime prefect at Toulon, tried to find a crew for *Bucentaure*. From Narbonne, Agde, Sète and Arles the recruiting officers only managed to find 200 of the 708 men listed. Fifty proved unfit to serve and fifty more deserted before they reached Toulon. In one instance eighty soldiers closed in on the village of Banyuls but all the seamen escaped the net and hid in the mountains.

In January 1804, a *levée extraordinaire* took place in Marseilles, executed with the help of an escort of *chasseurs à cheval*. They found several seamen with exemptions from naval service and some foreigners, but few experienced sailors. In the end, they kept only 150 men. A similar hot press was observed at Rochefort. In November 1804 one of Nelson's frigate captains, Thomas Capel of *Phoebe*, found a pilot of Marseilles 'accompanied by only one man both in a most wretched state and only keeping the sea from apprehension of being prest for the fleet in Toulon. They assured me that 3 or 4 nights past every individual in the shape of a seaman both from the Vessels and houses were seized and sent to the fleet.'

Captain Jean-Jacques Magendie took seamen for *Bucentaure* from wherever he could find them – on port vessels and merchant ships. On one occasion he intercepted two hundred black prisoners from

Guadeloupe who were being deported to Corsica in a vessel commanded by Gabriel Daudignon and recruited them and Daudignon for the Toulon squadron. The French colonies were considered part of France, so their citizens and recently freed slaves were automatically subject to conscription. However, a new law passed in Paris debarred foreigners from service in the French navy, and before he died Latouche himself discovered that he had to part with an American officer who had been with him for years, officially as his interpreter.

The French owed some of their difficulties in raising crews to the enforcement of such high legal principles. Not only did they debar foreigners but, unlike the British and Spanish, they had no system for supplementing their crews with landsmen who could be trained at sea. The seamen themselves had resolutely opposed dilution of the quality of their ships' companies. From 1804 onwards emergency measures were implemented. A plan was formed to raise 5000 seamen from Genoa in Napoleon's Italian domain. In the meantime, in the summer of 1804 two élite battalions of the 2nd Infantry Regiment were brought in to serve on the Toulon ships. The soldiers imagined that they were an expeditionary force intended for the invasion of Britain but they were put to work on the guns, liberating a thousand seamen for more skilled duties. Napoleon encouraged this sensible expedient.

Ganteaume concluded that 'the districts were almost depopulated of this precious class of men [experienced sailors] . . . English prisons, and the expeditions to Egypt and America have destroyed a great number of them'. However, French recruitment difficulties should not be exaggerated. British ships carried far fewer experienced seamen than their French counterparts. Even if the numbers had to be made up with soldiers and former slaves, there were as many actual seamen in the French ships at Cadiz as there were in their British opponents'.

Villeneuve's second-in-command was Pierre Dumanoir, who had commanded the squadron for four months after Latouche died and before Villeneuve was appointed over his head. Dumanoir had an influential uncle in Paris and had been one of the select band under Ganteaume who had helped Napoleon escape from Egypt after the battle of the Nile. During the brief period that he commanded it he had not won the squadron's confidence but he resented his replacement.

Apart from his Toulon squadron, Villeneuve's other ships-of-the-line were all originally from Rochefort. The people of Bordeaux and the south-western coastline who provided the men for the Rochefort ships (as well as many officers in those from Toulon) had good reason to hate the British. To many of them, trade with Saint-Domingue and the other West Indian colonies was their livelihood: most of the 15,000 French seamen employed in the West Indies trade came from this region. The British seizure in 1803 of sixty-three Bordeaux merchant ships that were at sea and ignorant of the outbreak of war, combined with the bombardment of French towns and villages along the coast that followed its declaration, had incensed the local population and generated an unusual degree of animosity towards the old enemy.

The captain of the *Aigle*, Pierre-Paulin Gourrège, was another who had been toughened by experience. In 1752 when he was born there Bordeaux was entering a period of prosperity. His father was a merchant captain whose ships picked up slaves from the Guinea Coast of Africa, sold them in Saint-Domingue, then returned to Bordeaux with a cargo of sugar or coffee. Gourrège's elder brother, Guillaume, had established himself as a merchant in Saint-Domingue to manage the family's affairs there. Gourrège himself had gone to sea as a boy and served in privateers in New England during the American Revolutionary War. He fought in two fierce boarding engagements; during one he was wounded in the thigh by a British pike. In 1802 Gourrège commanded the *Jean Bart* during the carnage in Saint-Domingue. He was briefly flag-captain to Latouche and host to the beautiful Pauline Bonaparte, Napoleon's sister. Then he returned to France to beg the government for the 4363 francs that he was owed in back pay. Now Bordeaux's trade was drying up and its population declining fast, owing to the collapse of trade with Saint-Domingue.

In November 1802 Gourrège was appointed to command the *Aigle*, which had been launched at Rochefort in 1798. 'This vessel is superb,' he wrote, to the minister of marine's secretary. The ship was immediately armed for Saint-Domingue. Her crew came from Bordeaux and the villages on that part of the French coast: they took part in the campaign to defeat the renegade slave leader Toussaint-L'Ouverture, then returned to France, taking refuge in Cadiz when war broke out. After Gourrège had left Saint-Domingue, his brother Guillaume was murdered by 'brigands' during another slave rising fomented by the British.

A penniless fifty-year-old Dutchman, Lieutenant Asmus Classen, joined Gourrège at Cadiz. As he was an experienced seaman and Gourrège was short of lieutenants, the French captain was glad of his presence and wrote to Decrès in support of Classen's claim for the 2273 francs he was owed in back pay. Like Gourrège, Classen had been an enthusiastic revolutionary and had fled to France when the Prussians and the British crushed Holland's own revolution in 1787. He was on the frigate *Concorde* when she took William Hargood's *Hyaena* in May 1793 off Saint-Domingue, and he had been a lieutenant for five years in *Jemmapes* under Julien Cosmao-Kerjulien, one of Villeneuve's best captains.

Aigle had remained at neutral Cadiz, getting repairs in the Carraca under the watchful eye of Nelson's spy, Consul Duff. During that time her crew repeatedly brawled with visiting English seamen, but Gourrège was well liked there and was now renewing acquaintance with his friends.

Of the other ships now under Villeneuve, five, *Fougueux*, *Redoutable*, *Argonaute*, *Héros* and *Duguay-Trouin*, had been blockaded at Ferrol for two years and were short of sea-going experience. Two other warships, *Algésiras* and *Achille*, both recently built and recently manned, had joined him in the West Indies, commanded by Rear Admiral Charles Magon, who was easily the most spirited and pugnacious of the French admirals. His father had been an administrator in Saint-Domingue and he himself had worked in the colonial office as well as on the committee charged with improving the organisation of the fleet. As he had married a viscountess just before the Revolution, Magon's career was dogged by accusations of royalism: he had to divorce his wife to save their property. His money – like that of several other French officers – was invested in the colonies and he viewed their retention as a matter of personal as well as national importance.

As a young man Magon had taken part in the action at Chesapeake Bay that had sealed the fate of General Cornwallis's army at Yorktown and with it that of the British in America. He had beaten British ships in actions in the Indian Ocean. He knew that the French navy was capable of better than its recent abject performances and he burned for revenge against the British.

In his naval history of 1823 William James asserted that 'no deduction need be made for inexperience in the Franco-Spanish crews'. This goes too far: some Spanish crews, especially, lacked sea-going experience. But it is not true that British blockades had kept all the enemy's ships in port for years, as some histories of Trafalgar claim: many French and some Spanish sailors had fought in Saint-Domingue, the Toulon ships had trained carefully under Latouche, and in 1805 many seamen in both squadrons had been to the West Indies and back, and had fought an even battle against Calder. Villeneuve was pessimistic because he thought Decrès wanted him to be so, but much of the muttering in the Combined Fleet as it arrived at Cadiz was born of frustration. Many, like Magon, were spoiling for a fight and must have wished Latouche was still leading them.

5

As Smooth as the Lake at Stowe

On 31 August Vice Admiral Sir Robert Calder arrived off Cadiz with his eighteen ships, and the imaginary fleet to which Collingwood had been making fake signals became real. Hoping the new arrivals had not been detected, Collingwood, who took charge as the senior admiral, kept Calder's ships over the horizon and tried to tempt the enemy out to fight his own small squadron.

George Duff, captain of *Mars*, wrote to his wife Sophia that their old friend Pulteney Malcolm of the *Donegal* 'is gone inshore with Admiral Louis, to get the combined fleet out, as we do not show our reinforcement, in hopes they may be tempted to come out; but I fear they will hear of it, and remain quietly at anchor'. He was right. Thomas Fremantle of *Neptune*, gloomily resigned to a long blockade, told his wife Betsy, 'as the combined fleets are safely lodged in Cadiz, here I conclude we shall remain until Domesday or until we are blown off the Coast, when the French men will again escape us'.

Edward Codrington, captain of the newly arrived *Orion*, also anticipated a prolonged blockade: 'Alas! I cannot look back to our little domestic enjoyments without feeling quite unmanned by the prospect of long, long absence from all hope of a renewal of them,' he wrote to his wife Jane. They had married in December 1802 and this was their first real separation. 'Surely Edward misses me, even if fat little William has lost all remembrance of my dandling him. His sweet laugh has, however, left such traces in my memory as will not be easily forgotten!' Codrington hoped for an early resolution but he didn't expect one. 'It would be very annoying to my feelings to see an inferior fleet of an enemy challenging that of the nation to which I belonged, even under the very walls of its principal harbour. The old Spanish pride, if there is any left, must be galled by it,' he went on, 'but the French I dare say console themselves under the knowledge that our fleet is wearing itself out whilst theirs is repairing; and I believe success from cunning is just as gratifying to a Frenchman as if gained in battle.'

Blockading had been the way of it in this war and the last. The French and Spanish kept their ships in port, rarely coming out unless the British were driven away by bad weather. The French asserted that the Royal Navy's ships were getting worn out by constant service. The British captains, who hated the boredom of blockading, worried that they might be right. The seamen loathed doing nothing (especially in rough winter weather off Brest) and the more truculent deserted whenever they could.

Blockading Cadiz in summer was tolerably pleasant from the climatic point of view. The sun shone and there was little for the seamen to do. Richard Anderson, master of the *Prince*, told his wife Mary that he spent much of his time playing his fiddle and reading books. But Fremantle and Codrington found the social life disappointing: isolated by rank on their own ships, captains liked to dine with each other and with a friendly admiral, but some admirals discouraged such familiarity. William Cornwallis, the admiral off Brest, was famously austere, and Fremantle and Codrington considered that Collingwood was of the same mould. 'Our Admiral is an humble follower of Cornwallis,' wrote Fremantle to Betsy, 'and I have not yet seen him or anybody else, I am entirely confined on board and know no more what is going on than you do.' Codrington agreed: 'We have got into the clutches of another stay-on board Admiral, who never communicates with anybody but upon service; and so, unless Bonaparte orders his fleet out, we stand a very good chance of forgetting that anything like society is known amongst men.' They were unlucky, but George Duff dined with his fellow Scot, Rear Admiral Lord Northesk, on *Britannia* and on *Canopus* with Admiral Thomas Louis and his flag-captain, Francis Austen, brother of the novelist Jane.

On 5 September Codrington finally met Collingwood. 'Finding that the Admiral rather thought me inattentive to one of his orders, I went on board, and rather surprised him by the account I gave of our various wants and inability to assist others.' He found Collingwood unexpectedly 'good-humoured, chatty, and communicative', but he noted critically that 'He seems to do everything himself with great attention to the minutiae.'

Fremantle, however, was growing ever more frustrated with Collingwood's inattention to him. 'What adds more to this cursed deprivation of Society is that the Weather has been remarkably fine and the Sea as smooth as the Lake at Stow,' he complained. He had heard nothing from his wife but he knew that she must be in the last stages of pregnancy. His mind returned to the famous house and landscape garden at Stowe in Buckinghamshire, which was where Betsy was. Each summer they, or she, spent some time at Stowe with Fremantle's patron, George Grenville, Marquess of Buckingham. Some weeks ago she had written to him about the festivities there:

> the Grotto being illuminated & the greatest concourse of people possible being assembled in the gardens, we all followed the Prince [of Wales] in Procession to the Grotto, among the shouts of the multitude, who crowded so much upon us we had some difficulty in reaching to the destined spot, which had the appearance of enchantment, the Grotto & surrounding scene being illuminated most brilliantly, the Bridge & Obelisk on the water had a charming effect. Several Maskers were pitched on the banks, & groupes of Morice Dancers, the Bands of the Pandeons, Savoyards, & of the Regiments who were on the water played in succession and enlivened the scene, the crowd was so great, there being at least 10,000 people.

She told him how she had watched all this 'snug in the Grotto by Charles Fox'. He wrote back asking what she made of Charles James

Fox, the great Whig leader, and wished he was not stuck in lone splendour on a ship hundreds of miles away while she might by now be in labour. He was becoming increasingly tetchy with everyone around him but chiefly with Collingwood. 'I wish and hope either Lord Gardner or Lord Nelson will soon be here as I confess I do not bear patiently from Collingwood what I should do more with a man of better pretensions to such severity.'

In London, Fremantle's wish was about to be granted. At five o'clock on the morning of 2 September Captain Henry Blackwood of the frigate *Euryalus* appeared on Nelson's doorstep with news of the arrival of the Combined Fleet at Cadiz. Blackwood had stopped on his way to the Admiralty with dispatches from Admiral Collingwood. The Prime Minister had already told Nelson to expect to resume command in the Mediterranean, and he followed Blackwood to Whitehall to join the inevitable council of war.

At the Admiralty Lord Barham invited Nelson to choose his officers. Nelson decided against altering the command of the ships already off the coast of Spain, but he had Sir Edward Berry, his old friend and comrade-in-arms, appointed to their old ship, *Agamemnon*, which was being prepared for action. William Brown and William Lechmere, commanders of *Ajax* and *Thunderer* from Calder's squadron, were ordered to join him as soon as their ships had been repaired. So was Richard Keats, another of Nelson's trusted 'Band of Brothers', but his ship, *Superb*, would take some time to repair. In *Euryalus*, Henry Blackwood would accompany Nelson to Cadiz while one of the Admiral's *protégés*, John Conn, a cousin by marriage, was to bring out the three-decker *Royal Sovereign*, which had been in Nelson's own Mediterranean squadron. On 5 September Nelson's servants, Henry Chevalier and Gaetano Spedillo, left Merton Place for Portsmouth with his heavy baggage.

On 6 September a note summoned Nelson to the Admiralty to collect his orders, and he attended a council at Downing Street. The news was mixed. Nelson wanted as many ships as the enemy had, but at present no more ships were available. They planned to send him out in *Victory* and reinforce him later. He could hope eventually for forty ships but for the time being he would have to make do with about twenty-seven. Nelson reminded the ministers that 'It is, as Mr. Pitt knows, annihilation that the Country wants.' They discussed the potential of Colonel William Congreve's newly invented rockets as a means of bringing the Combined Fleet out to fight but Nelson wanted enough ships to win a crushing victory and 'to bring Buonaparte to his marrow-bones'.

A few days later in the Admiralty waiting room he met Philip Durham, of the *Defiance*, another of Calder's ships that had come home for repairs. Nelson regretted that *Defiance* would not be ready to join his fleet. 'Ask Lord Barham to place me under your Lordship's orders, and I will soon be ready,' Durham replied. Next day at the George Inn, Portsmouth, Durham was delighted to receive the letter he had hoped for. It read: 'Pursuant to instructions from the Lords Commissioners of the Admiralty, you are hereby required and directed to put yourself under my command, and follow and obey all such orders as you shall from time to time receive from me for His Majesty's Service, Nelson and Bronte.'

In September 1805 France could put forty-four ships-of-the-line to sea, and Spain thirty, while Britain had an overwhelming 135. But every Royal Navy commander at sea wondered where those battleships were. They never seemed to be on the spot when they were needed. There was some truth in the French argument that because British ships were constantly at sea, blockading the enemy coast, they were repeatedly required to return to port to make repairs.

It would be some time before Nelson had a force likely to overwhelm the thirty-seven vessels known to be in Cadiz. Ships from his own fleet would have to be detached to guard convoys, obtain provisions and counteract the six Spanish ships inside the Mediterranean at Cartagena. Nevertheless, after years of British success there were now few enough French and Spanish ships left for the British to win strategically even if they lost a battle. One substantial engagement would put such a dent in French and Spanish resources that they would no longer pose a serious threat of invasion. In his mind Nelson was already designing a battle in which British casualties were not important. What mattered was that the battle caused as much destruction to the enemy as possible. They must not have the chance to slip away with only minor damage, as they had when fighting Calder and so many times before.

As he paced the new walk at Merton that he called the 'quarterdeck' Nelson explained his ideas to Richard Keats. 'I would go at them at once, if I can,' he told Keats, 'about one-third of their line from their leading ship. What do you think of it? . . . I'll tell you what I think of it. I think it will surprise and confound the enemy. They won't know what I am about. It will bring forward a pell-mell battle and that is what I want.'

'I have no reason to complain of my Ship, which is in real perfect order,' wrote Thomas Fremantle, 'but my temper naturaly hasty is often put to the trial by my First Lieutenant, who has so long been in the habit of governing the Ship in his way, that he cannot bear the smallest contradiction, which in turn obliges me to follow up my own System without benefiting by his assistance and advice, this added to the influence he has got in the ship obliges me to be very circumspect.' George Arklom had been the proud first lieutenant of *Neptune* since 1803, while Fremantle had only joined the ship in May 1805. *Neptune* was a three-decker of ninety-eight guns built in 1797. Fremantle didn't like to be in 'a large Ship that dont sail and must continualy be late in action', preferring smaller, faster vessels, but he could not complain about *Neptune*'s crew.

Her complement was 738, but she was eighteen men short. She had 116 marines commanded by Lieutenant George Kendall. There were thirty-four boys, divided by background and age into three categories: the first class were training to become officers, and the others were divided into second-class boys aged under eighteen and third-class under fifteen. The remaining 570 men were the ship's company. Some were old hands, and many of the new ones were good. The able seamen were an unusually cosmopolitan lot, even by the standards of the Royal Navy. There were men from all of the Baltic states, Spain, Portugal, Sardinia, Venice and Livorno, from Puerto Rico and Martinique, and the usual group from Canada and North America. Two seamen had brought their sons. Edward Nosworthy, rated gunner's mate, who had fought at the battle of the Nile in *Minotaur*, joined *Neptune* in November 1803 with his son William, aged eleven. David Ozaley had brought his nine-year-old son Joseph, the youngest boy in *Neptune*. Since Joseph had been born at sea his mother might also have been on board – petty officers and other old hands sometimes brought their wives with them. Since the women did not draw pay they do not appear in muster books, but their presence in small numbers was tolerated and possibly commonplace.

This, then, was the excellent crew joined by James Martin, aged twenty-six from Wivenhoe near Colchester, the author of one of the rare accounts of the Trafalgar campaign to have been written by a seaman rather than an officer. Martin had been born on 11 March 1778, and was picked up in late May 1803 in Guernsey by a press-gang from the frigate *Blanche*. What he was doing in Guernsey we do not know – Frenchmen sometimes went there to avoid conscription – but he had been bred to the sea and was rated able seaman. He seems to have been allowed to go home in late September, because his wife was about to give birth, on condition that he returned to the navy immediately afterwards. At any rate, a son was born on 5 October and on 19 November his father rejoined the navy as a volunteer. On the receiving ship, *Salvador del Mundo*, he was chosen for the *Neptune* and had been on her ever since.

Everybody was bored: 'The very sad sameness makes all days like one day . . . a life of misery and ennui,' wrote Fremantle. He had ordered the men to paint his lower cabins to keep them occupied. In *Orion* Edward Codrington had ordered harpoons from England: 'I do not expect to draw much blood with them, but if I can make the people amuse and employ themselves with them, it will answer my purpose.' The problem was, as Fremantle explained, that 'The large sum of money which was paid to our people, and which they have had no opportunity of getting rid of, is the cause of much drunkenness, thieving, and gambling.'

Neptune's crew had been paid in May and had had no chance to spend their money. The principal means by which Fremantle kept indiscipline at bay was flogging. The culprits were secured to a grating and the crew mustered to watch them beaten by a boatswain's mate with a rope cat-o'-nine-tails. The maximum penalty recommended by naval ordinance was twelve lashes, but by 1805 this was the norm. Fremantle was not over-enthusiastic in his flogging: between May and mid-October he punished thirty-eight of his men, 5.3 per cent of his crew. Three were punished twice, Daniel Barry, ordinary seaman from Limerick, three times, and John McGuire, landsman from Kilkenny, five. Drunkenness and neglect of duty were the usual offences, but if they were compounded by insolence or repetition, Fremantle would hand out twenty-four lashes, and in extreme cases thirty-six. Theft was always more heavily punished, and twenty-four was Fremantle's starting point for this offence.

Custom varied: no punishments are recorded in *Belleisle*'s log book, though perhaps this reflects lax recording. Thomas Hardy, of *Victory*, was among the most violent captains and thirty-six lashes was his normal response to drunkenness or neglect. A marine named John Moore was given seventy-two for theft and survived to fight at Trafalgar.

Charles Tyler, of *Tonnant*, who, according to Lieutenant Hoffman, never punished a man unless he richly deserved it, flogged ninety-four of his 673 men between March and mid-October, 14 per cent of the crew. In his ship, drunkenness was, overwhelmingly, the most popular misdemeanour, followed by fighting, and twelve lashes was his norm. He once handed out forty-eight to an Irish landsman for 'willfully cutting a man's hand with his knife'.

The ultimate sanction was a court-martial, which seamen underwent only for serious crimes, like mutiny or sodomy, punishable by death. Officers could be tried for apparently trivial offences, as was the case in the court-martial called on board Calder's flagship, *Prince of Wales*, on 18 September, in which Lieutenant Nathaniel Fish was removed from the *Minotaur* and placed at the bottom of the list of lieutenants for insolence to Captain Charles Mansfield.

For the captains off Cadiz, the court-martial provided a welcome occasion for what Codrington called 'as social a dinner as I was ever at; and the beautiful music [Calder's] band gave us to make our wine relish, made us all regret the more the difficulty of repeating our visit. It was really to me (and I am sure it would have been to you) a most animating sight; an admiral surrounded by twenty of his captains in social intercourse, showing a strong desire to support each other cordially and manfully in the event of a battle taking place.' They all wanted a battle that would cut short the war. 'Peace, peace, is the anxious cry here. Hope [George Hope of *Defence*] has been fourteen months at home in these eight years; and Captain Rutherford [William Rutherford of *Swiftsure*] told us yesterday, declaring that it was d—d foolish for a sailor to marry – that he had been in that happy state for nine years, one only of which had he been with his wife!' They also wanted to see Nelson with the fleet. As Codrington wrote, 'For charity's sake send us Lord Nelson, oh ye men of power!'

Nelson's last few days in England passed quickly. On 10 September he and Emma dined at the home of socialite James Crawford. Emma wanted Nelson to tell the company how he had been mobbed in the streets but he stopped her in mid-sentence. 'You like to be applauded – you cannot deny it', was her rejoinder. Nelson impressed his fellow guests with his unexpected modesty: 'Popular applause is very acceptable and grateful to me, but no man ought to be too much elated by it; it is too precarious to be depended upon, and as it may be my turn to feel the tide set as strong against me as ever it did for me.' When they pressed him they were even more impressed by the simplicity of his determination: 'Everybody joined in saying that they did not believe it could happen to him, but he seemed persuaded that it might, but added: "Whilst I live I shall do what I think right and best; the country has a right to that from me, but every man is liable to err in judgment . . ." ' Later Lady Bessborough reported more of this conversation: 'He says nothing short of the annihilation of the enemy's fleet will do any good. "When we meet, God be with us, for we must not part again till one fleet or other is totally destroyed." He hopes to be returned by Christmas.'

The next day at home at Merton Nelson received an unexpected but unrefusable invitation from the Prince of Wales for the next day. To the Prince's disappointment Nelson left Emma at home and squeezed him in before he met Lord Castlereagh, the secretary at war, and Lord Mulgrave at Downing Street. While waiting he met Sir Arthur Wellesley, the future Duke of Wellington, whose predisposition to find Nelson full of himself was at first confirmed and then dispelled. Eventually Wellesley concluded that Nelson 'really was a very superior man'.

At Merton, Nelson's dinner guests, Lord Minto, lawyer and former governor of Corsica, and James Perry, editor of the *Morning Chronicle*, were waiting patiently for their host to return from Pitt's home. At first Minto did not recognise Perry, who was a neighbour of Nelson, but as they chatted to fill the time it emerged that they had met before. Minto had jailed the Whig editor for libel during Pitt's crackdown on radicals in 1793. One of Perry's crimes had been to publish a series of 'Epigrammatica Bacchanalia' after the prime minister had appeared drunk in the Commons on the day that war was declared, of which one read, 'In what odd ways we taste misfortune's cup – / While France throws *down* the gauntlet, Pitt throws *up*.' After a while Nelson's chaplain Alexander Scott appeared, which probably eased the conversation. Finally Nelson arrived, two hours late. Minto could barely tolerate Lady Hamilton's theatrical sentimentality. She was in tears, 'could not eat, and hardly drink, and near swooning, and all at table'. It was not an easy dinner.

The admiral spent his last day at home, Friday, 13 September, with Emma, Horatia, his nephews and nieces, and left in the late evening. He travelled overnight to arrive at the George Inn at Portsmouth in the early morning. At the dockyard he found that Berry, Durham and Conn's ships were not quite ready for sea so he instructed them to follow him as quickly as they could. He collected the copies of Sir Home Popham's *Telegraphic Signals, or Marine Vocabulary* that had been sent from London. This was a new, flexible signalling system and Nelson had ordered sufficient copies for all the ships in his fleet. Then he pushed through cheering crowds to his boat and dined with Pitt's friends George Canning and George Rose on *Victory*. On 15 September *Victory* put to sea. The next day, to Nelson's frustration, the wind turned dead against him.

6

À la Nelson

As Nelson was leaving England, Napoleon was issuing new orders. On 14 September he wrote to Villeneuve, 'Having resolved to make a powerful diversion by directing into the Mediterranean our naval forces concentrated at the port of Cadiz, combined with those of his Catholic Majesty, we would have you know that our intention is that, immediately on receipt of these presents, you will seize the first favourable opportunity of sailing with the Combined Fleet and proceeding to that sea.'

Villeneuve was to play his part in the new campaign against the Austrians and Russians by contributing to a diversionary attack in southern Italy. He was to liberate the Spanish squadron at Cartagena, then sail to Naples and disembark the expeditionary force of infantry to reinforce the French army that was already there.

If you find at Naples any English or Russian ships of war, you will seize them. The fleet under your command will remain off the Neapolitan shores so long as you may judge necessary to do the utmost harm to the enemy, and to intercept an expedition which they intend to send from Malta. Our intention is that wherever you meet the enemy in inferior force you will attack them without hesitation, and obtain a decision against them. It will not escape you that the success of these operations depends essentially on the promptness of your leaving Cadiz.

This was Napoleon in restrained mood, but the next day he received a long and passionate letter from General Lauriston, his informant in Villeneuve's camp, denouncing the admiral for his cowardice and maintaining that he had never intended to go to Brest and had never supported the idea of invading Britain. This was too much. Napoleon immediately penned an angry note to Denis Decrès: 'As his excessive timidity will prevent him carrying out my order, you will dispatch Admiral Rosily to take command of the fleet, and give him letters instructing Villeneuve to return to France and account to me for his conduct.'

Decrès carried out these instructions to the letter. Self-preservation was one of his guiding principles and as an aristocrat, it had served him well during the Revolution. He had tried to place his friend Villeneuve in charge of the fleet, but if Villeneuve was to be dismissed Decrès was going to do it in such a way that neither his friend nor the Emperor could blame him.

On 16 September Decrès sent Villeneuve Napoleon's orders of two days beforehand, instructing him to leave Cadiz and head for the Mediterranean at the first opportunity. He did not mention that Villeneuve was about to be sacked, or that Rosily would soon be leaving France to replace him. However, he gave a hint of what was to come in an enigmatic covering note: 'I cannot too highly recommend you, M. l'Amiral, to seize the first favourable opportunity to effect your departure; and I repeat my most earnest wishes for your success.'

Then, on 18 September, Decrès told Admiral Rosily of his new appointment and instructed him to proceed with all haste to Cadiz. While Villeneuve had simply been ordered to go immediately to the Mediterranean, Rosily was told that he could remain at Cadiz if 'insuperable obstacles' prevented immediate departure, and to 'cause either the whole Fleet or several divisions to leave port whenever the weather permits'. Finally, on 20 September, Decrès wrote to Ville-neuve, telling him that Rosily had been appointed to command the forces at Cadiz and that he was to return to Paris to account for his behaviour. As Napoleon had ordered, he gave the letter to Rosily to give to Villeneuve. Rosily left Paris on 24 September.

Decrès appears to have constructed a delay so that Villeneuve had time to react to the Mediterranean order before Rosily arrived to supersede him. Between the lines his note suggested to Villeneuve that he should leave Cadiz as soon as possible. It was a discreet attempt to give his friend a last chance to redeem himself.

From the Tavira Tower at Cadiz, the watchman could just see the main body of Collingwood's fleet about twenty miles away, so the attempt to hide it and tempt Villeneuve to attack an apparently weak advanced squadron was futile. In any case Villeneuve had known that the British reinforcements were coming. Now Spain's spies brought more news. On 16 September General Lauriston forwarded to Napoleon important information sent to Admiral Gravina by a trusted informant in Tangiers: 'Reports from Tangiers, which Admiral Gravina regards as being very reliable, state that Admiral Nelson, with six more line-of-battle ships, is to arrive directly to take command.' That day Gravina reported to Decrès on how he had improved his squadron by exchanging poor ships he had brought with him for better ones at Cadiz but that 'it is seamen that we are lacking'. Villeneuve sent a pessimistic report on the condition of his ships and crews but promised that he was now waiting only for the last two Spanish ships to be ready before he put to sea.

The Spanish were energetically organising and instructing the crews and the troops were doing marine duty in naval and military drill. They were concerned to put the defence of Cadiz on a firm footing and, with this in mind, Gravina had prepared 'a considerable force of gun-boats, bombs, and bomb-ketches, feluccas, boats and barges that were able to work in heavy weather, to assist in the defence of the town and of the Squadron'.

On the streets of Cadiz there was considerable ill-feeling about the failure in late July of the French to support the two Spanish ships taken by the Royal Navy in the battle against Calder. It was said that the Spanish had done all the real fighting. Reports reached the British fleet, and through them the newspapers, that 'several Frenchmen have been assassinated, and the French in return are said to have hung up many Spaniards'. This was almost certainly exaggerated, but there was some substance to it. Antonio Galiano, whose uncle Rafael Villavicencio had commanded one of the ships that had fallen into British hands, recalled the Spanish seamen being angry with the French and their own generals for having meekly submitted to French leadership. Many French officers, equally frustrated with their own leadership, were becoming touchy about questions of honour.

By 24 September the Spanish ships were fully manned and had food and water for three months. They had more than enough inexperienced young landsmen, a surplus of 1500 soldiers above the normal complement and, on paper, they had an adequate number of seamen too, although the requirements had been relaxed a little to fill the books. But trained marine artillerymen could not be found. They had only 700, when there should have been twice as many, and fifty-three were in hospital. Also, most of the young recruits and a quarter of the seamen had never before sailed with the navy and Gravina warned that if they were not quickly supplied with clothing, or with money to buy it, they would soon be swelling the numbers in hospital. Villeneuve reported: 'It is very distressing to see such fine and powerful ships manned with herdsmen and beggars and having such a small number of seamen.' He was used to crews composed entirely of seamen – an unheard-of luxury for a British captain, who might have regarded the Spanish crews more charitably. Although Villeneuve was short of 2207 men (of whom 1731 were sick and 311 had deserted), his crews still contained more genuine seamen than British ships did.

Cosme de Churruca was painfully aware of the Spanish crews' lack of training. He had observed that the newly issued flintlocks had performed well in the battle on 22 July and he was sure that the gunnery would be even better when the men had been trained to aim properly. He had just published a manual on aiming guns and the mathematical principles that governed elevation and trajectory, to which he proposed adding an appendix that showed the measurements of different British ships.

He conferred with his friend Dionisio Galiano and, together, they proposed to train some seamen by carrying out a mission to fetch silver from New Spain. Churruca suggested that if anyone could get a ship out of Cadiz through the British blockade it was Galiano – he who had already done it once in the last war – and that he himself should undertake the easier mission of leaving Ferrol in one of the ships that had been left there. This would also give him a chance to visit his wife. Unfortunately, nothing came of the idea.

On receiving Gravina's report Villeneuve wrote to Decrès on 24 September to say that he was ready and would sail for the Channel – in accordance with the orders he then had – at the first opportunity. Reprovisioning and repairs had taken a month because there had been no money. Only the intervention of the French ambassador in Madrid, who persuaded a French banker to produce some cash, had allowed Villeneuve to get his ships in order.

On 27 September the Emperor's new orders to proceed to the Mediterranean arrived. By now a rumour was circulating in Cadiz that Decrès himself was coming to command the fleet, but there was no sign of it in Villeneuve's orders, and, beyond the minister's hint that he should sail immediately, no sign that the Emperor was displeased with him. A copy was sent to Gravina who rowed over to *Bucentaure* to tell Villeneuve that fourteen ships were ready to leave. Only the three-deck *Santa Ana* was still in dock. Villeneuve prepared his captains for immediate action.

The expeditionary troops will be embarked on Monday next [30 September] and immediately afterwards the Fleet is to set sail. The captains in command will realize from the position and strength of the enemy before this port that an engagement must take place the very same day that the Fleet puts to sea . . . The Fleet will see with satisfaction the opportunity that is offered to it to display that resolution and daring which will ensure its success, revenge the insults offered to its Flag, and lay low the tyrannical domination of the English upon the seas. Our Allies will fight at our side, under the walls of Cadiz and in the sight of their fellow-citizens; the Emperor's gaze is fixed upon us . . .

Then, as he wrote in a note to Decrès, he heard that three more British ships had arrived, taking the total in the area to thirty-one, and his old doubts piled up again.

The newly arrived ships were *Ajax*, *Thunderer* and *Victory*. Nelson had been travelling slowly: he reached Cape Finisterre on 23 September and passed Lisbon two days later. On board his flagship, he sifted the usual piles of correspondence: Newman of Oporto recommending him to buy genuine old port wine rather than inferior stuff from England; a demand from a merchant in Lisbon for the discharge of his servant, who had been pressed by the frigate *Phoebe* when it had called there; an anxious note from Lord Castlereagh about suitable presents for the Emperor of Morocco and the Dey of Algiers from whom he wished to secure supplies for the fleet. Nelson had told him how important it was to keep these potentates happy and had refused to intervene in favour of some seamen whom the Algerines had enslaved for piracy. Nelson knew their ship of old, knew that it had attacked Algerian vessels, and he was not going to upset the all-powerful Dey when he depended on him to provision the fleet off Cadiz.

Nelson excelled at both the gathering of information and the diplomacy that made war at sea possible off foreign shores. He turned his attention to the important letters that his secretary, John Scott, had marked 'Intelligence Spanish Fleet'. One spoke of news from Faro that in mid-September the admirals of the Combined Fleets had decided it was not yet possible to carry out Bonaparte's orders to sail for the Channel, another that the Spanish had prepared a flotilla of fireships and gunboats. This latter piece of news was not good: it suggested that, predictably enough, the Spanish wanted to prepare for a siege.

Nelson tried to address every detail. He warned Collingwood to drop the normal formalities of welcome, requesting that 'if you are in sight of Cadiz, that not only no salute may take place, but also that no Colours may be hoisted, for it is as well not to proclaim to the enemy every ship that may join the Fleet'. As an afterthought he added a postscript: 'I would not have any salute even if you are out of sight of land.' But Nelson's efforts failed to keep his arrival secret: the Spanish had known he was coming and learned quickly when he was on the scene.

Nelson worked with John Scott on correspondence in English, but on foreign correspondence he worked with *Victory*'s chaplain, Alexander Scott. He was fluent in Latin, Greek, French, Spanish, Italian and German – he had taught himself the last three languages on board ship – and translated letters from foreigners, summarised what Nelson did not have time to read, negotiated, and occasionally gathered information for the Royal Navy. As a first-class linguist he was an invaluable help to an admiral who had struggled in his youth to master French. Nelson had worked hard and long to prise Scott away from his original patron, Admiral Hyde Parker, having admired his negotiation skills and treaty drafting at Copenhagen in 1801. He finally got him in 1803, and the two had become firm friends.

Scott's daughter described how her father 'was in the habit of reading to his chief all the French, Italian, Spanish and other foreign newspapers, which were sent regularly to the fleet, and these were ransacked as well for amusement, as the information they contained'. Scott also waded through 'numberless ephemeral foreign pamphlets, which a mind less investigating than Lord Nelson's would have discarded as totally unworthy of notice; but he entertained a persuasion that no man ever put his hand to paper, without having some information or theory to deliver, which he fancied was not generally known; and that this was worth looking after, through all the encumbering rubbish'. Scott found Nelson impressive: 'His own quickness in detecting the drift of an author was perfectly marvellous. Two or three pages of a pamphlet were generally sufficient to put him in complete possession of the writer's object, and nothing was too trivial for the attention of this great man's mind, when there existed a possibility of its being the means of obtaining information.'

Day after day Scott and Nelson sat together in the admiral's cabin, unravelling correspondence and captured documents. 'They occupied two black leathern armchairs, into the roomy pockets of which, Scott, weary of translating, would occasionally stuff away a score or two of unopened private letters, found in prize ships, although the untiring activity of Nelson grudged leaving one such document unexamined.'

Nelson turned his mind to every facet of his job, to food supply, health, diplomacy, intelligence, innovation. As he approached Cadiz, he received a report from Henry Bayntun of *Leviathan*, a captain from his old Mediterranean squadron, who had recently questioned the captain of a boat that had left Cadiz on 21 September. It made interesting reading:

> There are 39 Sail of the Line & 6 Frigates ready and fitting, much jealousy between the Two Nations. – Villeneuve spoken ill of, – The Minister Ducré expected at Cadiz to take the chief Command. Admiral Magon is gone to France.

This was not true: his informant had perhaps confused Magon with Lauriston, who had indeed been summoned back by Napoleon.

> Gravina is highly spoken of for having done his duty. The Captain of the Pluton, Commander of a division, has received some mark of Honor from the King of Spain; he was supposed to have had more fight than the rest, had eight killed and fifteen wounded.

This was the sort of businesslike, dispassionate report that Nelson liked. Bayntun's source was evidently well informed, an American most likely. The British did not at this time prevent neutral ships trading with the enemy and Americans carried out a lot of trade with Cadiz. They divided on political lines with federalists helping the British while republicans were sympathetic to the French. The report proceeded from the officers to the men:

The ships in general are badly manned, the Pluton, Berwick and Intrépide have not more than 300 Men each and others whose names he forgot were in the like case. The Santa Anna has not a man. The Impress is very hot, but few men are got.

Bayntun had asked about health and received a picture rosier than that which Villeneuve was painting for Decrès:

The town is healthy and the ships not much otherwise; he knows in the Pluton there are 27 sick; when the fleet first arrived the sick were all sent to hospital, but soon were sent back to their ships, and none have since been landed.

Generally, the report was encouraging, chiefly because the French apparently expected to put to sea soon:

It is reported that the Troops are immediately to be embarked to their respective ships, he does not believe there are more than 3000 men; they were very sickly in the West Indies & on the homeward passage. The Troops are certainly the same that went from Toulon, he appears certain of this. He says L'Aigle is famously manned, & all stout fellows. The outward ship is the Swiftsure. They talk of sailing when all the ships are ready and Ducré is here to take the command. Six months Provisions are taken in.

As Nelson approached Cadiz the chances of an early battle rather than another long blockade suddenly looked better.

On the 28th of September was joined by H.M. Ship Victory Admirl Lord Nelson and the Ajax and the Thunderer it is Imposeble to Discribe the Heartfelt Satifaction of the whole fleet upon this Occasion and the Confidance of Success with wich we ware Inspired.

Thus wrote Able Seaman James Martin of the *Neptune*. The next day was Nelson's forty-seventh birthday, which reinforced the feeling of celebration throughout the fleet. 'Lord Nelson is arrived,' wrote Edward Codrington. 'A sort of general joy has been the consequence.' Moreover, *Victory* had brought post from England. 'This is a Great day all the Capts dine with Lord Nelson I Get a letter & some Clean Shirts from my dear Mary – Hurra,' noted Richard Anderson, the master of the *Prince*, in his journal.

Nelson liked to deliver letters for the captains personally, when each was rowed over to see him. Codrington reported that 'He received me in an easy, polite manner, and on giving me your letter said that being entrusted with it by a lady, he made a point of delivering it himself. I have no fear of obtaining his good will by the conduct of Orion; because I shall do my best to deserve it, and he is a man well able to appreciate such endeavours.' Thomas Fremantle was pleased to find Nelson so well: 'He looks better than ever I saw him in my life, and is grown fatter.' He, too, received a letter and it was the one he wanted. Nelson 'asked me if I would have a Girl or a boy, I answered, the former, when he put the letter into my hand and told me to be satisfied'. It was a girl.

A relieved Fremantle chatted about his family and Nelson delighted him by 'telling me that he should give me my old station, which is his second in the line of battle. This is very gratifying to me, as it puts me in a very prominent situation in the order of battle, and a very convenient and pleasant one in the order of sailing.' *Neptune* would be the ship immediately behind *Victory*, a position of great trust.

In *Victory*'s great cabin the captains dined with Nelson on two consecutive days, the order decided by seniority. Charles Tyler of *Tonnant* went to the first. Like Fremantle, he looked to Nelson as a patron. Tyler's son by his first marriage had deserted his frigate at Malta to run away with an opera dancer. Nelson had done his best to salvage the boy's career and now he told Tyler that he would notify his agents in Italy to make a discreet search for him and pay any money that he owed. About two in the afternoon the junior admirals and senior captains gathered for dinner. Around the huge mahogany table, set with silver and glass, in the heat of the afternoon, sat old friends from the Mediterranean, like Thomas Louis and Ben Hallowell who had fought under Nelson at the Nile, as well as men Nelson did not know well or had never met, like Eliab Harvey of *Téméraire* or Robert Moorsom of *Revenge*.

On 30 September, Edward Codrington wrote to his wife Jane, 'The signal has been made this morning for all of us who did not dine on board Victory yesterday to go there to-day. What our late chief will think of this I don't know; but I well know what the fleet think of the difference; and even you, our good wives, who have some causes of disapprobation, will allow the superiority of Lord Nelson in all these social arrangements which bind his captains to their admiral.' This was not the only change: the ships were suddenly allowed to buy fresh fruit and provisions from visiting market boats. 'The signal is made that boats may be hoisted out to buy fruit, stock, or anything from Teasels coming into the fleet; this, I trust, will be a common signal hereafter, but it is the first day I have seen it made.'

The junior captains came aboard in the early afternoon for dinner, and Henry Chevalier poured cooled wine. George Duff of *Mars* immediately concluded, 'He certainly is the pleasantest Admiral I ever served under.' John Cooke of *Bellerophon* had always wanted to serve under Nelson and must have been delighted to be present. Fremantle certainly was: 'The juniors and I never passed a pleasanter day. I staid with him until eight at night – he would not let me leave him before. He has obligingly desired me to come to him without ceremony whenever I choose, and to dine with him as often as I found it convenient.'

Nelson was happy too:

The reception I met with on joining the Fleet caused the sweetest sensation of my life. The officers who came on board to welcome my return forgot my rank as Commander-in-Chief in the enthusiasm with which they greeted me. As soon as these emotions were past I laid before them the plan I had previously arranged for attacking the enemy; and it was not only my pleasure to find it generally approved, but clearly perceived and understood.

Emma appreciated more animated language, so to her he wrote:

When I came to explain to them the <u>Nelson Touch</u> it was like an electric shock. Some shed tears, all approved – it was new – it was singular – it was simple! and, from Admirals downwards, it was repeated – 'It must succeed, if ever they will allow us to get at them! You are, my Lord, surrounded by friends, whom you inspire with confidence.' Some may be Judas's but the majority are certainly much pleased with my commanding them.

Most of the captains started to paint their ships 'à la Nelson' in imitation of *Victory*, black with buff-coloured stripes running between the gun-ports. Fremantle reported on 1 October, 'We are all busy scraping our Ships sides to paint them in the way Lord Nelson paints the Victory.' Anderson, master of the *Prince*, also noted that day that 'we are going to paint the ship'. Codrington and Duff were doing the same. Duff wrote, 'He is so good and pleasant a man, that we all wish to do what he likes, without any kind of orders.'

Ambitious captains, like Codrington, looked to their laurels. The crew that he had inherited in *Orion* came chiefly from two other ships, and each of their previous captains considered his men a poor lot, but Codrington had been working hard to improve his ship. 'As Croft, with the greatest perseverance and attention, is one of the ablest and best first-lieutenants I ever saw, and as I know how to do my part in improving the discipline of the ship, I have no doubt but we shall be in very good order ere long.' Fremantle had great faith in the beneficial influence of Nelson's example: 'We are a fine fleet, but three months will I think make us better; the energy and activity on board the Victory will make those who are slack keep a much better look out, and preserve better discipline.'

Having prepared to leave Cadiz on Tuesday, 1 October, Villeneuve changed his mind. He had aimed to take advantage of that morning's east-south-east wind, 'in my impatience to carry out the Emperor's orders, heeding neither the strength of the enemy nor the condition of the greater number of the ships in the combined fleet'. But the easterly wind was uncomfortably blustery that day. It rained, and if a strong easterly set in it would prevent him getting through the Strait of Gibraltar into the Mediterranean. This, at least, was what Villeneuve told Decrès. But at a council of senior officers held earlier that day he had been persuaded not to leave by Admiral Gravina, who had pointed out not only the east wind and the strength of the enemy now commanded by Nelson, but the virtues of defending the port as they had in 1797.

While Villeneuve dithered in Cadiz, the wind dropped, turned westerly, then fell calm. On 2 October Gravina was warned by the Spanish ambassador in Lisbon that Nelson intended to bombard Cadiz. It was one piece of information that the British admiral was keen to leak, but Nelson had bombarded Cadiz before without effect, and Gravina already had his flotilla of light boats prepared to attack bomb ships and repel any amphibious assault. He had a healthy respect for Nelson, though: he told the Spanish prime minister, Manuel Godoy, on 2 October that the British fleet had disappeared from view the moment Nelson arrived, and yesterday even the five ships of the advanced squadron had gone, leaving only frigates in sight. He reckoned that Nelson was telling his subordinates what he planned to do.

Napoleon's new instructions were difficult for the Spanish. Gravina had been born in Palermo, twin capital with Naples of the Kingdom of the Two Sicilies. Napoleon intended to take King Ferdinando's throne and territory. Gravina had explained to Villeneuve, Decrès and Godoy that he would not fight against his native land. This was not a problem exclusive to him since King Ferdinando of Naples was the brother of King Carlos of Spain. Godoy explained to Gravina that, in the event of hostilities against Naples, Napoleon had promised to consider Spain neutral.

Gravina was forty-nine and an old friend of Manuel Godoy. Both have frequently been described as pro-French, but they were trying to play a weak hand with Spain's best interests at heart. Gravina had got on well with Latouche when they were together at Brest between 1799 and 1801. He had taken a Spanish squadron to Saint-Domingue in 1802 and impressed the French with his conduct. Napoleon thought highly of him as an admiral, though he considered him unsuited to diplomacy. Gravina's duty now was either to preserve the Spanish navy or to win with it. His ships were universally admired but most of their crews needed more training. His sense of honour was as sharp as that of any other naval officer of his day, but it was his duty to prevent the unnecessary destruction of the navy in his charge, which was irreplaceable and vital to Spain's future. On the other hand his instructions from Madrid were, in the last resort, to obey Villeneuve.

On the morning of 6 October the wind was again east-south-east and Villeneuve, who must have been tortured by the conflicting pressures on him, appeared to find new strength of purpose. He 'informed General Gravina that he found himself obliged to leave port in order to comply with the orders of his government and that he desired to be furnished with certain replenishments of provisions of which he was in need; giving the requisite orders to the Spanish ships that they should be ready to sail as soon as the French.' Gravina replied 'that he considered it necessary, before weighing, to hold a council in which the opinion of all the commanding officers of both nations might be heard'. He gave orders to take the seamen out of the light flotilla of gunboats and return them to their ships.

The council of war took place on 8 October aboard the *Bucentaure*. The Spanish rear admiral Antonio de Escaño stated that 'our General received a very courteous letter from the French General, in which he, his Chief of Staff and other senior officers of the Spanish Fleet were invited to assist at the council'. Seven senior officers from each fleet signed the document that summed up its resolutions.

After holding discussions among themselves, the Spanish delegation was united behind Gravina. He had with him Escaño, widely considered the best naval tactician in Spain, and his squadron commanders: Vice Admiral Ignacio de Álava, recently governor of Manila, now commanding the newly cleaned and repaired three-decker *Santa Ana*, and Rear Admiral Báltasar Cisneros, commanding the four-deck *Santísima Trinidad*, one of few Spaniards who had distinguished themselves at the battle of Cape St Vincent in 1797. Commodore Dionisio Alcalá Galiano was now in command of the *Bahama*; Commodore Rafael Hore was captain of Gravina's flagship the *Príncipe de Asturias* and the last delegate was probably Commodore Enrique Macdonnell, an Irishman who had joined the Regimiento de Hibernia and later graduated to the navy.

The French deputation consisted of Villeneuve, Mathieu Prigny, his chief of staff, and his squadron commanders, Pierre Dumanoir and Charles Magon. The senior captains were Julien Cosmao-Kerjulien of *Pluton*, Esprit-Tranquille Maistral of *Neptune* and Guillaume Lavillegris of *Mont-Blanc*.

The laconic minute of this meeting that Villeneuve sent to Decrès glosses over a stormy discussion later described by Escaño, and Galiano's son, Antonio. Villeneuve told the assembly in confidence that he had pressing orders to take the fleet to sea and to attack the enemy whenever they were in inferior strength. However, his best information at present was that the enemy had either thirty-one or thirty-three ships outside Cadiz. Escaño spoke for the Spanish and asked whether in the circumstances 'it were preferable to leave port or to receive an attack at anchor'. He commented on the difference between the skilled seamanship of the British, who had been constantly at sea, and that of the French and especially the Spanish, 'who had spent eight years without putting to sea'. He pointed out that several of the Spanish ships 'have never yet been able to exercise their people at sea in any way and that the three-deckers *Santa Ana* and *Rayo*, and the *San Justo*, fitted out in haste and barely out of the dockyard, can in extreme necessity put to sea with the Fleet but that they are by no means in a state to render the service in action of which they will be capable when they are completely organised'.

Escaño suggested that a well-organised light force had beaten Nelson before and that a direct British attack on the port would fail. Also, the weather would soon break and storms might drive away the Royal Navy, providing an opportunity to put to sea without fighting a battle. He concluded that 'superior orders could not bind them to attempt the impossible, as nothing would serve as an excuse in the event of a disaster, which he saw to be inevitable if they weighed'.

The French were not as united as the Spanish. Chief of Staff Mathieu Prigny agreed with Escaño but others 'expressed various opinions with the warmth characteristic of their nation'. Some maintained that if they fought 'the result would be the rout of the opponent and the consequent ease of executing their orders'. Charles Magon was the most outspoken in refuting both the Spanish and his own chief of staff, and 'in his heated reply expressed himself with scant courtesy'. Galiano is said to have moved his hand to the hilt of his sword as he 'sought to make him retract several expressions'. Tempers frayed and Admiral Gravina, rising, 'requested that the vote be taken without further discussion'. They voted on 'whether, as they had not a superiority of force to counteract the disadvantage of their position, the Combined Squadron should leave port or no'. The result was no: they should remain at anchor. In consequence, the divisions of light craft were put back, with their crews and marines, 'in the stations that they had previously occupied' and the ships were positioned to withstand attack.

But Villeneuve was not absolutely bound by the decision of the council, as everyone knew. He renewed his order to be ready to weigh anchor at short notice should the situation change, and in his report on the day's events he promised Decrès that he would sail as soon as Nelson divided his force.

7

Signal Flag Yellow with Blue Fly

Nelson changed the system outside Cadiz. He posted Captain Henry Blackwood in *Euryalus* with four other frigates close to the city and gave orders that they should report all developments in the bay. Then the main fleet disappeared from the enemy's view. It would have been typical of Nelson if when he was previously in Cadiz he had checked the range of visibility from the Tavira Tower. What is certain is that he guessed it better than Collingwood had. Nelson's fleet cruised off Cape St Mary fifty miles to the north-west of Cadiz, while Collingwood's had been counted frequently from Cadiz, Nelson's strength was, from this moment, unknown. The advanced squadron formed a chain between the frigates and the main fleet, along which signals could be passed.

Nelson reported to Viscount Castlereagh that if William Congreve's newly invented rockets really would travel a mile and a half they might be useful. The defensive position taken up by the Combined Fleet abreast of the town exposed them to an attack launched across the spit of land that led to Cadiz. Nelson consulted Collingwood and decided that starving the enemy out with a blockade was likely to be more successful than an assault. Supplies were coming, in neutral Danish ships to the little neighbouring ports where they were transferred to small Spanish coasting boats for Cadiz. These were protected by

Spanish gunboats and sailed too close inshore to be attacked by warships. The supplies had to be intercepted earlier.

The problem was that the Danes pretended that the food was Danish property although it clearly came from Nantes and Bordeaux. Nelson asked Castlereagh 'to ensure that the Officers under my orders may not get into any pecuniary scrape by their obedience' when they seized the cargoes. Captains were personally liable for goods that they seized illegally, and Nelson envisaged that in some future foreign court of law it might be argued that Britain was not trying to blockade Cadiz but to usurp its trade. As an admiral, he tried to foresee and resolve all difficulties in advance, and if his officers knew that the government would protect them against liability their inspection of neutral ships would be a great deal more rigorous.

Nelson also decided to send the best ships of his old Mediterranean fleet, those commanded by Admiral Thomas Louis, away for supplies. 'I have no other means of keeping my Fleet complete in provisions and water, but by sending them in detachments to Gibraltar,' he explained, over dinner to Louis and to his flag-captain Francis Austen. 'The enemy *will* come out, and we shall fight them; but there will be time to get back first. I look upon Canopus as my right hand; and I send you first to insure your being here to help beat them.' On 2 October *Canopus*, *Spencer*, *Queen* and *Tigre* left, accompanied by *Zealous* and *Endymion*, both in need of repair.

They were intercepted next morning by Blackwood in *Euryalus*, who 'informed us by signal that he had received information by a Swedish ship from Cadiz that the troops had all embarked on board the men-of-war, and it was reported they were to sail with the first easterly wind'. Louis shot back with four ships to rejoin Nelson, only to be sent straight back to Gibraltar. Blackwood's report had been accurate, but nothing had happened. Villeneuve had been warned, among other things, against the onset of a strong easterly wind into which Louis now had to beat back for Gibraltar.

The news that the Combined Fleet was embarking its troops caused great excitement in Nelson's fleet and especially in George Duff's advanced squadron of *Mars*, *Defence* and *Colossus*. Nelson had already given Duff detailed instructions. He was to

> keep from three to four leagues between the Fleet and Cadiz, in order that I may get the information from the Frigates stationed off that Port, as expeditiously as possible. Distant Signals to be used, when Flags, from the state of the weather, may not readily be distinguished in their colours. If the Enemy be out, or coming out, fire guns by day or night, in order to draw my attention.

In bad weather the ships were to get close to *Victory*. One was to be placed well to the eastward to extend the range of vision and one of Blackwood's frigates would be placed to the west to be in sight. Presumably it was found that the chain needed to be longer because *Ajax* was quickly added to Duff's squadron. Duff was delighted to be given this job. He realised that Collingwood had got it for him 'as he was on board the *Victory* when I was sent for', but he was impressed that, even with Collingwood's recommendation, Nelson had chosen him over so many senior officers. Scots like Duff packed their ships with their own nationals and it is possible that sometimes they felt marginalised in English fleets.

Duff was not the only officer who hoped to impress Nelson. Through his captain, Israel Pellew of *Conqueror*, Humphrey Senhouse, a lieutenant from Nelson's Mediterranean squadron, volunteered himself to take part in an attack by fire vessels: 'Conceiving from my late observations that fire vessels may be successfully employed in destroying the enemy's fleets in Cadiz, I beg leave to request you will be pleased to tender the services of twelve volunteers with myself to the Commander in Chief.' This was among the most dangerous jobs because it involved sailing a burning ship among the enemy fleet to cause them to catch fire and blow up.

The dining arrangements continued as the captains got to know each other, renewed old friendships and exchanged information.

Thomas Fremantle met with Nelson again, stayed until eight and was then persuaded to remain longer 'to see a play that was performed by the seamen on board the Victory, I assure you it was very well conducted, and the voice of the seaman, who was dressed in great form and performed the <u>female part</u> was entertaining to a degree'. He was happy now: 'the whole system here is so completely changed, that it wears quite a different aspect we are continually with something to change the scene and know precisely how far we may go, which is very pleasant, Lord Nelson recounts many of our transactions when we were in this country before, and on every occasion is very kind to me.' He dined with Eliab Harvey of the *Téméraire*, his nearest ship, and then, a few days later, with Harvey, Philip Durham of *Defiance* and Pulteney Malcolm of *Donegal*. He managed to get three of the lieutenants from his previous ship transferred to *Neptune*, including his special *protégé* Andrew Green, 'a famous good fellow', who became signal lieutenant. Not only did this strengthen his hand over troublesome First Lieutenant Arklom in managing the ship, it brought in some battle-hardened men. Green had been at Toulon in 1793 and fought with Nelson and Fremantle in Corsica and Copenhagen. The only thing that still troubled Fremantle was the name of his daughter: 'I shall be outrageous if you do not christen my new tittler by the name of Louisa, I have taken such an aversion to Christine that I shall be sick, and melancholy,' he wrote to his wife.

The quality of the dinners was improved by 'all sort of fresh provisions', including bullocks from North Africa, but conversation centred, as Codrington reported, on 'a wish for peace and a disgust for the service'. But for peace they needed to fight a battle, and most captains were sceptical. 'Some are disposed to think the fleet will come out; but if they do, it will certainly be when they have a pretty fair chance of reaching Toulon or Carthagena before we can catch them. Brown [captain of *Ajax*] thinks they will steal off by small squadrons; which, as the weather advances, will become more probable.'

Fremantle dined again with Nelson on 11 October and found that he was optimistic: 'Lord Nelson expects the French Fleet will come out, I confess I do not, but I have no doubt as to the events of an action if our ships can get up with the enemy.'

By this time Nelson had put down on paper his battle plan. The memorandum he circulated among the captains of the fleet was dated 9 October and headed 'Secret'. He told his captains that the order of sailing would be the order of battle. There would be no time-consuming rearrangement, except that the flagships would move back from their exposed position at the head of each line. He was hoping to have enough ships to form into three columns, two divisions of sixteen ships each, and a fast squadron of eight. Collingwood, the second-in-command, was to have complete control of his division.

The essential concept was to attack the enemy centre and rear, leaving their vanguard untouched. Assuming that their commander-in-chief (whoever he was) was in the centre of the line, the area covered by the British assault would begin two or three ships ahead of him. Nelson reasoned that it would be some time before the enemy could react to this attack and especially before his van could turn back to help. He hoped to beat the enemy centre and rear before their van entered the fray, then beat the van. However the van reacted, the British were to place their own ships between it and the enemy ships that by then they would have captured.

Unconventionally, Nelson ordered that the attack would be carried out under full sail. This was liable to introduce confusion, since different ships sailed at different speeds, but it would reduce the amount of time spent in the approach phase when the attacking ships would be most exposed to enemy fire. He intended to cut through the enemy line himself at its centre, although he would conceal the direction of his attack until the last moment. The small fast squadron would cut through a little ahead of him to make sure of the enemy admiral. If the enemy was downwind of the British, Nelson anticipated that, just before they were in gunshot range, Collingwood's lee line would be told to turn simultaneously and attack in a line under full sail, each choosing an opponent beginning with the twelfth ship from the enemy's rear. If any captain was in doubt, 'in case Signals can neither be seen or perfectly understood, no Captain can do very wrong if he places his Ship alongside that of an Enemy'.

In the memorandum a note indicated the signal for the lee line to bear up. It was one that did not appear in the printed signal book but had been added by Nelson himself: 'Signal Flag Yellow with Blue Fly: Cut through the Enemy's line and engage them on the other side.' It was followed by a detailed explanation:

> NB: This Signal is to be repeated by all the ships. The Number of the Enemy's ship under the Stern of which the Van Ship is to pass and engage will be pointed out by Signal counting from the Enemy's Rear. The Ships being prepared are to make all possible sail (keeping their relative Bearings and close order) so that the whole may pass thro' the Enemy's line as quick as possible and at the same time. It is recommended to cut away the Studding sails if set, to prevent confusion and fire. Each ship will of course pass under the Stern of the one she is to engage if circumstances permit, otherwise to refer to the Instructions Page 160 Article 31 [the conventional admiralty advice on how to break the enemy's line]. The Admiral will probably advance his Fleet to the van of theirs before he makes the Signal in order to deceive the Enemy by inducing them to suppose it is his intention to attack their Van.

Clear communication was one of Nelson's great strengths. The memorandum and note about the new signal gave all of his captains as full as possible an account of what he intended to do and what he wanted them to do, right down to getting rid of their cumbersome studding sails (deployed for extra speed) as they reached the enemy line. It was a fairly simple plan, and although it allowed for contingencies nobody should have been in any doubt about the general principle.

Delegation was another strength. Nelson 'did nothing without my counsel,' Collingwood wrote a few days later. 'We made our line of Battle together, and concerted the mode of attack . . .' In fact, Nelson did everything possible to make Collingwood feel involved. He sent the memorandum to him on 9 October with a note:

> I send you my plan of attack, as far as a man dare venture to guess at the very uncertain position the enemy may be found in: but, my dear friend, it is to place you perfectly at ease respecting my intentions, and to give full scope to your judgment for carrying them into effect. We can, dear Coll, have no little jealousies: we have only one great object in view, – that of annihilating our enemies, and getting a glorious peace for our Country. No man has more confidence in another than I have in you; and no man will render your services more justice than your very old friend.

The two commanders then communicated the instructions to each of their own captains so as to clear up any doubts and invite their opinion on any difficulties. That Collingwood discussed the plan with his captains is proved by a crucial note written to Charles Tyler of *Tonnant* on 12 October: 'I have an order, and instruction about our battle – which I wish to give to the Captains – rather than send – that we might converse on the general plan intended to be executed – if there is opportunity pray come here for a quarter of an hour.'

Collingwood had kept his original Cadiz squadron and to it was added some of Calder's ships. Nelson's division was based on his old Mediterranean squadron with a similar addition. The line of battle drawn up on 10 October envisaged major roles for Thomas Louis's squadron of trusted ships and captains, and for Richard Keats's *Superb*, which had not yet arrived. With the exception of the two senior captains, Eliab Harvey in *Téméraire* and Richard Grindall in *Prince*, who claimed a place at the head of the line by right, Collingwood and Nelson put the men they knew best and trusted most at the front. After Thomas Louis in *Canopus*, Richard Keats in *Superb* and Ben Hallowell in *Tigre*, all Nile captains, Nelson's trust fell on Fremantle in

Neptune, Henry Bayntun in *Leviathan*, Israel Pellew in *Conqueror*, from his old Mediterranean squadron, and Sir Edward Berry of *Agamemnon*, who was on his way from England.

Nelson's plan envisaged close-quarters fighting during which his ships would depend for victory on their gunnery, their manoeuvrability and, most of all, the skill of their officers and seamen. The key to any gunnery duel was to position your own ship so as to bring as many of your guns as possible to bear against the enemy, while exposing her to the minimum of return fire. The perfect position was at right angles to an opponent from which position you could 'rake' her, firing along the whole length of her decks.

During the approach phase the bows of Nelson's ships would be exposed to raking fire from the broadsides of the enemy ships opposite them. However, when they broke the line and passed under their opponents' sterns, the British ships would be able to rake the enemy far more effectively and from extremely close range. Ships' sterns had wide windows to let in light to the cabins and gun-decks, so shots fired at the stern met with little resistance before they travelled the length of the gun-deck, knocking over guns and dismembering men. A 'raking broadside' occurred when all the guns from one side fired at once. But if you were close to the enemy and moving past, it was better to fire as the guns came to bear straight down the enemy deck. Once through the line, the British ships would manoeuvre to take up an advantageous fighting position on the far side of the enemy line, engaging from fifteen to thirty yards.

The warship of 1805 was essentially a floating artillery platform and it came in three standard sizes. Frigates had one deck of guns and carried between 200 and 300 men. They ran errands, did convoy duty and preyed on enemy commerce, often acting independently of the fleet. Command of a frigate offered a young officer his best chance to distinguish himself and to capture enemy ships. Ordinary seamen preferred to serve in a frigate for the prize money. But frigates rarely took part in big fleet actions, and stayed away from hostile ships-of-the-line for fear of being blown apart.

The standard battleship was the '74'. They were between about 168 feet and 182 feet long and all theoretically carried seventy-four guns. One ship off Cadiz carrying the traditional armament was the *Defence*. She had twenty-eight 32-pounders on the lower deck, twenty-eight 18-pounders on the upper deck, and eighteen 9-pounders on the quarter-deck and forecastle. Most two-deck ships like this went in fear of the taller three-deckers, which carried a hundred or more guns, often of slightly heavier calibre.

Ships were labelled according to their standard armament – *Achille*, 74, or *Neptune*, 98 – but the numbers are misleading. Trafalgar is usually described as if the ships actually carried their standard armament, but documents in the National Archive show that most of the British ships off Cadiz were considerably more heavily armed, with more guns – or, rather, with more carronades. Instead of eighteen 9-pounder guns above decks, *Achille*, 74, for example, had twelve 32-pounder carronades on her quarterdeck and forecastle and eight 18-pounder carronades on her poop, making a total of eighty-four rather than seventy-four guns. This increased her broadside weight by over a quarter, from 813 to 1064 pounds. *Revenge*, 74, was also carrying eighty-four guns, including sixteen 32-pounder and six 18-pounder carronades. Conventionally armed, she would have fired a broadside weighing 880 pounds; at Trafalgar her broadside weighed 1136 pounds.

The carronade had been developed by the Carron Company, based near Glasgow. First tested by the Royal Navy as long ago as 1779, it was adopted as standard for all ships equipped after 1794. By 1805 nearly all British line-of-battle ships had exchanged some or all of their quarterdeck guns for carronades. The great advantage of the new weapon was its weight, which was a fraction of that of the big cannon below deck. A 32-pounder carronade weighed about the same as a 6-pounder gun, but delivered a much more powerful blow. The low weight meant that carronades could be deployed on the ship's super-structure, operated by a smaller crew than a traditional gun, and easily traversed on a wheeled stand. Like giant shotguns, carronades were anti-personnel weapons with the potential to make it impossible for the enemy to operate effectively on his exposed decks. Their disadvantage was that they were only accurate at close range, but it was at close range that Nelson intended to fight. His tactics were designed to make the most of these new weapons, and massacre the enemy officers, sailors and marines on deck.

Captains had long debated when best to open fire. Some believed that firing from a greater distance caused more splinters, and so more casualties, because the ball was travelling slower when it hit and carved a more ragged hole. Others experimented with reducing the amount of powder to create the same effect. 'Point blank' – where the gun needed no elevation – judged to be 350 yards for a 32-pounder or 200 yards for a 24-pounder, was widely considered the maximum effective range. But Nelson and Collingwood both believed that getting even closer was best and the captains they trusted to lead the lines shared their view. Their guns, once double-shotted for the first broadside, were only accurate at less than a hundred yards and their carronades were optimised for fire at that distance.

A number of factors contributed to successful gunnery. Some were technical, such as the quality of the firelocks or the powder charge; British gunpowder, thanks largely to control of Indian saltpetre sources, was reckoned to be 20 per cent more efficient than any available to the French or Spanish. The British Blomefield guns were sounder and less likely to burst under strain than those used by the Combined Fleet.

At very close range, accuracy was not a factor. The key to success was a ship's rate of fire. Collingwood had reputedly drilled the crew of *Dreadnought* to achieve three broadsides in three and a half minutes – the best that a fully worked-up British crew might achieve. Several witnesses suggest that few British ships achieved anything like this rate, and the typical performance over a long period of time was almost certainly much slower. The French and Spanish ships, doubtless, also varied in performance. One shot every four minutes has been estimated as a decent rate to sustain over a long period of time. The very concept of repeated broadsides is flawed: after the first salvo or two, guns were fired as fast as they were reloaded.

The rounds fired by a crew while they were fresh were likely to be the best. As they got tired and their numbers dropped through injury, the need to fight on deck or pump ship, their fire became ragged. It was worst for the crews of the heaviest guns, and the French used heavier ones than the British did. The standard British heavy gun fired a 32-pound ball, which was difficult enough to lift. But the French 36-pound balls were even heavier.

On the night of 8 October, the day of Villeneuve's council of war, Admiral Rosily reached Madrid and revealed his orders to a surprised French ambassador. General de Beurnonville had just heard from Villeneuve that Nelson was at Cadiz, intending to 'fire the city and the Fleet' and that Villeneuve planned to 'take advantage of the earliest opportunity to get under way'. But the ambassador did not think that Villeneuve would really put to sea, 'as you have not given him orders to exchange shots with a superior force, and in case of a reverse we have nothing at Cadiz wherewith to effect repairs,' he told Decrès. De Beurnonville agreed with the Spanish assessment: 'As far as I can see nothing but storms or heavy weather would be to our advantage.'

Rosily arrived in a broken coach. While it was being repaired and measures taken to clear the road to Cadiz of brigands, de Beurnonville briefed him on finance, supplies and the broader situation in Spain. He believed that the Spanish 'do not like us and they detest our domination still more', and he was wary of their 'passive resistance' to French projects. Nevertheless, the latest news was that José Salcedo, the admiral commanding at Cartagena, was putting to sea in an attempt to attack the convoy of British reinforcements travelling from Gibraltar to Malta. Rosily and de Beurnonville were old friends: they had met in India many years before and enjoyed the enforced period of delay.

Rumours flew around wildly. The English newspapers had told

Nelson, Villeneuve and their fleets that Villeneuve had been sacked and replaced by none other than Decrès himself. This came as a surprise to Villeneuve, and although he knew it to be untrue, it was disquieting.

Tension was also building for Nelson. He had temporarily lost Louis and five of his best ships, but letters told him that reinforcements were on their way from England. He wrote to his chief watchdog, Blackwood, 'if Mr. Decrès means to come forth (if he would take my advice which I dare say he won't), he had better come out directly. Those who know more of Cadiz than either you or I do, say, that after those Levanters, come several days of fine weather, sea breezes Westerly, land wind at night.' He had evidently been talking to someone such as James Morris of *Colossus*, who had done Blackwood's job in 1797. With this weather, he warned Blackwood, it was possible to envisage a horrible scenario. If the enemy were heading for the Mediterranean they would come out at night as they had always done, stationing frigates to mark the rocks and shoals off Cadiz with lights. They would then run south and get through the Strait of Gibraltar on a sea breeze before Nelson, with little wind to help, could catch up. 'In short, watch all points, and all winds and weathers, for I shall depend upon you,' he commanded.

The man who had been appointed to replace Villeneuve, François Rosily, left Madrid on 14 October to begin the nine-day journey to Cadiz. That day a reassuring letter for de Beurnonville arrived from Villeneuve, written after the council of war, announcing that he could not leave port without some diminution in enemy strength or a change in the weather. Now de Beurnonville was confident that nothing would happen before the new admiral's arrival in Cadiz. But six days later the ambassador reported two unsettling pieces of news. First, he had learned that Villeneuve had discovered, through his own private sources, that Rosily was on his way to take over; second, that five of Nelson's ships 'are anchored at Gibraltar' and 'it is possible that others may be detached for victualling'. Moreover, Gravina had written to say that the Spanish ships were ready for action. 'It seems that he is complete, even to goodwill,' added de Beurnonville, with cool sarcasm.

If news that Nelson was under strength reached Villeneuve, he might suddenly decide to put to sea.

While Rosily was in Madrid, the reinforcements that the Admiralty had promised Nelson began to trickle in. *Defiance* and *Royal Sovereign* arrived on 8 October. On 10 October *Belleisle* appeared. She was a valuable addition, a powerful French prize launched at Rochefort in 1793, with eighty-eight heavy guns and carronades. Having been one of Nelson's Mediterranean squadron, her crew was well trained and her captain, William Hargood, was an old friend of Nelson. They had been shipmates on *Bristol* in 1778, shared a patron in Sir Peter Parker, and Hargood had been a guest at Nelson's wedding in 1787.

Another old friend arrived on 13 October in the shape of Sir Edward Berry. His *Agamemnon* was only a 64 (mounting sixty-six guns) but she was the fastest ship in the British fleet, according to Commodore Zacharie Allemand, whose Rochefort squadron had just chased *Agamemnon* through the Channel. Berry had fought with Nelson at St Vincent and had been his flag-captain at the Nile. 'Here comes Berry; now we shall have a battle!' exclaimed Nelson. The next day another little 64 appeared, the *Africa* under Henry Digby.

However, Nelson had lost a ship. He had brought out with him orders for Admiral Calder to go home and face a court-martial for his failure to defeat Villeneuve in July. Nelson urged him to stay for the battle, but Calder decided to go home. He was supposed to go in *Dreadnought*, which needed docking, but Nelson did not have the heart to turn him out of his own flagship and broke Admiralty orders by allowing him to go home in *Prince of Wales*. Both were three-deckers. Captains Brown of *Ajax* and Lechmere of *Thunderer* offered to go home with him and give evidence in his defence. They left on 14 October and their ships were taken over by their first lieutenants, so that John Stockham of *Thunderer*, who had recently written to Nelson asking to be a lieutenant in *Victory*, was now one of his captains – on an acting basis. Meanwhile, Collingwood was instructed to change ships into the newly

cleaned and therefore faster *Royal Sovereign*. Nelson allowed him to take
with him his first lieutenant, James Clavell, and signal lieutenant, Brice
Gilliland, on condition that he also took his flag-captain, Edward
Rotheram. This allowed Nelson's *protégé* John Conn to take over
Dreadnought with *Sovereign*'s first lieutenant, George Hewson.

Admiral Louis's five ships were still away and *Donegal* had followed.
With a 'nasty Levanter' blowing strongly against him, Louis did not
reach Gibraltar until 9 October. He spent three days loading stores,
and two at Tetouan loading water, then turned for Cadiz on 14
October, by which time the wind had dropped away to a calm.
'We are, of course, very anxious to get back to the fleet for fear the
enemy should be moving, for the idea of their doing so while we are
absent is by no means pleasant,' wrote Louis's flag-captain, Francis
Austen, to his sweetheart, Mary Gibson. But the wind went round to
the west and forced them back to Tetouan. There, Louis was ordered to
escort fifty transports bound for Malta past the Spanish ships at
Cartagena. Austen continued,

> I do not expect to derive any advantage from it, and it puts us
> completely out of the way in case the enemy should make an attempt
> to get to sea, which is by no means improbable, if he knows Lord
> Nelson's force is weakened by the detachment of so many ships.
> Having borne our share in a tedious chace and anxious blockade, it
> would be mortifying indeed to find ourselves at last thrown out of any
> share of credit or emolument which would result from an action.

Austen was to gain neither credit nor emolument for it, but he played
his part in the battle of Trafalgar. On 18 October Villeneuve wrote to
Decrès that he had just learned that four enemy ships were escorting a
convoy from Gibraltar, one remained at Gibraltar and one was going
there damaged. 'This force of six line-of-battle ships subtracted from
the English fleet seems to me to present a favourable opportunity to me
to get under weigh.'

Here was the excuse Villeneuve needed to order Gravina to leave port. The best guess in Cadiz was that Nelson had between twenty-seven and thirty-two ships in total. With six now gone Villeneuve might have the one-third superiority that he felt would make them about equal. In these circumstances Gravina could not prevaricate without incurring dishonour.

Villeneuve, who had been under pressure for some time, had made up his mind for different reasons. A few days later a French royalist who arrived at Cadiz *en route* to exile in America explained that Villeneuve

> had experienced much unpleasantness; many of his officers considered that he had carried prudence too far; and he had heard, from Paris, that his courage had been called in question in high quarters. Such circumstances were more than enough to exasperate an irritable and brave man. Perhaps, he was influenced less by prudence, than by the desire to vindicate his honour. He was heard to say angrily, one day: 'They shall see if I know how to fight.'

Then he had been told in private letters from Bayonne that Admiral Rosily was coming to take command of his fleet. He must have looked again at his last orders from Paris and at the subtle covering letter from Decrès. He and Decrès had previously colluded in a campaign of passive disobedience to the Emperor's unreasonable orders, but now that was no longer possible. It appeared that Decrès wanted him to put to sea, whatever the risk. Villeneuve wrote to his old friend just before he received the news that Nelson was short of six ships:

> I am informed that Vice Admiral Rosily has arrived at Madrid; the common report is that he is coming to take over the command of the Fleet; undoubtedly I should be delighted to yield him the foremost place if I am permitted to occupy the second; it is due to his seniority and to his abilities, but it would be too terrible to me to lose all hope of having an opportunity of showing that I am worthy of a better fate. Be that as it may, my Lord, I can only explain the silence that you

have maintained on Admiral Rosily's mission by the hope that I should have been enabled to accomplish the mission with which I am entrusted at this moment, and whatever may be the obstacles, if the wind allows me to work out, I shall put to sea the first thing tomorrow.

The day before Villeneuve and Gravina had decided to send out Magon's fast squadron, as soon as the wind was favourable, in an attempt to capture the British frigates that habitually cruised close to Cadiz at night. 'The secret orders for this operation having been given,' wrote Escaño, 'and the ships which were to carry them out being in readiness', at daybreak on 18 October Villeneuve unexpectedly came on board the *Principe de Asturias*. He informed Gravina 'that fresh orders and fresh considerations obliged him to order the whole Squadron to leave port'. There were no fresh orders, but Nelson's apparent numerical weakness made it impossible for Gravina to refuse with honour. 'The orders of the government to obey the French Commander-in-Chief being so explicit,' wrote Escaño, 'without the slightest reply, the Chief of the Staff was ordered in his presence to recall the light craft from their stations and to send the people back to their respective ships, everyone being ordered to prepare to set sail.'

8

Blue Lights

After his short conference with Gravina in the early morning of 18 October, Villeneuve climbed down to his barge, was rowed back to *Bucentaure*, then immediately signalled his fleet to weigh anchor and collect all of the smaller craft. Cadiz Bay swarmed with sudden activity. Seamen and gunners who had been serving for practice in the shore batteries were sent back to their ships while soldiers struck camp and prepared to embark.

Later in the morning the admirals drew up a line of battle. The main force, the *corps de bataille*, was divided into three divisions of seven ships each. This total of twenty-one was designed to match the number of ships that they thought (or rather hoped) that Nelson now had. Vice Admiral Ignacio de Álava in *Santa Ana* commanded the vanguard, Villeneuve in *Bucentaure* commanded the centre, with Rear Admiral Báltasar de Cisneros in *Santísima Trinidad* seconding him, and Pierre Dumanoir in *Formidable* commanded the rear. Admiral Gravina was given the Squadron of Observation, or tactical reserve, of twelve ships, with Rear Admiral Charles Magon as his subordinate leading six of them.

French and Spanish ships were alternated within each division. There was to be no question this time of the French failing to come to the support of the Spanish, or the opposite. Perhaps for the same reason ships crewed by Gascons were mingled with those from Provence, as were Andalucían and Galician ships.

Villeneuve's fighting instructions to his captains had not changed since he took over the Toulon squadron in December 1804. They were now reissued to all. Villeneuve had seen the Royal Navy in action many times before and he had first-hand experience of Nelson at the Nile. Whatever his faults, he was not a stupid man, and he predicted with remarkable accuracy what Nelson would do.

> The enemy will not confine himself to forming on a line of battle with our own and engaging us in an artillery duel, in which success is frequently with the more skilful but always with the more fortunate; he will endeavour to envelop our rear, to break through our line and to direct his ships in groups upon such of ours as he shall have cut off, so as to surround them and defeat them.

It has often been said that having defined the problem, Villeneuve had no real plan to deal with it. This is not true. He was well aware of the limited ability of his own French ships, never mind the even less experienced Spanish ones, to carry out complex manoeuvres so his instructions were devastatingly simple. If his captains found themselves to windward of the enemy they were to turn simultaneously and attack in line, each taking on the ship opposite; if he had the chance, each captain was to attempt to board his opponent. If, however, they were to leeward, they were to await the enemy's attack in a closely serried line of battle and do the same. They were not to wait for signals that might be obscured by smoke. Rather, any captain not 'in the fire, was not at his post'. Nelson could not have laid out his intention with greater clarity.

Once Villeneuve's line was broken, unengaged vessels were expected to come to the aid of their admiral or of other ships that had been attacked. Weakened and dismasted enemy vessels were to be attacked by the frigates. Nelson's apparent weakness produced one refinement: Gravina's detached Squadron of Observation. With several of the best ships and the most gifted, bold and enterprising captains, Gravina was equipped to make a decisive intervention wherever he was most needed.

If Nelson wanted a 'pell-mell' battle at close range, then Villeneuve wanted to get even closer. For years French propaganda had cast its people as virtuous republican Romans struggling against the perfidious, mercenary Carthaginians of maritime Britain. Perhaps the classically educated French officers remembered how the Roman fleet had finally defeated the superior Carthaginian seamen: they had stopped the Carthaginians manoeuvring by grappling them and turning every engagement into a land battle.

Like the Romans the French excelled at land battles, and some of the best French soldiers were on board Villeneuve's ships. The Spanish had also packed their ships with infantrymen, some doing duty on the guns, some on deck with muskets and bayonets. For months the soldiers and seamen of the Combined Fleet had been training to become adept at boarding tactics. Grenadiers and sharp-shooters would clear the decks and pick off the carronade crews and then they would storm aboard, surprising the British with a tactic rarely used in fleet actions.

Jean-Jacques Lucas, captain of the *Redoutable*, one of the ships from Ferrol, reported in detail to Decrès how he had prepared his crew for this style of naval warfare: 'I had canvas cartridge-cases made for each of the captains of the guns, to hold two grenades apiece; with, attached to the shoulder-belts of the cartridge-cases in each case, a tube of tin holding a piece of quick-match.'

On board ship Lucas made his men practise with pasteboard grenades, but he continually landed parties of men to throw real ones so that they would get used to the weight of the iron. By the time they left Cadiz the sailors he put up in his tops and rigging could toss down two grenades at a time. He had a hundred muskets fitted with long bayonets sent on board to be given to selected sailors, who were given special training in musketry and stationed in the shrouds. The rest were armed with cutlasses and pistols and were trained regularly at sword exercise and pistol shooting. Finally, after long practice, his 'men also learnt to throw grappling irons with such skill that we could count on being able to grapple an enemy's ship before her sides had actually touched ours'.

Lucas was not an isolated case: all the ships at Ferrol had been doing the same. James Duff, the Consul at Cadiz, had reported to Nelson as early as September 1803 that 'The French Ships at Ferrol are <u>daily practising Boarding</u> from one of their own ships to another, and when they are perfect they intend going <u>out</u> to board our Ships.' Moreover, it is clear from Villeneuve's instructions that his Toulon squadron had determined on the same approach to fighting the British and had been practising just as hard.

In hand-to-hand fighting, the larger size of the French and Spanish crews gave them another advantage. By regulation a French 80 carried 862 men, and a 74 carried 775. The numbers aboard French ships at Trafalgar are known precisely in only a few cases. *Redoutable* carried 643 men and *Fougueux* had 682. Both were 74s. By French standards Villeneuve's ships were probably undermanned. But by regulation a British 80 carried 700 and a 74 between 590 and 640, and most British ships were also slightly undermanned. So, weakened as they were, Villeneuve's crews still had a numerical advantage over their British counterparts.

Regulation Spanish complements were similar to British, but the Spanish always carried more soldiers than the British did marines. A Spanish 74 should have carried 614 men, including 170 infantrymen and fifty-five artillerymen. At Trafalgar all the Spanish ships but two were overmanned, carrying between thirty-two and ninety-eight men over their regulation complement, and the extra men were soldiers. Each ship had between 202 and 382 infantrymen on board. The Spanish looked to overwhelm the British with their soldiery.

On paper they had raised enough sailors, although their quality left much to be desired. Only *Rayo* left Cadiz seriously short – she was practically crewed by soldiers. The remaining Spanish weakness was in specialised gunners, the élite *artilleros de mar*, and they had sought to replace them with army gunners.

The French and Spanish were under no illusions about British armament. In fact, French estimates gave the British ships even more guns and carronades than they had in reality. But their own ships were heavily armed too. The French had no three-deckers, but they had four

80s, *Bucentaure*, *Formidable*, *Indomptable* and *Neptune*, and for their combination of fire-power and sailing qualities these were arguably the best type of ship on the oceans. French 80s were generally armed with 36-pounders on the lower deck and 24-pounders on the upper, while 74s had 18-pounders on the upper deck. Also, the French pound was heavier than the English equivalent, so French 36-pound balls weighed 39 English pounds. That was why French ships delivered considerably more punch than their conventionally armed British adversaries.

Napoleon, himself a gunner, had noted that 'In this war the English have been the first to use carronades, and everywhere they have done us great harm.' The French had introduced the carronade experimentally in 1793 and made them standard in 1799. Like the English, they had increased the number of guns and carronades carried by their ships. Ships-of-the-line now carried an extra six to eight guns above the number at which they were rated, but they had not begun the process of wholesale replacement of light-calibre quarterdeck guns with heavy carronades as the British had so they did not carry as many of these. In July 1805 Napoleon had written to Decrès, 'For God's sake, ship me some more carronades.'

The Spanish had some fine three-deckers. Indeed, they even had a four-decker, the *Santísima Trinidad*, the largest ship in the world, which carried 136 guns; *Principe de Asturias* and *Santa Ana* carried 120 and *Rayo* 100. They also had two fine 80s, *Argonauta* and *Neptuno*, each carrying about ninety guns. But although their heavy ships were armed, like the French, with 36-pounders, 24-pounders and 12-pounders, their 74s were only lightly armed with 24-pounders and 18-pounders.

They had invested heavily in carronades and, to some extent, balanced the weakness of their main armament with these new weapons. The *Santa Ana* carried twenty. It is unlikely that they were as reliably manufactured as the British weapons.

All three navies, then, had packed their ships with extra weapons designed for close-range combat. All three believed that their best chance lay in a bloodbath.

During the afternoon of 18 October the officers of the Combined Fleet attended mass in the Church of the Carmen. Rowing-boats carried them to the mole and they walked from the port along the shady Alameda to the convent that overlooked the bay. They pushed open the huge wooden doors into an interior of swirling baroque mahogany, marble and gold. Incense burners swung, the organ played and the Madonna del Carmen looked down upon them from high on the golden wall above the altar as they prayed.

Then there were fond farewells. Lieutenant Pierre Beaudran of *Bucentaure* was deeply in love with an Andalucían girl, who gave him a miniature of herself to carry in his pocket. A high proportion of the Spanish officers and crews resided in or near Cadiz so there were many tearful partings from wives and families. But there was no goodbye for Dionisio Alcalá Galiano: his wife had been ill and he had taken her and his son Antonio in *Bahama*'s barge to nearby Chiclana, where the wealthy citizens of Cadiz had their country villas. There she could convalesce in peace and quiet, and there his family would be safe in case Nelson decided to bombard or set fire to the city. Cosme de Churruca told his young brother-in-law, José Ruiz de Apodaca, to write to his parents and tell them he was going into a battle that would certainly be bloody. 'Say goodbye to them, because my fate will be yours. I shall not surrender my ship before it either blows up or sinks. This is the duty of those who serve their king and country.' He wrote to his own brother, 'If you hear that my ship has been captured you will know that I am dead.'

Red and gold flags fluttered bravely and the ships made an inspiring show. The turquoise water rippled and sparkled under cloudless blue skies. Families crowded on to the mole and the sea wall, or stood high on balconies and miradors to watch the boats pull over to the ships. But the farewells were laden with apprehension.

In the late afternoon Villeneuve signalled the fleet to unmoor, to hoist in their boats, to prepare to make sail and to send an officer to the flagship for their final instructions and order of battle. There was a stiff breeze from the north-west. The ships needed an east wind to get out of Cadiz Bay and although Magon's division was ready to leave, he would not be able to launch a surprise night attack on Blackwood's frigates.

Most of the ships remained deep in the harbour and had even greater problems with the wind. Baudouin's *Fougueux* was anchored between the forts of Puerto Real and Puntales, far too high up the bay to make for an easy departure in such conditions. And there was still much to do, not least recovering the guns that had been placed in longboats for port defence. But by nightfall all the ships were riding on one anchor, ready to leave in the morning.

By dawn the wind had changed direction, but was now only a whisper of an east south easterly breeze. Villeneuve signalled the fleet to sail and the French ships *Algésiras, Achille, Argonaute, Neptune, Héros, Duguay-Trouin* and Galiano's ship *Bahama* worked out on the tide with the frigates *Hermione, Rhin* and *Thémis*. But the feeble wind became more southerly and the remaining ships could do no more than get up into the bay. Baudouin sent out *Fougueux*'s boats and was 'warped' up as far as Cadiz harbour, the boats rowing forward, dropping an anchor ahead of the ship and the men in the ship pulling on its rope to haul the vessel forward.

Out to sea, the alert had been sounded. At first light Nelson's frigates were cruising four miles from Cadiz. William Prowse, closest in *Sirius*, inspected the enemy ships and telegraphed to Henry Blackwood, 'enemy have their topsail yards hoisted'. Blackwood watched through his telescope as topgallant yards went up and eight of the ships set topsails. He waited an hour and a half to see what would happen. At seven a.m. the nearest ships got under way, and once it was clear that they really were intending to put to sea, Blackwood sent Thomas Capel's *Phoebe* racing off west-north-west to repeat his signals to Duff's advanced squadron of battleships. Blackwood could just see George Hope's *Defence*, the nearest of Duff's ships. By eight o'clock he could see nineteen of the enemy under way. All the rest except two had their topsails to the masthead. Blackwood made signal 370, 'the enemy's ships are coming out of port, or getting under weigh'. Firing guns to draw attention to his ship, Capel repeated the signal. *Defence* saw *Phoebe* and repeated the news they had been waiting for to

Agamemnon. Berry repeated it to James Morris in *Colossus*. Morris sent it on to Duff himself in *Mars*.

Through his loud-hailer Blackwood shouted to Thomas Dundas in *Naiad* to sail closer to *Phoebe* and repeat signals along the chain. Using the Popham code book that Nelson had brought from England, he telegraphed Peter Parker in the *Weasel* to tell Admiral Louis and the ships at Gibraltar and nearby Tetouan what was happening, then sent *Pickle* south towards Cape Spartel to warn any ships there.

As Magon emerged into the open sea in *Algésiras* he saw those ships tearing off at top speed and sent his own frigate *Hermione* to scout out the British frigates as he organised his ships to chase. Then the wind dropped. By midday it was flat calm. Blackwood could see the enemy ships stranded in Cadiz Bay, powerless to move.

At nine o'clock in the morning, fifty miles away to the east, Nelson finished a letter to 'dear Coll' and considered dinner. 'What a beautiful day!' he concluded. 'Will you be tempted out of your Ship? If you will, hoist the Assent and Victory's pendants.' He sent this off to Collingwood, then signalled to his other prospective guests. *Prince* was in the process of transferring thirty butts of water from *Britannia*. Everything else was quiet. Captain John Cooke of *Bellerophon* accepted his admiral's invitation and *Victory* signalled to him to come closer.

On board *Bellerophon*, First Lieutenant William Cumby was ordering more sail when he noticed a signal flying from the masthead of the lookout ship *Mars*. He thought that he could make out 370 – the signal they had all been waiting for – and called to Cooke, asking his permission to repeat it to the admiral. 'The *Mars* at this time was so far from us that her topgallant masts alone were visible above the horizon; consequently the distance was so great that Captain Cooke said he was unwilling to repeat a signal of so much importance unless he could clearly distinguish the flags himself, which on looking through his glass he declared himself unable to do.' Cumby was sure of his own sharp eyes. Cooke asked if anybody would back up Cumby but none of the other officers or signalmen felt they could. 'I had the mortification to be disappointed in my anxious wish that the *Bellerophon* should be the first to repeat such delightful intelligence to the Admiral,' recalled Cumby.

> Soon afterwards the Mars hauled down the flags, and I said, 'Now she will make the *distant signal* 370,' which distant signals were made with a flag, a ball, and a pendant differently disposed at different mastheads by a combination totally unconnected with the colour of the flag or pendant used. She did make the distant Signal No. 370 as I had predicted; this could not be mistaken, and as we were preparing to repeat it, the *Mars*' signal was answered from the *Victory*, and immediately afterwards the dinner signal was annulled and the signal made for a general chase.

Nelson was sure that the Combined Fleet would head for the Mediterranean and steered south-east for its mouth, hoping that he might meet Admiral Louis there. *Prince*'s master, Richard Anderson, watched in horror as *Victory* made the signal for a general chase, then the signal to prepare for battle. His own boats were still racing back from *Britannia* with their heavy load of water. This was unfortunate because the admiral already thought both ships very slow. On *Neptune*, reported James Martin, Nelson's signal was 'Ancered with Heartfull Satifaction but it Being a Dead Calm we had but little hopes of falling in with them that day'. *Neptune* got under way within a quarter of an hour, and it was not long before *Bellerophon*, *Belleisle*, *Orion*, *Leviathan* and *Polyphemus* 'showed their superiority of sailing, and got far ahead of the fleet'. The admiral was still alert to every detail. As he watched these swift sailers pull away he noticed that neither the recently arrived *Belleisle* nor *Polyphemus* had yet painted their masts buff to distinguish British ships in action from the hooped masts of the French and Spanish. He sent his dispatch boat, *Entreprenante*, to tell them to paint them at once. Anything that might prevent ships opening fire on their friends had to be done.

Then he went back to writing letters. One was unfinished, of the type that superstitious men often wrote to their wives: 'My dearest beloved Emma, the dear friend of my bosom. The signal has been made . . . And as my last writing before the Battle will be to you, so I hope in God that I shall live to finish my letter after the Battle . . .' The next, to his daughter Horatia, confirmed for the first time that he was her father. 'My dearest Angel, I was made happy by the pleasure of receiving your letter of September 19th and I rejoice to hear that you are so very good a girl . . . Receive my dearest Horatia, the affectionate parental blessing of your Father. Nelson & Bronte.'

As they sailed they cleared the ships for action. The whistles of the boatswain's mates called all hands from below to a period of frantic activity, frequently rehearsed in exercises. In a Napoleonic sea battle, most injuries were caused not by the direct impact of cannonballs or lead shot but by flying splinters of wood. Elaborate preparations were soon in progress to minimise the risks. Hammocks were rolled up, carried on deck and stowed, mostly in netting at the side of the ship where they afforded protection against small arms and splinters with a few in the tops to protect the deadeyes and lanyards of the shrouds. All bulkheads and partitions were removed from the gun-decks and from beneath the poop. Some of the wooden partitions were hinged at the top and could be swung up to deck height. Others were pulled apart to be stowed in the hold. Lightweight canvas panels were either stowed or thrown overboard and canvas screens were treated similarly. The pillars between decks were knocked out, and all ladders that were not considered essential were removed and replaced with rope scrambling nets. Clearing space gave maximum room for manning the guns and made it easier to supervise and supply them with shot and powder. As well as minimising the danger from splinters, it helped to ventilate the crowded space and clear clouds of gunsmoke.

Cabin furniture, most of which was portable, was taken to the hold, but it was sometimes quicker to throw things overboard. Later, the carpenter would have to account for all that the crew, in their enthusiasm, threw away. *Ajax* jettisoned six ladders, ten cot frames, six staunchions, a grinding-stone, a set of screens for berths, four weather sails, thirty feet of copper funnelling and much more. The crew of *Neptune* behaved similarly. After the battle Thomas Fremantle found that some sections of his cabin had been thrown overboard although, to his relief, his prized mahogany writing-table had been spared. In *Tonnant* 'the Windsor chairs forming part of the ward-room furniture were suspended by a rope passed from the main to the mizzen mast' where they hung high over the deck. Nelson was better treated: all the furniture from his cabin, including his portrait of Emma Hamilton, was safely stowed below.

Dealing with injured or maddened animals was difficult in battle so most livestock were slaughtered. *Neptune* kept a goat for milk and had taken delivery of eleven bullocks on 8 October, a few of which might still have been alive. Some British captains tried to hold on to their beasts. Collingwood kept his pigs and Henry Bayntun preserved *Leviathan*'s goat.

Towards evening the wind got up and *Belleisle* won the race, with *Orion* just behind, doing four knots. Edward Codrington's cabin walls had disappeared and he was separated from the quarterdeck by a boat's sail as he wrote to his wife: 'How would your heart beat for me, dearest Jane, did you but know that we are now under every stitch of sail we can set, steering for the enemy . . .' He went to bed, he told her, 'full of hope that Lord Nelson's declaration would be verified; viz. that we should have a good battle, and go home to eat our Christmas dinner.' In *Bellerophon* William Cumby was more pessimistic, his joy at the prospect of battle and an end to long blockades 'considerably checked by the apprehension that it was merely a feint on their part'. Like many others, he feared that 'having no intention of giving us battle, that they would re-enter the harbour of Cadiz so soon as they discovered us in pursuit'.

This leading group was signalled to keep watch ahead through the night as they continued towards the Strait of Gibraltar. Cooke told Cumby that 'he should not feel comfortable unless either he or I were constantly upon deck till we either brought the enemy to action or the chase was ended'. Cumby volunteered to take two watches, 'adding my hope that the events of the following day would render our watching the next night unnecessary'. He watched till midnight, Cooke watched till four, then Cumby came on deck again. But morning brought no glimpse of the enemy fleet.

Admiral Charles Magon spent the day cruising at the entrance to Cadiz Bay. As a light sea breeze got up again in the late afternoon he formed his ships into a line of battle and sent *Hermione* and *Rhin* towards Blackwood. Blackwood stayed within a couple of miles, tacking when the French tacked. Magon ordered his ships to clear for action and they went through the same laborious process as the British. In the evening the wind faded away again and some of Magon's ships anchored at the mouth of the bay. The night was lit by flares fired by the British ships to the west, but otherwise it was uneventful.

In the morning there was a light south-easterly land breeze in Cadiz Bay and a fresher south-westerly wind at sea. Magon immediately chased Blackwood while the rest of the Combined Fleet in Cadiz Bay got under way. *Héros* got near enough to fire a broadside at *Sirius*, which had been searching an American merchantman. The frigates fled south-west and drew the Combined Fleet on to *Agamemnon*, which appeared to Blackwood to be oblivious to the danger and was certainly reluctant to abandon a brig that had been made a prize the previous day. All the ships of the Combined Fleet got out to sea by about ten in the morning, with only *Rayo* trailing behind, and cleared for action as they left Cadiz Bay.

Walking in the fields near Chiclana, Antonio Galiano met a peasant who asked him whether he had just climbed up to the hermitage of Santa Ana – the local viewpoint – to see which way the Combined Fleet was sailing. Galiano was astonished when the peasant told him he had seen the fleet leaving port with his own eyes. Galiano ran home to tell his mother the news.

Later in the morning it began to rain heavily, the first serious downpour in months. The wind strengthened. As the flagships reached the open sea, it grew stronger still and swung round to the south, scattering the ships. Villeneuve signalled to double reef the topsails, reducing sail in preparation for bad weather.

Around the mouth of the Strait of Gibraltar the sea was empty and British hopes were dashed. Codrington continued his journal to his wife in despair: 'All our gay hopes are fled; and, instead of being under all possible sail in a very light breeze and fine weather, expecting to bring the enemy to battle, we are now under close-reefed topsails, in a very strong wind with thick rainy weather, and the dastardly French we find returned to Cadiz.' They turned back and were sailing slowly north, most believing, like Codrington, that the enemy had gone back into port. Richard Anderson, master of the *Prince*, spoke for the less bullish: 'Well this Bustles over Enemy in Port again we Chaced all last Night & old ship Sailed well – I am Tired & we have bad w^r to day I am not sorry that the Enemy are in Port for they are 10 Sail of Line superior.'

It was not until the evening that most British ships realised the enemy were still out. Nelson was better informed: George Hope of *Defence* reported to him in the morning and was given instructions for Blackwood. The signal chain would be maintained until night. After dark, Blackwood was told, 'If the Enemy are standing to the Southward, or towards the Straits, burn two blue lights together, every hour, in order to make the greater blaze. If the Enemy are standing to the Westward three guns, quick, every hour.'

The weather remained gloomy with driving rain and low visibility. The wind was strong enough to split both of *Principe de Asturias*'s topsails despite the reefs. *Agamemnon* was more seriously damaged, losing her main topmast in a squall. In the afternoon the wind dropped a little and the Combined Fleet sailed with one reef as it tacked northwest and aimed out to sea to get far enough west to round Cape Trafalgar. They began to form in five columns, one for each division, with the Squadron of Observation furthest west. In the afternoon they wore round and steered south-west again. *Achille*, *Algésiras* and *San*

Juan Nepomuceno, along with the frigates, were out ahead, chasing the English scouts. At half past five *Principe de Asturias* signalled to them to rejoin before night and repeated the signal to clear for action and prepare for battle.

'Night fell,' *Principe*'s log recorded, 'with the sky and horizon misty and a choppy sea running from the north-west.' The wind had fallen away again to a moderate breeze. At seven 'a French ship came within hail, reporting that the *Achille* had made out as many as 18 enemy sail'. In the darkness they watched a firework display of flares and blue-coloured lights. Those on deck could both hear and see British signal guns. Escaño judged that 'from the interval which elapsed between the flash and the report, they must have been about two miles from us' and, using night signal lanterns, advised Villeneuve to form line of battle. Villeneuve agreed. He sent a brig to order them to form on the ships furthest to leeward. They beat to general quarters and everyone went to his post.

Principe de Asturias hoisted the signal to form in order of battle in line ahead, and to indicate that his flagship was leading the line Gravina showed a light at the mizen-mast head. Then they bore away south-east by south, giving orders to ships they met that the other ships should be directed to follow in their wake. 'The night being very dark, this movement was effected with a great deal of confusion,' noted Sub-lieutenant Désiré Clamart in *Achille*. Ships manoeuvred as best they could into several ragged lines.

All that Sunday it was impossible to see the enemy, even from the masthead of *Bellerophon*, and Cooke, Cumby and their crew remained tortured with doubt as to what the Combined Fleet was doing. The first positive and encouraging news came when an eager group clustered round Christopher Beaty, the yeoman of signals, pointing their telescopes at the flagship, read a telegraph signal from Nelson to Blackwood's *Euryalus*: 'I rely on your keeping sight of the enemy through the night.' They cheered. The Combined Fleet was still at sea and still in sight, and their hopes surged again. Cooke watched till midnight when Cumby relieved him, then took over again at four. All night they saw nothing but the blue lights and false fires that assured the admiral the frigates could still see the French and Spanish. Cumby turned in.

Nelson watched the hourly blue lights settle into a firm pattern. The enemy was heading slowly but steadily southwards. He, however, had turned south-west and out to sea in order to have the 'weather gauge' – the wind behind him – in the morning. Only at four in the morning did he turn back north-east towards the Combined Fleet.

On *Neptune* old tars sniffed the wind and watched the clouds anxiously whenever the flares illuminated them. The skies were clearing and there was a lovely moderate wind. It seemed as if, as James Martin recalled, the warriors of Great Britain were going to get the opportunity for which they had long waited: 'Now the moment was fast advancing which was to Decide wether the Boasted Herosum of France and Spain or the Ginene Valour of free Born Britans was to Rule the Main.'

9

A Forest of Masts

The first casualty of Monday 21 October 1805 was a young landsman from Bridgwater, Aaron Crocan. At five thirty, just before first light, he fell overboard from *Conqueror* into the heavy swell and was never seen again. Before anybody could lower a boat to search for him a shout from the masthead alerted the officers on watch to the sight they had been waiting for: the masts of the Combined Fleet, faintly silhouetted on the horizon to the east, about eleven miles away.

In the *Revenge* William 'Nastyface' Robinson remembered that 'a man at the topmast head called out, "a sail on the starboard bow," and in two or three minutes more he gave another call, that there was more than one sail.' The news spread very fast and, with cheers and feet pounding on ladders, the watch not on duty and all of the idlers surged up the hatchways. To Robinson the Combined Fleet 'looked like a forest of masts rising from the ocean'.

In *Bellerophon* Captain John Cooke knew that First Lieutenant William Cumby would want to see this sight and sent the master, Edward Overton, below to wake him. Overton had watched Cumby's hopes rise and fall over the previous days and roused him cheerily: 'Cumby, my boy, turn out; here they are all ready for you, thrice and thirty sail-of-the-line close under our lee, and evidently disposed to wait our attack.' Cumby shot out of his cot, pulled on clothes, and was about to rush up the ladder when, instead, he knelt for a moment. He 'put up a short but fervent prayer to the great God of battles for a glorious victory to the arms of my country', and thought for a moment of his wife Anne, their son Anthony, nearly two, and their six-month-old, whom he had not yet seen. Then he climbed the ladders to the quarterdeck and was soon watching the enemy through his telescope. They were steering south on the starboard tack and forming line of battle, just as Overton had promised. The rain had stopped and the wind had dropped to the lightest of breezes from the north-west.

From *Victory* Nelson issued a rapid series of signals to gather his fleet and direct them towards the enemy. The British ships began to form into two clusters behind *Victory* and *Royal Sovereign*, steering east-north-east not so much towards the enemy as to cut them off from Cadiz. The only exception was *Africa*, who had lost touch with the fleet during the night and was some miles away to the north-east.

In *Neptune* sixteen-year-old midshipman William Badcock had the first sight of the enemy. He ran aft to tell the officer of the watch, and Captain Thomas Fremantle was on deck in a moment with many of his men. One of them, James Martin, thought it was 'prehaps the Grandest Sight of Hosteil Fleets ever Behild being no less then 60 Sail of the Line Besides others of Smaller Force maned with the Flower of their Respective Nations'.

A few minutes after the British had seen the Combined Fleet, their own ships became visible to the enemy. Villeneuve dressed carefully and came on deck, meticulously elegant in a long-tailed navy-blue uniform coat with a high collar over greenish corduroy pantaloons with broad stripes down the sides. He wore black half boots with sharp toes and he carried his pocket watch in his waistcoat, its long gold chain dangling prominently.

Villeneuve signalled his ships to form up in the order that had been arranged before they left Cadiz. During the night he had told them to take station as most convenient and many now struggled to get into their proper place. In the darkness Louis Infernet, in *Intrépide*, had made for the spot immediately behind the admiral in *Bucentaure* but another ship had claimed the place so he had taken station two ships behind. The order of battle had him four ships ahead so now he put on sail to try to get into his proper place in front of the intervening ships.

Villeneuve also signalled to close the gap between each ship to a cable's length, or two hundred yards, which was considered to be close order. If they had been that close together his ships would have covered just over three and a half miles. As it was, their order was at present looser. It was also composed of several overlapping lines. They were about fifteen miles east of the low sandy bluff of Cape Trafalgar. Another fifty miles would get them to Tarifa and into the mouth of the Strait of Gibraltar, but with the wind almost calm it would take a long time. The British were about eleven miles further out to sea. Villeneuve sent the frigate *Hermione* to count the enemy ships.

At seven thirty *Hermione* signalled thirty sail, among which she made out twenty-seven ships-of-the-line. It was an alarming six more than Villeneuve had hoped. Evidently Nelson had been reinforced. He watched the British fleet carefully, and tried to work out what Nelson was doing. The British ships had turned towards the French in a disorderly mass with two three-deckers leading what might become two groups. The whole lot was heading towards the rear of the Combined Fleet, threatening at once to envelop it and to cut them off from Cadiz.

It was a hazy autumn morning of watery sunshine and by eight a.m. the temperature had reached a warm 65° Fahrenheit. Nearly all the ships in both fleets had already cleared for battle so there were only a few last-minute jobs to be done. The sailors' hammocks were taken down and put into their battle station as padding against small-arms fire. The lower yards were given slings of chain to stop the huge wooden spars falling on those beneath if the normal rope supports were shot away. The cloths separating the officers' cabins were removed and everything was wetted against fire. Observing from *Neptune*, Badcock recalled that 'all sail was set, and the different ships tried to form the line in two divisions, but the lightness of the wind, and the distance of the sternmost from the van, prevented anything like speed in the manoeuvre'.

At eight o'clock the British crews paused. It was normal to set aside half or three-quarters of an hour for breakfast and James Martin remembered that on *Neptune* Captain Fremantle 'allowed us the same Rest nearley as was ushall'. The officers gathered in the wardrooms. In *Belleisle* Paul Nicolas, second lieutenant of marines, was just sixteen. This was his first voyage and, understandably, he was nervous. He was impressed by the blend of eager confidence and fatalistic resignation to the certainty that some present would become casualties: 'Though each seemed to exult in the hope of a glorious termination to the contest so near at hand, a fearful presage was experienced that all would not again unite at that festive board.' First Lieutenant Ebenezer Geale was so convinced that he would not survive the day that he made a will for 'the necessary disposal of his property in the event of his death'.

In *Bellerophon* William Cumby had breakfast as usual at eight o'clock with the captain and his other officers. Afterwards Captain Cooke asked Cumby to wait behind and produced Nelson's secret memorandum. He asked him to read it through carefully then enquired whether Cumby 'perfectly understood the Admiral's instructions'. Cumby replied that 'they were so distinct and explicit that it was quite impossible they could be misunderstood'. Cooke explained that he wanted Cumby to know how to direct the ships according to Nelson's wishes in case Cooke himself was 'bowl'd out'. Cumby 'observed that it was very possible that the same shot which disposed of him might have an equally tranquillising effect upon me', and suggested that they should show the memorandum to the master, who would be the only senior officer remaining on the quarterdeck if they were both hit. He could then communicate Nelson's instructions to whichever lieutenant took over. Captain Cooke agreed, and Overton was called in to read the memorandum.

Premonitions and precautions were reasonable, given the vulnerability of the men on the exposed quarterdeck and *Bellerophon*'s history. She was among the most battle-scarred ships in the fleet. Launched in 1786, she was one of the smaller sort of seventy-four-gun two-deckers, which were the standard line-of-battle ships in all navies. She had fought in the famous victory over the French on the Glorious First of June 1794. At the Nile she had taken on the much larger three-decked

1. A portrait by Leonardo Guzzardi of Admiral Nelson aboard his Mediterranean flagship. Rolled hammocks provide added protection at the side of the ship and the sailor kneels by a carronade.

7. The Combined Fleet puts to sea from Cadiz, 20 October 1805, from William Heath's panorama of the battle of Trafalgar. The Spanish battery faces south across Cadiz Bay with the city just excluded to the right of this detail.

8. Vice Admiral Cuthbert Collingwood: 'in body and mind he was iron, and very cold iron'.

9. Captain Henry Blackwood of *Euryalus* was known as Nelson's 'watchdog' outside Cadiz, commanding the frigate squadron. 'He was rather short, but of extraordinary strength and finely made'.

10. Rear Admiral Charles Magon. Magon inflicted defeats on the British in the Indian Ocean and was considered the most aggressive of the French leaders at Trafalgar. Repeatedly accused of royalism and forced to divorce his wife, Magon defended himself in 1799 'I swear hatred to Royalty and anarchy; I swear attachment and fidelity to the Republic, to the constitution of the Year 3, and to the government'.

11. Vice Admiral Pierre Villeneuve 'a tallish thin man, a very tranquil, placid, English-looking Frenchman'. As a young man Villeneuve, like Magon, had fought in the French naval victory at Chesapeake that ensured the surrender of the British army at Yorktown and, with it, American independence. But in 1805 he considered his fleet too weak to do battle with the British.

12. Admiral Federico Gravina: 'all genius and decision in battle' (Napoleon, August 1805).

13. Commodore Dionisio Alcalá Galiano of *Bahama*, explorer of America's Pacific coast, learned English to read the works of British mathematicians.

14. A gun crew in action, by Thomas Stothard.

French flagship *L'Orient*, suffered 193 casualties and been totally dismasted. Nevertheless, it was not until the French flagship caught fire that *Bellerophon* had cut her cable and drifted away to safety. In 1794 her commander's leg had been blown off, while at the Nile the captain and the master were wounded and three lieutenants killed. It was sobering to think that they were all now in the same oak structure but with a much larger enemy fleet facing them.

Cooke, Overton and Cumby returned to the quarterdeck where Cooke told Cumby to beat to quarters. Cumby alerted Thomas Robinson, the boatswain, who ran with his two mates, Thomas Platts and William Hayter, to the hatches to call the men. Meanwhile Cumby gave the order to the drummers and they beat out the rhythm 'Heart of Oak', an old favourite from the Seven Years' War:

> Heart of oak are our ships, heart of oak are our men;
> We always are ready, steady, boys, steady!
> We'll fight and we'll conquer again and again.

When the drum beat to quarters each of the 550 other men and boys on board *Bellerophon* raced to his appointed battle station. For the vast majority, this meant the gun-decks.

Each gun-deck was commanded by one or two lieutenants and five midshipmen. On *Bellerophon*'s lower deck Lieutenant George Saunders controlled the forward fourteen of the twenty-eight 32-pounders. The first eight of Saunders's guns were commanded by William Fairweather, a forty-five-year-old midshipman who had either continuously failed his exams or been promoted from the ranks – the crucifix tattooed on his arm and his role as boatswain's third mate suggest the latter. He was born in Great Yarmouth and had a wife, Mary, waiting for him in Portsmouth. Robert Orchard, a dark thirty-four-year-old from Dorset, was one of Saunders's quarter gunners. He commanded the fifth and sixth pairs on the lower deck. Among Saunders's other men were prime seamen, like Henry Park from Whitby and John Legg from Dorchester, who were captains of their guns. Also in this group of seamen was John Signieur, an able seaman from Bordeaux, who had been pressed from an English merchantman in 1796, then made his home in the Royal Navy, and James Field, a twenty-one-year-old landsman born in Dublin, who had been a metal worker for two years before he volunteered. There was also the ship's butcher, thirty-six-year-old William Pallett, who had plied his trade in Hertfordshire before going to sea in 1791.

Fourteen men served each pair of 32-pounders on the lower deck, starboard and larboard. If the ship was firing from both sides the crew would be divided in half. The normal crew for an 18-pounder was eleven, eight for a 12-pounder. Of these crews, several had other duties that might call them away from serving the gun. In a crew of fourteen, two were conventionally designated boarders; two were sail-trimmers, who might leave to help with manoeuvre; two more operated the pump if enemy shot caused flooding in the hold; and one was charged to bring 'his Fire Bucket opposite his Gun, upon coming to action' and be ready 'to break off from his Gun to supply Water at whatever part of the Ship it is called for'.

From the gunroom, chests containing muskets, pistols and cutlasses were sent up to be distributed to each gun, with a salt-box containing two ready-to-use cartridges. Rope wads were placed in nets hung from the beams over the guns. Each gun captain was issued with a powder horn, spare gunlock flints, a slow-match in case the flints failed, cartridge prickers and reamers, and a pouch with firing tubes and spanners. The match was lit before the fighting started and inserted into a match-tub partly filled with water, the burning end poised above it.

A human chain of men and boys passed the powder cartridges in wooden cases from the magazines to the decks. From there, on the call to arms, 'the proper Men stationed to hand Powder' collected their salt-boxes and powder horns and placed them carefully on the side opposite that which was firing. If both sides were firing at once the powder was kept amidships. Among the 'proper men' in *Bellerophon* was Richard Bovett, a thirty-five-year-old married man from Devon who was instructed to guard his salt-boxes from sparks at all times. On this ship boys might have passed the powder cases to Bovett but, despite all that has been written about 'powder monkeys', in *Mars* Captain Duff did not trust boys to deliver powder to the guns. Instead they were given wet swabs to dampen any that was spilled on the deck.

Bellerophon's gunner, John Stevenson, moved between the lower gun-deck, his storeroom and the main magazine in the hold two decks below Saunders's forward guns. Fire in the magazine was a sailor's greatest fear. In 1796 a frigate commanded by *Conqueror*'s present captain, Israel Pellew, blew up at moorings in Plymouth with the loss of 300 lives when a trail of powder spilled by an embezzling gunner led flames to the magazine. Of course, the danger during a battle was much greater. No light was allowed inside the powder rooms or magazines. Instead, each was furnished with an adjacent light room in which lanterns shone from behind glass. The windows were protected with hinged screens with built-in water containers in case the glass broke. The master at arms, William Dowse, the ship's chief policeman, guarded the light room with the help of the cook, William Jefferys, an experienced old seaman.

As they prepared for action, Stevenson and his mates unlocked the magazines and powder rooms. They checked the emergency supply of cartridges already prepared for use and began to make more, measuring out powder with copper scoops. Behind them, screens were nailed above doors and soaked with water. Some captains flooded the lead-lined passage to the magazine to create a firebreak. One ship's corporal, Liverpudlian John Brown, stood in the passage and another, John Barton from Glasgow, guarded the magazine. A third corporal guarded the smaller after magazine where some trusty old seamen supervised the issue of cartridges.

Just above them on the semi-submerged orlop deck, carpenter Russell Mart and some of his crew, with caulker John Udell and his mate John Braithwaite, a former Yorkshire shipwright, went to the store to fetch their tools. They laid out wooden plugs of various sizes to repair holes made by round shot near the waterline, and sheets of lead or tarred canvas to nail over bigger holes. Udell prepared oakum to drive into the joints to seal them. During the battle they stationed themselves in the walks along the sides of the ship and the caulker periodically sounded the well for water seeping into the ship and, if necessary, supervised the pumps.

Surgeon Alexander Whyte, his assistant William Engleheart and the 'loblolly men' were transforming much of the space below the waterline into an operating theatre. They prepared saws and knives for amputation, probes and fleams to find and pull out splinters, extractors for bullets, ligatures to bind arteries, needles and twine for stitching, tourniquets, forceps and tweezers. Bandages were made from torn linen, and buckets of water placed nearby for washing wounds and to receive amputated limbs. Vinegar, to disinfect, and oil of turpentine, to seal stumps, were ready too. The edges of the deck were spread with canvas for the wounded to lie on while they waited for treatment, which was administered conventionally in strict order of arrival. This was the usual station of any women in the ship.

Up on the superstructure of the ship the boatswain, Thomas Robinson, and a lieutenant or mate responsible for manoeuvre commanded the forecastle. The boatswain's mates and some of the strongest and most reliable seamen were stationed here, where tight changes in direction might be needed in close proximity to the enemy. On the first pair of 32-pounder carronades were twenty-nine-year-old Peter McFarlane, a stout, muscular, fresh-faced Scotsman, and Peter Jansen, a thirty-seven-year-old Swede from Karlskrona with a flower-pot tattooed on his right arm. Jansen was an escaped white slave. In July that year the crew of *Bellerophon*, watering their ship in Turkish Oran, had taken him in, and when the Turks demanded his return, Lieutenant Cumby had negotiated his release in fluent French with the Bey.

On the quarterdeck, the command group consisted of Captain Cooke, William Cumby and Edward Overton, with three midshipmen as aides and William Hazard, the clerk, to take notes. A quartermaster and four seamen manned the helm. Above them on the poop were some of the marines and the nineteen-year-old signal midshipman, John Franklin, who would later become famous as an Arctic explorer.

With him was Christopher Beaty, the thirty-one-year-old yeoman of signals. About forty sailors and marines manned the guns. The captain of the starboard afterguard, Charles White, a thirty-nine-year-old former fisherman whose wife now lived in Gosport, was stationed above them in the mizen rigging with a musket. Other skilled and agile sailors were stationed in the tops. One was a Devonian named Ambrose Peake, another a red-haired Glaswegian called James Neblie, both in their twenties. They had muskets with which to pick off the enemy but their crucial role, which required considerable bravery, was to adjust the sail during the battle. If major changes were needed, other topmen would leave the guns and join them.

When the men were in place and everything seemed in order, First Lieutenant William Cumby toured the ship, then reported to the captain that *Bellerophon* was ready for action. On the lower deck George Saunders pointed to where some of his seamen had chalked 'in large characters on their guns the words "Victory or Death", a very gratifying mark of the spirit with which they were going to their work'.

Villeneuve, Magendie and the French command group on the flagship *Bucentaure* were still watching the British intently as Villeneuve tried to work out the best course of action. Villeneuve knew that Nelson had other ships in the area. The Spanish signal stations had not told him that these ships had passed by to rejoin their comrades so it was likely that they were still at Gibraltar and might be preparing to cut him off in the strait. Perhaps by threatening his rear Nelson hoped to trap him between two forces, one as yet unseen. Also, the swell promised bad weather and the rocky shoals of Cape Trafalgar were behind Villeneuve. If a storm struck, his only refuge was Cadiz. He weighed it all up and decided to counter the threat to his rear by turning his ships and moving back northward towards Cadiz.

This meant that the *Neptuno*, which had been the last ship, became the leader, while the *San Juan Nepomuceno*, which had been the pathfinder, now brought up the rear. 'My sole object being to protect the rear from the projected attack of the entire enemy force,' Villeneuve insisted later, aware that ill-intentioned colleagues might accuse him of attempting flight to Cadiz. But the principal result of his signal was to disorganise his fleet.

Captain Magendie watched what happened and reported that as the ships wore round, several of them, notably the Spanish three-deckers, fell away greatly to leeward – or downwind. In Gravina's Squadron of Observation, which was manoeuvring to cover the rear, several ships were soon dropping away. The problem was that the wind was extremely light. The ships were 'standing close-hauled' – moving slowly while steering as close to the wind as possible – and did not have enough wind to give them steerage way. To make matters worse, the heavy swell was hitting them full on the beam and driving them sideways in the same direction as the wind. To manoeuvre under these conditions would have been a trial for complete and experienced crews, but some of the Spanish seamen had only two days' experience of the open sea in their present ships. Even the French crews were short of practised sailors. In their efforts first to get into their proper station in the previously arranged line of battle and then to reverse direction, the Franco-Spanish line became ever more ragged and disjointed.

Magendie complained that 'the leading ship, the Spanish *Neptuno*, did not get up to windward; the signal for her to do so was made several times and some of the other ships did not take their stations'. Acting Lieutenant Auguste Gicquel, responsible for manoeuvre in *Intrépide*, not far from *Neptuno*, thought Villeneuve was giving Cayetano Valdés in *Neptuno* the wrong orders. He felt that what was needed was more speed to give the ships steerage way while they sorted themselves out. Instead of ordering *Neptuno* 'to carry full sail in order to rectify the line of battle, the admiral endlessly signalled to hug the wind'. With so little wind the ships that sailed worst fell to leeward and the line became increasingly deformed with 'ships doubled up at various points, leaving vast holes in the line for the benefit of the English'. Perhaps Villeneuve avoided any instruction to carry full sail in case it gave an impression of headlong flight. But he was also anxious to make his line as compact as possible so crowding might not have worried him as much as gaps.

Cosme de Churruca, the naval theorist who was captain of the *San Juan Nepomuceno*, was unimpressed with Villeneuve's leadership. He had thought Villeneuve's first signal to adopt the prearranged formation misguided: under the prevailing conditions simply to form a line in their current order was challenge enough for any fleet, but turning round was even more foolish as it compounded the problem. He stood on the quarterdeck with his old friend and second-in-command Francisco Moyua, who had sailed with him in all his voyages of exploration. They looked in professional disdain at the confusion that followed Villeneuve's order to sail in the opposite direction, with ships twisting, turning and dropping back to get into their proper place in the prearranged formation. He watched his own crew, straining on the ropes and tiring rapidly. Churruca turned to Moyua and remarked drily, '*El general francés no conoce su obligación, y nos compromete*': The French admiral does not know his business. He is putting us all in danger.

Over to the west the British were no longer in one mass. They were seen to have split into two main groups that were bearing down on Villeneuve's line. Where they might make their attack was not yet clear.

> The British Hearts did Lift for Joy
> the Sight for to Behold
> We Sone prepaird to fight them
> for Honnor and for Gold.

The motives that Able Seaman James Martin assigned to the British sailor in this doggerel verse are interesting. Honour is predictable, but gold less so. The Royal Navy was driven by prize money. When ships were captured they were valued and the proceeds were awarded to the captors. Money was allocated according to a complicated formula that gave most to those highest in rank and so downward. Victorious crews were also paid 'head money' for each French seaman they took prisoner. During the Seven Years' War the British had developed a policy of crippling the French navy by detaining as much of its skilled man-power as possible. Though cruel – many French seamen died in captivity – the policy was immensely successful because skilled seamanship required years of training and experience so the men could not be replaced. During the war of 1793 to 1801, 40,000 French sailors had spent time in British prisons.

Prize money gave the sea service its glamour. In 1780 a schoolboy watched some French prisoners landed by sailors and handed to soldiers, then heard the girls of Gosport sing:

> Sailors, they get all the money,
> Soldiers they get none but brass,
> I do love a jolly sailor,
> Soldiers they may kiss my arse.

While seamen might generally make enough to impress Gosport's womenfolk, officers sometimes made life-changing fortunes from prize money, usually in a frigate sent on a cruise to capture enemy ships. In 1799 when Henry Digby, now captain of *Africa*, helped to capture the *Santa Brigida*, his share of the prize money for the treasure she was carrying was £40,730 18s. 3$\frac{1}{4}$d. when a frigate captain's salary was under two hundred pounds a year.

Ships of war with no treasure on board were still worth having, and the aim in battle was not to sink or destroy the enemy, but to capture them as intact as possible. That way they were worth most. At Trafalgar everybody had their eyes on the Spanish four-decker, *Santísima Trinidad*. 'May God bless you, and send you alongside of the Santissima Trinidada,' Nelson had written to Collingwood in July. Henry Walker remembered that on *Bellerophon* that morning 'every one was in the highest spirits' and the men were so confident that 'they were employed in fixing the number of their prizes, and pitching upon that which should fall to the lot of each of our ships'. The oldest sailors on board – like forty-nine-year-old James Gill who had been in the navy for thirteen years – reckoned that *Bellerophon* would take on the 'Santisima Trinidada, the Spanish four-decker; and I dare say we were far from being the only ship in the fleet that fixed upon her'.

Most of the letters and accounts written soon after the battle maintain that the British crews were confident, even eager to fight. James Martin spoke of 'Coolness and Alacrity' and 'Resolute Itrepedity'. Marine Second Lieutenant Samuel Burdon Ellis, of *Ajax*, was sent below with orders 'and was much struck with the preparations made by the bluejackets'. Most had stripped to the waist – it was hot and airless down there – and had bound a handkerchief tightly round their heads and over the ears, to deaden the noise of the cannon, 'many men being deaf for days after an action'. Some were sharpening their cutlasses, others polishing the guns, and three or four were dancing a hornpipe. 'All,' he remarked, 'seemed deeply anxious to come to close-quarters with the enemy. Occasionally they would look out of the ports, and speculate as to the various ships of the enemy, many of which had been on former occasions engaged by our vessels.'

There was certainly nervous tension in the air and the men were well aware that some would not survive the day. William 'Nastyface' Robinson recalled some of *Revenge*'s sailors offering a guinea for a glass of grog. Others 'were making a sort of verbal will, such as, if one of Johnny Crapeau's shots [a term given to the French], knocks my head off, you will take all my effects; and if you are killed, and I am not, why, I will have yours'.

Many of the officers wrote letters home. Some were left half finished, like Nelson's to Emma Hamilton. John Aikenhead, one of Collingwood's midshipmen on *Royal Sovereign*, wrote: 'Should I, my dear parents, fall in defence of my King, let that thought console you. I feel not the least dread on my spirits. Oh my parents, sisters, brothers, dear grandfather, grandmother, and aunt, believe me ever yours!' He did not sign the letter, hoping to continue it at the end of the day.

Sometimes they wrote simple final messages to loved ones. Captain George Duff's son Norwich had joined his ship, *Mars*, in late September and was united with his cousins, Alexander and Thomas. Several of the other 'young gentlemen' on the ship were acquaintances from either Edinburgh or Perth. Having sent young Norwich and the three boys who had arrived with him down to the relative safety of the lower deck, Duff scribbled a note to his wife:

My Dearest Sophia, I have just time to tell you we are going into action with the combined fleet. I hope and trust in God that we shall all behave as becomes us, and that I may yet have the happiness of taking my beloved wife and children in my arms. Norwich is quite well, and happy. I have however, ordered him off the quarter-deck. Yours ever, and most truly, George Duff.

10

Putting a Good Face on It

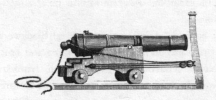

At first light the British had been about eleven miles away, and in the faint breeze they were approaching at no more than two miles per hour, a slow walking pace. It was a short late-October day and the sun would set early. Nelson's overriding concern now was speed so he wasted little effort on attempting to form up. His own division's prearranged order of battle was *Téméraire*, *Superb*, *Victory*, *Neptune*, *Tigre* and *Canopus*. But one of these ships was still in the English Channel and another two were near Cartagena – where the dispatch boat sent to summon them finally found them later that morning. *Prince* should have led Collingwood's column, but Richard Grindall's three-decker sailed, as Lieutenant Frederick Hoffman of *Tonnant* put it, 'like a haystack' and was signalled to take station where convenient, holding a line outside the two columns to avoid obstructing the faster ships. The same order was given to *Britannia* and *Dreadnought*. The columns sailed towards the Franco-Spanish line with *Victory* and *Royal Sovereign* in the lead. Nelson was determined to stop his enemy escaping and force a battle on them.

Early in the morning Nelson had signalled his frigate captains to come aboard *Victory*. Henry Blackwood announced that he was worried about Nelson's own safety and proposed that the admiral should hoist his flag in his frigate *Euryalus*, the better to control the battle. Nelson refused, as Blackwood had expected, and argued the importance of leading by personal example. Blackwood then tried to persuade him to allow *Téméraire*, *Neptune* and *Leviathan* to lead his column. Both Blackwood and *Victory*'s captain, Thomas Hardy, argued that it would be better for the fleet if Nelson kept out of the battle for as long as possible, and he eventually agreed to let *Téméraire* go in first. At that time *Téméraire* was sailing level with *Victory*, attempting to take what her captain, Eliab Harvey, thought was his prearranged station at the front of the line.

Harvey was just out of hailing distance so Blackwood was sent to pass the order on, only to discover that *Victory* was doing her best to stay ahead. Nelson had evidently changed his mind. Thomas Fremantle, in *Neptune,* had been promised the role of second to *Victory*. *Neptune* was normally reckoned slow, but she was sailing fast enough at about ten o'clock to threaten to overtake *Victory*. According to William Badcock, Fremantle 'had intended to pass her and break the enemy's line, but poor Lord Nelson himself hailed us from the stern-walk of the *Victory*, and said, "*Neptune*, take in your studding-sails and drop astern; I shall break the line myself."'

About a mile to the south Collingwood, in the newly recoppered *Royal Sovereign*, was pulling away from the ships behind him. His intended second, Charles Tyler's *Tonnant*, had not been cleaned for months and even with all sail set found it impossible to keep up. *Belleisle*, next astern, under topsails and topgallant sails, was having difficulty staying behind *Tonnant*. At nine twenty, *Belleisle*'s log notes, '*Royal Sovereign* made *Belleisle*'s and *Tonnant*'s signal to exchange places in line of battle.' Young Paul Nicolas, on board *Belleisle*, remembered that as the ships passed each other the captains shouted greetings through their loud-hailers. 'Captain Tyler exclaimed, "A glorious day for old England! We shall have one apiece before night!" This confidence in our professional superiority – which carries such terror to other nations – seemed expressed in every countenance; and as if in confirmation of this soul-inspiring sentiment, the band of our consort was playing "Britons strike home".'

Collingwood knew that his division was supposed to make its attack in echeloned line abreast. The plan anticipated that the change of formation would be made at the last moment by signal from Nelson to surprise the enemy. Collingwood realised that with the wind so light this wouldn't be possible and his journal records that he 'made the signal for the lee division to form the larboard line of bearing' early. He did it by signalling to three of his ships, *Belleisle*, *Achille* and *Revenge*, to alter course to starboard. He made no attempt to slow down in order to deploy properly, but these signals served to remind his captains that they were to engage the whole of the Franco-Spanish rear. He was supposed to aim for the twelfth ship from the enemy rear, but instead he aimed at the three-deck *Santa Ana*. If he thought she was the twelfth ship, the bunching of the Combined Fleet must have confused him: she was the sixteenth. By attacking so far forward he gave his lee line a much tougher task than Nelson had designed for them. Instead of outnumbering the enemy by a quarter as Nelson's plan intended, Collingwood's ships were themselves outnumbered.

Nelson, meanwhile, attempted to protect Collingwood and at ten o'clock *Victory* signalled *Mars* to lead the lee division. *Mars* acknowledged, but failed to catch up with either *Royal Sovereign* or the swift-sailing *Belleisle*, although she did overtake *Tonnant*. Collingwood himself made no attempt to slow down. No doubt he had observed Nelson's behaviour and determined to imitate him by leading the line personally. Midshipman John Aikenhead, writing home that morning, said the prospect of battle had made the old admiral 'quite young again'. Collingwood had indeed been cheerful all morning. He told his servant William Smith to take a look at the magnificent view of the enemy fleet and advised First Lieutenant James Clavell to change his boots for shoes and stockings, because in the event of a wound stockings were easier for the surgeon to cut away.

Nelson went down to his cabin, now bare of all furniture, and, kneeling at his desk, wrote up his diary, a private document of a public nature. He began prosaically enough, 'At daylight saw the Enemy's Combined Fleet . . .' but then moved into a carefully composed prayer:

> May the Great God, whom I worship, grant to my Country, and for
> the benefit of Europe in general, a great and glorious Victory; and

may no misconduct in any one tarnish it; and may humanity after Victory be the predominant feature in the British Fleet. For myself, individually, I commit my life to Him who made me, and may his blessing light upon my endeavours for serving my Country faithfully. To Him I resign myself and the just cause which is entrusted to me to defend. Amen. Amen. Amen.

This exists in two identical handwritten copies, possibly executed with a pantograph, and was clearly intended for publication. Nelson constructed his public image carefully, and the prayer would probably have been published in November even if he had survived. Many of the letters written home by captains (notably Edward Codrington's) seem to have been composed with at least half an eye on eventual publication, and much that is apparently private should be treated with caution for this reason. The sentiments Nelson expressed, identifying the British cause with that of 'Europe in general', were admirably diplomatic.

Nelson then asked Hardy and Blackwood to witness a public document of a more private nature. It sought national protection for his mistress and daughter in the event of his death. Having outlined Emma Hamilton's diplomatic achievements through her influence with the Queen of Naples, Nelson concluded:

I leave Emma Lady Hamilton, therefore, a Legacy to my King and Country, that they will give her an ample provision to maintain her rank in life. I also leave to the benificence of my Country my adopted daughter, Horatia Nelson Thompson; and I desire she will use in future the name of Nelson only. These are the only favours I ask of my King and Country at this moment when I am going to fight their Battle.

It was not unusual in the navy to bequeath one's children to king and country. When Captain John Morris was mortally wounded, commanding the *Bristol* in America in 1776, he left his young son James as a legacy to king and country: brought up in the navy, James

Morris was now commanding *Colossus*. Nelson's attempt to protect his loved ones in this manner was not as eccentric as it might seem.

Villeneuve was still uncertain as to where Nelson intended to attack. The British had begun by steering as if to cut him off from Cadiz. Then they had changed course to the east and had split into two columns, both aiming for the centre of the Combined Fleet. Then the leeward column had turned towards the fleet's rear while the windward column changed course slightly towards the north again, apparently aiming for the middle of Dumanoir's division at the front of the line. Nelson's design to 'surprise and confound' was bearing fruit.

Meanwhile, the bunching and confusion in the Combined Fleet had continued. One witness reported that 'the van was then becalmed and barely had steerage way, whilst the rear was already catching the breeze that was springing up in the south-west'. Both *Santa Ana* and then *Principe de Asturias* turned away from the wind to leeward to allow the ships that were behind and around them more room. At ten thirty *Principe* turned away again and *Achille*, still trying to take her proper position in front of *Principe*, collided with her; little damage was done.

Some ships were trying to form line of battle on the vessels furthest to leeward, as they had the day before. This was standard practice and made pragmatic allowance for the capabilities of the worst Spanish crews. Villeneuve's repeated signals to keep to the wind seem to have confused the issue. Of course, to leeward also meant towards the rocky shoals off the Spanish coast and, no doubt, the admiral wanted to keep as far from them as possible. The overall effect of the confusion was that 'several ships were doubling each other and were causing overcrowding in the *corps de bataille* and in the rear'.

Leading Pierre Dumanoir's van division and the line was Cayetano Valdés in *Neptuno*, a fine Spanish eighty. Although only thirty-four, Valdés was an experienced sailor (he had accompanied Galiano on one

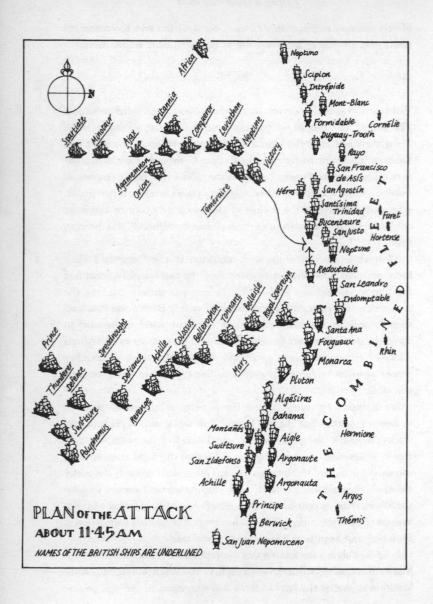

PLAN OF THE ATTACK
ABOUT 11·45 AM
NAMES OF THE BRITISH SHIPS ARE UNDERLINED

of his voyages of exploration) and a respected fighter who had helped to rescue the *Santísima Trinidad* at the battle of Cape St Vincent. *Scipion* was behind *Neptuno* and third in line was an unhappy Louis Infernet in *Intrépide*. He should have been four ships behind *Bucentaure* and was instead nine ships ahead. He had got out of position overnight, and in wearing had now overtaken the ships around him to find himself alongside Rear Admiral Dumanoir's *Formidable*. There was a gap ahead of *Formidable* because *Rayo* had fallen both leeward and backward, and Dumanoir ordered Infernet to fill it. The *Formidable* was the eighty-gun ship that had competed with *Bucentaure* in gun exercises at Toulon. The voyage to the West Indies had shown her up as a slow sailer – Villeneuve put it down to the poor-quality copper sheathing her hull – but she was a powerful vessel, nevertheless. Behind her *Mont-Blanc* and *Duguay-Trouin* were close to level with each other. The big but very old *Rayo* with her inadequate crew had already drifted some distance to leeward of them and to windward of her was *San Francisco de Asís*.

The leading ships of Villeneuve's centre division had bunched up with *San Agustín* to leeward of *Héros*, a new ship launched at Rochefort in 1803. Slightly to leeward and behind *Héros* was the massive *Santísima Trinidad*, the flagship of Spanish Rear Admiral Báltasar de Cisneros. This magnificent ship – the only four-decker in the world – was painted white, with red gun-ports creating the effect of four bold scarlet stripes down her sides, and her prow was ornamented with a colossal group of figures representing the Holy Trinity. Built in Havana of New World cedar, she had been launched in 1769 as a three-decker and converted in 1795 to accommodate an extra battery. She now carried 136 guns and four carronades and displaced 3100 tons. On board were 1048 men, including 382 soldiers. Some thought her top-heavy, but at the battle of St Vincent the Spanish had defended her with as much determination as the British had sought to capture her. Close behind was Villeneuve's own flagship *Bucentaure*, an 80, though James Martin believed, rightly or wrongly, that at Trafalgar she was mounting 102 guns. Villeneuve thought highly of her sailing qualities and of her tough Provençal seamen, rating his crew as 'one of the best in the Squadron'.

Her sister-ship *Neptune*, another brand-new 80, should have been behind *Bucentaure* but *Neptune*'s captain, Esprit-Tranquille Maistral, had been prevented from taking this place of responsibility and honour by *San Justo*, whose proper station was four ships further back. These two ships were attempting to exchange places and both had drifted to leeward:

> The *San Justo* not being in her station and edging down to place herself on my windward beam hampered me; I at once hailed her to enquire <u>if she knew her station</u>; I told her that mine was to be next astern to the *Bucentaure*; she replied that she was about to place herself astern of me, <u>which she did not do</u>, and continued to keep to the wind and to fore-reach on me, which made me fall off a little to leeward and to draw away from the flag-ship, of whom I had been within hail in the first place.

Maistral was one of those French captains who frequently found fault with their Spanish allies, but in this case he probably had a point. Like *Rayo*, *San Justo* was fresh out of the dock and this was her crew's third day at sea in her. Captain Miguel Gastón was critical of their training and blamed them for failing to hold the wind and consistently 'falling to leeward'. The confusion was unfortunate since *Neptune* was 'one of the finest and most sea-worthy ships in the Fleet', and the position immediately behind the flagship was likely to be the focus of British attention and best occupied by a powerful ship. The ship that should have been behind *Neptune*, *San Leandro*, had followed her to leeward, leaving a yawning gap behind the flagship. When he saw this potentially catastrophic situation developing, Jean-Jacques Lucas, commanding *Redoutable*, the last ship of Villeneuve's division, announced to his officers and men that they would second the flagship, to which they replied with cheers and shouts of '*Vive l'Empereur, vive le commandant.*' Lucas's crew of 643 men was highly trained and well motivated by their aggressive captain. Preceded by drums and fifes, Lucas led his officers through the batteries and was delighted to find his men burning with impatience to fight.

Behind *Redoutable* there was another yawning gap. Vice Admiral Ignacio de Álava's division should have been led by *Intrépide* but Louis Infernet's ship was miles out of position and *San Justo*, which should have been behind, was also ahead. Next in the line, but well to leeward, was *Indomptable*, a powerful 80. She had been hurriedly repaired at Toulon in 1804, and had received the dregs of the Hot Press that had provided better crews for *Bucentaure* and *Neptune*. Villeneuve thought her a fine ship with a bad crew. Then came Álava's flagship *Santa Ana*, leading a coherent line of four. Painted all black, she had just been recoppered and had retained the core of a decent crew that, with extra infantry, now totalled 1089. In theory she carried a formidable 112 guns with thirty 36-pounders, thirty-two 24-pounders, thirty-two 12-pounders, and eighteen eights on deck, but twelve of her 8-pounders had been exchanged for twenty carronades. Seconding *Santa Ana* was the seventy-four-gun *Fougueux* under the excellent Louis-Alexis Baudouin, a most promising young officer who had risen from the ranks. Villeneuve thought the ship in need of docking but she had a fine crew and Baudouin had already inspected the gun-decks and the various posts where the officers were greeted with the usual shouts of '*Vive l'Empereur!*' and '*Vive notre brave commandant!*' Behind *Fougueux* was Téodoro de Argumosa's *Monarca* and then the newly built heavy 74 *Pluton*, under the trusty and experienced Breton, Julien Cosmao-Kerjulien. The core of his crew was formed of fine Provençal seamen. He warned Rear Admiral Charles Magon in the ship behind that if the enemy tried to break the line ahead of him, or even ahead of the then stationary *Monarca* in front, he would accelerate away to prevent it.

Magon's *Algésiras* should have been in the centre of its division of the Squadron of Observation, but the ships had become disordered when reversing direction and Magon had instead taken the lead of what was now a densely packed cluster of ships. Astern was Dionisio Alcalá Galiano's 74, *Bahama*, mounting eighty guns and ten heavy carronades. The two men had almost fought each other during the council of war over points of national honour, but would now depend upon each other in combat. Galiano was painfully aware that his crew of 690 contained a high proportion of raw recruits of doubtful quality.

He had nailed the Spanish flag to the mast, however, to prevent anyone lowering it in surrender, and ordered a young relative, Midshipman Alonso Butrón, to look after it, telling him that no Galiano had ever surrendered and no Butrón should either. Seconding Galiano was the dependable Pierre-Paulin Gourrège in the equally dependable *Aigle* with its pugnacious crew of 'stout fellows'. Thanks to overcrowding and *Algésiras*'s movement forward, *Montañés* had never got into position and was exposed to windward of the line of battle, dropping back to be about level with *Aigle* and *Swiftsure*. The next ship in line should have been the elegant Spanish *Argonauta*, mounting ninety guns, but she had been overtaken by two French 74s, *Swiftsure* and *Argonaute*.

Magon's leading division of the Squadron of Observation was compactly grouped and Gravina's division, though in order apart from *Argonaute*, was so close behind as to make manoeuvre difficult. *San Ildefonso* was followed by *Achille*, followed by Gravina's flagship, *Principe de Asturias*. *Principe* packed a heavy punch with 120 guns consisting of 32-, 24- and 12-pounders and with an additional fourteen 48-pound and six 24-pound carronades in the stern. She carried 1113 men. Behind her was *Berwick* and bringing up the rear was Cosme de Churruca's *San Juan Nepomuceno*.

It is difficult to interpret what the experienced Admiral Gravina was doing with his tactical reserve. Its strength had probably been determined with reference to British numbers, and with an unexpected extra six British ships present, Gravina might have felt it necessary to extend the Combined Fleet's line. Villeneuve signalled him to hold the wind so that he could cover the centre of the fleet – presumably intending him to intervene with the advantage of the wind behind him. This was directly opposite to Spanish tactical doctrine. The sophisticated Spanish *Tratado de Señales* of 1804, probably edited by Escaño, provided a defence against an enemy fleet that attacked unformed with a following wind, broke the line and then sailed on the same course as the leeward fleet, as they now expected the British to do. The leading ships of the leeward fleet were to slow down, while the rear ships were to crowd sail, turn to leeward, then straighten up again to catch the enemy between two fires. Gravina might have had such a manoeuvre in mind, and in places something like this happened.

Despite its many problems and its irregular line the Combined Fleet succeeded in achieving a fairly closely serried formation. The occasional overlaps, accidental or otherwise, would present a serious problem for any British ships that broke through. A slight shift in the wind to westward, with the swell, had contributed to the line bowing at the centre into a horseshoe shape that might prove dangerous to ships sailing into it.

It was not until late in the morning that it finally became clear to all on *Victory*'s deck, from where Surgeon Beatty was watching, that 'from the very compact line which the enemy had formed, they were determined to make one great effort to recover in some measure their long-lost naval reputation'. It was what Nelson had wanted, but had he expected it he might have got his own fleet into a better shape for close support. Several times Nelson remarked to Blackwood and those around him that the enemy were putting 'a good face on it'. Blackwood agreed: 'They waited the attack of the British with a coolness I was sorry to witness.'

What was much more worrying was the absence of wind, which made Nelson's plan a great deal more risky than it would otherwise have been. His ships were moving too slowly for comfort. During the dangerous approach phase, those at the head of the line might take heavy casualties and good enemy gunnery might stop them dead in the water. As Lieutenant Humphrey Senhouse of *Conqueror* put it, 'An enemy of equal spirit and equal ability in seamanship and the practice of gunnery would have annihilated the ships, one after another in detail, carried slowly on as they were in this instance only by a heavy swell and light airs.' Nelson was now banking on inferior gunnery and seamanship from the enemy. Previous experience and knowledge of current circumstances led him to expect it, but it was not guaranteed and luck might play a part. There was also a dangerous possibility that the wind might drop away altogether.

But to change the plan at this stage would confuse his captains, who would then have to rely on signals to understand his new intentions. Nevertheless, Nelson seems to have considered it. He made up his mind to approach obliquely and open fire at longer range than he had intended. He ordered the gunner's son, Midshipman William Rivers who was on the quarterdeck, to go down and tell the lieutenants to reload the guns (which had been loaded with two balls to open fire at close range) with single shot.

Other officers certainly had their doubts about the disorderly version of the prearranged plan that was being adopted. Afterwards Captain Robert Moorsom of *Revenge* remarked, 'I am not certain that our mode of attack was the best.' Their anxiety was increased by the numerical superiority of the enemy. Nelson knew the Combined Fleet to be only six ships superior, but others expected it to be stronger. The British knew that there were thirty-seven line-of-battle ships at Cadiz and they anticipated fighting all of them. Richard Anderson, master of the *Prince*, had thought yesterday that they were '10 Sail of Line superior' and was relieved that they had apparently returned to port. In fact, because there weren't enough sailors for all of them, the four least battleworthy ships had been left behind. But the Franco-Spanish formation, or lack of one, made it difficult to count their ships so most Britons went in believing the enemy to be more numerous than they really were.

All these reasons for caution might have caused ships to lag behind. It is difficult to assess whether any did so, since some ships sailed with more speed than others. But some of the British ships did not get up fast, nor engage closely. After the battle Collingwood would hear no criticism of individuals but in his commonplace book Collingwood's captain, Edward Rotheram, noted against both Richard Grindall of *Prince* and Admiral Lord Northesk of *Britannia* that they 'behaved notoriously ill in the Trafalgar action'. The family of *Britannia*'s captain, Charles Bullen, told his biographer that there had been an argument between Bullen and Northesk during the approach when the admiral had ordered the captain to reduce sail. *Polyphemus*, a ship noted for her speed, reached the Combined Fleet's line five places behind her prearranged position between *Achille* and *Revenge*. Her captain, Robert Redmill, retired through ill health in 1806.

Whether or not there was reticence on the part of some captains during the approach phase, most were doing their utmost to keep up with their admirals. Collingwood and Nelson were racing ahead, challenging those behind not to leave them exposed and alone at the mercy of the enemy.

Nelson had put on his usual coat with all his stars and medals, but had forgotten to buckle on his sword. He toured the gun-decks and encouraged the men. He was euphoric as he always was when he was about to go into battle. He remarked that 21 October was his family's lucky day: it was on that date in 1757 that his uncle, Maurice Suckling, had distinguished himself in action. He told Blackwood that he would not be satisfied with the capture of fewer than twenty of the enemy.

Everywhere, last efforts were made to encourage the men. In *Tonnant*, twenty-five-year-old Able Seaman John Cash from Llangollen wrote that Captain Charles Tyler 'called all hands and said: "My lads, this will be a glorious day for us, and the groundwork of a speedy return to our homes for all." He then ordered bread and cheese and butter and beer for every man at the guns. I was one of them, and, believe me, we ate and drank, and were as cheerful as ever we had been over a pot of beer.' Most crews had an early dinner at around eleven o'clock. In *Bellerophon* Captain Cooke joined his officers in some cold meat, using the rudder head as a table since all the wardroom furniture had been stowed. In *Victory*, John Brown, a twenty-three-year-old able seaman from Waterford, wrote that 'we piped to dinner and ate a bit of raw pork and half a pint of Wine'.

Astern and slightly to larboard of *Victory*, Thomas Fremantle mustered the crew of *Neptune* at their quarters, as he did every Monday, even though they were about to fight. Her proper complement was 738 but that morning she had 707 aboard. James Martin recalled the gist of the Captain's speech:

> [He] adressed us at our Diffrent Quarters in words few but Intimated that we ware all alike Sensable of our Condition our Native Land and all that was Dear to us Hung upon a Ballance and their Happyness Depended upon us and their Safty allso Happy the Man who Boldly Venture his Life in such a Cause if he shold Survive the Battle how Sweet will be the Recolection be and if he fall he fall Covred with Glory and Honnor and Morned By a Greatfull Country the Brave Live Gloryous and Lemented Die

In *Defiance* Captain Philip Durham also 'turned the hands up and made a short, but very expressive speech to the ship's company'. Master's mate Jack Spratt, a handsome young Irishman, had taught the boarders their sword exercise and was put in charge of them. Durham told the boarders that he was sure Mr Spratt would lead them to glory. He gave a low bow and they gave three cheers. Then, with everything ready and the 'guns double shotted with grape and rounds', they too 'piped to dinner and had a good glass of grog'.

In *Minotaur*, landsman William Thorpe tried to remember Captain Mansfield's exact words:

> men, we are now in sight of the enemy, (the Men at this moment was going to Cheer, wich the Captn prevented & proceeded) wich, there is every probability of engaging, & I trust, that this Day, or to Morrow, will prove the most glorious our country ever saw, – I shall say nothing to you of courage, our country never produced a coward, for my own part I pledge myself to the officers & ships company, never to quit the ship I may get alongside of till either she strikes, or sinks, or I sink, I have only to recommend silence & a strict attention to the orders of your officers, be careful to take good aim, for it is to no purpose to throw shot away, you will now every man repare to your respective stations, & depend, I will bring the ship into action as soon as possible, God Save the King.

Almost everything was ready now, but those responsible for signals in the flagships were still busy. Nelson made a general signal to 'make all sail with safety to the masts'. Acutely aware that the shoals of Sancti Petri and Trafalgar were now to leeward, Nelson issued the signal to the fleet to 'prepare to anchor at the close of day'. Then the admiral signalled 'England expects that every man will do his duty'. 'It was answered by three hearty cheers from each ship, which must have shaked the nerve of the enemy,' recalled Lieutenant Frederick Hoffman, in *Tonnant*. In *Bellerophon* Midshipman Henry Walker said that cheers were followed by a general shout of 'No fear of that!' Nelson finally made the signal 'engage the enemy more closely' and left it flying.

In the Combined Fleet, preparations reflected the customs of the different nations. In *Bucentaure* the Imperial Eagle had been entrusted to two officers, Guillaume Claude Donnadieu and Charles Arman, who were to guard it throughout the engagement. Now they paraded it round the decks, followed by Villeneuve and his officers, and by the commander of the soldiers, Major General Théodore de Contamine. Each sailor and soldier of the crew put his hands between Villeneuve's and renewed his oath upon the Eagle entrusted to them by the Emperor to 'fight to the last gasp'. Shouts of '*Vive l'Empereur*' and '*Vive l'amiral Villeneuve*' rang out again as the officers 'returned to the upper works and each of us resumed our post'. The Eagle was displayed at the foot of the mainmast.

In *San Juan Nepomuceno*, Churruca gathered his crew and called upon Salvadore de Roque, his chaplain, to absolve the men. Then he spoke: 'My children, in the name of the god of battles I promise eternal happiness to anyone who dies in the course of his duty.' But, he warned them, he would shoot anybody he saw shirking it and even if such a man escaped him and his officers he would pass his remaining days in misery and disgrace. All gave three shouts of '*Viva el rey!*' and the crew dispersed to their quarters. As he watched Nelson's attack develop

around the junction of van and centre, Churruca realised that the van
division would be isolated and would have difficulty taking part in the
battle if they did not wear round at an early stage. He was waiting with
increasing impatience and anxiety to see a signal from Villeneuve to
this effect.

It did not come. Instead, at eleven forty-five, with *Victory* about a
mile to windward, Villeneuve 'made the signal to open fire when
deemed to be within range'. At this, reported Captain Magendie, 'we
ran up our admiral's flag and our colours, which were greeted with
shouts of "*Vive l'Empereur!*" repeated throughout the Fleet'. Just behind
Bucentaure, *Redoutable*'s ensign rose up the mizen mast. The drums beat
'*Aux drapeaux*' and the musketeers presented arms. Then officers and
men saluted the flag and shouted seven times, '*Vive l'Empereur!*' The
Spanish ships displayed a cross at the end of their spanker boom.

Bucentaure and *Redoutable* were still out of range of *Victory* but
Fougueux was much closer to *Royal Sovereign*. Her captain, Louis-Alexis
Baudouin, gave the signal to open fire, beginning with single ranging
shots. The best marksman fired a few guns in succession to try to find
the range of the *Royal Sovereign*.

Orders rang out on the decks below: '*Canonniers, chacun à son poste.*'
The men approached the guns, forming two files at either side. Soldiers
reinforced the sailors, but specialists from the marine artillery commanded the guns. '*Détapez, démarrez vos canons.*' The guns were
unleashed. Tompions were removed from the muzzles and aprons
taken off the gunlocks. The lids of the gun-ports were raised, making
chequers of contrasting colour along the side of the ship. The guns
were already loaded, and now they were hauled out: '*En batterie.*' On
the word '*palanquez*' from the marine artilleryman in charge, probably
an *aide-canonnier*, all the others hauled on ropes to run each gun into its
firing position pointing through the gun-port. '*Pointez.*' The marine
artilleryman, in his blue uniform, with one hand on the barrel and the
other on the wedge-shaped quoin beneath it, eased it to what he
judged to be the correct elevation and direction. He looked along the
gun to check his aim. '*Envoyez!*'

As the ship rose and fell on the swell the gun-captain chose his moment and pulled the lanyard that snapped the flintlock. With a loud explosion the gun shot backwards, held by its ropes. A stench of sulphur followed and, flapping at the black smoke, the gun crew tried to see where the shot had fallen. The officers with telescopes on deck sent a runner to give their opinion of whether it had flown over or fallen short. Soon one went straight through *Royal Sovereign*'s sail. Then, at musket range – about a hundred and fifty yards – Baudouin ordered the whole broadside to fire.

11

Go Through She Shall, By God

By midday the temperature had risen to 70° Fahrenheit and the sun was shining from a clear sky. From four hundred yards behind *Royal Sovereign*, the officers of *Belleisle* saw the French and Spanish raise their flags and Captain William Hargood gave the instruction to beat to quarters. 'Gentlemen,' he said, gesturing towards *Fougueux*, 'I have only to say that I shall pass close under the stern of that ship; put in two round shot and then a grape, and give her *that*. Now go to your quarters and mind not to fire until each gun will bear with effect.' Hargood then went and stood by the foremost carronade on the starboard side of the quarterdeck.

Ahead they saw two rows of red flame along the side of *Fougueux* and, seconds later, holes appeared in *Royal Sovereign*'s sails. A few short stabs of flame from Collingwood's forward guns followed and the flagship disappeared into a cloud of smoke.

In *Belleisle* thirty marines were stationed on the poop, with the three marine officers standing in front of them, looking down on the quarterdeck. The sixteen-year-old marine lieutenant Paul Nicolas was reassured for a moment by the sight of the crew, tanned, determined, some grinning. Some were stripped to the waist, others with collars open and sleeves rolled, handkerchiefs tied round their heads. To Nicolas, who had never before experienced combat, they all seemed eager for action.

Then, for the first time in his life, he heard the whistle of incoming fire, and as the first shot passed overhead he began to realise what they were about to suffer. Hargood ordered all the men in the ship to lie down, except for his officers who were expected to remain upright in the face of the enemy. Both Nicolas and his senior officer, First Lieutenant John Owen, were struck by the eerie, awful silence on board. The only noise was 'the commanding voice of Captain Hargood, "Steady! starboard a little! steady so!" echoed by the Master directing the quartermasters at the wheel'. Occasionally an officer shouted to an impatient sailor, 'Lie down there, you, sir!'

Then the ranging shots became broadsides. 'A shriek soon followed – a cry of agony was produced by the next shot – and the loss of the head of a poor recruit was the effect of the succeeding.' As the hits became more frequent Hargood himself was knocked over by a large piece of splintered wood. He got up again and climbed back onto the carronade.

Paul Nicolas, exposed on the poop with a full view of the quarter-deck, saw his first bloody corpses and heard the shrieks of injured and dying men. By his own honest account, the teenager was soon close to panic. Seeing marines lying down around him he was strongly tempted to imitate them. As he heard and felt shot pass close by, he could not stop himself crouching down. But, as he later recalled, an inner voice told him to stand up and do his duty, and he was inspired by the serenity of John Owen, who was coolly pacing up and down the exposed poop deck. Nicolas joined him and 'became somewhat infused with his spirit, which cheered me on to act the part it became me'.

Afterwards he thought Owen's behaviour an object lesson in just how influential an officer's example was to men under fire. But for all his apparent sang-froid, Lieutenant Owen found the inactivity trying, even as he admired the disciplined silence of his men. He was also alarmed by the number of casualties, which he later estimated at fifty men before *Belleisle* had fired a single shot.

First Lieutenant Ebenezer Geale asked Hargood whether it would not be best to get broadside on to the enemy and fire, if only to cover the ship with smoke? Owen admired the captain's stern and emphatic reply: 'No, we are ordered to go through the line, and go through she shall, by God!'

For twenty minutes, which seemed to last an age, Owen joined other experienced officers in trying to encourage the men by telling them, 'We should soon begin our work.' Then at last they heard Hargood shout, 'Stand to your guns!' and with great relief they sprang into action.

The French and Spanish ships were aiming to disable the oncoming British. For the most part they were firing bar and chain shot at the rigging, hoping to cut ropes and damage sails to make the enemy ships unmanageable. If they could prevent them moving or turning, they could pick them off as they wished, before they ever reached the line.

Their fire did considerable damage and certainly alarmed the foremost British crews, but slowly, inexorably, the British ships came on. The shortage of trained gunners was one factor limiting the Combined Fleet's gunnery but the great rolling swell was probably even more important. It hit the sides of the French and Spanish ships and made aiming at long range almost impossible. If they fired at the top of their roll their shot was directed skywards, if they fired at the bottom it would fly straight into the water. Also, smoke from previous shots, lingering in the faint wind, made it difficult for the French and Spanish gunners to observe the fall of shot and adjust their aim accordingly. In this battle more than almost any other, everything quickly became cloaked in smoke. A ship's horizon was limited to what happened immediately around it, and the moment she opened fire she was blind to what was happening elsewhere. For the British this provided a minor advantage. Their smoke drifted slowly downwind at the same speed as their ships, offering them prolonged protection.

Fougueux's master-at-arms Pierre Servaux deplored – in retrospect – 'our bad habit in the French Navy' by which *Fougueux* had 'fired away over a hundred rounds from our big guns at long range before the

English ship had practically snapped a gun lock'. They had perhaps fired the equivalent of three or four broadsides before *Royal Sovereign*, taller, with more men and guns, finally closed on them.

Royal Sovereign aimed for the gap in the line between *Fougueux* and Admiral Álava's conspicuous three-decked flagship, the black *Santa Ana*, intending to fire a raking broadside along the length of both. But as Collingwood approached, his enemies tried to prevent *Royal Sovereign* breaking through. The Spaniards backed *Santa Ana*'s mizen topsail to slow her down while Baudouin in *Fougueux* hoisted his topgallants to accelerate. Collingwood, however, was not to be denied and ordered Captain Rotheram to point the ship at the bowsprit of the *Fougueux*. When it became clear that *Royal Sovereign* would not turn aside, *Santa Ana* curved away to diminish the effect of her broadside and, rather than collide, Baudouin turned *Fougueux* suddenly to starboard, thus presenting her larboard broadside to *Royal Sovereign*.

As she steered between the two ships *Royal Sovereign* raked *Santa Ana*'s stern and then, from about fifty yards, fired her starboard broadside into *Fougueux*. Because she was taller than *Fougueux*, *Royal Sovereign*'s main- and upper-deck guns could fire directly down on to the French ship, leaving the sailors working on deck and the infantry marksmen in the gangways horribly exposed.

The impact of *Sovereign*'s opening broadside stunned Pierre Servaux:

> she gave us a broadside from five and fifty guns and carronades, hurtling forth a storm of cannon balls, big and small, and musket-shot. I thought the Fougueux was shattered to pieces—pulverized. The storm of projectiles that hurled themselves against and through the hull on the port side made the ship heel to starboard. Most of the sails and the rigging were cut to pieces, while the upper deck was swept clear of the greater number of the seamen working there, and of the soldier sharpshooters. Our gun-decks below had, however, suffered less severely. There, not more than thirty men in all were put hors de combat. This preliminary greeting, rough and brutal as it was, did not dishearten our men. A well-maintained fire showed the Englishmen that we too had guns and could use them.

Turning further to larboard, *Royal Sovereign* came so close up to *Santa Ana* that the two huge ships' yard-arms locked fast. As another broadside ripped into *Santa Ana*'s side, Captain Maistral of *Neptune*, several hundred yards away, was watching the Spanish ship and remarked, with characteristic disdain for his Spanish ally, that 'several men were hiding themselves outside the ship on the opposite side to the enemy'. Maistral wore his ship round to engage *Royal Sovereign* from long range. *Fougueux* had already delivered at least one full broadside on *Royal Sovereign*'s lee quarter as she turned and, from some 500 yards, the French warship *Indomptable* also fired into *Royal Sovereign*'s lee beam. From further away *San Justo* and *San Leandro* were also shooting into her bows.

On *Santa Ana*'s lower decks the gun crews moved from larboard to starboard and hit Collingwood's flagship with *Santa Ana*'s previously unused starboard broadside as she arrived alongside. Now it was *Royal Sovereign*'s turn to heel out of the water under the weight of at least 1300 pounds of metal thrown against her; since Álava would have expected these guns to be used for the first time at close range they were probably loaded with two balls, in which case they would have fired up to 2600 pounds of shot. For five minutes *Royal Sovereign* engaged six ships alone and unaided. It was perhaps during this time that Midshipman George Castle 'looked once out of our stern ports – but I saw nothing but French and Spaniards round firing at us in all directions'.

Santa Ana was the *Royal Sovereign*'s most powerful and immediate opponent, and for the next hour the great three-decked battleships slogged it out at close range. *Royal Sovereign* had the best of the fight, but not by a great margin. George Castle, on the lower deck, was in the thick of it: 'I can assure you it was glorious work, I think you would have liked to have seen me thump it into her quarter. I'm stationed at the heaviest guns in the Ship, and I stuck so close to one gun and poured it into her.' *Royal Sovereign*'s master, William Chalmers, was cut almost in two by a cannonball while talking to the admiral. 'He laid his head on my shoulder and told me he was slain,' Collingwood later wrote to his wife. The admiral himself was wounded in the leg by a splinter, but he continued to march up and down munching an apple as he encouraged the gunners on the quarterdeck. On the Spanish side, Sergeant Domingo Gallegos and Corporal Fernando Casal were later recommended for their great bravery while directing the fire of *Santa Ana*'s guns.

The story that the *Royal Sovereign*'s first raking broadside into *Santa Ana* killed 400 men and dismounted fourteen guns has figured repeatedly in histories of Trafalgar. It originated in William James's authoritative account of the battle, published in 1824, but it is manifestly false. Indeed, the idea that a single mighty broadside could knock a line-of-battle ship out of a Napoleonic sea battle is a fantasy.

William James's information came from English participants, who quoted 'the subsequent acknowledgement of the Spanish officers'. He evidently had his doubts, and qualified the figure with 'incredible as it may appear'. He did not know that a muster of the crew after the battle established that *Santa Ana*'s total casualties were 104 killed and 137 wounded. In the retelling, Spanish survivors, relieved to be alive, generously exaggerated the effect of *Royal Sovereign*'s opening on-slaught.

In piecing together the story of the battle, the habit of the defeated to exaggerate their losses has to be taken into account. Just as in the Second World War British prisoners-of-war in North Africa would generally claim to have fought the Afrika Korps rather than the Italians, the defeated French and Spanish at Trafalgar would later report seeing irresistible British three-deckers everywhere.

Nevertheless, survivors of the first British broadsides retained vivid impressions of their terrifying impact. Pierre Servaux left a graphic description of the effect of the opening double-shotted broadside of a three-deck warship, accompanied by carronade fire sweeping down and over his upper decks. But the effect on morale of this sudden violence might well have been more significant than its killing

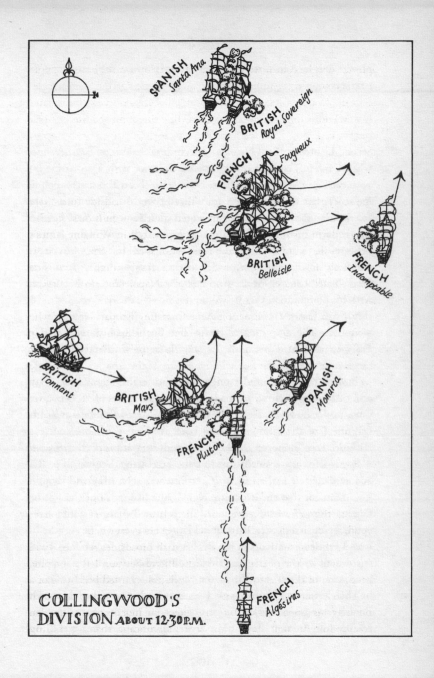

SPANISH *Santa Ana*

BRITISH *Royal Sovereign*

FRENCH *Fougueux*

BRITISH *Belleisle*

FRENCH *Indomptable*

BRITISH *Tonnant*

BRITISH *Mars*

FRENCH *Pluton*

SPANISH *Monarca*

FRENCH *Algésiras*

COLLINGWOOD'S DIVISION ABOUT 12·30 P.M.

power: it caused men to leave their guns in an attempt to escape the next blow.

Second Lieutenant Paul Nicolas's uncomfortable wait on *Belleisle* ended when Captain Hargood finally opened fire, not with a broadside but with each gun as it came to bear. *Belleisle* had been 400 metres behind *Royal Sovereign* and took eight minutes to cover that distance, as *Royal Sovereign* fought alone with her six adversaries. Some in *Belleisle* claimed that the wind dropped further as they reached the enemy line – sailors believed that gunfire stilled the wind – but these last few yards passed painfully slowly regardless, and under a terrifying hail of iron. First Lieutenant Ebenezer Geale, who had impressed everyone at breakfast with his premonition that he would not survive the day, was hit in the thigh and carried below. Lieutenant John Woodin was mortally wounded. The ship finally broke the line thirty yards astern of *Fougueux* and fired her guns as they bore most effectively on the target's stern quarter.

Belleisle was a captured French ship with eighty-eight heavy guns and carronades packing a broadside weight in excess of 1200 pounds. Once again, however, Baudouin turned *Fougueux* skilfully to avoid the full effect of the raking fire and bore away on the same course as *Belleisle*. Four hundred yards ahead and to starboard, the Spanish *Monarca* kept up a steady fire on the advancing British ship. The Spaniards cheered when *Belleisle*'s ensign was shot away and thought for a moment that she had surrendered. She had not, but she lost her flag twice more as she advanced. She returned *Monarca*'s fire, and a young Spanish officer called Manuel Ferrer never forgot the sight of his friend Prudencio Ruiz Alegria, in charge of *Monarca*'s own flag, being cut in half by one of the first British cannonballs to hit the ship. His head and torso fell into the water while his legs remained on deck.

Then Captain Hargood saw yet another ship ahead of him. The French *Indomptable*, apparently part of a second line of enemy ships, was raking him from in front. He now aimed to pass her stern, but

Belleisle's sails were in tatters, her rigging badly damaged, her speed ever slower. *Fougueux* completed her turn and followed *Belleisle* through the smoke, with Baudouin manoeuvring his ship into a position on *Belleisle*'s stern quarter, so close that his bowsprit was almost over her poop.

It was now *Belleisle*'s turn to be exposed to raking fire from *Fougueux*. Servaux remembered, 'We had the enemy's ship on the port quarter in such a way that whilst we could only receive a few shots from their stern guns, they were exposed to our whole broadside, raking the enemy, end-on, along all his decks.' On *Fougueux* they cheered when *Belleisle*'s mizen mast fell over the ship's larboard quarter. Then her rudder and steering gear were smashed so that she could no longer turn. 'Her sails flapped loose in the wind, and her sheets and running rigging were cut to pieces by our hail of shot. For some time she ceased firing. We, for our part, now redoubled our efforts and we next saw her main-topmast come down.'

On the battered *Belleisle*, Lieutenant Owen, Paul Nicolas and the other marines abandoned the exposed poop and went down to replace the many casualties on the quarterdeck carronades. Owen had been hit in the thigh by a splinter but he was still directing his men, trousers torn and bloody.

Some ten minutes or so behind *Belleisle*, *Mars* and *Tonnant* arrived to take some pressure off the first two British ships. *Fougueux*, which had just taken down a large portion of *Belleisle*'s rigging, was distracted by fire from *Mars* on her starboard quarter and by *Tonnant* at her stern. The French ship now lost most of her own rigging and her second-in-command, François Bazin, suffered several wounds.

Seeing that *Mars* was also threatening to break the line, Captain Julien Cosmao-Kerjulien of *Pluton* put on all the sail he could and closed the gap between his ship and *Monarca*, forcing *Mars* to change course and aim for the wide gap ahead of *Monarca*. *Pluton* kept going and Captain George Duff in *Mars* was forced to turn his ship on to a course parallel to hers. *Mars* and *Pluton* then engaged in a long running bombardment, but they were slowly approaching *Santa Ana*, who transferred some men to her larboard guns to fire raking shots at *Mars's* bows.

Mars was now in real danger of being trapped and, seeing an opportunity to grapple and board her, Cosmao called up his boarding party from *Pluton's* guns. Infantry Captain Pernot, whose men were to give covering fire from the poop, rushed towards the boarding station with his soldiers. But a round shot that had penetrated the second battery tore into them, killing three. Pernot fell, covered with his own blood and that of the others, and lost consciousness.

In any case Cosmao had changed his mind. He saw what he took to be 'a three-decker and another less powerful ship' – possibly *Tonnant* and *Belleisle* – manoeuvring to attack him astern. He threw back his sails, brought *Mars* on to his quarter, got one broadside to bear on *Tonnant* and, taking part of his crew over to the starboard guns, fired several raking broadsides into *Belleisle's* stern, claiming, as *Fougueux* also did, credit for bringing down her mizen mast and main topmast.

As *Pluton* turned, Duff on *Mars* bore up to avoid *Santa Ana's* raking fire, but at that moment Captain Thomas Norman, commanding Duff's marines on the poop, saw that *Fougueux* had now manoeuvred away from *Belleisle* and was getting into position to rake *Mars*. He climbed down to tell the captain. Duff asked whether the guns would bear on *Fougueux*. Norman thought not. ' "Then," replied the Captain, "we must point our guns at the ships on which they can bear. I shall go and look; but the men below may see better, as there will be less smoke." '

Duff went to the end of the quarterdeck and craned his neck over the side to see. He told his aide-de-camp, Alexander Arbuthnot, to go below and order the guns to be pointed more aft, against the *Fougueux*. As the boy turned, shots whistled in. Duff was decapitated and two seamen behind him were killed. Midshipman James Robinson told his father that 'when the men heard it, they held his body up and gave three cheers to show they were not discouraged by it, and they returned to their guns'. Nevertheless, *Mars* lost her main topmast and spanker boom as well as her captain, her rigging was badly shot up, several guns were smashed and the rudder was damaged. Twenty-nine men were already dead and sixty-nine wounded. The marine captain, Thomas Norman, was seriously injured and twenty-year-old master's mate Alexander Duff died in the arms of his younger brother, Thomas. First Lieutenant William Hennah took command, but *Mars* was almost unmanageable and could barely defend herself as she drifted away to windward of *Santa Ana*.

Pluton manoeuvred to take on new enemies. Captain Pernot regained consciousness, recognised the voice of one of his soldiers and implored him to carry him to the surgeon. The soldier replied that he would have done so already had he not thought him dead. In the cockpit Pernot was bandaged and examined: nothing was broken, but he feared for his left eye, his left hand was badly cut, and a splinter had smashed against his chest close to the collarbone. Pernot lay helpless on his mattress and listened to the noise of the battle.

Up on the quarterdeck, *Pluton*'s Captain Cosmao had no doubt of the identity of the enemy on which his starboard guns were now trained. He recognised the ship as one that the British had captured at the Nile, a ship he had himself captained in 1795 and in which he had taken his first English frigate. It was *Tonnant,* approaching under heavy fire with its band playing a song of the moment, an old favourite revamped in 1803 to suit the mood of the time and the threat of French invasion:

> The Gallic fleet approaches nigh, boys,
> Now some must conquer, some must die, boys;
> But that appals not you or me,
> For our watchword it shall be.
>
> Britons, strike home,
> Revenge your country's wrongs . . .

A hundred yards from the Combined Fleet's line *Tonnant*'s studding sails were shot away and 'Britons Strike Home' reached a jarring crescendo when a 40-pound cannonball obliterated two of the bandsmen. At about twelve thirty Captain Tyler directed *Tonnant* between the Spanish *Monarca* and the French *Algésiras*, then steered to larboard and came up behind the Spanish ship. *Tonnant*'s raking broadside of 2300 pounds from forty-six double-shotted guns and carronades produced confusion and carnage on *Monarca*'s gun-decks. Lieutenant Ramón Amaya, commanding one, was killed outright and Sub-lieutenant Ignacio Reguera was wounded but stayed at his post. A second broadside brought down *Monarca*'s fore and cross-jack yards. A Spanish soldier named Amor Seco was given credit for saving the ship by discovering and extinguishing a blaze that had caught below decks. For a while the Spanish ship's fire was much reduced, and as she pulled away *Tonnant*'s port guns were trained on *Pluton*, but the British ship concentrated her resources against *Algésiras*, her principal French opponent on the other side.

'Although I wish very much to be able to give you a circumstantial account of the calamitous battle,' went a letter sent from Cadiz to Bernardo de Uriarte on 25 October 1805, 'the reports in circulation here are so vague and uncertain, that I have my doubts if the Admirals themselves could do it with any degree of accuracy . . . the disorder and confusion which reigned throughout this fearful battle, have rendered it almost impossible for the commanders themselves to know what occurred on board their own ships.'

Even today no two accounts of Trafalgar are the same. The discrepancies do not lie simply in the small details or the weight of importance given to aspects of the battle. After all the logs and accounts have been put together, the exact course of events remains unclear: different authors have different ships fighting each other.

In truth, it was an unusually confused and confusing battle. At the time captains did not know what had happened with any accuracy, and when they tried to work out afterwards which ships they had encountered they often got it wrong. It was not until 1907 that the French historian Edouard Desbrière analysed the reports of the captains of the Combined Fleet and established the order in which their ships were sailing. Previous accounts had been based upon the order in which they were supposed to be sailing and on inaccurate plans drawn immediately after the action. Eyewitnesses are unreliable. Many wrote twenty years or more after the event, used later sources, exaggerated, were wise with hindsight, and conflated their own impressions with those of others they conferred with afterwards.

Most of all, everyone made mistakes. This was a battle in which the metaphorical fog of war was made denser by huge quantities of real smoke, with little wind to clear it. Ships emerged from thick, drifting banks of it, then disappeared again. Others took their place. Flags were shot away. Were the enemy ships they glimpsed through the smoke in fact friends? Or were ships that they feared were about to attack them already engaged in fighting each other?

Algésiras had eighty-two guns against *Tonnant*'s ninety-two, and her main armament of 36- and 18-pounders was heavier than *Tonnant*'s 32- and 18-pounders by little more than the extra weight of a French pound. Nevertheless, her crew of 850, many of whom were soldiers, was more than a match for *Tonnant*'s 673, of whom only eighty eight were marines.

Algésiras had filled her main topsail and was gliding slowly towards *Tonnant*. In her final approach she put in a raking broadside that smashed into *Tonnant*'s stern, causing great damage despite Captain Charles Tyler's evasive action. His sudden turn caused *Algésiras* to crash into *Tonnant*'s side, entangling her bowsprit in *Tonnant*'s main shrouds. The two ships pounded each other from the closest range, but *Tonnant* had an advantage in the angle at which the ships had collided and could bring more guns to bear. Volleys of grape from her 32-pounder carronades ripped away much of *Algésiras*'s rigging. Lieutenant Benjamin Clement, commanding on the forecastle, ordered his men to turn their 32-pounder carronades, again loaded with grape, towards *Algésiras*'s deck. Clement was one of the more battle-hardened lieutenants in the navy and this was his fifth fleet action. As a midshipman he had been wounded three times at the battle of Camperdown, and he had commanded a flat-bottomed boat at Copenhagen. With him on the forecastle he had boatswain Richard Little and some of the strongest, most experienced able seamen.

But *Algésiras*'s own gunners were doing almost as much damage to *Tonnant*. Admiral Magon was wearing his finest uniform, including a gilded shoulder-belt awarded to him by the Spanish in 1798 for escorting home two of their treasure ships. Before the action commenced he had promised to give it to the first man to board an English ship. Now he sounded the drum to call his boarders. They surged up behind Lieutenant Guillaume Verdreau with supporting fire from the soldiers of the 1st Swiss Regiment and men of the 20th Regiment who were serving as marines.

This was the moment for which the crew of *Algésiras* had trained, their chance to turn a naval battle into hand-to-hand combat. As on other French ships, sharp-shooters were sniping from the tops, and killed or injured many of the men on the *Tonnant*'s upper decks but, critically, they did not hit enough of those manning the 32-pounder carronades. Just as Verdreau led the charge on to *Tonnant*, Benjamin Clement's forecastle carronades and the remaining 18-pounders and carronades on the quarterdeck delivered another devastating volley of grape that all but massacred the boarding party. Verdreau was killed outright, as was Michel Mennet, who commanded the marines, and Magon received a bullet in the arm although he refused to go below. Lieutenant Frederick Hoffman, on *Tonnant*, recalled proudly that 'Only one man made good his footing on our quarterdeck, when he was pinned through the calf of his right leg by one of the crew with his half-pike, whilst another was going to cut him down.' Hoffman intervened and ordered that the Frenchman be taken to the cockpit for medical treatment.

Monarca, meanwhile, had returned to the offensive and manoeuvred into a dangerous position on *Tonnant*'s opposite bow, from which position she put in a broadside that cut in half fourteen-year-old Midshipman William Brown and brought down *Tonnant*'s fore topmast and mainyard. Benjamin Clement, on the forecastle, realised that *Pluton* was in a position from which she could put in raking fire on *Tonnant*. From *Pluton*, Captain Cosmao eyed *Tonnant*, the ship he had briefly commanded. There might be a chance to get her back now – as Clement fully appreciated: 'Seeing the situation we were in, I went aft to inform Captain Tyler, when I found he been carried below wounded.' First Lieutenant John Bedford had become captain and told Clement he had sent for the officers to consult over what was best to be done. At that moment Second Lieutenant Charles Bennett came up and the three 'agreed to keep the boarders aft, and turn to on those gentlemen on the Bow'.

Charles Tyler had been shot through the thigh, and although he was conscious he could not stand. *Algésiras*'s sharp-shooters had also succeeded in clearing *Tonnant*'s poop, where the 18-pounder carronades had now been abandoned while the remaining marines sought less exposed positions. Two of their three sergeants had been killed. Clement went forward again, to direct as many guns as possible against *Monarca* and *Pluton*. One of *Tonnant*'s shots went straight through *Pluton*'s hull into the orlop deck: splinters hit Captain Pernot in the head, where he lay wounded on a mattress, and killed a surgeon. Pernot was temporarily blinded, then almost suffocated when a dozen wounded men fell on him. He was rebandaged and moved into an officer's cabin.

Up ahead *Fougueux* had suffered serious damage from her long duel with *Belleisle* and from *Mars* and *Royal Sovereign*. Her mizen mast had gone and the sails and rigging were lying in wreckage along the sides of the ship. Fire had broken out in the stern walk and the poop, as burning wads caught on fallen sails. Pierre Servaux, responsible as master at arms for fire-fighting, and his men 'tried our best, in spite of the hail of shot, to put the fire out, and with hatchets to cut adrift the mass of wrecked top-hamper from the fallen masts and yards and cordage'. The wreckage was lying along the ship's sides and hanging over the gun-ports. Baudouin ordered Servaux 'to climb outboard and see if the wreckage of the mainsail was not in danger of being set on fire from the main-deck guns'. He obeyed and had just clambered over the gangway and into the chains when 'one of the enemy fired her whole starboard broadside. The din and concussion were fearful; so tremendous that I almost fell headlong into the sea. Blood gushed from my nose and ears.'

To be hit by a broadside when on the wrong side of the ship's protective woodwork must have been terrifying indeed. The assailant was probably once again *Royal Sovereign*, since Baudouin was sailing *Fougueux* towards the British three-decker. His second-in-command, François Bazin, noticed that her rigging was in an even worse state than *Fougueux*'s own, and claimed that 'we succeeded in dismasting her entirely'.

Certainly *Royal Sovereign* lost her own mizen and mainmast at about this time and became completely unmanageable. *Fougueux*'s mainmast also fell: shot through some ten or twelve feet above the deck, it tumbled over to larboard. Pierre Servaux and his men set to work again on the shrouds with their tomahawks, but they were now almost engulfed in fallen rigging. Servaux's impression was that by this stage more than half of the crew were wounded. Then the foremast fell over the forecastle. 'Our flag, however, was still flying. It was the only thing left above the deck,' he recalled.

Belleisle was not yet in so bad a state but her mizen mast had fallen in such a way that it masked most of the guns at the stern. Seeing that this blind spot existed, Captain Cosmao now placed *Pluton* there, and proceeded to batter *Belleisle* further, suffering minimal return fire.

Admiral Villeneuve could see nothing of the battle to the south through the enveloping smoke. Although he could not know it, his men were inflicting substantial damage on the first enemy ships to break their line.

Anxious British officers, watching from ships further back, had a much better view. Lieutenant Humphrey Senhouse of *Conqueror* later wrote that the leading ships were placed in such situations at the onset, that nothing but the most heroic gallantry and practical skill at their guns could have extricated them. If the enemy's vessels had closed up as they ought to have done, *from van to rear*, and had possessed a nearer equality in active courage, it is my opinion that even British skill and British gallantry could not have availed.

Many later commentators looked at the opening phase of the battle and wondered at the risk Nelson took. The seaman and novelist Joseph Conrad spent years in merchant ships in those waters. He remembered vividly that, in that locality, once the wind went north of west as it had the previous night, it was quite capable of veering right round to the east at a moment's notice. This would have left the leading ships isolated and stranded under the French guns. 'The mere idea,' he wrote, 'of these baffling easterly airs, coming on at any time within half an hour or so, after the firing of the first shot, is enough to take one's breath away.'

From the head of his own column, Nelson had watched Collingwood's leading ships go through the Combined Fleet's line to the south. One of the aides on the quarterdeck, Midshipman George Westphal, remembered the admiral's enthusiasm for the way that Hargood held his fire until he broke the line. 'Nobly done, Hargood!' he exclaimed. But he was anxious. Signal Lieutenant John Pasco had his telescope focused on the action. 'There is a topgallant yard gone,' he observed.

'Whose? Is it the *Royal Sovereign*'s?' asked the admiral.

Pasco assured him that it was an enemy's. Nelson smiled, and said, 'Collingwood is doing well.'

Before Collingwood reached the enemy, ranging shots from *San Agustín* and *Héros* began to make splashes in the water ahead of *Victory*. When one passed overhead Nelson sent the frigate captains back to their ships. William Prowse of *Sirius* said goodbye to his nephew, Captain Charles Adair, who commanded the marines in the flagship. Soon *Victory* would face a battering every bit as severe as that being endured by *Royal Sovereign*, *Belleisle*, *Mars* and *Tonnant*.

12

Take Your Choice

The first shot to strike *Victory* tore a hole in her main-topgallant sail. For at least a minute nothing happened. Then two hundred guns fired on Nelson's flagship all at once. The three nearest ships, *San Agustín*, *Héros* and *Santísima Trinidad*, all opened up with their full batteries, and from longer range several of Dumanoir's ships in the vanguard joined in. Having drawn this fire and partly blinded Dumanoir with the smoke that billowed from the French and Spanish guns, Nelson turned to starboard, hauling into the fitful westerly wind, and ran down the line searching for the French admiral.

A hundred yards or so behind *Victory,* on *Neptune*, young William Badcock was still gazing in awe at *Santísima Trinidad* and adding up his prize money: 'She was lying-to under topsails, top-gallant sails, royals, jib, and spanker; her courses were hauled up; and her lofty, towering sails looked beautiful, peering through the smoke, as she awaited the onset.' In *Neptune*, as in other British ships, they were tying extra Union Jacks and ensigns to the fore and fore-topmast stays, the mizen rigging, and the peak, to try to ensure against fire from their own side in the smoke and confusion. As the first cannonballs splashed around *Neptune*, Badcock returned to his station in the middle of the lower deck. Captain Fremantle ordered all the men to lie flat on the deck to avoid raking shots.

It was always Nelson's intention 'to deceive the Enemy by inducing them to suppose it is his intention to attack their Van'. Commanders of ships in the Combined Fleet's van and centre, such as Dumanoir, Valdés and Felipe Cajigal, insisted that Nelson 'steered for the centre of the van, and thence, hauling to the wind, towards the centre'. Xavier de Uriarte, captain of the *Santísima Trinidad*, stated positively that *Victory* formed 'with the three-deckers *Téméraire* and the *Neptune,* a line almost parallel to that formed on our side by the . . . *Bucentaure* . . . *Trinidad* . . . and . . . *Héros* – with the gallant and most intrepid intention of breaking the line between the *Trinidad* and the *Bucentaure.'*

Several British witnesses confirm that Nelson did not head straight for *Bucentaure* but, rather, sailed along the Franco-Spanish line. An unpublished account by *Victory*'s assistant surgeon, William Westemberg, records that the enemy opened fire on *Victory*, who returned it soon afterwards 'with our larboard guns at their van in passing down their line'.

By twelve twenty the flagship was drawing concentrated fire that became more accurate as she drew within effective range. Nelson's secretary John Scott was talking to Hardy when a cannonball cut straight through him. Charles Adair and a seaman hauled Scott's shattered remains over the side. Nelson asked, 'Is that poor Scott that is gone?' Adair confirmed that it was and Nelson muttered, 'Poor fellow!'

Spinning double-headed bar shot from *Santísima Trinidad* screamed along decks and scythed through ropes. One cut down a file of eight marines lined up on the poop. Second Lieutenant Lewis Roteley, a twenty-year-old Welshman, was so struck by the power of a single iron bar sixteen inches long that after the battle he kept it as a gruesome souvenir. Nelson ordered Adair to disperse his marines just before another shot splintered the forebrace bitts on the quarterdeck and ricocheted between Hardy and himself. They stopped and examined each other for injuries. A wooden splinter had ripped the buckle from Hardy's shoe and bruised his foot. Nelson smiled. 'This is too warm work, Hardy, to last long.' He had brought on the battle he had wanted.

But *Victory* was suffering now. The mizen topmast and all the studding sails and their booms were shot away. The loss of sail reduced her speed from a slow walk to a crawl, but she was still moving, her remaining huge sails still holding the faint breeze.

At about twelve twenty-five, having changed the charge of the larboard guns from double to single shot, *Victory*'s men were waiting for the order to open fire. Gun captains bent over their guns, the pans of their gunlocks filled with powder, with more on the vent pan just in case. Each captain took the tallow cap from the firing tube, cocked the gunlock and warned his men to 'make ready'. They shuffled clear of the gun's line of recoil. Two hundred yards from *Santísima Trinidad*, standing safely away from the gun, the captains tugged on the trigger lines, the guns roared and shot backwards, and immediately the men fell into the familiar drill. 'Sponge out': the sponger and his assistant forced the wetted woollen sponge down the gun to stifle any sparks or embers, while the second captain closed the vent with his finger. 'Load with cartridge': the powderman passed a charge to the loader, who stuffed it into the muzzle and rammed it home. The captain stuck his cartridge pricker into the vent to check it was in place. 'Load with shot': the loader placed a single round shot into the barrel, then rammed it home. 'Wad the gun': he took a disc of junk wadding from the stack by the gun and rammed that in to hold the ball in place. 'Run out the gun': the whole crew hauled on the ropes to roll it into its firing position with the muzzle protruding from the gun-port. They levered it into line, the captain checked elevation, his second pricked the cartridge to expose the powder, put in a new firing tube and took off the top. The captain half cocked the gunlock, primed it with powder and they were ready again. 'Make ready. Fire!'

As the British ships approached, Jean-Jacques Lucas, captain of *Redoutable*, had called some of the captains of his guns to the forecastle to observe how most shots fired from the Combined Fleet were falling short of *Victory*. 'I then gave orders to aim for dismasting, and above all to aim straight.' Very early in his career, Lucas had been a *protégé* of Latouche-Tréville. In the American war he had sailed in Latouche's frigate and had shown such promise that Latouche had put him in charge of one of their prizes. Lucas came from the same sort of middling background as the English captains Hargood and Cooke. But this, in the Marine Royale, would almost certainly have prevented him rising above warrant-officer status. For this reason, among others, Lucas had welcomed the Revolution and the new régime had soon made him an officer. He was a small, slight man, but very determined, and he had whipped up his crew to be equally so. He saw his first ranging shots cut through the foretopsail yard of the *Victory* and cheers resounded through his ship.

Captain Jean-Jacques Magendie of *Bucentaure* realised that *Victory*, on which he had now identified Nelson's flag, was aiming to pass between his ship and the *Santísima Trinidad*, less than two hundred yards in front. 'We rejoiced at this, everything being ready prepared to board him,' Magendie reported. Xavier de Uriarte backed *Santísima Trinidad*'s main and mizen topsails to slow his ship and close the gap between it and *Bucentaure* while Magendie sailed forward. Both ships had crews larger than *Victory*'s, and *Trinidad* had nearly four hundred soldiers on board. If they managed to get aboard *Victory* in numbers, Nelson's flagship would be in extreme peril.

But when *Victory* was at 'short musket range' – about a hundred yards – from *Bucentaure* she changed course to starboard as if to pass *Bucentaure*'s stern. Perhaps Nelson and Hardy judged it impossible to get through ahead of *Bucentaure*, but the change may have been involuntary. About now the *Victory*'s steering-wheel was smashed by a cannonball, leaving her briefly out of control. Thomas Atkinson, a Yorkshireman who had served as master of Nelson's successive flagships for seven years, ran below to the gunroom to rig the reserve gear to the tiller. On *Redoutable* Lucas realised that his was the only ship that could now close the gap astern of *Bucentaure* and help his admiral battle the celebrated Lord Nelson. He crowded on sail to do so.

Bucentaure's soldiers were now pouring musket fire into *Victory* and the combined gunnery of *Bucentaure*, *Santísima Trinidad* and *Redoutable* was doing great damage to her masts and rigging. The air was full of grape and bar shot. Casualties were mounting, almost all from the men on the exposed superstructure. According to Surgeon William Beatty, about twenty men were dead and another thirty wounded before *Victory* reached Villeneuve's line. Lieutenant Pasco had gone down, his forearm and side torn by grape shot. A marine corporal's arm had been shot off. A large splinter had scalped Jerry Sullivan, a young Irish able seaman. *Victory's* mizen mast was shot through, and then her main topgallantmast and fore topmast came crashing down in quick succession in a tangle of ropes and canvas.

But on *Bucentaure* Captain Magendie was not satisfied. He thought that by now they should have dismantled *Victory* completely, but had failed owing to the effect of the swell and of the smoke that swirled around his gunners and masked their target. As *Victory* closed on *Bucentaure's* stern, Villeneuve hoisted signal number five, which ordered all ships not in action to get into a position from which to fight effectively.

If Pierre Dumanoir, commanding the vanguard of the Combined Fleet, saw Villeneuve's signal number five through the smoke, he did not take it as an order to change course and double back towards the fighting.

Signal number five carried the same force as Nelson's 'engage the enemy more closely' and was a reminder of the admiral's general instructions, which might have been designed specifically to cover the present situation. They advised the captains not to wait for further instruction from Villeneuve, who might himself be in action and enveloped in smoke, but to be guided by '*son courage et . . . son amour de la gloire*'. They also stated unequivocally that a captain who was not in the heat of the action was not at his post and, further, that if the line was broken all efforts should be made to support the ships that had been attacked and to get close to the flagship. If Dumanoir's squadron was going to intervene decisively in this battle then this was the moment to do so and his squadron had to go about immediately. In the near calm, reversing direction was difficult and would take time.

The captains around him looked to Dumanoir for a lead, but he did not give one. Auguste Gicquel recalled that aboard *Intrépide*, Captain Louis Infernet had his eyes fixed on *Formidable*, Dumanoir's flagship, waiting for the admiral to hoist the signal to go about in order to get into action. 'This signal did not appear. Time passed and the van slowly drew away from the battlefield. It soon became all too clear that its commander was leading it away from the fight.' Gicquel effectively accused Dumanoir of cowardice. If things were as clear as he remembered them, then it is difficult to find any excuse for Dumanoir. But Gicquel's recollections were not always accurate. If there was an excuse it was probably smoke. As a result of Nelson's feint in their direction, Dumanoir's ships had engaged *Victory* and each then fired on the little sixty-four-gun *Africa* as she passed by, as fast as possible, on her way to rejoin the fleet after getting lost during the night. These distant exchanges did not do much damage but for a time they might have made it genuinely difficult to see what was going on.

Meanwhile *Victory* had almost reached the Combined Fleet's line.

In *Redoutable*, Lucas had now come so close to *Bucentaure* that they were shouting warnings from the flagship that he would hit them. His bowsprit actually touched the railing on *Bucentaure*'s poop, but through his loud-hailer Lucas assured Captain Magendie that he had nothing to fear.

With the reserve steering gear working, *Victory* could now cut the line but Hardy saw no chance of getting through without hitting either *Bucentaure* or *Redoutable* and consulted Nelson. The admiral said, 'I cannot help it. It does not signify which we run on board of. Go on board which you please. Take your choice.' Hardy decided on the smaller of the two. Twenty men hauled on ropes attached to the tiller and got the helm to larboard.

The choice was sensible. Villeneuve had won the first round of the tactical battle by closing his line so efficiently, but in choosing to hit

Redoutable Hardy greatly assisted the other British ships coming in behind him. Although she was travelling at under two knots, *Victory*'s weight and momentum when they smashed together threw men off their feet and guns off their mountings. The impact forced *Redoutable* to swing round and to leeward with the British flagship alongside. As *Bucentaure* moved slowly forward, a large gap opened in the enemy line behind her for the ships following *Victory* to exploit.

On *Bucentaure* Captain Magendie felt cheated and frustrated. As she turned towards *Redoutable*, *Victory* passed so close to him and his waiting soldiers that her yards crossed *Bucentaure*'s poop. But *Victory* was always fifteen yards away and the French seamen could not throw their grappling hooks that far. This was a decisive moment. Had *Bucentaure* managed to get hold of *Victory* then, Nelson and Hardy would have faced the boarding parties of two of the toughest French ships in action that day. As it was, the aftermost guns of *Bucentaure* did what damage they could, but *Victory* towered above them. From close range her larboard guns raked *Bucentaure*'s stern. Then her huge 68-pounder forecastle carronade, loaded with a round shot and a specially made canister of over three hundred musket balls, fired for the first time. The guns on her upper deck blasted *Bucentaure* with grape shot to murderous effect. Magendie's exposed upper-deck guns aft were all knocked out, their crews and the soldiers on the poop killed, maimed or driven below. Meanwhile *Victory*'s starboard broadside, fired for the first time with each gun still loaded with two shot, smashed into *Redoutable*. The junior marine lieutenant Lewis Roteley had been sent down to the middle gun-deck to fetch more marines to replace casualties above. He found the experience astonishing:

We were engaging on both sides; every gun was going off. A man should witness a battle in a three-decker from the middle deck, for it beggars all description: it bewilders the senses of sight and hearing. There was the fire from above, the fire from below, besides the fire from the deck I was upon, the guns recoiling with violence, reports louder than thunder, the decks heaving and the sides straining. I fancied myself in the infernal regions, where every man appeared a devil. Lips might move, but orders and hearing were out of the question; everything was done by signs.

Eliab Harvey's *Téméraire*, another three-decker, was astern of *Victory* and some distance to starboard. She had followed *Victory*'s lead during the approach and had fired successively at *San Agustín*, *Héros*, *Santísima Trinidad*, *Bucentaure*, and *Redoutable*, but none gave her the same volume of fire that they lavished on the flagship. For a time Harvey lost sight of her and ordered his guns to cease fire, 'fearing I might from the thickness of the smoke be firing into the *Victory*'. When he saw her again she was side by side with *Redoutable*. *Téméraire* was being engaged from ahead by *Santa Ana*, *San Justo*, and *San Leandro*, but although her rigging was suffering Harvey still had control of the ship and got her into position to rake *Redoutable* as he passed her. Then he turned to cut the line the far side of *Redoutable*.

As he did so he exposed himself to raking fire from the eighty-gun French *Neptune*, sister ship to *Bucentaure*. Esprit-Tranquille Maistral was one of the few captains to see Villeneuve fly signal number five, instructing his captains to get into close combat, and took it as a personal reproach. He abandoned his distant cannonade of *Royal Sovereign* and wore back to support the admiral. He completed the manoeuvre in time to blast *Téméraire* as she emerged. The latter had been aiming to break the line just astern of *Redoutable*, but now found herself exposed to crossfire from five enemy ships. The effect was dramatic. With help from the others *Redoutable* brought down *Téméraire*'s mizen topmast, and fire from *Neptune* destroyed her fore yard, main topmast and rigging. A tangle of sails and rigging crashed down in confusion towards the deck of the British ship and it was all she could do to fire some larboard guns at *Redoutable* as she drifted out of control.

By now *Victory*'s momentum had forced *Redoutable* around, placing *Redoutable*'s poop level with and at the same height as *Victory*'s quarterdeck. On his orders, Captain Lucas's men hurled their grappling irons on to the British flagship and bound it tight. Some of those at the stern broke, but the forward grapples held. Now Lucas had the battle he wanted, and a bloody duel began, from so close that it was difficult to fire the guns. The French 'had to use rope rammers in several cases, and fire with the guns run in, being unable to bowse them, as the ports were masked by the sides of the Victory'. But their heavily armed men were making things uncomfortable for *Victory*'s gunners. 'By means of muskets fired through the ports into those of the Victory, we prevented the enemy from loading their guns,' Lucas claimed.

Lieutenant Roteley found it difficult to persuade the marines to leave the guns and join the fight on deck, so engrossed were they in the struggle. 'In the excitement of the action men had thrown off their red jackets and appeared in check shirts and blue trousers. There was no distinguishing Marine from Seaman – they were all working like horses.' Eventually he located four sergeants and corporals, and with their help he forced about twenty away from the guns and led them towards the quarterdeck.

About this time *Redoutable*'s crew unexpectedly slammed shut the lower deck portholes and took to their small arms. The tactic caused uncertainty on board *Victory* where, with *Redoutable*'s great guns silent, it was thought for a moment that she had surrendered and *Victory* twice ceased fire. Then her guns opened up again, *Victory*'s firemen throwing buckets of water after the shot to stop the flaming wadding, blasted out with the shot, setting fire to the French ship.

At Lucas's bugle call, hundreds of his men left the lower decks to swarm on to the poop and into the netting and shrouds. From there, and from the tops, *Redoutable*'s musketeers and grenadiers put all their effort into clearing *Victory*'s upper decks. Her own 36-pounder carronades poured grape and canister into *Victory* so fast that one of them burst. Upwards of two hundred grenades were thrown on board and almost all the 12-pounders on *Victory*'s top deck were soon put out of action, although her boatswain, William Willmot, continued to sweep *Redoutable*'s gangways with the starboard carronade.

Victory's surgeon later admitted that 'at this period, scarcely a person in the *Victory* escaped unhurt who was exposed to the enemy's musketry'. Midshipman William Rivers's foot was almost completely blown off by a grenade, left attached to him 'by a Piece of Skin abought 4 inch above the ankle'. Rivers asked first for his shoes, then told the gunner's mate to look after the guns and informed Captain Hardy that he was going down to the cockpit. Nelson remarked, 'Hardy, mind he is provided for. It is my Desire,' and they told him to ask 'Putty Nose' – their nickname for James Cosgrove, the purser's steward – when he reached the cockpit 'for a knife to Cutt the foot off'.

Midshipman Robert Smith lost both legs, and a ball that tore through the deck at his feet hit newly appointed Lieutenant William Ram. The popular young Irishman had been looking forward with impatience to the battle, but he died, horribly wounded, as he was carried down to the orlop deck. Captain Hardy's clerk, Thomas Whipple, also died before he reached the surgeons so there was nobody left on the quarterdeck to record what happened. Lord Nelson and Captain Hardy continued to pace its twenty feet, but they were losing the battle up there. Fewer and fewer men were around them as Lucas's crew made preparations to board.

If all was chaos around *Victory*, the ships immediately behind her were carrying out their part of Nelson's plan with clinical precision. The systematic destruction of *Bucentaure* and *Santísima Trinidad* was perhaps the one perfect tactical manoeuvre that the Royal Navy achieved that day. Thomas Fremantle's *Neptune* was ideally placed to take advantage of the hole in the enemy's line that *Victory* had punched by driving aside *Redoutable*. Fremantle steered his powerful three-decker across *Bucentaure*'s stern and, at about one o'clock, delivered a raking broadside from a range of only thirty yards.

Neptune then turned immediately to leeward of *Bucentaure* and stopped on the French flagship's bow quarter. When *Victory* turned to run along the Combined Fleet's line, the ships behind *Neptune* cut the corner and were close behind her when she reached the line. *Leviathan* followed the same course, raking *Bucentaure* in her turn, then carried on to engage *Santísima Trinidad* and *San Agustín*. *Conqueror*

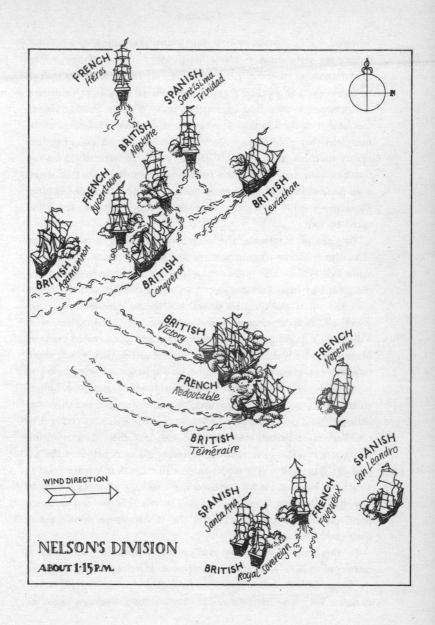

FRENCH
Héros

SPANISH
Santisima
Trinidad

BRITISH
Neptune

FRENCH
Bucentaure

BRITISH
Leviathan

BRITISH
Agamemnon

BRITISH
Conqueror

BRITISH
Victory

FRENCH
Neptune

FRENCH
Redoutable

BRITISH
Téméraire

SPANISH
San Leandro

WIND DIRECTION

SPANISH
Santa Ana

FRENCH
Fougueux

BRITISH
Royal Sovereign

NELSON'S DIVISION

ABOUT 1·15 P.M.

N

followed, raking *Bucentaure* for a fourth time and taking up a position on her lee stern quarter just behind *Neptune*. With *Victory* having drawn most of the anti-personnel fire, all of these British ships sustained damage to their rigging but suffered only light casualties. At some point, according to master's mate William Pringle Green, *Conqueror* took the additional precaution of sending below most of the men from her poop, quarterdeck and forecastle and pounding the enemy with her main guns. With the gap to leeward of the enemy flagships crowded, *Agamemnon* took position to windward of them, with *Britannia* contributing more distant fire and *Africa* approaching. *Bucentaure* was hit from close range by at least six British ships and raked by four.

To Captain Magendie, the succession of raking broadsides was 'disastrous': 'all the rigging was cut to pieces, the masts wounded by a number of shot, the guns in the upper works dismounted'. Once the guns had been knocked over they could not fire and the fall of sails and masts made others unusable. *Neptune*, *Leviathan* and *Conqueror* all escaped almost unscathed from their encounter with Villeneuve's flagship, but their carronades and guns caused carnage. Magendie, who had thought a few minutes earlier that he was about to grapple and board *Victory*, was hit by a splinter and went below to have his wound dressed. First Lieutenant Joseph Daudignon limped aft from his station on the forecastle to take command, but there was little he could do. With no rigging he could not manoeuvre, and he could see more British ships arriving. On deck there were few guns left to fire so Villeneuve sent the surviving gunners below to the 24-pounder gun-deck while, under intense fire, his best seamen tried to repair the rigging. As he surveyed the wreckage all around him he saw that Dumanoir was still sailing north. He hoisted a signal positively instructing the ships in the van to come to the aid of their comrades.

By this stage there was open dissent in Dumanoir's squadron. A quarter of an hour earlier Jules-François de Martinencq, commanding the frigate *Cornélie*, had signalled to *Formidable* that the van had no one to fight. They were not far away but turning back with practically no wind was no easy matter. Most had to lower boats to drag the ships round and for angry, frustrated or guilty officers it seemed to take for ever. Gicquel claimed that *Intrépide* had made several unsuccessful attempts to tack before Villeneuve made his second signal, but with the lack of wind and the surging swell the ship would not respond to the helm. Valdés reported that he wore *Neptuno* round on Villeneuve's signal without waiting for Dumanoir's, which finally came a few minutes later. Dumanoir claimed to have made his signal before he saw Villeneuve's second.

Wearing and tacking are alternative methods of reversing direction. Villeneuve's signal instructed the captains to wear but Dumanoir's called for them to tack. Some captains tried one approach and some the other. *Intrépide* finally wore round with the help of a boat, then collided with *Mont-Blanc* as she tried to tack. *Rayo* and *San Francisco de Asís* also wore round but fell yet further to leeward in doing so. *Formidable* tacked with the aid of a boat and, after more than one attempt, *Scipion*, *Duguay-Trouin* and *Mont-Blanc* (with a broken jib) joined her.

Dumanoir then ordered his ships to hold the wind and aimed to the south of the main battle. The rumour in Cadiz after the battle was that Valdés told Dumanoir that 'the Admiral's orders were superior to his, and that in a battle, the only route he saw, was the one that led to the fight'. He aimed straight for *Santísima Trinidad*. *Rayo* and *San Francisco de Asís* probably tried to get back into the battle, but their sailors were incapable of doing so and they ended up joining the frigates and the other ships to leeward. When he had finally got *Intrépide* about, Infernet roared out in the broad Provençal that he and his crew spoke most fluently, '*Lou capo sur lou Bucentauro!*' – Lay her head for the *Bucentaure*! – and without replacing the foresail she had split on *Mont-Blanc*'s jib, *Intrépide* took the shortest route to the flagship. It was glorious but it was too late. Infernet should probably have disobeyed orders earlier.

By now *Neptune* and *Conqueror* had shot through the *Bucentaure*'s mizen and mainmasts, which fell forward over the starboard side where the tattered sails masked the guns facing her principal assailants. The ship was paralysed. They tied the colours to the stump of the mainmast and tried to clear away enough wreckage to make use of the lower deck 36-pounders. William Pringle Green reckoned that *Conqueror* eventually cut away the wreckage with her own shot. Considering *Bucentaure* beaten, *Neptune* moved forward to place herself on *Santísima Trinidad*'s stern quarter, joining *Leviathan*.

Santísima Trinidad had been engaging successive ships of Nelson's column as they came down, but *Neptune*'s arrival on her unprotected starboard stern quarter was a more urgent problem. From here *Neptune* could rake her mercilessly, while the Spanish ship could return fire with very few guns. Admiral Cisneros had already been wounded and he was joined below by Second Captain Ignacio Olaete and First Lieutenant José Sartoria. As in all the other fights, the men on the quarterdeck were being mown down. But Commodore Uriarte was still there, directing the defence. He had repeated Villeneuve's signal number five, which caused *San Agustín* to wear round and come to *Santísima Trinidad*'s aid. *Héros* also came, but more slowly because her captain, Jean-Baptiste Poulain, had just been killed and there was a delay while her first lieutenant, Jean Louis Conor, took over and worked out what to do.

Both admirals were in deadly danger in the thick of the fighting. Nelson had taken the most tremendous calculated risk: weighing the lack of wind against the swell; his slow approach against the rolling French gunnery; British skill and discipline against his enemies' lack of practice; his own exposure to fire against the moral effect of this on his subordinates.

His opponents had a clear plan, but they had to work out what was happening before they could respond. By concealing and changing his line of attack, Nelson had sown uncertainty among the enemy. His plan to 'surprise and confound' was succeeding. His enemies genuinely did not know 'what I am about'. By doing this he had gained just enough time to strike heavily at the centre of Villeneuve's line and to ensure that no fresh initiatives would come from him before more British ships arrived.

In Nelson's own area the plan was working fairly well, but towards the rear the outcome was much less certain. In breaking the line too far from the rear ship, Collingwood had bitten off rather more than his captains could chew. The ships that had followed him closely were in danger of being overwhelmed before those further behind could come to their aid.

13

Incredible Fury on Both Sides

Bellerophon was the fifth ship of Collingwood's division to open fire. She was leading a second cluster further towards the rear of the Combined Fleet and was about four hundred yards from Dionisio Alcalá Galiano's *Bahama*. In this slow-motion battle it would take ten minutes to cover that distance.

Captain John Cooke had not intended to use his guns until he cut the line, but with at least four ships shooting at his own during the interminable final approach he decided to create a smokescreen. At twelve twenty George Saunders passed the word to William Fairweather and his 'victory or death' boys on the lower deck. Then, in his broad Norfolk accent, he gave the familiar commands to men relieved to be in action at last. The ship had been taking casualties and the rigging was suffering serious damage. In front of them, *Bahama* closed up on *Algésiras* to prevent the British ship breaking through ahead of her, so Cooke altered course slightly to pass her stern. As *Bellerophon* finally slipped between *Bahama* and the more distant *Montañés* she fired from both sides at once. The ship was moving so slowly that, according to Lieutenant William Cumby, while she was in a position to rake *Bahama*'s stern, 'We fired our carronades three times, and every long gun on the larboard side at least twice.'

Bellerophon was relatively lightly armed but her veteran crew was

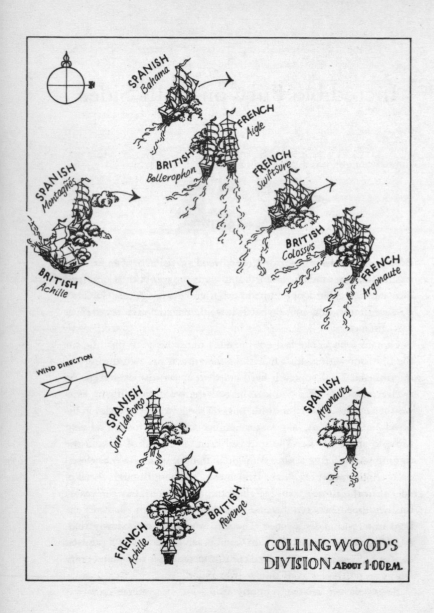

COLLINGWOOD'S DIVISION ABOUT 1.00 P.M.

highly experienced and her guns hurled a devastating shower of metal along the length of the Spanish ship. Boatswain Thomas Robinson, the burly Peter McFarlane and the former white slave Peter Jansen on the forecastle 32-pounder carronade swept *Bahama*'s quarterdeck with grape, leaving Galiano bleeding profusely from a splinter wound in the face. His coxswain, an old family retainer, sprang to his assistance but Galiano refused to go below, realising that the ship's morale might collapse if he did so. Somewhere in *Bahama* there was an explosion that Cumby thought was a small powder magazine going up.

It was fortunate for *Bellerophon* that this explosion and her captain's wound temporarily distracted the crew of *Bahama*. Just as Geordie William Ferguson and his mates swung *Bellerophon*'s wheel to turn her to larboard to continue the battle with *Bahama* from alongside, they saw looming over the smoke the topgallant sails of another ship right on top of them on the starboard bow. Robinson, McFarlane and the other old hands on the forecastle leapt from carronade to ropes to haul the foresail into the wind to try to stop the ship, but it was too late. William Cumby had just time to register the name *Aigle* on the French ship's stern before they crashed into her larboard quarter, 'our foreyard locking with her mainyard, which was squared'.

The *Aigle* was much taller, giving her poop and gangway command of *Bellerophon*'s upper decks, and her 36- and 18-pounder guns were heavier than *Bellerophon*'s 32- and 18-pounders. The French ship also had a larger crew and she was crowded with soldiers, far outnumbering *Bellerophon*'s eighty marines. Sharp-shooters sniped from the tops and grenadiers hurled bombs from the gangways as another close-quarters slugging match began. *Bellerophon*'s only advantage was the experience and discipline of her crew of hardened seamen. They were considerably older than the average, had been together in this ship for four years, and included only a hundred landsmen.

At first more of *Aigle*'s cannons would bear since *Bellerophon* could only fight with her forward guns and Thomas Robinson's forecastle carronades. But the two carronades proved their worth as their opening volleys roared across *Aigle*'s quarterdeck and Captain Pierre-Paulin Gourrège fell in a hail of bullets, hit five times. He was carried below and his second, Jean-Pierre Tempié, took over. But as the ships drifted alongside, *Aigle*'s sharp-shooters began to gain the upper hand above decks, driving the British crews from their guns and carronades. This truly was the land battle at sea on which Villeneuve had pinned his hopes, 'Romans' against 'Carthaginians', and the fighting between them was furiously intense. Captain Cooke himself was firing his pistols. In the midst of the action he told Cumby to hurry down to explain to George Saunders and the other officers on the main and lower decks how the ship was placed and order them to direct their main cannon fire effort against *Aigle*, taking the beds and quoins from under the guns and firing upwards directly through the French ship's decks.

Lieutenant Cumby clambered down the ladders deep into the hot, smoky heart of the ship to where the ancient midshipman, William Fairweather, and the ship's butcher, William Pallet, were sweating at the forward 32-pounders. Cumby shouted into Saunders's ear over the chaotic din. He checked the deck, and ordered the gun-ports to be hauled up close against the side, to prevent them being torn off their hinges when the ships ground into each other as they were hurled together by the rolling sea.

Aigle and *Bellerophon* fought side by side for nearly half an hour until the British ship's main and mizen topmasts crashed down over the starboard side. The sails hooked on to something in the main chains and hung like a curtain directly in front of the muzzles of the ship's guns. The canvas quickly caught fire and the sail trimmers were detached from the gun crews to hack it away. The sight encouraged the French, who attacked with new vigour. A shot smashed the leg of the master, Edward Overton, on the quarterdeck and he collapsed. Captain John Cooke was reloading his pistols for the third time when at eleven minutes past one he, too, was hit and pitched forward on to the deck. Fourteen-year-old George Pearson ran to help him but was felled by a splinter. A quartermaster came from the wheel to ask if he should carry the captain below. Cooke gasped, 'Let me lay one minute,' and never spoke again. When they got him to the cockpit the surgeon, Alex Whyte, opened his waistcoat and found that a musket-ball or canister-shot had hit his right breast, broken two of the ribs, passed through the lungs and killed him.

William Cumby was returning from the lower gun-deck and was weaving his way between the recoiling guns and busy crews on the main deck when he met Overton, 'carried by two men, with his leg dreadfully shattered'. Overton died soon afterwards. Before he reached the quarterdeck ladder, having stopped to give some orders, Cumby was located by 'a quartermaster, who came to inform me that the Captain was very badly wounded and, as he believed, dead'. Cumby, who had never fought in a big fleet action before, now took command of the ship. He was the only one of the three who had read Nelson's memorandum that morning and was still on his feet.

There was no doubt that they were in trouble. *Bahama* had now moved forward to pelt them with more fire, and *Monarca* and *Pluton* were hitting them from a distance, but the immediate problem was *Aigle* to which ship they were locked fast. The fighting grew desperate as the French crew prepared to board. The marine captain, James Wemyss, still commanded a knot of men in action on the poop. Among them were the signallers John Franklin and Christopher Beaty, who saw that for the third time *Bellerophon*'s ensign had come tumbling down when the ropes that held it had been shot away. Realising that the men might think they had surrendered, Beaty grabbed the largest Union Jack he could find and climbed up the mizen rigging. He spread it as wide as he could and tied the four corners to the shrouds. Franklin was surprised that he was not shot by the French riflemen in the tops and on the *Aigle*'s poop, who had ruthlessly picked off anyone who had gone up to mend rigging before. Instead, the French marksmen, it was later claimed, 'seeing what he was about, and seemingly in admiration of such daring conduct, suspended their fire for the few seconds that he remained aloft'.

The French had closed the gun-ports on their lower deck and their crews, mainly soldiers, were massing above. At the level of the upper gun-decks the ships were so close that opposing crews were pulling the ramrods out of the hands of their enemies. French musketeers were seen firing through the British portholes and fizzing grenades ran along *Bellerophon*'s forecastle and gangway. Cumby himself picked one off the gangway with the fuse still burning and threw it overboard. Others exploded and caused serious burns. Midshipman Robert Patton watched one burning man throw himself out of a stern port.

One grenade, thrown in at a lower-deck gun-port, nearly blew both ships sky high. Its explosion blew off the scuttle of the gunner's storeroom, causing a fire and forcing open the door into the magazine passage. 'Most providentially', Cumby wrote later, the doors were so placed that the same blast that blew open the door from the storeroom into the passage blew shut the door from the passage to the magazine. If it had not done so both ships would certainly have exploded. John Stevenson, the gunner, had fortunately been in the storeroom and reacted immediately and calmly. He went quietly up to Lieutenant Saunders on the lower deck, told him the storeroom was on fire and asked for some men to extinguish the blaze. He returned with the lower-deck firemen, who put it out before anybody else knew that there had been the greatest possible reason to panic.

Cumby sounded Cooke's bugle for the boarders. They left their guns and gathered in their divisions ready to defend the ship. They did not have to wait long.

Jean-Pierre Tempié shouted, 'À *l'abordage!*' and the French surged towards the sides of their ship, hurling themselves across the gap between *Aigle* and *Bellerophon*. British sailors slashed at them with cutlasses, stabbed at them with half-pikes and clubbed at their clinging hands with anything they could find. French sailors fell into the sea between the two ships to be crushed or drowned, but the soldiers of the 67th Regiment, commanded by Lieutenant-Colonel Jacquemet and with the regiment's Eagle in their midst, moved to press home the assault.

British marine captain James Wemyss was reportedly shot eight times, but still stood tall as he led and encouraged his outnumbered men on the poop. Up ahead, at the front of the ship, five Frenchmen 'had got upon our starboard sprit-sail yard-arm, and were making their way to the bowsprit'. The stout, muscular Scotsman Peter McFarlane saw them and responded like the vastly experienced seaman he was. He went over to the cleat on the starboard side of the forecastle and, untying the rope, 'let go the sprit-sail brace [a rope supporting that end of the yard] which suddenly canting with their weight, they all fell into the water'. A grenade badly wounded boatswain Thomas Robinson in both hands and he was forced to go below.

The Bellerophons held off the first assault but Cumby saw that the position on deck was hopeless. 'Our quarterdeck, poop, and forecastle were at this time almost cleared by musquetry from troops on board *L'Aigle*, her poop and gangway completely commanding those decks, and the troops on board her appearing very numerous.' He called down the men from the poop and mustered the boarders in cover under the half-deck. There, he held them in readiness to repel further attempts to board, 'their position rendering it quite impracticable for us to board them in the face of such a fire of musquetry so advantageously situated'.

Cumby went below, touring the decks 'to encourage the men and stimulate their exertions at the guns, observing that we had nothing else to trust to, as the ship aloft had become an unmanageable wreck'. On the lower deck the British guns were firing upwards to kill men on the decks above. But both crews were tired by their efforts and their wounds, and there was a lull in the fighting. *Aigle* had sustained heavy casualties from *Bellerophon*'s gunnery and in her attempts to board, and those of her guns that had not been dismounted or disabled were much quieter.

On the quarterdeck, the remaining officers moved cautiously now. John Franklin was having a private duel with a sniper 'in the foretop of the enemy ship wearing a cocked hat who had during the engagement taken off with his rifle several of the officers and men'. One was Franklin's close friend John Simmons. They had been talking together earlier when the sniper shot him and he fell dead at Franklin's feet. Just now Franklin and a marine sergeant 'were carrying down a black seaman to have his wounds dressed, when a ball from the rifleman entered his breast and killed the poor fellow as they carried him along'. Franklin said to the sergeant, 'He'll have you next.' But the sergeant had other ideas. He announced that he would find a position below in cover 'from which he could command the French rifleman, and would never cease firing at him till he had killed him'.

Franklin climbed back on deck, dodging rapidly behind a mast as he 'saw the fellow lift his rifle to his shoulder and aim'. The ball thudded into the deck a few feet away. So few guns were firing that Franklin could hear the sergeant firing away with his musket from below and, peering from behind the mainmast, he saw the rifleman fall head first into the sea. 'Upon the sergeant coming up, he asked him how many times he fired: "I killed him," he said, "at the seventh shot."'

At this point the two ships drifted apart. Just how and why is unclear. British accounts claim that the French deliberately withdrew. But *Aigle*'s Dutch second lieutenant, Asmus Classen, reported that his ship was winning the struggle, that 'the well-sustained musketry fire and the grape from our upper works had cleared those of the enemy; the fire from her gun-decks slackened considerably and we were about to board and carry her'. His view was that 'The two ships were separated by accident and we were deprived of the hope of seizing our prey.' But whether they had won or narrowly survived through luck, the much-relieved crew of *Bellerophon* triumphantly raked *Aigle* as she went.

Out of the forty-seven men who had been on *Bellerophon*'s quarter-deck at the start of the action only seven were now unwounded. Twenty-eight were dead, 127 badly wounded and forty slightly. Over the coming days twenty-three of the wounded would die. Boatswain Thomas Robinson reappeared on the deck, his mangled hands roughly bandaged by the purser's steward, and volunteered to do whatever Cumby thought he was fit for. The queue for the surgeons had been so long that he had not waited for Whyte and Engleheart to treat him properly, but had hurried back to the fray.

Midshipman Henry Walker reckoned that *Aigle* and *Bellerophon* 'were well matched, she being the best manned ship in the Combined, and we in the British fleet'. To judge from the British muster books and from what was said of *Aigle*, he was not far wrong. In both ships the chief burden of responsibility fell on the same key figures – officers obviously, but also the petty officers and experienced seamen. Given the difference in numbers, the burden was probably greater on the British ship. People like Thomas Robinson, the boatswain, Christopher Beaty, the yeoman of signals who climbed the mast, Peter McFarlane, credited with tipping five of the boarders into the sea, and the calm gunner John Stevenson bound a ship's crew together and knew what to do next in combat when less experienced men became confused.

Peter McFarlane seems to have been remarkable chiefly for being alarmingly stout and muscular: the Kirkcaldy-born gorilla of the forecastle, with the sun, moon, stars and a mermaid tattooed on his right arm. He was still in his twenties but had served in the navy for seven years and had spent five years in the Baltic trade before that. The way that he used his wits and strength on this occasion was presumably celebrated over drinks for years to come. William Ferguson, the grey-eyed man from North Shields with a Newcastle accent whose battle station was the wheel, had been in the navy constantly for thirteen years. 'This man has never been paid off. A trusty fellow' was the comment on him in *Bellerophon*'s description book. It took courage to play such important roles in the ship because casualties were distributed disproportionately. Those on the superstructure suffered most, which was where many of the officers and the best of the experienced seamen were stationed.

Throughout Nelson's fleet, captains suffered 22 per cent casualties, lieutenants 19 per cent and marine officers 18 per cent. Some junior officers were, of course, stationed on the gun-decks below and their relative invulnerability reduced the proportion of officer casualties. Masters on the quarterdeck suffered 30 per cent casualties, and boatswains, who served on the forecastle, 33 per cent. The courageous Thomas Robinson, the boatswain who had trained *Colossus*'s crew before he switched to *Bellerophon*, never went home to his wife and two small children in Portsea. Eleven days after the battle he was one of many to die in the foetid, overcrowded, fly-infested misery of Gibraltar hospital.

While *Bellerophon* battled *Aigle*, Thomas Robinson's previous charges on *Colossus* were giving a good account of themselves. Captain James Morris had also chosen to open up with his starboard guns to create a smokescreen as he approached the line. The French *Swiftsure* was nearest him, and she had just been forced to throw back her sails and turn away to avoid a collision with the ships in front, which left her vulnerable to *Colossus*. Morris's double-shotted larboard broadside killed seventeen of her men. *Colossus* was firing furiously from both sides of the ship but Morris could see nothing to starboard through the smoke until the French ship *Argonaute* emerged from it and crunched against *Colossus*'s starboard side. There was nothing that either captain could do to avoid the collision in which gun-ports were ripped away and men knocked off their feet before the yards locked together with the two ships feet away from each other.

Once again, the British ship was at a disadvantage. *Colossus*'s 32- and 18-pounders were up against heavier French batteries on either side. According to *Argonaute*'s officers, Captain Epron had held his fire until now so *Colossus* 'received the full brunt of our double-shotted broadside'. For perhaps twenty minutes the two ships swept each other's decks with grape and canister. But, unlike *Bellerophon*, *Colossus* had twelve 32-pounder carronades. They won the battle above decks and fourteen of *Argonaute*'s officers were killed or wounded. After a short time it seemed to Morris that nobody was alive on his opponent's deck, and most of her men might have taken refuge below from where they continued a furious battery with their guns.

Colossus was suffering, too, from the continuous fire of *Argonaute*'s lower-deck guns. Her master was killed, her boatswain mortally wounded, and she had at least a hundred other men down. Nelson had just promoted Sir Edward Berry's cousin William Forster from midshipman in *Victory* to acting lieutenant in *Colossus*, and in his eagerness to emulate his dashing relative, the Norfolk boy was one of those who fell. Captain Morris himself was grazed by a shot on the outside of his knee. It was painful and he bound a tourniquet round it to stop the bleeding, but he refused to leave the quarterdeck.

Argonaute's officers reported that, after half an hour or more, 'the Captain judged the moment propitious and gave orders to board; but at the minute that we were all coming up from below, the English, who had heard the order, braced their main-sail aback and began to draw clear'. However, Morris's log reported that it was the French ship that pulled away. Most probably, as with *Bellerophon* and *Aigle*, the swell that had been rocking both ships up and down now unlocked their yard arms, pulled them apart and set them drifting into the smoke.

Argonaute's officers might have exaggerated her chances of success against *Colossus*, but once again a promising opportunity to board a British ship had been frustrated. *Argonaute* withdrew, according to Morris with only a gun in the after part of her cabin still firing, which is consistent with her officers' assertion that the men had left their guns to board. It is a tribute to the training of *Colossus*'s crew, a bunch that two years before had looked so unpromising, that *Argonaute* had suffered over two hundred casualties. Men like the brothers Venus from North Shields, though pressed into the navy, had turned out to be first-class recruits. William Venus was promoted midshipman after Trafalgar and went on to become a lieutenant.

Colossus had no leisure to pause. She was still fighting the French *Swiftsure* on her larboard quarter and the wounded Dionisio Galiano had cleverly manoeuvred *Bahama* into a position from which she could fire on both *Bellerophon* and *Colossus* further off.

Montañés was next in action. She had never got into position and was out to windward of the line of battle, about level with *Aigle* and *Swiftsure*. After firing on the approaching *Bellerophon*, *Aigle* had interrupted her line of fire and *Swiftsure* was in her way to leeward. Unable to move, her officers found it impossible to see through 'the dense smoke in which we were enveloped on every side, so that with this and with the calm it was difficult to distinguish the colours'. She ceased fire until suddenly the British *Achille* emerged. This ship, which Lieutenant Alejo Gutiérrez de Rubalcaba (who was below at the time), took for a three-decker, 'approached to place herself a pistol-shot from us, pouring a terrible fire into our larboard quarter, which caused great havoc among the people, to the hull and to the rigging'.

Montañés fell away. The seamen went into action, despite the bullets from Richard King's *Achille*, 'setting the topgallant sails and the main topmast staysail, with the intention of getting more headway'. They luffed up as they did so in order to bring their broadside to bear on *Achille*. But the British ship had slipped by, raking them as she rounded their stern. *Montañés* had to change direction sharply, bearing away before the wind again to avoid *Swiftsure* and *Argonaute*.

Gutiérrez' account more or less honestly represents the confusion that must soon have become widespread in both fleets. It was compounded for *Montañés* by the loss of the senior officers, Francisco Alcedo and Antonio Castaños. Captain Alcedo was killed and Castaños horribly wounded by *Achille*'s raking fire. Like *Colossus*, *Achille* was armed with twelve 32-pounder carronades as well as six 18-pounders, and their anti-personnel fire, directed at the quarterdeck, was ruinous. After some time Lieutenant Melitón Perez found Gutiérrez and told him that he was now in command.

When he reached the deck he realised that in continuing to sail westwards they had gone some way to leeward of the battle. He gave orders 'to luff up into the wind at once with the intention of filling the nearest gap to enter into action'. But once again friends and foes, including the British *Achille*, had disappeared into the enveloping smoke and he judged it unsafe to continue firing 'lest we hit our own ships'.

Revenge was leading another posse of British ships but had become isolated out in front. As *Revenge* sailed well, Collingwood had signalled Captain Robert Moorsom to keep a line of bearing from him. *Revenge* was on a slowly converging but almost parallel course with the remainder of Gravina's Squadron of Observation. Like other British ships, *Revenge* was under fire for some time before she replied. Down in the darkened lower deck William 'Nastyface' Robinson remembered, 'Many of our men thought it hard that the firing should be all on one side and became impatient to return the compliment.' But Captain Robert Moorsom, a steady North Yorkshireman, had made his wishes quite clear. 'We shall want all our shot when we get close in,' he had told them. 'Never mind their firing: when I fire a carronade from the quarterdeck, that will be a signal for you to begin, and I know you will do your duty as Englishmen.'

Finally they heard the carronade and instantly fired off their heavy, double-shotted guns. Moorsom bore in and steered for a gap between *San Ildefonso* and the French *Achille*. But these two ships closed up well. *Achille*'s captain, Louis Deniéport, was a seaman from Dieppe and another who owed his status as an officer to the Revolution. His men were all prepared to board and he forged ahead so that *Achille*'s jib boom ripped away *Revenge*'s mizen topsail as Moorsom tried to break through ahead of her. *Achille* failed narrowly to jam *Revenge* up against *San Ildefonso* and would have done so had not her mizen and main topsail been shot away at the crucial moment. 'Those ships we had thrown into disorder turned round, and made an attempt to board,' recalled Nastyface. One 'ran her bowsprit over our poop, with a number of her crew on it, and, in her fore rigging, two or three hundred men were ready to follow; but they caught a Tartar'.

They had indeed. *Revenge* was the most heavily armed 74 in the British fleet. On her main deck she had 24-pounders instead of the usual 18-pounders and on her forecastle and quarterdeck she had sixteen 32-pounder carronades with six 18-pounder carronades on the poop. These swung into action: 'Our marines with their small arms, and the carronades on the poop, loaded with canister shot, swept them off so fast, some into the water and some on the decks, that they were glad to sheer off.'

But Captain Moorsom's problems were not yet at an end. 'The Frenchman wore under my stern and I was obliged to endure a raking fire for a considerable time without being able to help myself, for all our ropes were cut to pieces in going down and the wind so light that we were a long time exposed to their fire before we got near.' He was being peppered and threatened with boarding by *San Ildefonso* on the other side and soon he perceived that a three-decker with a flag, which he made out as that of Admiral Gravina, was approaching his leeward quarter.

The French *Achille* raked *Revenge* repeatedly, dismounting three of her guns. On one occasion, Nastyface reported, 'what was termed a slaughtering one, came in at one of the lower deck ports, which killed and wounded nearly all at the gun'. Among them was the ship's cobbler, 'the very life of the ship's company, for he was ever the mirth of his mess, and on whatever duty he might be ordered, his spirits made light the labour'. At the gun he 'was so completely stunned by the head of another man being knocked against his, that no one doubted but that he was dead'. British sailors cleared their dead out of the way as they fell, so the cobbler was carried over 'to be committed to the deep, without any other ceremony than shoving him through the port'. Just as they were about to let him go he started kicking and they hurriedly pulled him back in again. He recovered so quickly that he fought the battle out. Afterwards the cobbler joked, 'It was well that I learned to dance; for if I had not shown you some of my steps, when you were about to throw me overboard, I should not be here now, but safe enough in Davy Jones's locker.'

He would have had plenty of company there. *Achille*'s own officers were falling fast under the British grape shot that was sweeping the upper decks. Once again, the carronade was proving its worth and extracting a heavy price in French blood. First, Pierre Montalembert, second-in-command, fell mortally wounded. Then Captain Louis Deniéport's thigh was broken by a grape shot before a second hit killed him outright. Sub-lieutenant Jean Jouan came up from the lower deck to take command. He lasted only ten minutes on the quarterdeck before he was hit in the chest.

It was a long, hard struggle and it was at least half an hour before any other British ship came near. Eventually *Defiance* came up to windward and engaged *San Ildefonso*, but at the same time the three-decker *Principe de Asturias* appeared to leeward. The much-damaged *Achille*, now commanded by a very junior officer, took the oppor- tunity to bear away into the smoke. *Principe de Asturias*, the Spanish flagship, with her 114 heavy guns, was a more than adequate replacement.

Revenge's chaplain, John Greenly, remembered that Captain Moor- som had told the men that 'he would act as Lord Nelson had always done, lay his ship alongside the largest he came near and would leave the rest to his men, they gave him three cheers and they fought like lions'. They needed to. Although Greenly's place was with the wounded on the orlop deck he kept going up to see what was happening, even though Moorsom twice ordered him off. Once he 'had a very narrow escape, a 42 pounder came within 6 inches of me, and entirely shattered a beam'. He found that he had been 'wounded in twenty places by splinters of shot that came close to me, but mere scratches'. Up there, as Nastyface put it colourfully, 'the shots were playing their pranks pretty freely, grape as well as canister, with single and double headed thunderers all joining in the frolic'. He reckoned that there was so much crossfire that the enemy must have been damaging their own ships.

Principe de Asturias had stopped *Defiance* breaking through the line but Midshipman Colin Campbell, in *Defiance*, had reckoned her fire pretty harmless at that time. Although she did considerable damage to *Defiance*'s rigging, she only killed one man. However, she was closer to *Revenge* and although she completed the destruction of the British ship's yards and rigging, her gunners were also firing grape and canister to kill.

'We had a dreadful carnage,' the chaplain reported. Twenty-eight men were killed and fifty-one wounded – forty-five seriously, accord- ing to the chaplain. The prime seamen turned over from the *Centurion*, who formed the core of *Revenge*'s crew, had suffered very badly. 'All our yards were shot away and topmasts and lower masts terribly mauled', and eight shots had gone through the copper below the waterline. Captain Moorsom, Greenly said, although slightly wounded in the cheek would not quit the deck and 'fought his ship as coolly as if at dinner'. But it is hardly surprising that Moorsom was 'not certain that our mode of attack was the best'. At this stage, between one thirty and two o'clock, almost all the eight ships of Collingwood's division that had broken the line had been isolated and severely battered. But their discipline, armament, rate of fire and resolution had saved them.

14

A Mere Matter of Fact

For about twenty minutes *Redoutable*'s men had been trying to drive the British from *Victory*'s upper works so that they could board her. Nelson knew that the French had spent months practising close fighting and boarding but *Victory*'s crew was both surprised and alarmed at the intense musketry, carronade fire and grenades that poured out of Jean-Jacques Lucas's ship. Captain Charles Adair, of the marines, was hit and he withdrew the remaining marines from the poop, taking up a less exposed position on the starboard gangway. Both senior marine lieutenants had been 'wounded dangerously' and taken to the cockpit. The junior lieutenant, Lewis Roteley, had also gone below to fetch more marines. Then Adair was shot for the second time, in the back of the neck, which killed him instantly.

At about one fifteen, when the battle reached its height, the most infamous musket ball in British history left a barrel high in *Redoutable*'s mizen top. Thirty feet below and fifteen yards to larboard Horatio Nelson was pacing the quarterdeck alongside Captain Hardy. He had just turned at the hatchway to face the stern when the lead ball, five-eighths of an inch wide, struck the epaulette on his left shoulder. It plunged downward into his thorax, fractured two ribs, punctured a lung, severed his pulmonary artery and lodged in his spine, driving fragments of coat and gold lace before it. Nelson slumped to his knees, trying to support himself on his left arm. Hardy, who had been walking slightly ahead, turned to see his friend and admiral collapse into the slicks of blood left by the earlier destruction of Nelson's secretary. Marine Sergeant James Secker, Able Seaman James Sherman and another sailor eased Nelson from the deck and shuffled towards the hatchway. 'They have done for me at last, Hardy,' Nelson gasped, through great pain. 'My backbone is shot through.'

Any naval commander who led from the front invited death in battle, and this was not the first time that Nelson thought he had been fatally injured. At Tenerife in 1797, when his arm was smashed by a musket ball, he collapsed into his barge muttering, 'I am a dead man,' to his stepson Josiah. At the Nile, his forehead slashed open to the skull by a splinter, he fell into the arms of Edward Berry, saying, 'I am killed. Remember me to my wife.'

The men in *Redoutable*'s tops were certainly aiming to kill Nelson if they identified him, but even from close range it was not easy to hit a particular person with a musket. The weapon was inaccurate; a targeted man was sometimes concealed by thick smoke or protected by intervening obstacles as he moved; the platform from which the sniper had fired was rocking and swinging dramatically. Nearly all of the officers on the quarterdeck were hit. Nelson was merely unlucky to be wounded fatally.

In the mid-nineteenth century an account appeared purporting to have been written by Sergeant Robert Guillemard in which he claimed to have been the assassin. Further investigation suggested that it had been invented by two writers who published the story in a book of adventures from the Napoleonic Wars. Second Lieutenant Lewis Roteley, who led twenty fresh marines to the deck just afterwards, was adamant that his men, furious that Nelson had been shot, wiped out the sniper in the mizen top.

The marines became exasperated. I was now in command, and the first order I gave was to clear the mizzen top, when every musket was levelled at that top, and in five minutes not a man was left alive in it. Some Frenchman has vaunted that he shot Nelson and survived the battle, and I have heard a book has been published so stating, but it must be a romance. I know the man was shot in five minutes after Nelson fell.

The man who came to be known as 'the man who shot the man who shot Nelson', although he never made such a definite assertion, was Midshipman John Pollard. With the fifty-six-year-old signal quartermaster, John King, Pollard remained on the poop when the marines left. He later wrote that 'my attention was arrested by seeing in the tops of *Redoutable* a number of soldiers in a crouching position, loading and directing their fire on the quarterdeck of the *Victory*'. Pollard pointed them out to King, and 'there being a number of spare muskets on the signal chest for the use of the marines, I took one of them, King supplying me with ball cartridge from two barrels kept on the after part of the poop for the use of the marines'. Since the marines had left the poop Pollard made free with their ammunition and was joined for a shot or two by another midshipman, Edward Collingwood. 'I remained firing at the top till not a man was to be seen; the last one I discovered coming down the mizen rigging, and from my fire he fell also' Just before he fired this last shot, 'King the quartermaster in the act of giving me the last parcel of ball cartridge was shot through the head and fell dead before me'.

While Pollard and Roteley's marines concentrated on avenging Nelson, *Redoutable*'s soldiers and sailors were getting much the better of the general firefight, and in fifteen minutes *Victory*'s decks were almost cleared. About eighteen seamen and marines were killed and twenty-two wounded, including Lieutenant George Bligh, shot in the head, and Midshipman Alexander Palmer, shot through the thigh. As he directed this musketry and the grenade-throwing, Jean-Jacques Lucas felt a surge of pride. His keen young officers were standing by their boarding-nets armed with carbines, pistols and cutlasses and waiting for his command. The guns and the two big carronades on

Victory's forecastle and quarterdeck had been abandoned and the guns below had temporarily fallen silent.

Lucas thought his moment of glory had come. 'The upper deck of the *Victory* became deserted, and she again ceased firing, but it proved difficult to board her because of the motion of the two vessels, and the height of the *Victory*'s upper tier and battery.' Eager to secure his triumph, Lucas 'gave the order to cut the supports of the main-yard so that it might serve as a bridge'. While the ropes and slings were cut away, Midshipman Jacques Yon led four seamen on to *Victory*'s forecastle by climbing up the anchor. To cheers from the French crew they emerged unscathed and reported it deserted. The yard fell and Lucas's boarders swarmed towards it.

Suddenly, at this critical moment, *Téméraire* appeared out of the billowing smoke and crashed, out of control, into *Redoutable*'s other bow.

By now Pierre Villeneuve should also have been fatally injured. After successive raking broadsides from four ships almost everybody else on *Bucentaure*'s quarterdeck had been hit, but the French admiral led a charmed life. His flagship, though, was helpless, dismasted, surrounded and unable to move.

Once again Villeneuve was frustrated, as each of his contingency plans failed. His supporting frigate *Hortense* had specific orders to come to the aid of vessels under pressure and tow them away from trouble. Captain Louis La Marre La Meillerie should have made some attempt to rescue his admiral, however suicidal that course of action might have seemed. But evidently La Marre had no ambition to be covered in the glory that Villeneuve had promised to enterprising captains of frigates, especially not posthumously. *Hortense* made no attempt to help and suffered no casualties from dawn to dusk. Villeneuve had kept one of *Bucentaure*'s boats in the water so that he could transfer to another vessel if his flagship was dismasted. He called for it now, but it was no longer there. It had either been shot to pieces or smashed by falling masts. The other boats had all been riddled by shot.

By now most of the guns in *Bucentaure*'s 24-pounder battery had been knocked over and bodies were heaped around them. The men still fit to fight were sent down to the 36-pounder battery while sailors worked to clear the debris from in front of the starboard guns. On the quarterdeck a splinter smashed Daudignon's left hand and another went straight through his lower abdomen. Lieutenant Fulcran Fournier was called up from his post on the lower deck to take command of the ship. Villeneuve was remarking to Mathieu Prigny, his chief of staff, on how extraordinary it was that 'he was spared amidst so many balls grape and splinters' when Prigny collapsed, his leg pierced by a piece of wood.

For a moment a gap appeared in the banks of smoke surrounding the ship, and Villeneuve was able to assess his situation. He saw that his centre and rear were giving ground, that the *Bucentaure* was the furthest to windward of the entire fleet and that there were several undamaged ships to his leeward. Sensing a chance of escape, he ordered Fournier to use the foremast to run before the wind towards safety. But there was neither room nor time for such a manoeuvre. As *Bucentaure* got under way, the navigating officer, Blaise Gaudran, was shot and the jib-boom broke against *Santísima Trinidad*. A moment later *Conqueror* shot down *Bucentaure*'s foremast, leaving her completely dismasted. Villeneuve hailed the *Santísima Trinidad* to ask for a boat and a tow, but her crew was fully occupied with *Neptune*'s attack on her stern and did not answer.

Villeneuve decided to surrender in order to prevent further deaths. It was just after two o'clock. Captain Magendie, who returned to the quarterdeck at this moment, estimated that they had 450 casualties out of a complement of about 870. In reality the ship had probably suffered about two hundred. The Imperial Eagle had been shot to pieces and Fournier had the shards thrown into the sea, 'not wishing that the relics should provide a trophy for the enemy', along with all the ship's signal books. They removed their ensign from the stump of the mainmast but *Conqueror* was still firing so they waved handkerchiefs in her direction until she stopped.

On perceiving this pathetic acknowledgement of defeat, Captain Israel Pellew sent his senior marine, Captain James Atcherley, in a cutter to take possession of the *Bucentaure*. As soon as he had lowered the boat Pellew moved on to help *Neptune,* with *Santísima Trinidad* and the other ships ahead. When Atcherley came aboard, Villeneuve, Magendie and Contamine approached him.

'To whom have I the honour of surrendering?' Villeneuve asked.

'To Captain Pellew of *Conqueror*,' replied the marine.

'It is a satisfaction to me that it is to one so fortunate as Sir Edward Pellew that I have lowered my flag,' said the ever-polite Villeneuve, pleased to surrender to a man renowned for his fighting and his chivalry.

'It is his brother, sir,' mumbled Atcherley in confused apology.

'His brother?' Villeneuve stumbled, then recovered his wit: 'What? Are there two of them? *Hélas!*'

Seeing that *Conqueror* was now fiercely engaged with *Santísima Trinidad*, Atcherley had the senior French officers and their junior aides rowed over to *Mars*, which had drifted towards them. There, according to Midshipman Thomas Robinson, the exchanges were less courteous:

The French commander in chief came aboard about the middle of the battle and seeing Captain Duff lying dead upon Deck began to smile to some of his attendants which one of our sailors observing came running up to him and laid hold of him and said when my captain lived he was able to avenge an insult now he is dead it is my duty to revenge it for him at the same time throwing Villeneuve from him covered the dead body with a flag that was laying near him.

Like *Victory, Téméraire* was taller than *Redoutable,* but for close-quarter anti-personnel fighting she was much more heavily armed than *Victory*. The seven 32-pounder carronades and sixteen 18-pounder guns on the larboard side of her upper deck and superstructure commanded *Redoutable*'s decks. As the two ships collided she fired off a full broadside of grape and canister at what was almost the whole of Lucas's crew as they massed to storm aboard *Victory*. It was a massacre – a shattering moment for Lucas. 'It is impossible to describe the carnage produced by the murderous broadside of this ship,' he reported later. 'More than two hundred of our brave men were killed or wounded by it.'

In this one decisive moment *Téméraire* turned *Redoutable* from a ship about to fight for a prize to one now fighting for her life. Lucas escaped the volley with only a slight wound, but his second-in-command, Henri Dupotet, fell with a ball through his left knee, Captain Charles Chafange, leading the infantry of the 16th Regiment, was killed and Captain Louis Guillaume, leading the marines of the 79th, was seriously wounded. The captain and lieutenant of marine artillery were both killed leading the grenadiers. Six other officers were killed and six wounded. *Redoutable* should probably have surrendered immediately, but she kept fighting.

Victory opened up again, with her heavy guns firing downwards through *Redoutable*'s hull. Ostensibly this was done to avoid hitting *Téméraire*, but it was angry fire, perhaps influenced by the injury to Nelson, and calculated to sink the French ship. It also caused hideous casualties in the crowded operating theatre in the orlop deck, killing or further injuring many of those lying wounded there. Lucas ordered his men to fire into *Téméraire* whatever guns had not been dismounted by the collision, but the British ship had much the better of what could only be an uneven artillery duel. The heroic Lieutenant François Briamant, whose previous fighting record was tremendous, had survived the attempt to board and was commanding on the lower deck. He died, hit three times by the crossfire from the two British ships.

At this moment the much-damaged *Fougueux* emerged from the

smoke on *Téméraire*'s other side. *Téméraire* fired her starboard broadside at *Fougueux* before all four ships drifted into each other. By this time *Fougueux* was totally disabled and powerless to avoid collision, 'having the topsail and lower yards shattered and all in disorder, having not the slightest catspaw to give us steerage way', according to François Bazin. *Téméraire*'s seven starboard 32-pounder carronades swivelled round and sprayed murderous grape over *Fougueux*'s decks. Captain Louis Baudouin, whose conduct on the day could not be faulted, was hit in the chest and lost consciousness. François Bazin was wounded but took over command and attempted to resist, sending men to repel *Téméraire*'s boarders and firing what guns could still be made to work. At first they even forced the *Téméraire* crew on to the defensive, but the British carronades gradually cut down those Frenchmen who dared remain above decks.

Bazin called for the first lieutenant, only to be told that he was dead. The second lieutenant was mortally wounded and the third had a ball in the leg. The fourth lieutenant reported that the main battery was nearly silenced and Sub-lieutenant Jean Drudésit said that he had only fifteen men left in the 18-pounder battery. Twenty seamen and six marines from *Téméraire* had a foothold on *Fougueux* now and Bazin gave the order to cease fire. He dragged himself down to the captain's cabin and threw the box of signals and instructions into the sea. Lieutenant Thomas Kennedy found Captain Baudouin dead on the quarterdeck. Shortly afterwards Bazin was taken to *Téméraire* to surrender formally to Captain Eliab Harvey.

Victory finally disentangled herself from *Redoutable* and got her head to northward. Harvey now hailed Jean-Jacques Lucas and offered him the chance to surrender to avoid further slaughter. Lucas ordered some soldiers standing nearby to fire back in reply. Immediately after that *Redoutable*'s mainmast fell on to *Téméraire* and the English ship's two remaining topmasts fell in turn on to *Redoutable*. Despite Lucas's bravado, his ship was now little more than a floating heap of debris. The poop looked as if it had been crushed, the helm, rudder and stern post had been smashed to splinters. The stern and the decks were shot through and all the guns were smashed or dismounted. An 18-pounder on the gun-deck and a 32-pounder carronade on the forecastle had exploded, causing many casualties. The hull was riddled with shot that had passed straight through it, deck beams were shattered, port-lids torn away. Four of the six pumps no longer worked. The quarterdeck ladders were broken. The decks were strewn with dead bodies, and many injured men were trapped under debris. Some tarred canvas at the stern had caught fire. Henri Dupotet gathered the surgeons and those passing powder to put it out.

Grenades had also set fire to *Téméraire* and one had rolled dangerously close to the powder room where the master-at-arms was credited with saving the ship. For some time *Téméraire* also stopped firing while the blazes were extinguished. Finally Lucas decided to surrender, but his flag had already fallen with the mizen mast so he had no sign to show to the British. Unable to leave the quarterdeck, he had difficulty communicating his intention to his own people. When Lieutenant John Wallace from *Téméraire* boarded *Redoutable* one of his marines was bayoneted before it could be made clear to everyone concerned that the fighting had ended.

Nelson heard the British cheers that greeted this surrender as his lungs slowly filled with blood. Three separate witnesses recorded what happened in *Victory*'s cockpit during what was the most minutely described hero's death in British history.

Nelson had always admired prints of Benjamin West's painting, *The Death of General Wolfe*, the hero of the Seven Years' War who had died in the hour of victory at Québec. Nelson had even met the artist at Fonthill Abbey, Wiltshire, in 1800, and had asked him why he had never painted anything else like it. 'Because, my lord, there are no more subjects,' West replied. 'Damn it!' said Nelson. 'I didn't think of that.'

It came as no surprise to anyone that, just days after news of Nelson's own death had reached London, West had struck a bargain with the engraver James Heath for a print of the scene. Such detailed engravings took years to complete, but on publication it was a sensational bestseller. For authenticity West made portrait sketches of around thirty of *Victory*'s officers, sailors and marines. But he chose to set the hero's death on *Victory*'s quarterdeck rather than on the crowded, dimly lit orlop deck far below. A painting by Arthur Devis for a rival publication that showed Nelson's death as it actually happened enraged West:

> Wolfe must not die like a common soldier under a Bush, neither should Nelson be represented dying in the gloomy hold of a ship, like a sick man in a Prison Hole . . . No Boy, said West, would be animated by a representation of Nelson dying like an ordinary man, His feelings must be roused & His mind enflamed by a scene great & extraordinary. A mere matter of fact will never produce this effect.

Arthur Devis worked in the rival stream of English painting that took the illusion of documentary realism one stage further: he produced a record so accurate of Nelson's situation at his death that in 1999 the picture helped *Victory*'s curator rediscover the exact spot in the ship where Nelson died. His strategy was to take 'a mere matter of fact' and attempt to imbue it with the numinous significance of a religious scene. To twenty-first-century eyes, Devis was right and West was wrong. But Devis lied too: the uncluttered serenity of his painting belies the noisy confusion and agony around the dying hero.

Alexander Scott, *Victory*'s chaplain and Nelson's right-hand man, was a nervous intellectual, temperamentally ill-suited to the chaplain's traditional battle station in what he described as 'a butcher's shambles'. After watching friends come in horribly mangled he lost control, tore up the slippery ladders gasping for air, and reached the quarterdeck just in time to see Nelson shot. Immediately sobered, he followed those carrying the admiral back down to the cockpit. Surgeon Beatty had just determined that Hardy's secretary, Thomas Whipple, was dead, despite the apparent absence of any wound to his body, when his attention was caught by a whisper going round that the admiral was there, gravely wounded.

With the help of purser Walter Burke, Nelson was laid on a bed in the midshipmen's berth behind the larboard cable tier. The space normally occupied by casualties was already full. 'Ah, Mr. Beatty, you can do nothing for me. I have but a short time to live: my back is shot through,' Nelson said. He had made a study of a similar case that Beatty had treated a year ago and recognised the symptoms in himself. Beatty removed his clothes and examined him thoroughly. His probe confirmed Nelson's own diagnosis: the bullet had indeed lodged in the spine. There was no exit wound. 'Doctor, I told you so. Doctor, I am gone,' said Nelson, and then low, after a short pause, 'I have to leave Lady Hamilton, and my adopted daughter Horatia, as a legacy to my country.' He said that he had felt the bullet break his back, that he felt blood gushing into his breast and that he had lost all sensation in his lower body. They were all symptoms that Beatty and he had discussed with regard to the surgeon's previous case. Beatty accepted that nothing could be done for Nelson and left him with the grief-stricken Scott, along with Walter Burke and his servants Gaetano Spedillo and William Chevalier.

According to Scott, Nelson was in agonising pain. It was oppressively hot and stuffy and *Victory*'s heavy guns rolled and thundered five feet overhead. They responded to his requests of 'Fan, fan' and 'Drink, drink' with lemonade, wine and water. In his lucid intervals Nelson said short prayers with Scott.

To the south *Royal Sovereign* and *Santa Ana*, whose exchanges had begun the battle, were still firing at each other and the ships about them. Collingwood's young *protégé* from Durham, George Castle, was shocked 'to see many brave seamen mangled so, some with their heads half shot away, others with their entrails mashed lying panting on the deck'. In *Royal Sovereign* forty-seven men were killed, and ninety-four wounded. Collingwood's leg was badly bruised by a splinter and what he took to be 'the wind from a great shot' hurt his back as it flew past him. But, once again, the superior quality of British cannon and carronade fire meant that, in a straight duel, the Royal Navy inflicted more damage. Casualties on board *Santa Ana* were almost double those on *Royal Sovereign,* and Admiral Ignacio de Álava lay seriously wounded in the head.

At about ten past two *Santa Ana*'s firing petered out and many in *Royal Sovereign* thought that she had surrendered. Instead, she crossed ahead of *Royal Sovereign* and raked her. *Royal Sovereign* brought her starboard guns to bear and fired back. Jolted with the motion, *Santa Ana*'s fore- and mainmasts fell over the side, and at two twenty she surrendered. At almost the same time *Royal Sovereign*'s mainmast fell too. George Castle found that 'She rolled so much after her masts were gone we could scarcely fight the lower-deck, the water was almost knee deep.' The one benefit, he said, was that the seawater washed away the blood.

In his moment of triumph, Collingwood received news from *Victory*. A boat came alongside and Lieutenant Alexander Hills climbed aboard, asking to see him. He told Collingwood, who had a bandage round his own leg now, that Nelson had been wounded. Collingwood asked if Nelson's wound was dangerous. Hills 'hesitated; then said he hoped it was not; but I saw the fate of my friend in his eye; for his look told what his tongue could not utter'.

Collingwood realised that he might now have to take command. At three o'clock he signalled to Henry Blackwood in *Euryalus* to come and take *Royal Sovereign* in tow because his ship was incapable of movement. He then sent Henry Blackwood on board *Santa Ana* to fetch Admiral Álava. Blackwood returned soon afterwards with Captain Gardoquí, who delivered Álava's sword and the news that the admiral was at death's door. With the humanity that was characteristic of him, Collingwood sent Gardoquí back with instructions to take care of Álava. It was a generous gesture that he would later regret.

The great *Santísima Trinidad* was now under attack from *Neptune*, *Agamemnon* and *Conqueror*. Fremantle skilfully manoeuvred *Neptune* into a position across her stern and repeatedly raked her. Her captain, Xavier de Uriarte, tried to make sail to break out of the ring of British ships that had now formed around *Santísima Trinidad*, but the moment she did so they concentrated their fire on her rigging. Admiral Báltasar Cisneros saw that the masts were in danger before he was carried away injured. *Neptune* and *Conqueror* maintained a better rate of fire than *Santísima Trinidad*, which had already lost a number of guns. Firing from advantageous positions, they were causing more casualties than they were suffering although William Badcock on *Neptune* was alarmed when one man was killed and three wounded close to him in the choking smoke of the main deck. As on other ships, most of *Neptune*'s casualties were experienced seamen working on the quarterdeck. Of only nine men killed in action, one was the veteran gunner's mate Edward Nosworthy, who had survived the Nile, leaving his young son an orphan in the ship. But he and his cosmopolitan shipmates delivered some of the most impressive gunnery in the British fleet with their heavy guns and 24-pounder carronades.

At two forty the Spanish ship's huge mainmast came down with a tremendous crash. Able Seaman James Martin, in *Neptune*, recalled that 'We then gave them three Hearty cheairs and they did the same but we accompanyed our with a Broad sider.' *Santísima Trinidad* swung away to leeward bringing *Neptune* on to her beam, and at once her mizen mast came tumbling down. It made a vivid impression on those who saw it:

This tremendous fabric gave a deep roll with the swell to leeward, then back to windward; and on her return every mast went by the board, leaving her an unmanageable hulk on the water. Her immense topsails had every reef out, her royals were sheeted home but lowered, and the falling of this mass of spars, sails, and rigging, plunging into the water at the muzzles of our guns, was one of the most magnificent sights I ever beheld.

With almost all her guns masked by the fallen sails, *Santísima Trinidad*'s fire died away.

On seeing her without a flag and hearing the cheers, *Africa* sent a lieutenant to take her surrender, but Uriarte informed him politely that his ship had not struck. About ten minutes later her foremast fell 'along on her deck with the mast head on her stearn'. The second-in-command, Ignacio Olaeta, came below wounded and told Cisneros that *Santísima Trinidad* was totally dismasted, that many guns were out of action, and the others were unable to fire because the decks were smothered with a chaos of masts, rigging and sails, and strewn with dead and wounded. Soon afterwards Uriarte was brought down, knocked unconscious by a splinter wound to the head. He had been the last unwounded officer of those stationed above decks. Cisneros sent his aide, Francisco Basurto, to direct the third-in-command to consult the officers who remained on duty and authorised them to strike if they felt there was no other course.

At about three o'clock an officer draped a Union Jack over the starboard quarter, hailed *Neptune* and told them they had struck. According to Martin, a couple of guns opened up from *Santísima Trinidad*'s middle deck, to which *Neptune* replied forcibly, but then the surrender was explained or enforced and *Santísima Trinidad* was silent. The crew of *Neptune* had achieved their ambition: the largest ship in the world was their prize. *Santísima Trinidad* had ninety-seven dead on board and more than two hundred wounded. Hercules Robinson, who was watching the battle from the frigate *Euryalus*, wrote later that 'If I were to select the most seamanlike act I witnessed I should name the "Neptune" rounding to on the quarter of the "Santissima Trinidada" and keeping the ship in command until she brought down her opponant's three masts altogether.'

Fremantle immediately ordered men to inspect *Neptune*'s rigging, yards and masts and carry out what repairs they could. Others were sent down to fetch more shot since they had almost used up the supplies they had laid in. 'We had now Been Enverloped with Smoak Nearly three Howers,' remarked James Martin. 'Upon this Ships Striking the Smoak Clearing a way then we had a vew of the Hostle fleet thay ware scattred a Round us in all Directions Sum Dismasted and Sum were Compleat wrecks Sum had Left of Fireng and sum ware Engagen with Redoubled furey it was allmost imposeble to Distinguish to what Nation thay Belonged.'

As they planned the wars of the twenty-first century, military theorists in America studied the battle of Trafalgar and declared it a dramatic illustration of the importance of what they called 'command and control'. According to Edward Smith of the Pentagon's Command and Control Research Program, writing in 2002, successful commanders push their enemy 'beyond the edge of chaos'. This, Smith judged, was exactly what Nelson had done at Trafalgar when he managed to fight at the outer limit of his own ability to command and control his forces, but just beyond that of his opponent. He argued that 'The real key to Nelson's success was the effect that his bold manoeuvre had on the French and Spanish ability to control their forces and the chaos it created.' Nelson's ships could still perform well because of what Smith called the 'cerebral networking' between the commander and his key subordinates, formed by many years of shared combat experience and by thorough explanation of his battle plan. Nelson knew that his captains would perceive the developing battle in the way he expected them to, and that they would possess, in Smith's words, 'a shared situational awareness . . . and carry out mutually supportive actions without further directions'.

Villeneuve's situation was different. Many of his captains distrusted him, each other, or both, and they struggled – due to lack of experience – to co-ordinate even simple pre-battle manoeuvres. Forming and holding a crude line under fire was the limit of their ability. Nelson pushed them over it into confusion and self-doubt with the impact of his 'pell-mell' battle. From the moment he broke the line he forced on them his own pace of operations. Separated from each other and from Villeneuve, few managed an effective response and Villeneuve himself was unable to control his forces in any meaningful way.

Smith concluded, 'The range of combinations of scale/scope and pace of operations that the French and Spanish could handle, their edge of chaos, clearly lay inside that of the British fleet. This gave the British the decisive advantage in what was otherwise a symmetric conflict.'

Undoubtedly Nelson laid great stress on communication of his plan and the importance of well-informed initiative from his captains. His conversation in the garden of Merton Place with Captain Richard Keats amply demonstrated his desire to confuse and confound the enemy, to wreck their decision-making, while imposing on them his own pattern of operation.

Once he had brought on the battle he wanted, Nelson was confident in the power of close-range British gunnery, on superior armament and manoeuvre as well as in rate of fire. His faith was well founded, as had already been proved. In some instances the Franco-Spanish attempt to counter the power of British carronades with overwhelming small-arms fire had worked, but they had not yet won a battle between two ships. The main batteries on the British ships repeatedly dominated their adversaries, whatever they could do above decks. Elsewhere, the packing of British quarterdecks, forecastles and poops with heavy carronades had proved devastatingly efficient, knocking ships out of action through the destruction of rigging and key personnel.

Confused by smoke and demoralised by their first encounters with British gunnery, ships such as *Montañés* and *Argonaute* fell away rather than closing in around isolated enemies who might, with their help, have been put under greater pressure. Ships such as *San Justo* whose power to manoeuvre was inhibited by an inexperienced crew, failed to engage closely at all. The result was that the first British ships to reach the Franco-Spanish line survived even though they were outnumbered by sixteen to eight when Nelson intended them to have a numerical advantage of fifteen to twelve.

Now, belatedly, a stream of fresh British vessels was arriving with some headway to manoeuvre. Most appeared towards the rear, giving the British a local numerical advantage. Some were in a position to intervene at the heart of the action and to support or attack wherever their presence seemed most useful. What their captains now chose to do would have a decisive effect on the outcome of the battle.

15

The Edge of Chaos

Further to the south, in what was left of the Combined Fleet's line, *Pluton* was still fighting hard. She was firing on *Belleisle* who could barely respond because the guns facing *Pluton* were covered by the fallen wreckage of the mizen mast and its sails. Despite the Royal Navy's success elsewhere it looked, for a while, as if *Belleisle* might be the only British ship forced to strike as retreating French and Spanish ships poured their fire into her. *San Justo* and *San Leandro* found her a convenient target, as did *Aigle* when she had pulled away from *Bellerophon*. At ten past two Paul Nicolas, the young marine lieutenant, 'was at the time under the break of the poop aiding in running a carronade, when a cry of "Stand clear there! Here it comes!" made me look up, and at that instant the mainmast fell over the bulwarks just above me. This ponderous mass made the ship's whole frame shake.' It just missed crushing all those who remained on the poop.

Esprit-Tranquille Maistral, captain of the French *Neptune,* was eventually driven from his position near *Téméraire* by British reinforcements. At two thirty he closed in on *Belleisle*, took up a position from which to rake her bow, and by two forty-five had shot away her foremast and bowsprit. Refusing to surrender, *Belleisle* raised a Union Jack on a pike on the stump of her foremast. But she was being shot to pieces and, as Nicolas admitted, was unable to manoeuvre to return

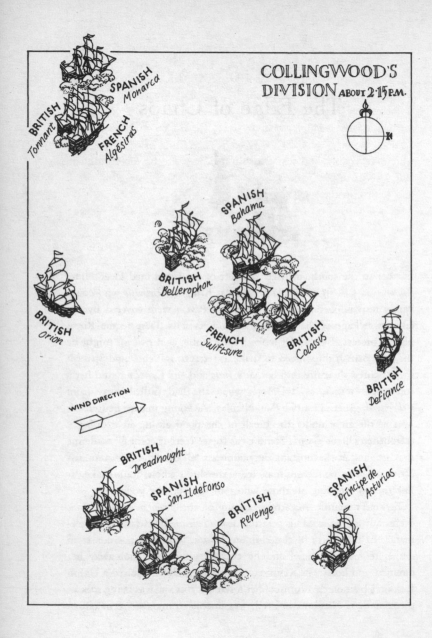

COLLINGWOOD'S
DIVISION ABOUT 2·15 P.M.

N

BRITISH
Tonnant

SPANISH
Monarca

FRENCH
Algésiras

SPANISH
Bahama

BRITISH
Bellerophon

BRITISH
Orion

FRENCH
Swiftsure

BRITISH
Colossus

BRITISH
Defiance

WIND DIRECTION

BRITISH
Dreadnought

SPANISH
San Ildefonso

BRITISH
Revenge

SPANISH
Príncipe de
Asturias

fire: 'The only means at all in our power of bringing our battery towards the enemy, was to use the sweeps [long oars] out of the gunroom ports; to these we had recourse, but without effect, for even in ships under perfect command they prove almost useless.'

Lieutenant John Owen recalled that, at this time, 'The Captain, seeing me actively employed in my duty, was kind enough to bring me a bunch of grapes, and seemed pleased when I told him that our men were doing nobly, and that the ship had been greatly distinguished.' But, as Nicolas put it, *Belleisle* was now 'a mere hulk covered in wreck and rolling in the swell'.

A short distance away *Algésiras* and *Tonnant* were still blasting away at one another. The sides of the two ships were grinding together and on the lower deck the guns had to be run back inside their ports to fire, creating even more noise and clouds of choking smoke. Considering his position critical Admiral Charles Magon strode round *Algésiras* encouraging his men and cheering his officers with a display of cool courage. Although pale with loss of blood after a splinter had torn open his thigh, he refused to leave the action for treatment.

On *Tonnant*, quartermaster's mate James White, a thirty-three-year-old from Somerset, was captain of a carronade on the poop. Suddenly he found one of his big toes hanging by a piece of skin. He cut it off with his knife and bound the wound with his neckcloth. He was as reluctant to go below as the French admiral he was fighting: 'No, sir, I am not the fellow to go below for such a scratch as that. I wish to give the beggars a few more hard pills before I have done with them.' Moments later, when his 18-pounder carronade's carriage was smashed, White hopped over to another.

Although their main and mizen topmasts had fallen some time ago, James White's shipmates were threatening to board *Algésiras* and the few Frenchmen still above deck were forced to defend themselves desperately. Laurent Le Tourneur was badly hurt in the shoulder, the navigating officer, Pierre Leblon-Plassan, was shot in the chest and so was First Lieutenant Luc Morel. Blazing wads from *Tonnant*'s guns set the boatswain's storeroom on fire and three men burned to death before the blaze could be extinguished. *Tonnant* had also caught fire and used her fire-engine to spray water on both ships.

Daniel Fitzpatrick, a twenty-eight-year-old from Kilkenny who, in April, had been given twenty-four lashes for theft, leapt across the gap between the ships and ran up the French rigging. Cutting away one of *Algésiras*'s four ensigns, he tied it round his waist, and darted back towards *Tonnant*. Just as he was climbing across a rifleman shot him and he pitched into the water. By now the battered crew of *Algésiras* had abandoned its 18-pounder battery and everyone fit to serve a gun had gathered in the lower 36-pounder battery. As he tried to rally his men for one final effort, Magon was hit by a bullet in the chest and fell dead. News of their admiral's death spread though the ship just as *Algésiras*'s mizen and mainmast fell, tearing away the rigging and hurling the remaining sharp-shooters into the sea. Both ships' boats had been shot to pieces so those in the water could only cling to wreckage and hope to survive until the shooting stopped.

Fourteen of the French ship's 36-pounders had been dismounted and most of the starboard guns were now masked by fallen sails. They double-loaded the few forward guns that could be fired at *Tonnant* and their impact completed the destruction of her stern, holing her below the waterline. Her replying broadside finally drove the French from their guns.

Led by Second Lieutenant Charles Bennett and Marine Lieutenant Arthur Ball, *Tonnant*'s boarders cheered and rushed on to *Algésiras*. They found Magon's body at the foot of the poop ladder, then came face to face with the dangerously wounded Laurent Le Tourneur, who surrendered control of the ship. On *Algésiras* seventy-seven had been killed and 142 wounded. *Tonnant* had lost twenty-six killed and fifty wounded, each recorded in detail in the ship's muster book. Cornishman William Knight, who had been punished for drunkenness three times during Captain Tyler's brief period with the ship, had drunk his last.

As *Tonnant*'s boarding party took possession of the dismasted *Algésiras*, Lieutenant Benjamin Clement directed the fire of *Tonnant*'s forward guns against *Monarca*. According to the account of Manuel

Ferrer, *Monarca* was making three feet of water an hour, even after the men who could be spared had been transferred to the pumps. Not long after *Algésiras* surrendered *Monarca* did likewise and the flags that her captain Teódoro de Argumosa had nailed to the mast before he was wounded were taken down.

Benjamin Clement hailed *Monarca* to ask if they had struck. They replied that they had, so he went aft to tell First Lieutenant John Bedford, who ordered him to row over and take possession. All their boats had been holed, Clement recalled, but 'he told me I must try; so I went away in the Jolly Boat with 2 Men, and had not got above a quarter of the way, when the boat swampt'. Clement, who could not swim, was thoroughly alarmed but he was saved by the prompt action of the two other men in the boat. Charles Macnamara, a twenty-one-year-old black volunteer from Barbados, had been with the ship for almost a year. John McKay, aged thirty-eight, was an experienced Scottish quartermaster. They took hold of Clement on either side and supported him until he was able to get hold of the rope attached to the jolly-boat to enable it to be hoisted in. Clement hooked his leg between the rope and the boat, but every time the boat fell with the swell he was dragged under. Macnamara swam back to the ship for a rope and tied it under Clement's armpits. Then the crew hauled Clement up the ship's towering side and pulled him into a stern port.

With no boats, *Tonnant* was powerless to secure *Monarca* or to take men off *Algésiras*. The party that had boarded that ship under Charles Bennett remained in her as a prize crew, but their position would have been more comfortable if it had been possible to remove some of the French officers and fighting men.

Collingwood's first eight ships had attacked at an angle of seventy to eighty degrees to the enemy line. The ships that locked together, like *Tonnant* and *Algésiras*, lost headway and drifted to leeward. Most of the rest bore away downwind to avoid being raked, or to rake, or to avoid a collision. The result was that the course steered by the rear ships of

Gravina's division, seeking to reinforce their friends towards the centre, became easterly rather than northerly. In consequence the ships at the back of Collingwood's division found themselves chasing from almost astern at the same pace as their adversaries. Moreover, thanks to the light wind, the ships under full sail in the rear of the British columns had little more than a knot advantage over those drifting to leeward ahead of them.

This goes some way to explaining how they came to be an hour or even two hours behind the first ships to break the line. But at last the rear ships were coming up and the numerical disadvantage of the British in the rear was slowly evening out. By two o'clock a confused gun battle raged in this area and Gravina's ships split into two groups. *San Ildefonso* and *San Juan* held the wind and headed towards *Bellerophon*. *Achille*, then *Principe de Asturias* and *Berwick* headed further to leeward where *Argonauta* was fighting the British *Achille*. *Dreadnought*, *Thunderer* and *Defence* were pursuing to windward. In their eagerness to contribute to a battle that was literally drifting away from them, some of the late-arriving British ships indulged in a lot of ineffectual long-range gunnery. They also hit each other. *Swiftsure* shot away *Polyphemus*'s ensign halyards and Captain Redmill had to hail Captain Rutherford to ask him to cease firing on his friends.

Thunderer opened fire on *San Ildefonso* for a time before pushing on after *Principe de Asturias*. *Ildefonso*'s rigging was already badly damaged from her encounter with *Revenge*. Captain José de Vargas had gone below, wounded in the left arm by a splinter. The carpenter reported to Commander Anselmo Gomendio that the ship was leaking badly from some hits below the waterline, and he ordered men from the guns to operate the pumps. Gomendio was also fighting a fire on the quarterdeck and poop. George Hope in *Defence* caught up with *Berwick*, got alongside, and began to shoot it out at close range.

Cosme de Churruca in *San Juan Nepomuceno* was heading to support his friend Dionisio Alcalá Galiano whose ship *Bahama* was still exchanging shots with *Bellerophon* when he was cut off by John Conn's *Dreadnought*. This painfully slow three-decker had been ordered to take a line between the two columns, which had effectively become a short-cut. Under Collingwood, who had been her captain until a week before, *Dreadnought* had trained to fire three broadsides in three and a half minutes, a rate unsurpassed in the British fleet. Since the ship had over a hundred guns of heavier calibre than *San Juan*'s this was a starkly uneven contest.

Churruca had been directing both manoeuvre and fire on *San Juan* through his loud-hailer, choosing his targets economically and concentrating on accurate fire. He was just returning from the bows where he had been pointing a cannon at *Bellerophon* when a ball almost ripped his leg off at the top of the thigh and pitched him on to the deck. His brother-in-law, José de Apodoca, ran to him and Churruca said calmly, 'Pepe, tell your sister that I died honourably.' Apodoca reported that Churruca told him that he died at peace with God and that he wished to thank the crew for their courageous conduct. At first he refused to leave the quarterdeck but realising he would have to hand over command, he called for his inseparable friend and second, Francisco Moyua, only to find that Moyua had just been killed. Apodoca fetched the navigating officer, Joaquín Ibañez de Corbera, who sent him to look for the senior lieutenant, Joaquín Nuñez Falcon. Falcon was badly wounded but came up anyway. Churruca died without losing consciousness.

For a while *San Juan* fought on, but some 250 of the crew had been killed or wounded and only the mainmast was standing. Falcon held a council with Ibañez de Corbera and two other surviving officers and they decided to surrender. *Dreadnought* sent a boat to take possession, and moved on towards *Tonnant*, now a little way north-east.

That Monday morning Antonio Alcalá Galiano, whose father was commanding *Bahama*, had travelled by coach to Cadiz with his aunt. As they drove along the beach they could make out big ships in the far south but no sign of smoke or fighting. They entered the gates of Cadiz and soon learned the circumstances in which the fleet had put to sea, and that Antonio's father, like many others, had been given no time to say his goodbyes. Antonio had not been back in Cadiz long when he went to the house of a close friend, the wealthy merchant José Gutiérrez de la Huerta. They had just begun to talk when another visitor arrived and said that they should go up to the tower as quickly as possible because the watchtower had signalled that a battle was taking place within sight.

Gutiérrez's house had one of the tallest and best placed of the miradors with an unobstructed view to the southern horizon. Antonio had an unpleasant sensation of dread in his stomach and was uneasy at the thought of watching the battle, but he was 'seized by one of those inexplicable impulses, and climbed up with the others to the tower'. When they reached the roof they saw that all the other towers of Cadiz were crowded with people eagerly pointing their telescopes towards Trafalgar.

The battle in which he knew his father was fighting was barely visible on the horizon. With the aid of a powerful telescope, Antonio said, 'You could tell, despite the dense smoke, that various vessels had been dismasted, a certain sign that the fighting had been hard and that it had begun some time ago. That was as much as it was possible to find out, and on that my imagination went to work, conjuring up visions of horror and desolation.'

Dionisio Alcalá Galiano was still in action but was becoming increasingly isolated. He had positioned *Bahama* between *Bellerophon* and *Colossus* and for two hours had been engaging them both. The French *Swiftsure* had also been fighting *Colossus* from closer to, while *Bellerophon*'s attention had been absorbed by her long struggle with *Aigle*. At about two thirty *Swiftsure* lost her main topmast and dropped astern with her guns more or less silent, enabling *Colossus* to concentrate all her fire on *Bahama*. Unluckily for *Bahama*, *Aigle* had also lost contact with *Bellerophon* a little earlier, and *Bellerophon* was also now firing on Galiano's ship. Each of the English ships was about a hundred yards away and two more British ships, *Orion* and *Defiance*, were advancing on *Swiftsure* and *Aigle*. *Bahama* was exposed in a horribly dangerous position.

Galiano, who had already been injured earlier in the battle, considered withdrawing as other ships of the Combined Fleet had begun to do, but he decided that if he did so its whole position in the centre would collapse. It was a brave but fatal decision as, shortly afterwards, a hail of British bar and grape shot swept across his decks. The wind from one shot knocked the telescope from Galiano's hand and he stumbled. His coxswain came over to pick it up but as he handed it back to his captain a cannonball cut him in half, showering Galiano in blood. An instant later another shot tore along the deck. It took off the upper part of Galiano's skull. His men threw a Spanish flag over his body, but they soon lost heart.

Bahama's rigging had suffered to the point that the ship could not have escaped even if she wanted to. The mizen and mainmast had fallen and the water in the hold was rising. The new commander, Tomás de Ramery, was soon wounded and Roque Guruceta took command. He held a council of officers and they decided to surrender. The young midshipman Alonso Butrón – whom the dead Galiano had told not to surrender at any price – had been carried away wounded and his flag had been shot down. The Spanish spread out Union Jacks on the parts of the ship that faced their antagonists. *Colossus* and *Bellerophon* ceased firing on *Bahama* immediately. Within a few minutes and a few hundred yards, Spain had lost her two foremost mariners and explorers, Galiano and Churruca. While other ships withdrew, they had carried the fight to the enemy with extreme courage, even though it was a battle contested against their better judgement.

'It must be admitted that the Dons fought as well as the French in that battle; and, if praise was due for seamanship and valour, they were well entitled to an equal share,' wrote William Robinson who, in *Revenge*, had had personal experience of determined resistance from *San Ildefonso* and *Principe de Asturias*. Other front-line Spanish ships fought until they were so disabled that they could no longer fire and paid a considerable price in blood, especially that of their quarterdeck officers. Usually outgunned, the Spanish upheld national honour despite all their misgivings about the wisdom of inviting battle.

Having seen the Union Jacks appear on *Bahama*, the attention of Colossus's captain James Morris was diverted elsewhere. The crew of the French *Swiftsure* had recovered control of the ship and Captain Charles-Eusèbe L'Hospitalier-Villemadrin was attempting to rake his stern. *Colossus* reacted quickly. As Morris wrote, 'we, wearing quicker, only received a few of her larboard guns, before giving her our starboard broadside, which brought her mizen mast down.' At that moment Edward Codrington appeared with *Orion*.

Codrington had been closing in upon the battle and watching the action for some time, determined to hold his fire until he was close enough to do significant damage to a worthwhile target. He found this meant that 'As we were the only ship thereabout not firing . . . we were the only people who could have a distinct uninterrupted view of that grand and awful scene.' The view impressed him so much that he called up all his lieutenants to share it. He passed *Santa Ana* and *Royal Sovereign* dismasted on his left and, further off to his right, a cluster of wrecks including *Tonnant*, *Algésiras*, *Monarca* and *Mars*. Shot from ships of both sides was 'flying about us like hailstones' but did hardly any damage. The crew was perfectly disciplined and only one officer irritated Codrington by repeatedly pressing him to open fire.

When he came upon *Swiftsure* Codrington realised that he had finally found a suitable victim for *Orion*'s guns 'and going close under his stern we poured him in such a dose as carried away his three masts and made him strike his colours. Having repeatedly pointed out to my men the waste of shot from other ships, I had now a fine opportunity of convincing them of the benefit of cool reserve.'

The lesson was certainly appreciated by Villemadrin on board *Swiftsure*, who imagined that he had been raked by a three-decker 'and as it was almost a calm at that time, she had leisure to discharge three broadsides into me which brought down my mainmast, carried away part of the taffrail, the wheel, and dismounted most of the guns on the main deck'. *Swiftsure*'s surgeon was sending messages to say that he had no space in the orlop deck or the hold for any more wounded. Briefly, Villemadrin fought on from the lower gun-deck. Then he, too, lowered his flag. As British voices let out another cheer, it was now clear that the day was turning into a rout.

Codrington had done exactly as Nelson had wanted, using his own judgement to intervene decisively with *Orion* at a point where support was needed. *Colossus* had suffered forty killed and 160 wounded, the highest casualties on any British ship. As Morris turned his ship back to windward her mizen mast fell over the starboard quarter. She would not be able to contribute much more, but she had already accounted for three enemy ships, after what might be considered the best performance on the British side.

After dealing the final blow to *Swiftsure*, Codrington ordered *Orion* to make for Admiral Gravina's flagship, *Principe de Asturias*, and attack her from ahead. But fire from the *Dreadnought* prevented *Orion* getting close to the Spanish three-decker. Codrington 'had therefore to undergo what always alarms me, a distant cannonade, for a considerable time, and what mischief we met with was from that said *Prince of Asturias*'.

Principe de Asturias bore away north by east in order to bring her broadside to bear on *Orion*. To avoid the full blast Codrington steered to escape larboard without replying to the Spanish fire, but his own initial raking shots had caused a serious blow. Admiral Gravina's left arm was smashed by a grape shot.

Bellerophon had only her lower masts standing after *Aigle* drifted away from her. She fired on *San Juan Nepomuceno* and was relieved to see *Dreadnought* engage her closely. Then she fought *Monarca* and *Bahama* until they both surrendered.

Ten hours beforehand, William Cumby had been woken to see the enemy's masts on the horizon. Now he was acting captain. He sent Lieutenant Edward Thomas, Midshipman Henry Walker, and eight men to take possession of *Monarca*. At this moment the surgeon sent him a message to say that the cockpit was seriously overcrowded with wounded and to ask permission to use the captain's cabin for the amputation cases. Cumby said that they must evacuate back to the cockpit if any more enemy ships attacked.

The first of those to be treated was being carried up the quarterdeck ladder as Cumby approached to go down. 'It had been my unvarying rule from the commencement of the action to avoid speaking to any of my messmates and friends who might be wounded,' Cumby recalled, 'not wishing to trust my private feelings at a time when all my energies were called for in the discharge of my public duty.' He had passed Overton without a word. But Wemyss was right in his path 'and not being able to avoid speaking to him without apparent unkindness I said: "Wemyss, my good fellow, I'm sorry you've been wounded, but I trust you will do well;" to which he replied with the utmost cheerfulness, "Tis only a mere scratch, and I shall have to apologise to you by and by for having left the deck on so trifling an occasion': he was then entering the cabin to have his right arm amputated!' Wemyss survived to become a lieutenant colonel.

About this time *Defiance* came across the badly damaged *Aigle*. She ran up alongside and they pounded each other with guns from close range until *Aigle*'s fire appeared to slacken. According to master's mate James Spratt, the young Irishman commanding *Defiance*'s boarders, there was an eerie pause while they watched each other. The other officers in *Defiance*, who were almost all Scottish, prepared her men to board and the enemy got ready to repel them, 'each viewing the other with glistening arms in hand impatient for the encounter'. The problem was that, thanks to *Defiance*'s earlier duel with *Principe de Asturias*, and *Aigle*'s long struggle with *Bellerophon*, 'both ships' boats had been shot through and rendered useless'. They wondered how to complete the conquest.

Spratt asked Captain Philip Durham for permission to board by swimming 'as I well knew 50 or 60 of the boarders who I taught for some years could swim like sharks'. At first Durham demurred, 'saying I was too prompt', but in the end he agreed. Spratt shouted, 'All you, my brave fellows, who can swim, follow me,' and 'plunged over board from the starboard gangway with my cutlass between my teeth and my tomahawk under my belt'. He swam to the stern of the *Aigle* 'where by the assistance of her rudder chains I got into her gunroom stern port'. But he was alone. For whatever reason his men had not followed.

Aided no doubt by surprise, Spratt fought his way to the poop and 'showed myself to our ships crew from the enemy's tafrail and gave them a cheer with my hat on the point of my cutlass'. At that moment Durham succeeded in bringing *Defiance* alongside and his boatswain, William Forster, lashed the ships together. In doing so he was killed, 'shot through the breast by a rifleman from the fore cathar springs and received a second shot as he was carrying below'.

A division of Spratt's men scrambled on to *Aigle* and began to fight their way towards him. They distracted attention from the lone Irishman in the nick of time. Spratt was fighting an individual battle against three grenadiers with fixed bayonets. He swung on a signal halyard over their heads to an arms chest and disabled two before they could react. He grabbed the third round the neck and threw him over the edge of the poop deck, but the Frenchman pulled Spratt with him in his fall. Spratt landed on top and the grenadier broke his neck as he hit the quarterdeck. There, a desperate mêlée was in progress. The crew of *Aigle*, now commanded by Lieutenant Louis Huissier, defended their ship resolutely. The sharp-shooters of the 67th Regiment were still firing on the British sailors and throwing grenades from the tops. More grenades were being hurled through *Defiance*'s gun-ports and in the hand-to-hand fighting the French had the advantage. The first division of British boarders was badly cut up and driven back. Spratt's friend First Lieutenant Thomas Simons was shot by a rifleman.

Seeing that *Aigle* was not as ripe for conquest as he had thought, Durham opened up again with *Defiance*'s guns. Many of *Aigle*'s were already dismounted and they made little reply. Flaming, sulphur-saturated wads from *Defiance*'s set fire to the French ship's gunroom close to the cable tier. Then a second party from *Defiance* swarmed aboard and these fresh reinforcements finally turned the tide. Spratt watched 'a red-headed tobacco twister' from Dublin fight a powerfully built Frenchman. They fixed their eyes on each other, then each shot his pistol and missed; they fought with cutlasses and then they wrestled. The Frenchman found a pistol on the deck and shot the Irishman through the body, but the Dubliner killed him with a knife.

Soon one French officer was fighting a rearguard action on the quarterdeck as his men made their escape. When he tried to get down the hatch he was seized by 'two of our men with uplifted tomahawks'. According to Spratt, the Frenchman 'cryed for quarter and threw himself at my feet and I was obliged to throw myself on him and cover his body to save him from our men who said they would open his soul case in a minute'.

As Spratt got to his feet a grenadier charged at him with a fixed bayonet. Spratt parried the thrust with his cutlass. The grenadier stepped back a pace or two and levelled his musket to shoot. Spratt deflected the barrel downward with his cutlass so the ball intended for his chest hit his advanced right leg and shattered the bone. 'I felt something like an electric shock and darted at him but my right leg turned up between my thighs with my shin bone resting on the deck.' Spratt 'backed in between two of the quarterdeck guns with my back to the bullwark to prevent being cut down from behind where I was immediately attacked by my old tormenter in front and one at each side slapping at me furiously.' He shouted for help and when the smoke cleared his men 'saw my perilous situation and ran my old tormenter through the body and nearly put me on the same spit'.

On *Aigle* Lieutenant Huissier saw three more British ships closing in around him and decided that further resistance was pointless. At about three thirty he surrendered. A good half of his men had been killed or wounded in their brave struggle against two British ships. Somewhere in the fighting the 67th Regiment lost its Eagle, although Colonel Jacquemet had rescued the colours.

Spratt helped to haul down *Aigle*'s ensign, which he sent across to Captain Durham in the hands of a black man who was one of his boarders. He found himself weak from hard work and loss of blood. He tried to swing back across to *Defiance* on one of the ropes for hoisting boats, but missed the deck and landed painfully but fortunately on a raised gun-port. From there his shipmates hauled him in and carried him to William Burnett, the ship's excellent surgeon, a veteran of St Vincent and the Nile.

Philip Durham sent Lieutenant James Purches to take possession of *Aigle* with a prize crew that was later reinforced. He left Captain Gourrège and *Aigle*'s many wounded in the hands of the French surgeons.

The crew of *Belleisle* saw a three-decker approaching through the smoke and realised that, one way or another, their fate was sealed. Depending on whether she was friend or foe they were saved or they would have to surrender. About a fifth of the crew were casualties and the upper deck had been more or less abandoned but, fortunately for those sheltering below, until now there had been no fresh enemy ship to come in close and smash in the hull. Paul Nicolas remembered 'with what anxiety every eye turned towards this formidable object, which would either relieve us from our unwelcome neighbours or render our situation desperate. We had scarcely seen the British colours since one o'clock, and it is impossible to express our emotion as the alteration of the stranger's course displayed the white ensign to our sight.'

They were saved. The approaching three-decker was *Dreadnought*. She turned aside, but the two ships with her did not. Men from the British *Swiftsure* climbed into the rigging and cheered as they passed *Belleisle*, then steered for *Pluton*, forcing Cosmao to withdraw. Soon afterwards *Polyphemus* drove off Maistral's *Neptune*. *Belleisle* now ceased fire 'and turned the hands up to clear the wreck'. They could not yet relax. To leeward, ships were rallying in something like a line of battle while, more dangerously, the fresh ships of Dumanoir's division could be seen returning from the north.

Whenever they saw another ship surrender *Victory*'s crew cheered. Once, Nelson asked what the cheer was for and Lieutenant John Pasco, who was lying badly wounded nearby, eased himself up and pleased the admiral by telling him an enemy ship had struck. Scott and Burke tried to persuade him that he would recover to bring the news of a great victory back to Britain, but Nelson was convinced he was dying. He was also very worried for Hardy. Beatty sent frequent messages requesting that Hardy come down, and when he didn't appear Nelson suspected they were hiding from him that Hardy had been killed. 'Will no one bring Hardy to me? He must be killed: he is surely destroyed.'

Then Hardy's aide, Richard Bulkeley, came down with a message that Hardy 'would avail himself of the first favourable moment to visit his Lordship'. 'Remember me to your father,' Nelson told Bulkeley. About an hour and ten minutes after Nelson had been shot the tall captain finally appeared, stooping low in the dimly lit cockpit. Those present tried afterwards to recall exactly what was said.

'Well, Hardy, how goes the battle? How goes the day with us?'

'Very well, my lord, we have got twelve or fourteen of the enemy's ships in our possession; but five of their van have tacked and show an intention of bearing down upon the *Victory*. I have therefore called two or three of our fresh ships round us, and have no doubt of giving them a drubbing.'

'I hope none of our ships have struck, Hardy.'

'No, my lord, there is no fear of that.'

'I am a dead man, Hardy. I am going fast: it will be all over with me soon. Come nearer to me. Pray let my dear Lady Hamilton have my hair, and all other things belonging to me.'

Hardy said he hoped Nelson might yet survive.

'No, it is impossible. My back is shot through. Beatty will tell you so.'

Hardy went back on deck. At present he was commanding Nelson's division of the fleet, but he sent a message to Collingwood telling him what had happened. Beatty visited again, but Nelson told him to look after less hopeless cases: his four carers were doing all that could be done.

Hardy had seen that Dumanoir had got some of his ships round and had hoisted the signal to come to the wind on the port tack. *Leviathan*, *Conqueror*, *Neptune* and *Agamemnon* began to form a rough line and move north between Dumanoir and *Rayo*, *San Francisco de Asis*, *Héros* and *San Agustín*.

In his plan for the battle Nelson had envisaged two phases. In the first, he would isolate and capture the enemy admiral while Collingwood employed superior numbers to defeat the enemy rear. In the second, his own ships would defeat the enemy van while Collingwood made sure that the prizes were protected from any enemies who were still at large. The first phase of the battle in which Nelson looked to obtain a 'Victory before the Van of the Enemy could succour their Rear' had been won. Even so, there were still enemy ships at large to windward and towards the rear, where Collingwood had taken on sixteen ships instead of twelve, and the second phase was still to come. Determined intervention from the fresh enemy ships might yet spoil the day.

16

Death or Victory

As he said, James Martin had 'but a few minets to take a peep a Round us' before he and his mates in *Neptune* 'precived the van ships of the Enemy had wore Round and ware coming Down on us to suport their admirl'. Five fresh vessels apparently heading straight for them was an alarming sight. He calculated that 'had thay Closed upon us we must [have] Sunk as Death or Victory was the Gineral Resolution of our Ships Crew'. But *Leviathan*, *Conqueror* and *Agamemnon* came rapidly to *Neptune*'s support and together they formed a barrier at the northern end of the line.

Nelson's memorandum had given his captains instructions on how to secure the prizes and their own disabled ships against fresh enemy attacks. They adapted them to suit the current situation. Further to leeward *Africa*, *Britannia*, *Ajax* and *Orion* put themselves between the unengaged enemy ships and the damaged flagships of both sides. The British frigates went in to help the disabled three-deckers and tow them into positions from which they could defend themselves. Further south *Dreadnought*, *Thunderer*, *Swiftsure* and *Polyphemus* were threatening the retreating *Principe de Asturias*, with *Prince* now almost in range behind.

Within this protective cordon the remaining British ships completed the destruction of the enemy ships that they had cut off.

Richard King's *Achille* had trapped Antonio Pareja's already damaged *Argonauta* and, after a sharp fight, silenced her guns and wounded her captain. King was trying to force the surrender of the Spanish ship when the French *Achille* appeared out of the smoke. Her latest commander Sub-lieutenant Charles Cauchard manoeuvred his ship into a position from which he could rake King's and delivered some tired broadsides. He was not there long before *Polyphemus* had come to King's rescue, brought down the French *Achille*'s tottering mizen mast and smashed the wheel. *Polyphemus* then put on sail to cut off the French ship from any possibility of escape to the remnant of the enemy squadron, who were forming up to leeward. She shot away *Achille*'s fore yard and saw that she was on fire at the fore top. *Achille* seemed to have stopped firing and *Polyphemus* thought she saw someone waving a Union Jack from her cathead so she steered away to help elsewhere.

The French *Berwick* had lost her captain, Captain Jean Filhol-Camas, cut in half by a bar shot. She pulled away from *Defence* with her mizen mast over the side, only to run straight into Richard King's British *Achille*. Another fierce gun battle developed. George Hope's *Defence* joined *Revenge* in bombarding the already damaged *San Ildefonso* and together they shot away her mizen and mainmast. With thirty-four men dead and 126 wounded, second-in-command Anselmo Gomendio went below to tell the wounded Captain Vargas that he judged it necessary to surrender. *San Ildefonso* hauled in her colours, which were hanging over the stern, and someone waved a Union Jack to make plain her surrender. Just after a boat from *Defence* took possession of this thirteenth prize, the foremast fell over the side.

None of the British ships had succeeded in cutting off Gravina's powerful flagship, *Principe de Asturias*. Edward Codrington had tried to get close 'but we could not get within three cables' length [600 yards] of him and his supporters'. First the cumbersome *Dreadnought* got in his way and then *Britannia* starting firing across his line, aiming at Gravina's flagship from very long range. *Principe de Asturias*'s own gunnery helped to dissuade her enemies. She was nursing a weakened mainmast and trying to come to the assistance of the stricken but not yet captured *Argonauta*. She had lowered a lieutenant into the water in a boat to take command of the apparently leaderless ship if necessary.

This delay allowed *Prince*, the last of the English three-deckers to get into action, to come within grape-shot range. Two raking broadsides from astern crashed into the Spanish flagship. Chief of Staff Antonio de Escaño, who had taken charge when Gravina was wounded, was hit in the leg and lost consciousness from loss of blood. The flag was shot away and for a time the *Principe de Asturias* ceased to resist as she fled and British ships closed in.

She was saved by the intervention of Maistral's *Neptune* and *San Justo*. Supported more distantly by *San Leandro* and *Pluton*, they closed in around the flagship and drove back her British assailants. After a few minutes Escaño came to and rehoisted the colours. But in the anxiety to escape, *Argonauta* had been left behind. The fine Spanish eighty-gun ship's rudder had been shot away in the last exchanges and she had several holes beneath the waterline. Her rigging was so disabled that, with the masts in danger of falling, she could not make sail to escape. Isolated and abandoned, she became the fourteenth ship to surrender.

Principe de Asturias had now gathered around her a group of ships that were damaged but still seaworthy, with *Indomptable*, *Montañés* and *Argonaute* further behind. Their problem was that they were downwind of the battle and could not sail directly into the wind to intervene where the British were most vulnerable.

Nelson was losing sensation in his lower body, a symptom he recalled from the case of the man who had died on *Victory* some months earlier from an injured spine. He was in such intense pain, he told Beatty, that he wished he was dead. 'Yet,' he added, 'one would like to live a little longer, too.' After a pause of a few minutes, he added, in the same tone, 'What would become of poor Lady Hamilton, if she knew my situation?'

Hardy descended to the cockpit to make a second visit. He clasped Nelson's hand as he congratulated him on a brilliant victory that 'was complete though he did not know how many of the enemy were captured, as it was impossible to perceive every ship distinctly'. He was certain that fourteen or fifteen had surrendered.

'That is well, but I bargained for twenty,' Nelson said, then added forcefully, 'Anchor, Hardy, anchor!'

Hardy replied that he supposed Collingwood would now take charge of affairs.

'Not while I live, I hope, Hardy!' exclaimed Nelson, attempting to get up. 'No, do *you* anchor, Hardy.'

'Shall *we* make the signal, sir?' asked Hardy.

'Yes, for if I live, I'll anchor.' He told Hardy that he expected to live only for a few more minutes, then continued, in a low tone, 'Don't throw me overboard, Hardy.'

'Oh, no! Certainly not.'

'Then you know what to do. And take care of my dear Lady Hamilton, Hardy. Take care of poor Lady Hamilton. Kiss me, Hardy.' The captain knelt and kissed his cheek. His lordship said, 'Now I am satisfied. Thank God, I have done my duty.' Hardy stood for a minute or two in silent contemplation. Then he knelt down again and kissed his lordship's forehead.

Nelson asked, 'Who is that?'

The captain answered, 'It is Hardy.'

'God bless you, Hardy!'

Having spent eight minutes in the cockpit, Hardy returned to the quarterdeck. Nelson asked Chevalier to turn him on to his right side, then said, 'I wish I had not left the deck, for I shall soon be gone.' He was failing, breathing with difficulty, his voice faint.

At the northern end of the battle Dumanoir's squadron split into three groups. The admiral in his eighty-gun *Formidable*, with *Mont-Blanc*, *Duguay-Trouin* and *Scipion* in line behind him, kept tight to the wind and exchanged long-range fire with *Neptune*'s blocking group as they passed. *Neptuno* was behind the French ships and aiming more directly for the *Santísima Trinidad*. They were coming, but they were already too late. Uncertainty, confusion, poor visibility, technical difficulty in turning with no wind and perhaps a little cowardice had delayed the ships of the van to the point where Nelson had already won the battle in the centre of the battlefield before they could intervene. As Dumanoir got closer he surveyed the flagships, saw that they were completely dismasted, and decided that he could no longer help. To the relief of James Martin and his shipmates, he did not close with *Neptune*.

Instead he aimed to cut off *Minotaur* and *Spartiate*, the rearmost ships of Nelson's division, which had still not reached the enemy line. He failed. With a strengthening west-south-west wind filling their sails, *Minotaur* and *Spartiate* reached the point of junction first, passed close ahead of *Formidable* and raked her bows as they did so, causing numerous casualties and putting several shots through her hull beneath the waterline. Then they sailed along the French line under topsails, exchanging distant fire with each ship in turn.

As *Formidable* cleared *Spartiate* and *Minotaur* she was engaged at long range by *Victory* and *Mars*, who managed to bring their guns to bear, disabled as they were. *Royal Sovereign*, towed round by *Euryalus*, joined in, while *Téméraire* cut loose *Redoutable* and *Fougueux* and brought her starboard broadside to bear on the French ships too. The range was so long that Harvey reckoned he did no damage. According to Jean-Jacques Lucas, the leg of British Midshipman William Pitts, in the prize *Redoutable*, was shattered by a shot fired by one of Dumanoir's ships. He was carried below to have it amputated by the French surgeon, Alain Bohan, but died soon afterwards. *Tonnant* and *Bellerophon* also contrived to open fire as Dumanoir passed. The French ships' return fire hit *Monarca* as well as *Bellerophon*, according to Midshipman Henry Walker, who was aboard the Spanish prize.

At about four o'clock Collingwood signalled to *Dreadnought* and the British ships around her to come to the wind on the port tack. *Dreadnought*, *Thunderer* and *Revenge* turned away from Gravina's flagship, *Principe de Asturias*, and offered their support to the ships to windward. The sight of these relatively undamaged ships finally deterred Dumanoir from any attempt to recover the prizes. At about

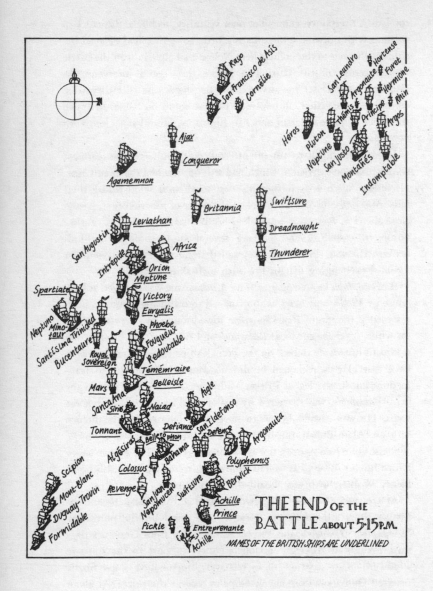

THE END OF THE BATTLE ABOUT 5.15 P.M.

NAMES OF THE BRITISH SHIPS ARE UNDERLINED

four thirty he ceased fire and sailed off with his four ships to the south.

Dumanoir's other ships had not followed him. *Rayo* and *San Francisco de Asís* aimed to come to the aid of *Principe de Asturias* when they saw her under threat but the strong British squadron heading towards them cut them off. After some brief resistance they and *Héros* bore away north-eastwards towards the group of friendly ships to leeward.

The remaining three ships of Dumanoir's division, *Intrépide*, *Neptuno* and the frigate *Cornélie*, continued obstinately southwards. When they got close enough to see *Bucentaure* and *Redoutable*, it was clear that they were dismasted and had probably surrendered. Nevertheless, Captain Louis Infernet told his officers that he intended to rescue Villeneuve, get him on board *Intrépide*, and rally round them those ships still fit to fight. To Auguste Gicquel, it was evident that the enterprise was insane, but he realised that Infernet, too, knew that. The project was merely a pretext to engage for the sake of their honour, so that no one could say that *Intrépide* had left the battle without fighting.

Infernet's crew seemed to share his wish to fight. Many of them had been together since 1802 and had jointly experienced the horrors of Saint-Domingue. According to Gicquel, 'Our crew was understrength, but at least it was good, something that could not be said of the crews of the Spanish vessels.'

Their ship was one of the vessels that Napoleon had extracted from Spain a few years earlier. She was slow because she was long overdue for docking and to French eyes she was too lightly built and undergunned: 'Though she was supposed to be an eighty, her fabric was so weak that her batteries could only be armed with 24- and eighteen-pounders instead of carrying thirty-sixes and twenty-fours.'

Cornélie was the only one of Villeneuve's frigates to make any attempt to obey the admiral's instruction to join in the fighting. Her captain, de Martinencq, had also determined to rescue *Bucentaure*.

Ahead of them was Felipe Cajigal's *San Agustín*. She had been much closer to *Santísima Trinidad* and had responded much more quickly to the instruction to come to her aid. She had suffered considerably from a gunnery contest with *Britannia*, and now found herself isolated under the fire of several British ships, with *Leviathan* trying to get close to finish her off. As *Leviathan* came within a hundred yards Cajigal put *San Agustín*'s helm hard to starboard, hoping to rake the British ship from ahead. On seeing the danger, Captain Henry Bayntun swung the helm to port and, because he was moving faster, *Leviathan* responded more quickly. The British ship's guns came to bear first and Bayntun fired off an admirably accurate double-shotted broadside into *San Agustín*'s starboard quarter from a range of less than fifty yards. He brought down the Spanish ship's mizen mast and her colours with it.

Bayntun was now afraid that *San Agustín* would be able to wear under his own ship's stern and rake him in return. His rigging was so damaged that he could not prevent this by backing his sails to slow down. So he kept going and, putting the helm to starboard, he ran on board *San Agustín* in such a way that his larboard main rigging became entangled with the Spanish ship's jib-boom. Having skilfully put *Leviathan* into a position to rake *San Agustín* from the front, he poured the full weight of his larboard broadside into the Spanish ship, which could hardly bring to bear any guns to return fire.

After half an hour's pounding from a few yards away *Leviathan*'s first lieutenant, Eyles Mounsher, led a boarding party on to *San Agustín* and quickly carried her. Only two men were killed in the attempt, one – marine Peter Smith – squashed between the two ships as he crossed. Cajigal estimated his own ship's losses at 180 killed and 200 wounded, and although he had doubled the number of dead his casualties were genuinely heavy.

While *Leviathan* was boarding *San Agustín*, Louis Infernet's *Intrépide* finally arrived in the thick of the fighting. The little 64 *Africa* tried to intercept her, but *Intrépide*'s fresh crew outmanoeuvred and raked her and the British ship's guns fell silent. During the lull that followed Gicquel offered the young midshipman stationed near him a glass of wine. The boy's hand was trembling so much that he spilled it. His face had been calm and his deportment courageous, but this evidence of his fear humiliated him. Gicquel seized his hand and assured the boy of his esteem, telling him how well he was doing at concealing his emotion.

San Agustín had shot away *Leviathan*'s tiller and completed the destruction of her rigging, leaving Bayntun unable to manoeuvre and powerless to intervene against the new assailant. *Leviathan* was in a vulnerable position but *Intrépide* edged on past her, her captain still intent on recapturing *Bucentaure*.

Edward Codrington of *Orion* had got out his studding sails again to come to *Leviathan*'s aid. 'It was seeing Leviathan so harassed by the shy van which made me push to her assistance, & could I have passed through the fire of our friends I should have succeeded sooner in my object,' he wrote to Bayntun the following Saturday. Like Bayntun, he believed in getting close and settling things. He did not wish to see this last French prize turn away and escape. But, once again, he found his attempts impeded by inaccurate fire from other British ships shooting at long range. 'After several fruitless attempts to pass by one or two of our ships, who kept up a distant cannonade on her, I managed, first, to back all sail so as to get under *Ajax*'s stern, and then to make all sail so as to pass close across *Leviathan*'s head.' As *Orion* passed *Leviathan*, where the men were making running repairs to their damage, Bayntun hailed Codrington cheerfully 'and said he hoped, laughing, that I should make a better fist of it'.

On *Intrépide*'s forecastle Auguste Gicquel saw *Orion* coming. He was there with the best seamen to advise Captain Infernet on manoeuvre, to implement his instructions, and to command the forward musketeers and boarders. He had set his heart on boarding and, in his imagination, he saw his men storming the isolated British ship and carrying it as a prisoner to Cadiz. He sent a second midshipman to Infernet, advising him of the course to cut off *Orion*. But Gicquel had chosen the wrong boy. Minutes passed and nothing happened. He went to the quarter-deck and, on the way, found his messenger lying down, terrified, on the gangway to avoid the grape shot screaming across the ship. By the time Gicquel reached Infernet the moment had passed.

Codrington got *Orion* close enough 'to get our starboard guns to bear on *L'Intrépide*'s starboard quarter, and then to turn gradually round from thence under his stern, pass his broadside, and bring to on his larboard bow'. Intense, accurate fire from *Orion* pounded *Intrépide*. François Grévillot was one of the ship's old hands. Gicquel had won the esteem of the ship that summer by rescuing him when he fell overboard in mid-ocean. The two were standing side by side on the forecastle when a wooden splinter caught Grévillot. As he was carried away another shot smashed his skull.

Cayetano Valdés in *Neptuno* was pursuing his own death-or-glory mission. Cut off from Dumanoir by *Spartiate* and *Minotaur* he continued on towards *Santísima Trinidad* and *Bucentaure*. Valdés had helped rescue *Santísima Trinidad* at the battle of St Vincent and he intended to do so again. Sailing through the fire of *Victory* and *Neptune* he got very close to her before *Minotaur* and *Spartiate* closed in. Valdés wanted to launch his boats to attempt to recapture the flagship, but he found that they had all been riddled with shot. Then *Minotaur* and *Spartiate* brought down his mizen mast. Some of the debris hit Valdés on the head and neck and he was carried below, unconscious, leaving his second, Joaquín Somosa, in charge of the ship.

Nelson said to Alexander Scott, 'Doctor, I have not been a great sinner', and after a short pause, 'Remember that I leave Lady Hamilton and my daughter Horatia as a legacy to my country.' He added, 'Never forget Horatia.' He thought of Scott, too. Having told George Rose to look after Scott if anything happened to him, he reminded Scott to apply to Rose for employment. He spoke in half-sentences between bouts of intense pain. He was very thirsty and called, 'Drink, drink!' 'Fan, fan!' and 'Rub, rub!' with garbled urgency. Scott was rubbing Nelson's chest with his hand. Burke was keeping the bedding behind his shoulders in place. This held him in the semi-recumbent position that was the only one he could bear. Every now and then he enunciated clearly. Scott heard him say again, 'Thank God, I have done my duty'. When he had said nothing for about five minutes Chevalier went to Beatty and told him that they thought the admiral was dying. When

Beatty came he found Nelson's hand cold and could feel no pulse in his wrist. When he felt his forehead, Nelson opened his eyes, looked up, and shut them again. Beatty left him again. Five minutes later Chevalier came over to say that he thought Nelson had died. It was true. Beatty recorded the time of death as four thirty.

Fire from the van ships had shot away the stream cable with which *Euryalus* had been towing *Royal Sovereign*. Blackwood turned his ship about and went over to *Victory* instead. He was one of the first to learn of his commander's death.

Nelson never knew how close he had come to his bargain for twenty. With fifteen enemy ships down there were still three to fall.

At much the same moment on the Spanish flagship *Principe de Asturias*, Admiral Antonio de Escaño hoisted a signal to rally the remaining ships of the Combined Fleet around him. With Villeneuve in British hands it fell to him to decide whether to fight on in a hopeless cause or to salvage what he could. Ten ships, with the frigates and brigs, headed towards the Spanish flagship.

Intrépide was left surrounded. From a distance *Agamemnon* and *Téméraire* joined their fire to that of *Africa* and *Leviathan*, but the real damage followed *Orion's* progress round Louis Infernet's gallant ship. His mizen yard was shot away, the wheel and tiller were smashed and then the mainmast fell. By five o'clock the foremast was the only one still standing. At this stage Infernet decided that it was now honourable to surrender. About half of his crew had been killed or wounded.

Neptuno fought on for fifty minutes after Valdés was knocked unconscious, but shortly after Infernet gave in, the ship's second-in-command, Joaquín Somosa, was also hit. By then, in addition to the mizen mast, *Neptuno* had lost the fore-topmast and part of the foretop together with most of the shrouds, the main stay, the fore yard, and the main topmast. The mainmast was damaged in five places and all the shrouds and preventer-shrouds to larboard had been cut away. Her casualties were not excessive (twelve dead and forty-seven wounded) but the British were firing high to disable her and ensure that she did not escape. Believing Valdés to be dead and further resistance point-less, *Neptuno*'s first lieutenant, Antonio Miranda, surrendered.

Marine Second Lieutenant Thomas Reeves went aboard *Neptuno* from *Minotaur*, with a prize crew of forty-eight men, and took possession at five-thirty. He sent Miranda on board *Minotaur* to deliver Valdés's sword to Captain Charles Mansfield, and took off another lieutenant and twenty-five men. Then they secured the other prisoners, disarmed them, locked away their firearms and put a guard on the magazine.

The battle was almost over but having been deprived of any aggressive role so far, Captain Richard Grindall and his officers in *Prince* were looking for a prize. *Achille* was the only accessible French ship that had not yet surrendered. She was drifting south-eastwards, and a fire in her foretop had spread, despite frantic attempts by the carpenters and most of the crew to cut away the foremast. The ship's fire-engine had already been shot to pieces in the fighting. *Polyphemus*'s officers 'observed the *Prince* range alongside the *Achille*, who was on fire, and fired several broadsides into her, not supposing she had struck to us'. Had *Achille* already surrendered this might have been considered a war crime, but since none of *Achille*'s officers complained, it is fairly certain that they did not think she had.

The second of three broadsides from *Prince* brought down *Achille*'s remaining masts, which fell amidships. The sails tumbled into the flames and set fire to the ship's boats. Now the entire ship was on fire and it was only a matter of time before her magazine exploded. When they realised their situation was desperate, the remaining men in *Achille*'s 36-pounder battery came up on deck and began to throw into the water any debris that would float, then jumped in after it.

One of those still below was a woman in her mid-twenties, named Jeanne Caunant. The wife of a maintopman, she had been employed in the powder room. When the firing stopped she climbed up to the lower deck and tried to reach the main deck in search of her husband, but found that the ladders had all been shot away. As she tried frantically to find a way up she heard cries of 'Fire!' from above. It burned downwards, trapping her on the lower deck. With no one to help her she ran from place to place among mangled bodies and dying men. Finally, some guns from the main deck fell through the burnt planks, allowing her to scramble out of the gunroom port and climb down the chains to the back of the rudder where she stayed, as she couldn't swim. Later she said she had prayed that the ship might blow up and put an end to her misery.

Captain Grindall put *Prince*'s boats into the water to save as many of *Achille*'s crew as possible before he took his own ship to a safe distance. The British schooner *Pickle* and the cutter *Entreprenante* also sailed up to help with rescue and lowered their boats. The frigate *Naiad* sent three 'under the direction of Lieutenant Mainwaring, Hugh Montgomery, mate, and Mark Anthony, Midshipman, which saved about 190 amongst which was the surgeon who informed Mr Anthony that there was nearly 300 wounded below when he left the ship'. But because the ship was bound to explode, only the most daring boatmen went within two hundred yards to save those capable of swimming or paddling to them.

At five-thirty *Achille* erupted. Désiré Clamard, the sub-lieutenant who wrote one of the official reports, said that it 'was not very violent seeing that we had taken the precaution of drowning the remainder of our powder' but it impressed others. An officer from *Defence* wrote, 'The hull burst into a cloud of smoke and fire. A column of vivid flame shot up to an enormous height in the atmosphere and terminated by expanding into an immense globe, representing for a few seconds, a prodigious tree in flames, specked with many dark spots, which the pieces of timber and bodies of men occasioned while they were suspended in the clouds.'

When this column had collapsed into the water the boats closed in and saved all those they could find in the gathering twilight. Jeanne Caunant had stayed by the rudder until the lead that lined its trunk melted and fell upon her. Her skin burnt, she stripped off her clothes and jumped. The water was rough but not cold, and by luck a piece of cork was within reach. Clinging to it, she kicked herself away from the burning wreck. A man swam to her with a six-foot plank, which he pushed under her arms. After what she later imagined was two hours in the water, but was probably much less, Hugh Montgomery, commanding one of *Naiad*'s boats, saw her 'floating by the assistance of the ship's quarter billboard' and pulled her in. His men rowed her to *Pickle* where her burns were treated and she was given clothes. Harry Andrews, master of *Naiad*, wrote, 'Lieut. Mainwaring and Mr. Anthony was within a cable length when the explosion took place, and did not reach us until 1.30 a.m. which we were happy to see, as we had despaired of seeing them any more they retired unhurt.'

The explosion marked the end of the battle. Soon afterwards Escaño turned his flagship for home, followed by eleven ships, some seriously damaged, with the frigates and two brigs. The fighting had lasted about five and a half hours, and officially cost 449 British lives; 1214 men were reported wounded and dozens, perhaps even hundreds, would die of their injuries over the coming days and weeks.

French and Spanish casualties are impossible to calculate since we do not know how many Frenchmen fought, and the fate of the crews of some ships is obscure. Perhaps two thousand Frenchmen were killed that day. For the Spanish, the historian Ferrer de Couto gave the plausible figure of 1022 for those killed in battle (not including those who died of wounds or subsequently drowned); our own guess, based on numbers reportedly taken off Spanish ships by the British, is about 860. At the end of the battle the British had in the region of 11,230 prisoners on their hands, many of them wounded. Seventeen ships had been captured and one had blown up. This total might have been two short of what Nelson had wanted but by the standards of the age it was amazing. The previous record for a modern fleet action was the seven captured and four destroyed at the battle of the Nile.

Watching from the mirador in Cadiz, not knowing that his father was already dead, Antonio Galiano saw a terrible portent in the end of *Achille*:

It had got very late in the day. Suddenly, an enormous blaze appeared on the horizon and as if drawn in the midst of this terrible splendour the shape of a ship. The light disappeared and the sound of the explosion was heard, a bang that felt far off but very powerful. There could be no doubt that a ship had blown up. As was natural, though without any foundation and wrongly, I believed that it was my father's ship that had suffered this horrible disaster. I threw myself down the stair and fled from the tower, overwhelmed with horror and dread.

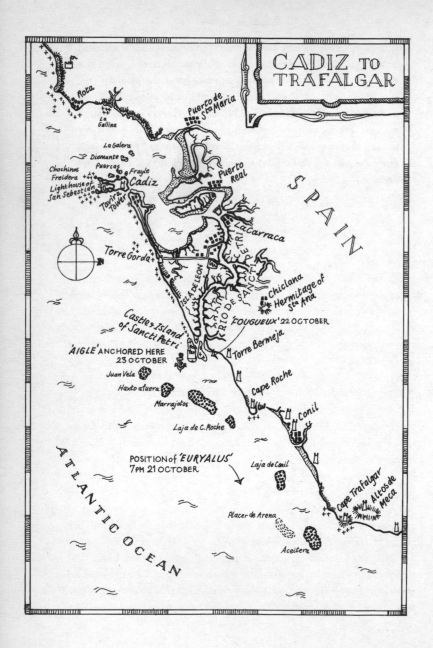

17

The Dangers of a Lee Shore

'Anchor, Hardy, anchor!' Surgeon Beatty's care in reporting this repeated injunction in his minutely detailed account of Nelson's death was his contribution to an acrimonious and long-running controversy. In the 1820s, when the war against Napoleon was over and the histories of it were being written, debate about the way in which the battle had been fought was restrained compared with the furore surrounding what happened immediately afterwards.

There can be no doubt that Nelson wanted the fleet to anchor. He had made the signal 'prepare to anchor at the close of day' before the battle started so that the captains knew what he intended to do and so that the crews could get the spare anchors and cables ready in case of damage to the main ones. Ships carried four large anchors, two on the catheads projecting from the bows and two spares on the forecastle. When the battle was over one of the crew's most urgent tasks was to repair or replace damaged anchor cables or catheads and get undamaged bower anchors and cables on to the catheads from where they could be dropped as soon as the admiral gave the signal.

There were several good reasons to anchor. First, the battle was drifting ever closer to a coastline that was notorious for its dangerous shoals, and the wind was blowing in that direction so that the shore was in the lee of the wind. Any mariner was aware of the dangers of a lee shore. Second, although we do not know whether the fleet fully expected a storm, the westerly swell that had been troublesome all day was a known sign of an approaching gale. The barometers in the British ships were presumably behaving like the one at the Royal Observatory just south of Cadiz for which records survive. This had risen between readings taken at eight in the morning and two in the afternoon of 21 October, so that when Nelson gave the instruction to anchor his barometer was suggesting that the weather was improving.

But it might not have been the weather that prompted his decision. The final and most important reason to anchor was to facilitate repairs to battle damage and to reorganise. Any captured enemy ships had to be secured, large numbers of foreign seamen, especially officers and petty officers, removed from the prizes and competent British personnel put in their place while the battle damage was patched up to make them seaworthy.

There were arguments against anchoring too. If the damaged British fleet, with all its even more damaged prizes, anchored in their present situation and the onshore wind became fiercer there was a strong possibility that they would be stuck there for as long as bad weather persisted. It was easy to become trapped in Cadiz Bay and anchors might not hold. To get out they required several miles of sea room to round either Cape St Mary far to the north or the much nearer Cape Trafalgar in the south. By the time Collingwood had made his decision about anchoring, the barometer was probably falling – the one at the Cadiz Royal Observatory dropped sharply overnight. That evening, with the wind still mostly westerly and light, it was possible that the ships might find enough sea room to get round the shoals off Cape Trafalgar and escape southward, then eastward to Gibraltar before the weather closed in. Soon after Nelson had died Captain Blackwood ferried Thomas Hardy from *Victory* to meet Collingwood in *Royal Sovereign*. There, Hardy, who had been acting as admiral, surrendered to Collingwood the authority he had borrowed from Nelson and told him how Nelson had died, and that his dying wish was to have the fleet and prizes brought to anchor. Collingwood's reported response was 'Anchor the fleet? Why, it is the last thing I should have thought of.'

Collingwood's partisans assert that he was a better seaman than Nelson and a good, proud seaman was always reluctant to anchor. He would try to manoeuvre off a lee shore by skilful sailing and would only anchor when desperate. To anchor off a lee shore was a course to be taken only when all else had failed.

Collingwood ordered Blackwood to make the general signal to all ships to come to the wind on the starboard tack, and to take the disabled and captured ships in tow. This recall to the pursuing ships finally silenced the guns. Having no masts, *Royal Sovereign* could not make signals so just before six p.m. Collingwood transferred to *Euryalus* and hoisted his blue flag at the foremast. *Euryalus* put a cable across to *Royal Sovereign* and took the badly damaged ship in tow.

Collingwood ordered *Thunderer* to take *Santa Ana* in tow, and *Prince* to look after *Santísima Trinidad*. They were both under way before midnight. He saw that Thomas Capel's frigate *Phoebe* was already towing a prize – *Fougueux* – and that *Naiad* had *Belleisle*. He sent *Euryalus*'s boats to the nearest and least damaged ships to repeat his signalled orders verbally and to tell the captains to follow the admiral. But as darkness fell only a few of his ships received these instructions – *Neptune* had them from *Pickle* at four the next morning. A dangerous confusion about the fleet's orders was thus established.

Collingwood never explained his decision and subsequently he did his best to conceal that he had done anything controversial. Perhaps he was merely anxious to get further offshore, which was a perfectly reasonable instinct, especially since he had no idea how many ships might be in a position to anchor effectively. But Captain Eliab Harvey, the only captain to speak to Collingwood that evening, stated plainly that 'at this time our object was to go to Gibraltar' and evidently believed that Collingwood was hoping to get round the Cape that night.

Aboard *Belleisle*, exhausted, relieved men were in an emotional state. 'Eager inquiries were expressed, and earnest congratulations exchanged at this joyful moment,' wrote Paul Nicolas. The crew was securing the guns to stop them rolling around dangerously, and clearing and cleaning the ship. Marine Lieutenant John Owen, William Hudson, the master, and a handful of men took the pinnace to the *Argonauta*. When they climbed up the side the ship appeared deserted: 'I found no living person on her deck,' Owen recalled, 'but on making my way, over numerous dead and a confusion of wreck, across the quarterdeck, was met by the second captain at the cabin door.'

Pedro Albarracin surrendered his sword, explained that Captain Antonio Pareja was wounded and the crew had taken cover below. Owen returned Albarracin's sword, requiring him to surrender to Captain Hargood on *Belleisle*, and left Hudson in charge of the prize. A little later *Polyphemus* had *Argonauta* in tow, having taken several more Spanish officers on board.

By the time Owen returned to *Belleisle* with the Spanish officer, the full extent of her losses had become clear. The two dead lieutenants, Ebenezer Geall and John Woodin, 'were lying beside each other in the gunroom preparatory to their being committed to the deep,' wrote Paul Nicolas, 'and here many met to take a last look at their departed friends'. Any other bodies remaining in the ship were thrown overboard. One sailor was found still to be breathing a second before he was heaved over the poop and, according to Nicolas, 'after being a week in the hospital, the ball which entered the temple came out of his mouth'.

The upper deck was still a tangle of masts, sails, ropes, and fragments of wreck: 'Nothing could be more horrible than the scene of blood and mangled remains with which every part was covered, and which, from the quantity of splinters, resembled a shipwright's yard strewed with gore.' The cockpit was worse. Nicolas, like others, went down to ask after a friend and was appalled by the scene of crowded carnage: 'On a long table lay several anxiously awaiting their turn to receive the surgeon's care, yet dreading the fate which he might pronounce. One subject was undergoing amputation, and every part was heaped with sufferers: their piercing shrieks and expiring groans were echoed through this vault of misery.'

He was relieved to receive an invitation to tea in the captain's cabin, where he was introduced to Pedro Albarracin. The room was still hung round with bunches of grapes, alhough they had been liberally plundered for refreshment during the battle.

Now the officers were overcome with exhaustion and depression. Some were mourning friends; most were wounded to some degree and all were filthy. Their gloom deepened when a lieutenant from *Naiad* came aboard and told them of Nelson's death. *Belleisle* had been part of Nelson's fleet for two years and Hargood had been a guest at Nelson's wedding in 1787. They took the news badly and 'even the Spanish captain joined in our regret'. When he noticed that Owen's trousers were torn and bloody, Hargood sent for William Clapperton who came 'reeking from the cockpit' to examine his wound. Hargood himself had 'an extensive bruise reaching from the throat nearly to the waist, but he desired not to be returned wounded'.

The seamen on *Revenge* cleared their decks with similar emotions: 'as each officer and seaman would meet . . . they were inquiring for their messmates,' wrote William Robinson. Orders were given to fetch the dead bodies from the cockpit of those who had bled to death waiting for attention or had died during amputation, and throw them overboard. Then the men were given a gill of rum each. Robinson recalled that 'they much needed it, for they had not ate or drank from breakfast time: we had now a good night's work before us; all our yards, masts, and sails were sadly cut, indeed the whole of the sails were obliged to be unbent, being rendered completely useless, and by the next morning we were partly jury-rigged'.

The day's work did not end with the last shots from the cannon, especially not down on the orlop decks where, partly below the waterline, the surgeons of all nations were still working hard. Forbes MacBean Chevers of *Tonnant* performed amputations by the light of tallow candles, held by his loblolly boys. He instructed them, 'If you look straight into the wound, and see all that I do, I shall see perfectly.' The next day he found that his eyebrows had been singed off. He 'described the agony suffered by strong, muscular sailors torn by splinter wounds (these wounds being generally much more formidable than those inflicted by shot) as being terrible, even to a surgeon'.

In theory a British 74 had a surgeon and two assistants. In practice this was rarely the case. Chevers had just one mate in Robert Evans. The loblolly men did the unskilled work and it was customary in battle for the purser and the chaplain to lend a hand in the cockpit. In *Tonnant* there was no chaplain, but the purser George Booth and his Carmarthen-born steward, Mansel Rees, enjoyed the able assistance of 'a very powerful and resolute woman, the wife of a petty officer'.

We do not know how many other women helped. Jane Townshend of *Defiance* later claimed a Trafalgar medal; presumably she was the wife of Thomas Townshend, an able seaman from Great Yarmouth. Although her presence during the battle was well attested, her claim was refused on the grounds that many other women had served in the fleet that day and they were not going to give medals to them all.

French and Spanish ships were generally better equipped with medical staff. *Monarca* had a physician, two surgeons and a surgeon's mate, with two chaplains. *Leviathan* later embarked five surgical staff as prisoners from *Swiftsure*, which was the proper medical complement for a French 74: a chief surgeon, two deputy surgeons and two assistant surgeons. French and Spanish surgeons, unlike their English collea-gues, received a formal training and qualified at schools of surgery established at the major naval bases.

On a ship with heavy casualties the scene in the cockpit was gruesome and the comparison with a slaughterhouse was a common-place: 'The surgeon and his mate were smeared with blood from head to foot. They looked more like butchers than doctors . . . The task was painful to behold, the surgeon using his knife and saw on human flesh and bones as freely as the butcher at the shambles.' Amputation was undertaken chiefly where limbs were smashed and nerves and vessels damaged. There was no anaesthetic. If the patient was lucky there might be some opium afterwards to dull the pain.

Only a few surgeons' reports survive from the battle. The most coherent is that of William Shoveller, the thirty-two-year-old surgeon of the *Leviathan*. He worked with the help of his assistant, Paul Johnstone, and his mate, Mattio Capponi, from Corfu. Shoveller amputated the right arm of Hugh Baimbridge, a twenty-three-year-old seaman, at the shoulder below which it had been shot off by a cannon shot. Then he cut off above the elbow the left arm of the popular Thomas Main, the captain of the forecastle, after it was shattered by a grape shot. Main told his messmates, who had offered to help him to the cockpit, 'I thank you, stay where you are; you will do more good there,' then climbed down alone. Shoveller, 'who respected him', offered to treat him immediately but the seaman replied, 'Avast, not until it comes to my turn, if you please,' and waited.

A tourniquet, usually a silk strap, was applied above Main's arm. The skin was stretched upwards towards the root of the arm. The soft tissues were cut with a scalpel. Then the periosteum, the membrane enveloping the bones, was sliced through with a sharp, round-bladed knife so that the initial movements of the saw should not shatter it. The bone had to be cut higher up to help the flesh to heal over it. The surgeon began to saw carefully, then rapidly as soon as he had purchase. A skilled practitioner could perform the entire procedure in only a few minutes. Thomas Main sang 'Rule Britannia' while Shoveller was sawing. Then a haemostatic ligature was applied to seal the blood vessels, the wound was bandaged and the patient given something to drink. Chaplain Alexander Scott served lemonade in *Victory*.

Shoveller and his mates also had to deal with several clean canister and grape-shot wounds, where bullets needed extracting, and several splinter wounds that were usually messier. Fred Brown had a wound in his forehead complicated by bruising: he had fallen from the main top after the splinter hit him.

But the most daunting wounds in *Leviathan* were caused by the explosion of one of the lower deck 32-pounders, when the breach blew out backwards. David Morris was the worst hurt, 'severely burnt over his forehead, face, neck and over the whole of his breast and belly . . . both eyes much injured'. He was dosed with opium and terebinth. At least four other men suffered lesser burns from the same explosion. *Victory*'s gunner William Rivers had been clearing up his ship and found that numerous 'marines lay on the Forecastle dead with their muskets to their breast as if they were going to fire the sight was shocking to behold'. Afterwards he went to the cockpit to ask after his son, whose leg had been sawn off four inches below the knee. The seventeen-year-old midshipman called out from the other side of the deck, 'Here I am, Father, nothing is the matter with me; only lost my leg and that in a good cause.' When, that night, they were collecting the sawn-off limbs to throw them overboard, young Rivers 'asked the men if they had his leg, they said that they did not know and he joked, "I understand old putty nose was to have them for fresh meat for the sick."'

As the sun sank into the cloudbanks on the horizon at around seven p.m. Lieutenant Humphrey Senhouse, on *Conqueror*, looked out over four miles of sea, and contemplated 'a melancholy instance of the instability of human greatness'. Two of the finest fleets that had ever put to sea, 'which only a few hours previously had been towering in all their pride on their destined element', had been reduced to wreckage all around him. Dismasted ships were 'lying like logs on the water, the surface of which was strewed with wreck from various vessels and their hulks interspersed with the remaining part of the fleet in a most shattered state'.

Several of the British ships had lost some or all of their masts, rigging had been shot away and few were in a condition to carry much sail. Out of the twenty-seven in the fleet, fourteen had fairly serious damage to their hulls. Of the prizes, eight had no masts and none had all of them. They had suffered considerable damage below the water-line and hundreds of the men in them were badly wounded.

In the gathering dusk the British crews tried to count their prizes, but with so many ships dismasted it was difficult to tell friend from foe at a distance. *Phoebe* calculated fifteen or sixteen. Collingwood made the total nineteen, including the one that had blown up. In fact, without counting *Achille*, there were seventeen – eight French and nine Spanish. Over the next few days ignorance of what ships were in whose possession introduced confusion. It was gradually clouding over and the gentle wind, which had strengthened slightly, was blowing from west-south-west directly on to the shore. The uneasy swell troubled the ships with damaged masts and threw about those that had none. But now there was little time before it became completely dark and much needed to be done.

In later years Senhouse was one of the most outspoken of the 'we should have anchored' school. 'It is impossible to conceive why it was not done,' he wrote. In his view the issue was not whether it was best to anchor off a lee shore to ride out a storm. The reason for anchoring was much more immediate and practical: 'The great difficulty, the first night, was in getting the hulks clear of their shattered rigging, and taking them in tow. Under circumstances like these, occasioned by the want of boats, and the disabled state of the ships, it was almost impossible to accomplish it under sail. At anchor it might have been done with ease.'

At anchor the ships could have been kept reasonably close together and repairs effected before any attempt was made to get under way. Leaking hulls could have been plugged, water pumped out and everything made shipshape before the bad weather, which they probably expected, hit them. Fitter ships could have helped the weaker ones and supplied them with whatever they lacked. Adequate crews could have been put aboard all the prizes, sufficient to guard the prisoners and sail the ship the next day. Assuming their anchors held, they would have remained where they were during the first night, safe from the offshore shoals. If any anchors dragged, some nearby ship would have seen and aided any in trouble.

'If Lord Nelson had lived the fleet would have anchored immediately after the action,' wrote Senhouse elsewhere. 'As we were only five leagues from the land and in shoal water where our anchors would have rode the ships securely, and having nothing else to attend to, we could have employed ourselves in rigging jury-masts and in securing the prizes; but this was neglected. A considerable time elapsed before the ships were in a condition to take the more disabled vessels in tow, during which time they were drifting fast on a lee shore.'

While there was still enough light Blackwood and Collingwood took a bearing on Cape Trafalgar and reckoned it to be about eight miles east-south-east. This put them only about two miles to windward of the nearest shoal, the Laja de Conil, and far too close to land for comfort. The admiral steered southwards and as close to the westerly wind as possible, towards the open water beyond the banks off Cape Trafalgar.

When the ships lit their lights William Cumby and his fellow officers in *Bellerophon* 'observed that the *Euryalus*, to which ship we knew Vice Admiral Collingwood had shifted his flag, carried the lights of the Commander in Chief, and that there were no lights on board the *Victory*; from which we were left to draw the melancholy inference that our gallant, our beloved Chief, the incomparable Nelson, had fallen'. Many ships did not see this and did not know for days afterwards that Nelson was dead.

Collingwood had only been sailing for half an hour close-hauled on the starboard tack when a sudden squall from the south hit the wrong side of *Euryalus*'s sails and drove her backwards. Then the heavy swell threw *Royal Sovereign* against her. 'At 7.36, took aback,' reported *Euryalus*'s log, 'and the *Royal Sovereign* fell on board of our starboard beam.' The huge three-decker 'took away the main and mizen topgallant masts, lost the royals and yards. Tore the fore and main sails very much, and took away a great part of the running rigging.' The loss of masts and sails impaired the frigate's performance and her men spent the rest of the night attempting to repair the damage. To add insult to injury, apart from smashing the railings and the jolly-boat, *Royal Sovereign* swept away the hammock cloths, hammocks and bedding that were still lining the ship's side, leaving some of the crew with nothing to sleep in.

The collision ended any hope Collingwood had entertained of rounding the Cape. By the time they were moving again they had made too much leeway for the project to be at all safe. That evening Collingwood was very much alone. He had left his right-hand man, Lieutenant James Clavell, severely wounded and unconscious in *Royal Sovereign*. He was a sentimental man and he had loved Nelson. He was exhausted by the battle even before the responsibility of being commander-in-chief had dropped heavily on to his sagging shoulders. One of *Euryalus*'s midshipmen, Joseph Moore, described, many years later, how Collingwood had stood on the deck for hours 'now and then tugging at the waistband of his unmentionables . . . his only food a few biscuits, an apple and a glass of wine every four hours'. He never found decision-making easy. Having got clear of *Royal Sovereign*, he again made sail on the starboard tack but at nine o'clock, having sounded in twenty-three fathoms, he made the night signal to prepare to anchor. The historian William James – a trenchant critic of Collingwood's leadership that evening – who was writing in 1823 with information from eyewitnesses, noted drily that the signal came 'about four hours too late'.

Some of the ships of the fleet were able to keep quite close to Collingwood. *Agamemnon* took *Colossus* in tow early in the evening. *Téméraire*, towed by *Sirius*, was also in company. John Conn of *Dreadnought* had efficiently put a prize crew into *San Juan Nepomuceno* and taken 160 officers and men off her in the late afternoon. As it got dark she left the Spanish ship to fend for herself and set off after the admiral, mending her rigging and her main topsail yard as she sailed. *Neptune* got some new sails up and accompanied the admiral. Even some of the prizes were on the move. Richard King's men in the British *Achille* threw sixty-seven empty barrels overboard from the forward hold to make room for thirty-eight prisoners from *Berwick* and made sail with the admiral, towing the French ship.

But most British ships were unable to move off when the admiral did, either because of their own injuries or because of the state of the prizes and the difficulty of getting them in tow. The crew of *Defence* began to clear their own ship and their prize *San Ildefonso*. Her wounded captain, José de Vargas, brought aboard as a prisoner, impressed his captors by coolly lighting his cigar from a match-tub next to a gun. The Spanish ship's foremast fell just after *Defence* put the first watch aboard, leaving her without any masts. Midshipman Thomas Huskisson was rowed over during the evening: he 'found the decks both above and below covered with the killed and wounded'. They threw what Huskisson estimated was more than a hundred dead bodies overboard and, with their boats, finally got *San Ildefonso* in tow at about ten o'clock.

Humphrey Senhouse's *Conqueror* received orders to take *Bucentaure* in tow. At ten thirty Captain Israel Pellew sent Lieutenants Richard Spear and Nicholas Fischer with four midshipmen, fifty-three seamen and twelve marines to take charge of her. Within an hour they had a tow-rope between the ships and had begun to throw corpses over the side. But the tow parted as soon as they set sail so Pellew decided to heave to and wait until daylight. Both ships drifted towards the shore but the dismasted *Bucentaure* drifted further and faster.

Philip Durham sent one of *Defiance*'s lieutenants with twenty men to take possession of *Aigle* and took off fourteen French officers and eighty-seven men. A further forty-four of *Aigle*'s crew were put aboard *Britannia*, and Admiral Lord Northesk reinforced the prize crew aboard the French ship with a lieutenant and sixty men. The prisoners who were removed included Colonel Jacquemet and the officers of the 67th Regiment, as well as Lieutenant Louis Huissier, who had become acting captain of the French ship. Lieutenant Asmus Classen and Sub-lieutenant Louis Tanguy insisted on remaining in *Aigle*, 'in order to give such assistance as was still in our power to our unfortunate comrades and to the wounded among the crew'. Their much-admired captain, Pierre Gourrège, was among the seriously wounded.

In both ships the British crews set to knotting and splicing the badly damaged rigging. Philip Durham, in *Defiance*, sounded in fifteen fathoms with a sandy bottom and decided to let go the best bower anchor. When the whole length of the cable had run out the ship did not appear to have stopped. It was dark and Durham was nervous and, 'being near the shoals of Trafalgar, cut the cable and made sail, by which was lost one bower anchor and cable, buoy and buoy rope'. He made sail but endeavoured to stay close to his prize and they kept in touch with the prize crew by loud-hailer all night.

Marine Second Lieutenant Thomas Reeves went aboard *Neptuno* from *Minotaur* with a prize crew of forty-eight men and took posses-sion. One of his team was William Thorp, a twenty-four-year-old landsman from Coventry, who wrote a detailed account of the experience. They secured the prisoners, disarmed them, locked away their firearms and put a guard on the magazine. When the prize crew inspected the ship they 'found she was very leaky', as William Thorp reported, and 'having no shot Plug on board, sent on board the *Minotaur* for some, received six and proceeded to plug up the shot holes that appeared most Dangerous'. They then had to free some of the prisoners and make them 'ply at the Pump as at this time she had 5½ feet Water in her hold'. *Minotaur* found herself in only thirteen fathoms at ten o'clock and signalled that she was in shoal water.

Captain Richard Grindall of *Prince* sent Lieutenant William Kelly, Mate Peter Hambly and some men to take charge of the *Santísima Trinidad*. They made repairs and took her in tow at eleven o'clock. As soon as the wind changed they sailed west, away from the land. 'Our first night's work on board the *Trinidad* was to heave the dead overboard, which amounted to 254 killed, and 173 wounded, several of which are dead since.' Immediately after the battle *Trinidad* had sixty inches of water in the hold and since there were not enough Britons on board to undertake this job, even if they had wanted to, the unwounded Spaniards pumped in relays all night.

Mars and *Bellerophon* remained under sail near the site of the battle, making repairs. On *Monarca* the Spanish crew was also pumping, for until morning the British prize crew consisted only of Lieutenant Edward Thomas, Midshipman Henry Walker and eight men from *Bellerophon*. *Tonnant* wore round and began to clear the wreckage off her decks. Her carpenters cobbled up one of her cutters in which Frederick Hoffman was sent to *Royal Sovereign* to report her condition and request a tow, *Tonnant*'s rudder having been smashed. *Spartiate* made repairs to her rigging, put a party of men on to *Algésiras*, then tried to take *Tonnant* in tow, but did not finally succeed until ten o'clock the next morning.

Edward Codrington sent a boat to bring Louis Infernet and his eleven-year-old son from *Intrépide*, which left Auguste Gicquel as the senior unwounded French officer in the ship. Codrington's first lieutenant, John Croft, took charge with a powerful prize crew that was reinforced with men from *Ajax* and *Africa*. With Gicquel's help, they began to take the seriously injured men out of the French ship, lowering them into the boats with a box fixed to bars taken from the capstan. Cass Halliday, *Orion*'s master, reported that they got under *Intrépide*'s stern 'with a rope to take her in tow, but they slipped it'. According to his own account, Gicquel deliberately cut the tow-rope, presumably hoping to escape. Finally *Ajax* managed to attach a rope to *Intrépide* very late at night and got under way.

Most of the ships, then, remained near where the battle had taken place while a few sailed southwards with Collingwood in *Euryalus* and found themselves ensnared by shoals. Having finally signalled the fleet to prepare to anchor at nine o'clock, the admiral again changed his mind. Twenty minutes later he sounded in thirteen fathoms. Perhaps he feared that if he dropped anchor and veered out a cable some of the ships might swing on to a bank or rocks. In the dark, and not knowing exactly where he was except that it was close to danger, he kept going. Every few minutes an experienced seaman, tied to the side of the ship, heaved the lead into the dark water and read the coded line. Coloured rags or scraps of leather were tied to it at every fathom to help him find the depth in the dark. The shallow water suggested that they were close to the sandbank then known as the Placer de Arena (now the Placer de Meca). But there was a worse possibility: they might be approaching the vicious rocks of the Bajo Aceiteira four to five miles west by north of Cape Trafalgar. According to the notebook of *Naiad*'s master, Harry Andrews, the worst of these had only five feet of water over it and the sea always broke two hundred yards away. Straying into this area would be ruinous.

Euryalus edged slowly on, taking a series of irregular soundings from thirteen to twenty-two fathoms. Collingwood was increasingly uncertain of where he was and fearful of running aground. Then, at about midnight, the wind veered round to the south. To Collingwood's enormous relief, it was now blowing his ships northwards and away from the rocks and shoals that reached out from the Cape. It also allowed him to tack out to sea. At midnight, with lights and a gun, he made the signal to wear round and steer westward.

As he celebrated the change of wind direction, Collingwood should have recognised another sign. He had spent a considerable amount of time blockading Cadiz over the years and he would have known the weather there quite well. He might even have seen a document that at least one of his captains had read.

In the record office at Bedford town hall there is a small collection of documents that once belonged to Captain Henry Bayntun. Along with Bayntun's own copies of Nelson's orders for the battle is the rough log of *Leviathan*, water-stained and bound in oiled sailcloth. It is the log that was actually on board the ship during the battle of Trafalgar and the storm that followed, with remarks rapidly penned in the hand of each successive officer of the watch. There are also books such as William Nichelson's *Treatise on Practical Navigation and Seamanship*, an up-to-date manual written by an experienced master mariner and published in 1792, and Vicente Tofiño's 1789 *Atlas Maritimo de España*, the project on which Dionisio Galiano had worked as a young man. The charts are beautifully lucid products of the Enlightenment, their very appearance inspiring confidence in their accuracy. Bayntun left a letter carefully tucked into the volume. It was sent to him on 6 April 1804, just before he left England to join Admiral Nelson in the Mediterranean. The writer attached a watercolour sketch showing how Jervis and Nelson had blockaded Cadiz in 1797 and marking a rock that was not shown on the charts but was discovered when a Spanish ship hit it while attempting to run the blockade. The rock and bearings from it in the sketch have been carefully copied on to Bayntun's Tofiño chart of the approaches to Cadiz. This strongly suggests that in 1804 and 1805 Bayntun was using this atlas in the Mediterranean.

But it was another document that the same writer had given to Bayntun, thinking it might prove useful, that suddenly became profoundly relevant towards midnight on 21 October. This was 'a remark or caution of a SW gale when in Cadiz Bay', which was 'a copy of a memorandum given out to the Fleet' during the previous blockade of Cadiz. It began: 'People who are ignorant of the Navigation of the Coast between Cape Trafalgar and Cape St Maries are much alarmed with the Idea of a S.W. Gale; and for want of a proper knowledge how those Gales come on, frequently get into difficulties.' Then it warned, 'The Gale is always far southerly in its outset for six or eight hours; but at the same time the sea will make for the westward.' The junction of a southerly wind with a westerly swell was what had just occurred, and, according to this 'caution', it was a very dangerous sign. Harry Andrews, master of the frigate *Naiad*, transcribed this same memorandum into his commonplace book, so knowledge of it might have been widespread in Collingwood's fleet. To those who could read the signs that the document pointed out, it became clear at about one o'clock in the morning of 22 October that a south-west gale was on its way and that the fleet had about seven hours in which to try to secure its safety.

The instinct of inexperienced captains, the fleet advice went on to explain, was to head south to try to make the Strait of Gibraltar. But in a strong south-west wind that became extremely difficult, requiring some thirty miles of clearance to get round Cape Trafalgar. The shoals around it were perilous, much the most dangerous in the area. If you did get round the cape you would still be exposed, blind and short of seamarks, in water too deep to sound and in danger from the rocks off Tarifa. The best thing to do was to head north, taking advantage of the early phase of the storm when the wind was just west of southerly. If you set off quickly and steered as far west as possible, then allowing four points of leeway, your real course would take you to Ayamonte or, failing that, Huelva. In either area regular soundings allowed perfect judgement of the distance from a relatively safe coastline.

This advice did not allow for the idea that a fleet might have fought a battle during the hours before they had warning of the oncoming storm, or cover the problem that to sail north-west in darkness after such a battle was tantamount to an invitation to the prizes to attempt to escape into Cadiz harbour. Its use to Collingwood at this moment was limited. But it is clear that the writer was firmly against the course of action that the fleet was currently taking in attempting to move south-west.

At the close of the battle the French and Spanish had lost eighteen ships, and the Royal Navy had seventeen of them. If all went well, Collingwood would take them to Gibraltar and then to Portsmouth, returning with a fleet substantially larger than the one he and Nelson had taken into battle. This promised a further change in the balance of power in Britain's favour and a considerable financial bonus for the government: ships usually cost much less to repair than they did to build from scratch.

For captains and crews alike, there was a further incentive to keep the prizes afloat: the money that would be paid for them. They represented real riches for the men who had captured them, especially the admirals and captains. All captains in sight of the enemy were entitled to an equal proportion of a quarter of the total prize money awarded to the fleet. The marine captains, naval lieutenants and masters shared one-eighth. Warrant sea officers, chaplains, surgeons, masters' mates and marine lieutenants shared an eighth, midshipmen, petty officers, surgeons' mates and marine sergeants also shared an eighth, and a quarter was divided between the marines and seamen. The remaining eighth went to the admirals commanding. The calculation was done across the fleet so that all men of the same rank received the same reward.

In many a wardroom and gunroom, off-duty officers calculated their likely prize-money, and some came up with plausible estimates. The Reverend John Greenly, chaplain of the *Revenge*, reckoned on £500, while Midshipman Henry Walker of *Bellerophon* had calculated his reward at £100. Oddly enough, the ratio between the two amounts (which was nearly correct) implied that they had attached roughly the same value to the seventeen prizes, a little under £1.5 million. By this calculation a captain's share would have been in excess of £10,000, enough to buy a country estate, and each seaman would have received about £30, not much less than three years' pay. The battle of the Nile, the record so far for a fleet action, had brought each seaman only £7. 18s.

However, even the most optimistic British seamen were sceptical about bringing two of the prizes home to Portsmouth. The hulls and bottoms of *Redoutable* and *Fougueux* had been shot full of holes.

William Rutherford's *Swiftsure* took *Redoutable* in tow at nine p.m. Jean-Jacques Lucas reported, 'We spent the whole of that night at the two pumps which were all that remained workable, without, however, being able to keep the water under.' The Frenchmen who were fit enough to work joined the English prize crew in pumping, stopping leaks, blocking up the portholes and attempting to hammer wooden planks over sections of the poop, which appeared ready to collapse. Lucas wrote of 'turmoil and horrible disorder' and described a scene that was hideously Gothic: there had been no time to clear the ship so the poorly lit gun-decks remained choked with dead bodies. Lucas noted that some of his men, notably the young midshipmen, were going around picking up weapons and hiding them on the lower deck. They whispered to him that if the opportunity presented itself they would retake their ship.

Things were even worse on *Fougueux*, now being towed by Thomas Capel's frigate *Phoebe*. At eight p.m. the foremast went overboard, leaving the ship without any masts. At ten she requested assistance, reporting that she was sinking. Whatever pumps were still functioning were not working well enough to keep the leaks at bay. At eleven *Phoebe*'s boats started taking people off. None of the French ship's boats were usable. From accounts that he heard afterwards, Commander François Bazin reported that the British rescued about forty Frenchmen, including several wounded men. Presumably they also took off most of the prize crew although some men from *Téméraire* were still on board in the morning. As the night went on the wind rose, and when dawn broke it was very strong. The seas were so dangerous that small boats could not get near the ship. In driving rain the attempt to transfer people was abandoned. Pierre Servaux, who had been in charge of discipline in *Fougueux*, recalled that 'the scenes of horror on board the ship that night were really the most awful and fearful that imagination can call up.' There were no masts or sails or rigging.

> [The hulk] was as full of holes as a sieve, shattered from stem to stern, and with two enormous gaps forced in on the starboard side at the water line, through which the sea poured in a stream. The water had

risen almost to the orlop deck. Everywhere one heard the cries of the wounded and the dying, as well as the noise and shouts of insubordinate men who refused to man the pumps and only thought of themselves.

The men were exhausted, drunk, mutinous, despairing. They thought they would die. At daylight they could hear the breakers on the rocky shoals of the Marrajotos to seaward of Sancti Petri. The water had reached the lower deck.

18

The Seaman's Last Shift

By first light on Tuesday, 22 October, it was clear that the British fleet and its prizes were trapped in Cadiz Bay.

To Collingwood in *Euryalus*, daylight revealed *Naiad* towing *Belleisle* and *Agamemnon* towing *Colossus* ahead of him to the south-west, and forty more ships straggling behind him and towards the shore, stretching over about twenty miles from the east to the north-east. He realised that his fleet was dangerously scattered. The wind had risen to force five and was strengthening all the time. The barometer had dropped two inches overnight and was still falling. His first priority now had to be to get his ships back together.

Euryalus cast off *Royal Sovereign* and Collingwood ordered *Neptune* to take his former flagship in tow and to lead the fleet westward. At eight a.m., as it began to rain, he headed back inshore to collect the more distant ships, sending his little schooner *Pickle* and the cutter *Entreprenante* to tell everyone they met to close around *Neptune*. He passed *Prince* towing *Santísima Trinidad*, and *Thunderer* with *Santa Ana*. *Spartiate* was struggling to get *Tonnant* back in tow, *Dreadnought* was picking up *Swiftsure*, and *Britannia* was aiming towards *Berwick*.

As he returned to the site of the battle, Collingwood could see that many of the ships had never got under way with their prizes. During the night they had drifted on a predominantly westerly breeze towards land. Now, reinforced by inshore currents, the wind was driving the ships northwards, back towards Cadiz, while the great westerly swell still nudged them incessantly east towards the shore. For the ships close to the shore there were rocky shoals around Sancti Petri to the north and around Trafalgar to the south. By mid-morning the wind had reached force six, a 'strong breeze', creating large white-crested waves and spray. The rain was heavy and visibility was getting worse all the time. As the wind increased, new dangers entered the equation. The sea began to break on the sandbanks three to four miles off Cape Roche and Conil and on the Placer de Arena off Trafalgar, making them a great deal more dangerous than they had been the previous night. A tidal race, with fast, treacherous currents, also developed as far as eight miles offshore.

In one of the first squalls of the morning, *San Agustín* lost all of her weakened masts. The fall of one killed Able Seaman George Knowles of *Leviathan*'s prize crew, the first of many post-battle casualties. His comrades managed to anchor *San Agustín* to prevent the ship drifting further towards the rocks, and everyone resumed pumping for all they were worth. *Leviathan* was standing guard close to her when Collingwood approached. *Conqueror* had hove to for the night close to *Bucentaure*, and briefly succeeded in getting her in tow during the morning and hauling her slowly seaward.

Edward Codrington's prize, *Intrépide*, was being towed by *Ajax* so, he wrote the following Saturday, 'in the morning I ran down to three others near Trafalgar – I took the worst & weakest manned in tow, went in to pick up another'. The worst and weakest manned was *Bahama* with a prize crew of only four men from *Bellerophon* under Lieutenant George Saunders. He succeeded in getting a tow attached, using 'two 8-inch hawsers on end'.

Having double-reefed her topsails against the southerly squalls, *Phoebe* had gone inshore and spent the first part of the morning in a hopeless attempt to get the waterlogged hulk of the *Fougueux* in tow, before giving her up as lost and making an equally fruitless attempt on *Aigle*. She lost 'three whole hawsers and 100 fathoms of rope' in the process. The swell made unstable ships roll wildly and *Aigle* had 'rolled away' all of her masts in the early morning and was drifting north-wards, along with what was left of *Fougueux*, with Philip Durham's *Defiance* in attendance. For a while they would be in open water, but the isle of Sancti Petri and its rocky shoals lay in wait to the north.

The moment when *Phoebe* abandoned *Fougueux* and sailed off towards the nearby *Aigle* was the moment at which master-at-arms Pierre Servaux decided it was time to think of himself. He jumped out of a lower-deck port and fought his way through the turbulent sea towards *Orion*'s boats. By mid-morning, with seventeen other strong swimmers, he was safely in the hands of the surgeons on the orlop deck of Edward Codrington's ship.

Collingwood could now count fourteen prizes in tow, all heading south-west towards *Neptune*. At that moment, to his relief, a fresh frigate, the *Melpomene* under Captain Robert Oliver, joined the fleet: he gave her immediate orders to take any disabled ship or prize in tow. Oliver tried to pick up *San Juan Nepomuceno*, but this was not easy: the wind was now blowing a fresh gale, about force eight, punctuated by violent gusts of fifty miles per hour.

As the wind grew stronger, the desire to preserve the prizes came into conflict with the overriding priority of all seamen: the need to preserve their own ships. Most sailors felt a strong emotional attachment to their ship and this formed a unifying bond between captain, officers and crew. How far the ship might be endangered to help secure the prizes was a difficult judgement to make.

For the prize-masters and prize crews the issue was different. Saving the prize and saving their own lives were the same thing, but their new vessels were usually even more badly damaged and encumbered with corpses and wounded men. In most cases the British prize crews were dependent on the surviving French and Spanish seamen for the tasks that required large numbers of men, such as pumping out water, weighing the anchor or tacking the ship. Their defeated enemies could not simply be locked up.

Small prize crews were vulnerable to attack. Lieutenant Edward Thomas, Midshipman Henry Walker and the eight men from *Bellerophon* who were in charge of *Monarca*, and the twelve from *Bellerophon* in *Bahama*, must have felt particularly vulnerable. However, *in extremis*, the prize crews had one option: they could hand the ship back and give their former prisoners the chance to sail for the relative safety of Cadiz; so long as they were not lynched by an angry mob, they could expect to be exchanged for some of the many captured Spaniards.

For the defeated and exhausted Spanish and French crews the outlook was bleaker. It was an established principle of British naval warfare that, in the long term, depriving ships of experienced seamen could defeat any enemy. The French, at least, could be certain that they faced a long period of captivity in England. Officers might pass this in tolerable comfort, but many of the men had already sampled life in a British prison hulk. In the revolutionary navy, Auguste Gicquel had spent the freezing winter of 1795 in an ancient, rotting ship no longer fit for sea service, moored offshore as a prison, guarded by the dregs of the navy and retired soldiers. Gicquel owed his life to a French sailor who had made him a pair of trousers when otherwise he might have perished of cold. Before being dumped on the coast of France he had lost a front tooth and his nose had been broken. But even a British prison hulk was preferable to a watery grave.

A third option, retaking the ship followed by escape to Cadiz, must have looked especially attractive. As the escorts began to lose contact with their prizes in the worsening weather, French and Spanish sailors were soon casting mutinous looks at the prize crews.

In driving rain Philip Durham, of *Defiance*, came aboard *Aigle* to inspect her and decided that he was not going to succeed in towing her off the shore. The most honourable course was to hand her back to her original officers and allow them to take their chances. *Defiance* sent out boats to evacuate her prize crew.

Durham's decision appears to have been conveyed to Asmus Classen, the fifty-year-old Dutch lieutenant who was now the senior officer aboard, by a subordinate, almost certainly Lieutenant James Purches, the prize-master. Classen reported that he was told it had been decided 'she should be abandoned to the French after her cables had, by the order of the admiral, been cut into fragments'. Destroying a ship's cables ensured that she could never anchor again and, in the *Aigle*'s situation, this meant almost certain destruction on the nearby rocky shoreline.

If Collingwood gave such an order there is no record of it. There might have been a misunderstanding; Classen might have lied; or Durham might have demanded such a ruthless course of action on his own account. Either way, Asmus Classen 'prevailed upon the officer in command not to carry out this barbarous order'. Perhaps the twenty-two-year-old Purches changed his mind when he realised that he was about to be left behind on the condemned ship. *Defiance*'s log reports tersely, 'Got all on board except Lieutenant Purchase and twelve seamen, which could not be got without risking the loss of the Defiance, being so close on a lee shore. Up boats and made sail.' In his ten-year naval career, Purches had already been wrecked once, six years previously, on the Goodwin Sands. According to Asmus Classen, fifty Englishmen remained on board *Aigle*, so Durham must also have abandoned men from *Phoebe* and *Britannia*.

Further out to sea, on *Algésiras*, Lieutenant Charles Bennett from *Tonnant* had spent the night clearing the French ship's deck of fallen rigging and masts. The prisoners were sent below, and the gratings secured over them. He hailed several British ships that passed close by to give him a tow but none was willing to try. In the morning Bennett started firing guns every quarter of an hour for assistance and in the early afternoon a ship and a frigate again refused his request for help, instead steering, as Lieutenant Pierre Philibert noted, 'to rejoin the main body of their fleet which was running west-north-west'.

At two in the afternoon Collingwood noted that his ships were failing to get the prizes in tow because of the 'great sea and fresh wind', which was now blowing a 'strong gale', force nine, and had swung to the south-west, a highly dangerous angle for the ships so near to the shore. With visibility so low that he could not exercise control by signal, Collingwood wore *Euryalus* round and set her head westward again. At four o'clock he caught up with *Minotaur*, whose tow-rope had broken. He signalled her to stay close to *Neptuno* and to the other drifting prizes rather than rejoining the fleet. William Thorp and the other seamen in the prize crew of *Neptuno* had begun to clear away the wreckage at first light. They threw the mizen mast, the foreyard and the main topgallant mast overboard and cut away a number of loose spars and some rigging. *Minotaur* had taken them in tow at three thirty but, in Thorp's words, 'the wind continued to increase to a hard Gale' and 'soon after the Hawzer broke'. They were then 'left to the Mercy of the Waves the gale continued to menace the Ship a mere wreck on a lee shore possessed by the enemy'.

A ship off a lee shore was in great jeopardy when the wind was blowing a gale. The lee shore north of Cape Trafalgar was particularly dangerous because of the rocky shoals. While the wind continued to blow strongly towards the shore there was no possibility of getting round the cape to escape to Gibraltar.

To appreciate what a perilous situation the men were in, it is necessary to understand some of the technicalities of nineteenth-century seamanship. Square-rigged sailing ships could not sail directly into the wind. The nearest they could normally manage was 67 ½° off the direction from which the wind was coming. They had to tack first one way and then the other to make ground at an oblique angle to the wind. The wind that hit the hull caused the ship to make 'leeway' – drift off the course it was trying to steer and back towards the shore.

As any storm worsened crews had to strike a fine balance between having enough sail to keep the ship away from the shore and not having so much that the ship was damaged. First they got rid of the higher sails that put most pressure on the masts. During 22 October Collingwood's ships lowered their topgallant masts and yards to the deck, then took in four reefs in their topsails (that is, they were 'close-reefed'). A ship sailing close-hauled (her sails positioned as near to the wind as possible) under close-reefed topsails made so much leeway that she could not increase her distance from the shore. If the wind became strong enough to force the captain to reduce sail still further, the ship would be driven, very slowly, ever closer to it. Most of the hulks could carry hardly any sail at all and were being blown much more rapidly shorewards.

If a ship was getting dangerously close to the shore, the only thing to do was to anchor and pray that the cables would hold.

As *Defiance* left *Aigle* and disappeared into the murk to the north-west, Asmus Classen took stock of his new command. His captain, Pierre Gourrège, was fighting for his life below in the care of the surgeon, but Classen had been at sea since he was thirteen and had served for twenty years in the Dutch navy before joining the French in 1787. He had been an officer under Julien Cosmao-Kerjulien for four years and had commanded several small ships already, so he was accustomed to such responsibility. With the soldiers at the pumps, Classen soon had his sailors at work, hoisting spars to rig studding sails and topgallant sails on the stumps of the masts. The aged carpenter, Louis Colombel, and the master caulker, Pierre Martinet, had already been working steadily since the battle to repair the most dangerous shot holes and leaks.

Classen does not say whether the fifty British on board helped to sail the ship or whether he held them prisoner, but his silence suggests that they joined in this attempt to preserve all their lives. In these circumstances, every fit man was needed. Classen took a bearing on Cadiz, which he reckoned was twenty-one miles away to the north. Then he tried out his improvised sails. The swell and the wind were immediately too much for them. The ship would not answer to the helm and he found himself carried inexorably towards the coast. 'This desperate situation, when it happens,' wrote William Nichelson in his *Treatise on Practical Navigation* (1792), 'is the seaman's last shift, when a ship is so entangled with a lee shore, with the wind and seas so high, and right upon the shore, that it is found impossible to keep off the shore, with all the sail she can carry, so that her safety must depend entirely upon the management of the ground-tackle, that is to say the anchors and cables.'

Classen succeeded in anchoring close to Sancti Petri, rather more than three miles from the shore. He was in a horribly exposed position, right on top of rocky shoals and far too close to land for comfort, but since Sancti Petri was a Spanish outpost there was some faint hope of rescue. Classen 'fired distress signals and passed a most critical night owing to the hurricane and the heavy seas'.

The desperation of the men in *Aigle* was not diminished by what they saw at last light. They watched helplessly as, only six hundred yards away, the waterlogged wreck of *Fougueux* was ripped and broken as it was driven through the rocks of the Haxto Afuera shoal. A little later they saw it break up completely in the distance on the savage brown rocks on the shore between Torre Bermeja and the mouth of the Sancti Petri river. *Fougueux* had been abandoned by the Royal Navy some hours before *Aigle*. Now, despite frantic efforts from Spanish gunboats based at the little fishing village in the estuary, almost all of her remaining crew perished. Acting Captain François Bazin estimated later that only about thirty men reached land. With those whom the British had as prisoners he guessed that perhaps 110 or 120 men had survived out of the ship's company of 682. He did not bargain for the forty-seven men saved by *Phoebe* and *Orion*, but the true total of survivors was only 165. Twenty-four British seamen from *Téméraire* and one from *Phoebe* also drowned in the wreck of the *Fougueux*.

Further out to sea, *Redoutable* was also in trouble. In the morning, as the wind strengthened, *Swiftsure* had sent her boats to take off Captain Jean-Jacques Lucas with twenty of his officers and men, then to put on a prize crew under Lieutenant Thomas Read. She seemed to be floating quite well, until early in the afternoon when, as Midshipman George Barker recalled, 'from her rolling so violently in a heavy sea, she carried away her fore Mast, the only mast she had standing'.

With no sail to keep her steady, *Redoutable* rolled sickeningly and at about five it became clear that the prize crew was losing the battle against the rising water. Pumping was extremely hard work. *Redoutable* had six pumps, all operated from around the mainmast on the lower deck, but four had been wrecked in the battle. Each pump pulled up water from the well and diverted it towards the scuppers at the side of the ship. Handles turned the wheels that drove the pumps. These could be extended to allow twenty or thirty men to work each one at once. But, as a British manual explained, it was the most uncomfortable and least popular work on a ship: 'Few officers of any experience must not have known the difficulty with which men are almost drove to return to the pumps of leaking ships, when obliged to keep them going. It strains their loins, affects the muscular parts of their arms like violent rheumatic pains, and galls their hands.' On *Redoutable* the men worked the two remaining pumps in relays. With the ship actually sinking, they had an extra incentive to work, but exhaustion set in nevertheless.

Prize-master Thomas Read realised that he would have to abandon the ship, but with the sea so rough he was uncertain whether his shipmates would be able or willing to save the men on board. If no help arrived they would all drown. He made a distress signal to *Swiftsure* and peered through the pouring rain to see what her crew would do. The response was instantaneous. Captain William Rutherford and his men lowered all *Swiftsure*'s boats into the heaving water. There were five, between twenty-five and thirty-two feet long, and the little eighteen-foot jolly-boat.

Minimally crewed, they put out into the huge seas with dense foam blowing across their bows and curling waves breaking over them. The spray was blinding as the British sailors tried to get close to the rolling wreck that towered over them. As it became clear that the ship was going down, the French crew carried up their wounded into the open air and laid them on the quarterdeck. The injured men must have realised they had little chance: it was difficult even for fit men to climb from the ship to the boats. *Swiftsure*'s boats rowed back carrying Thomas Read and most of the seamen of the prize crew, with about a hundred Frenchmen and some men from *Téméraire*.

It was now almost dark and Rutherford decided it was too dangerous to risk the boats going back. The tow-rope was still in place and there was an outside chance that the *Redoutable* might float till morning, but nobody really believed it. 'What added to the horrors of the night,' wrote Midshipman George Barker, 'was the inability of our saving them all, as we could no longer endanger the lives of our people in open boats, at the mercy of a heavy sea and most violent Gale of Wind'.

Lieutenant Thomas Sykes begged to be allowed to make one more run. Reluctantly, Rutherford gave him the launch, the most capacious of the boats, and he set off into the darkness. It was now so rough that there was no way of tying up close to the French ship. But Sykes found that it was possible, as the dying ship rolled to leeward, to 'drag into his boat as many of the half-drowned wretches as could be laid hold of'. He remained out for so long that Rutherford became sure the launch must have gone down. Thomas Read, who had been the prize-master, asked to go back and look for him. Rutherford gave Read the pinnace and he returned to the French ship. When he found Sykes still trying to lift men off *Redoutable*, Read joined in the heroic effort. They kept at it until both boats were full. Altogether they got off another ninety-seven of the crew.

By the time they left, *Redoutable*'s stern was almost entirely under-water and shortly after seven she sank with about 300 men still on board or swimming nearby, most of them wounded. With the wind blowing even stronger Captain Rutherford refused to send the boats out again in conditions where they would all surely be lost. George Barker was haunted by the voices in the storm: 'This was the most dreadful scene that can be imagined as we could distinctly hear the cries of the unhappy people we could no longer assist.'

Towards dawn the wind dropped to a moderate breeze, although the swell remained a problem. But daylight revealed nothing but wreckage. *Redoutable* had disappeared and there was no sign of survivors. Then, around nine, the lookout shouted that he could see some improvised rafts made from wreckage with figures clinging to them. The boats were lowered again and circled around, patiently hauling exhausted bodies from the sea. They came back with fifty-four men, and tried to help them from the bobbing boats up the steep sides of the rolling *Swiftsure*:

> When the Boats came alongside many of these unfortunate men were unable to get up the Ship's side, as most of them were not only fainting from fatigue, but were wounded in the most shocking manner, some expired in the Boats before they could get on board, completely exhausted and worn out with struggling to preserve their lives, having been the whole of a Tempestuous Night, upon a few crazy planks exposed to every inclemency of the weather.

The survivors saved in the morning brought the total of Frenchmen taken off *Redoutable* to 169, of whom seventy were wounded. *Neptune* found three more floating on a piece of wreckage and hauled them in. Five of *Swiftsure*'s own men were drowned in the French ship along with twelve from *Téméraire* and two from *Phoebe*.

Francis Beaufort invented his 'Beaufort Scale' for measuring wind speed in the autumn of 1805, at the time that this storm was taking place. As he chose the original terms to denote different strengths of wind, Beaufort, a lieutenant in the navy, 'merely formalised and adopted terms that had by then entered common usage'. Naval logs were already employing nearly all the terms that Beaufort used with the same meanings that Beaufort gave them.

The logs of the ships in Collingwood's fleet record the wind on 22 October rising from 'moderate breezes', to 'fresh breezes', to 'strong breezes' in the morning, to 'fresh gales' by noon and 'strong gales' in the early afternoon. Wind strength remained at 'strong gales' with 'violent squalls' until around daylight on 23 October.

The amount of sail carried by the ships, as recorded in their logs, matched conditions for a strong gale of force nine to force ten. They took down their topgallant masts and close-reefed their topsails. One or two, such as *Defence*, went one stage further and took in their topsails completely, relying on the courses, the sails set from the lower yards, instead. Some still ran into trouble, probably because of the violent squalls and sudden, treacherous changes in wind direction that were a feature of this storm as it developed (for it was not yet at anything like its height).

In the afternoon *Achille* lost two cutters, which she had been towing astern. *Mars* lost one of hers. *Ajax* had her sails reefed and was pumping constantly, her carpenters hard at work on the shot holes and repairing the boats to transport prisoners. *Belleisle* was pumping furiously. In mid-afternoon *Leviathan* had to 'cut away the fore and main courses to save the masts'.

Towards evening, as the rain fell in driving torrents, Lieutenant William Hennah held a funeral service on *Mars* and 'committed the body of Captain Duff to the deep', watched by Pierre Villeneuve, his little huddle of staff, and young Norwich Duff, the dead captain's son. In *Bellerophon* William Cumby read the funeral service over the bodies of Captain John Cooke and Edward Overton.

After darkness fell, *Prince*'s mizen topsail split. *Dreadnought*'s fore topsail blew away and at ten thirty she was 'taken aback', thrown off course so that the wind hit her sails from the wrong direction, losing a cutter as a result. *Neptune*'s main topsail blew to pieces. For all Collingwood's vaunted seamanship, *Euryalus* herself was 'took aback' for the second time since the battle at eleven thirty. Despite reefed sails *Mars*'s main topmast broke just after midnight, leaving the crew struggling to clear the resulting wreckage all night in the raging storm. *Conqueror* was in particular trouble, having tried to maintain touch with *Bucentaure* close to the shore. Soundings revealed that she was in only thirteen fathoms of water, close in among the shoals, when the main topsail sheets gave way. Captain Israel Pellew remembered seeing 'all adrift, the clewlings and buntlings gone, and the sail all flying'. He called for an officer to lead the seamen up aloft into the violently tossing rigging sixty feet above the deck and Humphrey Senhouse was 'the only officer that volunteered the hazardous expedient of going aloft to cut away the sail, by which means alone we saved the mast'. But as they struggled to save their own ship, they lost touch with *Bucentaure*.

Conqueror's master's log gives the impression that she was in constant touch with *Bucentaure* until late next day. The truth was somewhat different.

Conqueror pulled out to sea where she and *Defiance* could still be seen with *Phoebe* rather closer, keeping a distant eye on *Bucentaure*, which was not far to windward of the abandoned *Aigle* and the wreck of the *Fougueux* in the area of Sancti Petri. The French ships were in real danger, being blown north-east on to the shore by a violent, squally wind in extremely high seas.

Looking north-north-east from *Bucentaure*'s quarterdeck, Lieutenant Fulcran Fournier, the senior officer fit for service, thought he made out the lighthouse tower of San Sebastian about nine miles away and covertly took a bearing on it. All day, in murmurs, *Bucentaure*'s crew had discussed retaking their ship, and by nightfall Fournier knew that they were resolved to act. There were about five hundred of them against about eighty British seamen and marines. With their friends so far away, the British were looking nervous about their prospects for surviving the night. Fournier sent a message to the wounded Mathieu Prigny, Villeneuve's chief-of-staff. Prigny agreed that this was a chance worth taking: 'The circumstances were as urgent as the opportunity was favourable; we took advantage of it.' But he wanted to do it without bloodshed.

Fournier invited Lieutenant Richard Spear and marine Second Lieutenant John Nicholas Fischer to go with him to Prigny's dimly lit cabin. The ship was now swaying violently and the men had to brace themselves against the cabin walls and door. Prigny, a man of considerable charm, suggested that the British officers surrender to him so that they could all try to run for Cadiz, pointing out that if they refused his offer the French would be obliged to retake the ship by force. After a hurried consultation, Spear and Fischer agreed. They must have realised that the last thing any of them needed was further conflict on a crippled ship in the middle of a storm. Even if the prize crew prevailed, they could not keep the *Bucentaure* afloat on their own.

The British and their French prisoners-turned-captors set to work, clearing away the wreck of the foremast and rigging one of the smaller sails on its stump, and discovered that they could get the ship to bear up towards Cadiz. To Fournier's delight, *Bucentaure* was soon making almost five knots in the favourable wind, but with night falling and only his uncertain bearing to steer by, he was still uneasy. He fired a gun at regular intervals to warn the San Sebastian lighthouse of their approach, but it was far from certain that the Spanish would light it for what might be a hostile ship. At seven the flame shone out from the lighthouse and they celebrated.

But the light on the tower of San Sebastian was all they could see: in the torrential rain the night was pitch dark and the land was soon invisible. They all knew that there were dangerous rocks at the entrance to Cadiz harbour. The *Bucentaure* had been given three Spanish pilots to advise on coastal navigation, one of whom had told Fulcran Fournier that he had fished the waters off Cadiz for six years, and 'promised to take the ship within the Puercas'. Fournier could not refuse his advice: 'He therefore took the helm.'

The anchorage at Cadiz is not easy to reach in pitch darkness with a raging gale. After clearing the rocks off Sancti Petri, mariners have relatively clear water ahead until they make Cadiz. On the map Cadiz looks like the head of a dragon. A long neck of a peninsula stretches northward to the city, set in the middle of a rocky island, and from there two rocky jaws gape north-eastwards into the sea as if to devour the unwary mariner. At the tip of the more powerful lower jaw stands the lighthouse tower of San Sebastian. Behind it, the forts of San Sebastian and Santa Catalina guard the entrance to the harbour in the bay that opens above the city. From the south, ships have to sail past the lighthouse, giving it a wide berth because the rocks spill out way beyond it, then turn in well to the north, clear of the Puercas, the first of several dangerous rocky shoals at the entrance to the bay. The safest deep-water channel lies between the Diamante rocks and the Galera further north. All of these rocks hide innocently under the sea at high tide but at low tide their jagged, dirty-brown features are revealed, with the water crashing against them.

It was almost low tide, with many of the most dangerous rocks exposed, but no one on the *Bucentaure* could see or even hear them in the gale until they were on top of them. In the dirty blackness of this foul night of driving rain, the light from the San Sebastian lighthouse looked much further away than it otherwise would have done, so the *Bucentaure*'s fisherman-pilot miscalculated and turned south-eastwards a few hundred yards too soon.

At eight fifteen Fournier 'felt a very severe shock which unshipped the rudder and carried away two planks in the 24-pounder battery'. They had come in far too close to the town and had crashed into a rock off Santa Catalina fort. The sounding said that they were in seven and a half fathoms (forty feet) of water so they lowered two anchors and cut away their rudder because it was hammering against the hull and might stave it in completely.

The heavy sea continually rolled the ship against the rocks but fortunately the water level did not drop much further and at nine thirty the tide began to rise. 'We worked all night,' Prigny reported, 'to start the water casks and to throw overboard provisions, wood, spare spars and the boats – which, riddled as they were, could be of no help to us – in order to lighten the ship.' To signal their distress they continued to fire a gun.

At about two in the morning of 23 October a small boat arrived from *Indomptable*, one of the French ships that had escaped after the battle, to ask what their problem was. They sent it back with a request for a longboat, an anchor, some hawsers, and as many other boats as possible. If a boat with another anchor could come while the tide was high, Fournier felt that he might yet preserve the ship. But no boat returned, and at three the tide began to ebb once more. If no help arrived soon the bottom of the ship would certainly be smashed in.

Bucentaure and *Aigle* were not the only ships to escape towards Cadiz on 22 October. From a mile or two further south and to windward on *Algésiras* the late Admiral Magon's two aides, Voldemar de la Bretonnière and Pierre Philibert, watched *Defiance*, *Phoebe* and *Conqueror* sail away from 'the *Bucentaure* and another ship that we did not recognize' towards a British fleet that was no longer in sight. They checked to see that they were unobserved by any of the prize crew from *Tonnant*, then covertly took a bearing on Cadiz lighthouse. Like Fulcran Fournier before them, they saw an opportunity to escape as soon as it was dark.

Charles Bennett, the prize-master from *Tonnant*, was probably somewhat shamed and frustrated by his repeated failure to obtain help from his own side. Now he was also alarmed. De la Bretonnière and Philibert pointed out the rocks around Sancti Petri a mile and a half away and 'observed to him that we should be lost with all hands'.

Bennett did not have enough men to rig masts and sails and guard the 650 fit Frenchmen and decided to free the crew of the *Algésiras* so that they could rig topgallant masts on the stumps of the masts. This 'was very soon done, our crew lending them a hand, and as soon as the topgallant-sail serving as a foresail was trimmed, the ship bore up and we got clear of the shoal'.

At five thirty the French officers met secretly 'and decided unanimously that as soon as it was night we should retake the ship'. At seven they invited Bennett and the marine Captain Arthur Ball to join them in the great cabin, where Admiral Magon's secretary, Pierre François Feuillet, who spoke the best English,

> informed them in the name of the executive that after the noble . defence of our ship we had a right to expect that assistance from the English fleet which they themselves had vainly demanded; that feeling ourselves thereby released from the obligations that we had assumed when placing ourselves in their power, we had decided to retake our ship, but that they might expect to be treated with consideration on our part, provided that they did not compel us to employ force by a resistance after which they would still find themselves obliged to yield.

Bennett and Ball 'displayed a great deal of resistance and the greatest firmness', but eventually yielded, after insisting upon a promise of liberty for the British crew whenever the ship reached a port. Shouts of '*Vive l'Empereur!*' rang out around the ship.

Voldemar de la Bretonnière now took charge. He was a handsome twenty-nine-year-old, born in Martinique in the West Indies, but he was no novice, either as a fighter or as a seaman. He had first fought the British as a boy and had been in charge of a little boat in the rearguard when the former black slaves first burned Cap François in Saint-Domingue. He had helped evacuate fleeing civilians to the waiting French fleet (William Hargood, now captain of the *Belleisle*, then a prisoner-of-war, was one of those they saved). Later, he had been a sub-lieutenant in the famous frigate *La Forte*, which as part of a frigate squadron led by Magon, had fought off two English 74s, then 'terrorized the Indian seas'.

By about seven thirty de la Bretonnière and his officers had restored order and calm on the ship, locked the disarmed prize crew in the council chamber and their officers in a private cabin. The surviving accounts are generous to the men of both ships but, given what is known about other ships, the officers might have had to suppress panic and drunkenness, especially among the soldiers who had never before been to sea.

Then the *Algésiras*, under French command once more, ran before the wind for Cadiz, with the two topgallant sails rigged on the stumps. They were working to rig a third on the stump of the mizen mast when several guns broke loose and began to roll around. This was very dangerous since the guns were heavy enough to smash through the sides of the ship. They hauled to the wind and lay-to while they secured them, taking advantage of this pause to secure a cable to the only bower anchor they had left.

At eleven they got under way once more, approaching cautiously because they were terrified of hitting a rock before they found an anchorage. There was no Spanish pilot on *Algésiras* so the best advice they had came from a reliable quarter-gunner named Legris, who had helped take ships into Cadiz harbour several times in his past life as a merchant seaman. They neared Cadiz in the dark, eyes straining in the rain and wind for rocks or signs of land. They fared better than the *Bucentaure* and at two in the morning they anchored in Cadiz Bay to the north-east of the San Sebastian lighthouse.

It was only as it began to get light and the tide fell that they saw how close they were to the Diamante rocks.

ARENAS GORDAS
TO CADIZ

'BAHAMA' ANCHORED HERE
24 OCTOBER

'BERWICK'
27 OCTOBER

'RAYO'
27 OCTOBER

'MONARCA'
25 OCTOBER

Placer de Jacinto

RIO GUADALQUIVIR

Sanlúcar

Chipiona

Punta Regla
Baja Salmedina

SPAIN

Rota

La Gallina

'NEPTUNO'
24 OCTOBER

La Galera
Diamante

Cochinas

Puerto de Sta María

'SAN FRANCISCO de ASIS'
24 OCTOBER

'AIGLE'
26 OCTOBER

'BUCENTAURE'
23 OCTOBER   Freidera

Puercos
o Frayle

Cadiz

Porto
Real

ATLANTIC OCEAN

Torre Gorda

la Carraca

ISLA DE LEON

RIO DE SANCTI PETR

Chiclana

Hermitage
of Sta Ana

'FOUGUEUX'
22 OCTOBER

19

Cosmao's Sortie

The shift in wind direction to the south that had blown Cuthbert Collingwood off the Trafalgar shoals on the night of the battle prevented the remnant of the Combined Fleet getting into Cadiz Bay. They sailed slowly north to Cadiz on a gentle westerly that, had it lasted, would have carried Antonio de Escaño's surviving French and Spanish ships into the safety of the bay. But the squally southerly that took over at midnight made getting past the rocks at the harbour entrance perilous in darkness, so the eleven ships, their frigates and brigs anchored outside the harbour off Rota. At first light on 22 October, although the squalls were becoming increasingly frequent and fierce, they could at least see where the rocks were. The ships edged slowly towards the shelter of the bay, leaving two frigates and the *Héros* under sail outside on the lookout.

According to the Spanish account, at nine a.m. Escaño called the four senior captains to a council of war in *Principe de Asturias*. This concluded that any ships that were in a state to do so should put to sea when the weather eased in the hope of rescuing as many of their comrades as possible. The Spanish captains, who knew these waters, reasoned that with the wind now blowing straight up to Cadiz, the British would struggle to keep control of their prizes and some might be recaptured. However, the wind had risen during the meeting,

removing any possibility of putting the plan into execution immediately. Even in the bay the seas were so mountainous that small boats
were in danger of being swamped and the four captains could not even
return to their own ships.

That morning Antonio Alcalá Galiano went in search of news of his
father with a feeling of foreboding. The weather reflected his melancholy. The horizon was ringed with black clouds, and agitated waves
crashed against the sea wall. The wind whirled in fierce gusts along the
narrow streets of Cadiz and rain stung the faces of hundreds of anxious
men and women enquiring after fathers, husbands and brothers. At
breakfast time it was 63° Fahrenheit, noticeably cooler than it had been
the day before but still essentially warm. Galiano hurried to the
Alameda, from where he could get a wide view to the mouth of the bay
and across to Rota and Puerto Santa Maria.

From there he was shocked to see the handful of ships under Escaño
anchored, pitifully insecurely, at the edge of the bay, battered by the
wind and the heavy seas. All looked as if they had suffered serious
damage. Galiano tried to find out what had happened to his father's
Bahama but nobody knew. People said there had been a tremendous
battle, that the Spanish and French ships had suffered heavily but that
the British were in just as bad a state. 'The rumour was even going
round that we had won the victory.'

The spectators gradually identified the ships but the *Bahama* was
not among them. A crowd rushed to the mole whenever wounded men
were landed. But this happened rarely because, with the sea as high as
it was, it was dangerous to bring little boats close to the tall-sided
ships, especially since they were anchored a long distance outside the
harbour. Anxious as they were, the people of Cadiz did all they could
for the few wounded who came ashore: the principal families had
servants posted on the mole with instructions to bring them to their
houses. Galiano satisfied himself that there was no reliable news and no
possibility of getting any, abandoned his apparently futile enquiries

and went home. After he had discussed the situation with his aunt, they decided to lock up the house, leave it in the hands of a trustworthy servant and go back to Chiclana, where his mother was waiting.

They soon discovered that every carriage in the city had been commandeered by the governor to carry the wounded from the quay to the Royal Hospital or other accommodation. 'I hurried to see general the marquis of Solana in order to ask for a pass for a small calash in which my aunt and I could go to where my mother must by now be consumed by pain and doubts, and also to find out whether he, better informed about what was going on, knew anything about the *Bahama*, object of my unflagging curiosity.' The general gave him a pass. Solana wanted to be helpful and was sympathetic to Antonio, but he knew nothing about *Bahama* either. He had only learned a little from the ships that had come into port. It had been a defeat, not the rumoured victory, but that was about all he knew for certain. In this weather communication with the ships was all but impossible and no reports had come in from individual captains.

Antonio and his aunt got on the road, 'lashed by the wind and the constant downpour, with the sky as sad and overcast as our spirits'. It took long hours to cover the few miles separating Cadiz from Chiclana, and night was falling when they arrived. 'My afflicted mother already knew about the battle, but not about its result and we could add very little to what she knew.'

In Cadiz Bay the French and Spanish ships took down their topmasts and yards and prepared for a storm. Early in the afternoon the rain-drenched crowds lining the sea wall in Cadiz were just able to make out *San Leandro*'s mizen and mainmast blown into the sea by a violent squall from the south-south-west. The mountainous waves, 'as they do in Cadiz in the great storms, broke against the sea wall with appalling noise, spraying nearby places with spume'. The sea seemed determined to rip down the buildings close to the shore. After two hours of this the two frigates that had been on the lookout anchored, and *Héros* came in afterwards, having broken away from her anchor outside.

'Night closed in, thick on every side and raining, with a very high wind from the south,' reported *Principe de Asturias*'s log. They heard the gunshots fired by the approaching *Bucentaure* but could see nothing. They assumed that the shots were distress signals but there was nothing they could do. Julien Cosmao-Kerjulien explained in his report that *Pluton*'s boats were all shot to pieces, but even undamaged boats would have been at great risk in attempting to help *Bucentaure* in the darkness close to the rocks. Admiral Escaño himself was distracted by a disaster on his own ship. At eight in the evening, after a great lurch, *Principe de Asturias* rolled her mainmast overboard and the mizen mast followed immediately afterwards.

Dawn on 23 October was almost calm with the lightest of north-west winds, although the sky was overcast and the horizon looked ominously dark and squally. It was still raining but visibility had improved and this brought surprises all round. The crew of *Algésiras* perceived to their alarm that they had anchored far too close to the Diamante rocks and were still in danger. The crew of *Principe de Asturias* had not expected to see either *Algésiras* or *Bucentaure*, which, to their horror, was being beaten against the rocks near the fort of Santa Catalina on Cadiz Point.

On board *Bucentaure* Lieutenant Fulcran Fournier had given up hope of saving his ship. She had started to ground two hours after the tide had turned. Small boats came to offer help, but only one longboat from *Neptune*. By first light seawater was pouring into the hold through the broken hull. The water reached the orlop deck at midday. Most of the British prize crew was put on to one of the frigates where, contrary to propaganda published soon after in the *Gibraltar Chronicle*, they were well treated. *Indomptable*'s boats took many others, including a few Britons. At one thirty, when the last of the men had been taken off, Acting Captain Fournier and Prigny left the ship. By mid-afternoon the ruined hull was submerged although the stumps of the masts remained visible.

Further out in the bay other ships tried to help *Algésiras*. *San Justo* and *Indomptable* proposed towing her further from the rock. But with the capstan damaged it took the seamen in *Algésiras* a long time to raise the anchor and by that time both ships had been diverted to other tasks. All morning and all afternoon Voldemar de la Bretonnière fired distress signals from *Algésiras*, but it was not until early evening that a Spanish boat from Cadiz brought a little stream-anchor, a hawser and a pilot. Several ships also sent small boats but *Algésiras* needed a longboat with a much larger bower anchor, or a frigate to take her in tow.

That Wednesday morning of 23 October the watchman in the Tavira Tower confirmed that what Escaño had anticipated was indeed coming to pass. Whether by their own volition or by the caprice of wind and current, the prizes were escaping. *Neptuno*, with *Santa Ana* a little way beyond, was closest to the port, less than six miles to the south-west. Even closer, but to the west, was *Bahama*. Antonio Alcalá Galiano would have seen his father's ship clearly, had he not returned to Chiclana. Those were the three most accessible vessels. The tower would soon identify *San Juan Nepomuceno* and was already reporting a French ship in difficulty close to the shore to the south, requesting assistance that could not be given to her because of the high seas. The watchman thought it was *Fougueux*, but she had already been smashed to pieces and the one he could see was *Aigle*. *San Agustín*, *Monarca*, *Argonauta* and *Swiftsure* had also broken away from their escorts and were drifting towards Cadiz. For the most part the British ships had maintained some degree of contact and were tracking their charges from a mile or two out to sea.

This was the chance to implement the bold rescue plan that the senior captains of the fleet had conceived the previous day. At six thirty the commanders who had met to hold council returned to their ships. The old Irishman commanding *Rayo*, Commodore Enrique Macdonnell, and the senior French officer, Commodore Julien Cosmao-Kerjulien hoisted senior officers' pennants and ordered the other ships to prepare to set sail.

In his report Cosmao claimed sole credit for the sortie. His account mentions no council of war. It is possible that he was telling the truth and *Principe*'s log was lying. But the participation in the sortie of Macdonnell, a Spanish officer of equal rank, lends credence to Escaño's version of events. Whoever was responsible for this courageous and enterprising initiative, the beaten and battered ships of the Combined Fleet prepared to renew the fight. With Cosmao and Macdonnell flying commodore's pennants, *Pluton*, *Neptune*, *Héros*, *Rayo*, *San Justo*, and *San Francisco de Asís* got under way together with the frigates and despatch craft. With *Pluton* leading they tacked to the north. While this was going on, the dismasted *Principe de Asturias* and *San Leandro* were towed down the deep-water channel into the shelter of the inner harbour and anchored in relative safety near the fort at Puntales.

Out in the bay the aggressive move caught the British completely by surprise. The three pairs of ships in most danger were *Minotaur*, which was closing in to take *Neptuno* in tow again, *Thunderer*, which had already made contact with *Santa Ana*, and *Orion*, which had recovered *Bahama* to the north. *Minotaur* raised the alarm, although her log does not say when – probably at ten twenty when Henry Bayntun in *Leviathan* repeated to Collingwood a signal flown by a ship to the north-east that the enemy were coming out of port.

Collingwood was slow to react. His first orders of the morning were to get the fleet to close up again and head out to sea. Initially he might not have believed the news or appreciated the danger. *Leviathan*'s signal log reveals that, at twelve ten, *Euryalus* issued a general signal to prepare for battle and for anchoring with springs. If it proved necessary, he intended to anchor before fighting in defensive positions protecting the prizes. The springs – ropes attached to the anchor cable – enabled anchored ships to turn to face whatever danger might threaten.

Collingwood sent Thomas Capel's *Phoebe* north at top speed to find out what was going on. At this time the sloop *Scout* and another frigate, *Eurydice*, joined the fleet.

Forty minutes later, in response to a signal from *Phoebe*, Collingwood finally began to organise the main body of the fleet to move north with the prizes and damaged ships towing behind. He freed up

15. The *Santísima Trinidad*, the largest battleship in the world:
'[Our prize], by the calculation of the oldest sailors on board, was to have
been the *Santísima Trinidada*, the Spanish four-decker; and I dare say we
were far from being the only ship in the fleet that fixed upon her'.

16. The battle of Trafalgar as seen from the mizen starboard shrouds of *Victory* by
J.M.W. Turner. Nelson has just been shot from *Redoutable*'s mizen top and
Roteley's marines (*centre*) are exacting revenge on the sharpshooters (*upper right*).

The artist is standing close to where Midshipman John Pollard was. 'At this period, scarcely a person in the *Victory* escaped unhurt who was exposed to the enemy's musketry'.

17. After the battle the ships were in no condition to endure a storm.

18. The end of the battle: the French ship *Achille* in flames with *Prince* (*left*) sending boats to rescue survivors.

19. Jeanne Caunant (decently clothed in this print) pulled from the water by Hugh Montgomery, mate of the *Naiad*, after *Achille* blew up.

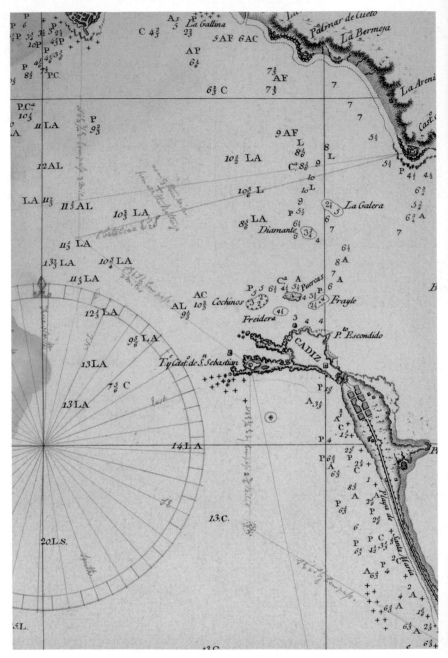

20. Bayntun's chart of the approaches to Cadiz. He added his own bearings in pencil – and drew in a group of rocks south of the town, which had not been marked on the printed chart.

21. Prizes in the storm: the ship in the foreground is believed to be the *Santísima Trinidad* seen on 22 or 23 October.

22. The frigate *Naiad* tows the dismasted *Belleisle* over the final few calm miles towards the safety of the Rock of Gibraltar on 24 October.

23. *The Apotheosis of Nelson* by Scott Pierre Nicolas Legrand, one of many tributes to the fallen hero. Either this painting was made for engraving (during which process it would have been reversed) or the artist mistakenly thought Nelson retained his right arm not his left.

Neptune by having *Mars* take over the care of *Royal Sovereign* from her. *Britannia*, *Defence*, *Dreadnought* and *Leviathan* were similarly disengaged to deal with the threat emerging from Cadiz. While this was going on Admiral Villeneuve and his small suite transferred from *Mars* to *Neptune*. All this took a considerable time and it was not until three o'clock that they were ordered to make all sail to the north. At four forty-five Collingwood repeated the signal to prepare for battle and to anchor with springs.

The most vulnerable prizes were in a poor way. The previous night at midnight the pressure of the wind had got the better of *Neptuno*'s damaged mainmast, which crashed down on to the poop, smashing through it and the great cabin beneath. This was where the Spanish officers had been locked away and the paymaster, Diego de Soto, was crushed as he slept. One of *Minotaur*'s seamen was killed too. The quarterdeck was also badly damaged, so William Thorp and the rest of the British prize crew went to work to shore up the broken beams to try to ensure that the decks didn't collapse on top of them. They were now drifting hopelessly, blind to where they might be until, in Thorp's words, 'about three oclock cleared away the best bower Anker on Account of seeing Cadiz light now close under our lee, having only 18 fathom water'. This must have been a shock. They let go the anchor and brought up for the night just south-east of Cadiz. In the morning the watchman, who was peering through the misty drizzle, saw a squadron of five ships-of-the-line, three frigates and a brig. It did not take him long to identify the ships as hostile. 'Thus situated we expected assistance from our own Fleet, but lookt in vain,' William Thorp recalled. Captain Charles Mansfield, in *Minotaur*, was not far away but he decided in favour of discretion and withdrew.

The drizzle turned to a sheet of pouring rain through which they could dimly make out the enemy getting closer. Frantically the prize crew of *Neptuno* tried to improvise sails on what was left of her masts. Thorp wrote that they 'Riggd a spar to the stump of the Main Mast and an other to the Taffrell set a top Gallant upon each, and got an other to the Fore Mast, in lieu of a Fore sail'. By the early afternoon they could see British ships approaching in the distance with the strengthening wind in their favour, but the enemy were nearer and their frigates were fast. They cut their cable and 'stood toward our own Fleet with all sail we could set, but the enemy was gaining upon us fast from Cadiz'. They cleared away the stern-chasers, the long guns in the captain's cabin pointing backwards at the enemy, and opened up the powder magazine. This was too much for the Spaniards, who were presumably still pumping. They decided to make sure of the outcome. 'The prisoners observing this rose upon our people and retook the ship,' Thorp reported. There was little opposition. The seventy-five Britons were outnumbered by ten to one. Thorp's view was that 'It would a been madness to resist, a slight resistance was made by some men who narrowly escaped with their Lives.' With Cayetano Valdés still unconscious in the surgeon's care, one of the junior lieutenants took command. He wore the ship round and headed towards Cadiz.

Lieutenant Stockham, in *Thunderer*, was a little further from the advancing enemy squadron but he did not reckon he could escape with the badly damaged and unmanoeuvrable hulk of *Santa Ana*. Instead, he took his own people off the prize, abandoned the valuable but badly damaged Spanish three-decker to its former officers, and made off before the ships coming out of Cadiz could trap him.

Edward Codrington was cooler: his *Orion* had got hold of *Bahama* in the early morning but had trouble getting her moving because there was little wind to provide headway and the swell kept throwing the ships off course. At around nine thirty, 'in a calm, heavy swell, and violent rain, we were obliged to anchor within a few miles of Cadiz to prevent being driven in nearer', Codrington wrote. At eleven o'clock he saw that the enemy were coming out of the harbour. With only a handful of Britons on *Bahama* the prisoners would certainly overwhelm them and retake her if it came to a fight, so at twelve he cut his anchor cable and made off northwards with his prize in tow. He had looked closely at the situation and reckoned he could get away with it.

Codrington was being pursued and fired upon by a frigate but he was still confident of escaping with *Orion* and *Bahama*: 'They re-took one two-decker which was left to herself and also the *Santa Anna*, three-decker, which the *Thunderer* had in tow; but although to leeward of the *Thunderer* much, and so situated that they could easily have come up with me, and with one of their frigates then within shot firing at us, I persevered in retaining the ship in tow.' If he could clear Rota Point, Codrington reasoned, then even if he was forced to abandon *Bahama* in order to escape, she would be driven by the wind on to the shores of Portugal rather than Spain. 'I was the more encouraged to do this, because, had they attacked me, they could not have again fetched into Cadiz, and would have risked an action with some of our fleet then to windward.'

Bahama was still in the hands of the Royal Navy but two of the prizes had gone, taking the total lost to six, four escaped and two destroyed. However, Collingwood's captains had taken some successful measures to secure other potential escapees. *Leviathan* picked up *San Agustín* at ten a.m. and turned her over to *Bellerophon* at four o'clock when *Leviathan* was required to be free to fight. Between them, *Dreadnought* and *Phoebe* took care of *Swiftsure*. The frigate *Melpomene* secured *San Juan Nepomuceno*. *Achille*'s log reports that she took *Monarca* in tow before noon, but this does not seem to have been noticed by anyone on board *Monarca* and perhaps *Achille*'s log for 23 October is largely fictional. According to Henry Walker, one of the prize crew on *Monarca*, the ship continued to drift or ride at anchor in the greatest distress. *Conqueror* had pulled away from *Bucentaure* the previous afternoon. Pellew's log states that he spent the morning trying to take 'the prize' in tow (*Bucentaure* is not named specifically) and that he abandoned her when the enemy came out in force. Whether *Conqueror* ever got close enough to identify 'the prize' is not clear. She might have mistaken *Aigle* for *Bucentaure*.

Lieutenant Asmus Classen, *Aigle*'s acting captain, reported that at daybreak two British ships approached to tow him off the shore, but he decided that he did not want to be saved. The only escape was to go further inshore, pretending to be adrift and about to be lost, and risk actually running aground. There was just a chance that he could get between the rocky Juan Vela and Haxto Afuera shoals three miles off the island of Sancti Petri. If so, he might be able to anchor in the mile or so of water between them and the terrifying rocks that stretched out on either side of the castle on the island. Modern yachtsmen are warned not to dream of trying to approach Sancti Petri when waves are breaking on the offshore banks. The sandbanks closer in shift constantly, bemusing even the local tuna fishermen, but Classen reckoned he had no choice but to try to find the inner channel. The British would be convinced he had gone aground and would not dare to follow. He cut through his anchor cable and 'steered amid the breakers for the coast, going before the wind, and most fortunately found coarse sand bottom inside, where I let go one damaged anchor in eight fathoms'. Incredibly, *Aigle* had survived. They were now tantalisingly close to their would-be rescuers at Sancti Petri, but still in acute danger. The men on board, French and British alike, must have sent up prayers for that symbol of hope, their last anchor, already damaged in the battle.

By the time that the bulk of Collingwood's fleet came within sight of the French and Spanish ships that had ventured out of Cadiz, Cosmao's men were already heading for home. The brief spell of moderate weather in which they had put out had not lasted and the wind was growing ever more squally and dangerous. The French frigate *Hermione* took *Neptuno* in tow and brought her to the mouth of the bay 'where whe brought up amongst some of their disabled ships,' William Thorp recalled. He was now a Spanish prisoner and was probably taking his turn at the pumps. *Santa Ana* was also towed into the bay.

All the Spanish and French ships came in, except *Rayo* because exposure to the angry elements had proved too much for her incompetent crew and she was already nursing a badly damaged mainmast. In the increasingly strong south-south-east wind they couldn't get back into the harbour. According to Enrique Macdonnell, few of his sailors dared go up to reef the sails, even when the repeated creaking of the masts suggested they would break if nothing was done. 'They were not men for this sort of work,' he reported afterwards. Eventually the main topmast crashed down at ten o'clock, followed shortly afterwards by the mizen and mainmast. The mizen crushed the tiller in its fall, so they could no longer steer. *Rayo* came to an anchor eighteen miles from Cadiz off Rota. The other ships came back safely but *Pluton* had to be nursed into port. She was making a great deal of water and returned 'in a sinking condition'.

The weather that night was worse than anything seen so far. In the harbour they reported it as a full gale with repeated fierce squalls from the south-west. It had started to rain heavily again at four in the afternoon and continued in torrents until morning. The weather closed in very dark and misty with poor visibility, bringing on the blindness that seamen detested, especially when they knew that there were dangers nearby to be avoided.

As the frigates returned from the sortie they sailed straight past *Algésiras*, even ignoring the boat that de la Bretonnière had sent to wait in the path of the last one, begging for help. As the tide fell, apprehension mounted in the French ship, dangerously anchored close to the Diamante rocks. Around ten o'clock the inevitable happened and the ship bumped on the rocks, but 'most fortunately the wind shifted to the east in a violent squall that made us drag, so that we rounded and got clear of the Diamond'. The hawser split and they lost their new stream anchor and waited tensely for the tug when their only anchor would be at full stretch. Their cable would be chafing on the rocky bottom. It held. They breathed again. Then, through the blackness, another ship loomed up, dragging its anchor, broadside on and out of control. If it hit, their cable would certainly break and they would be carried ashore. But it missed, even though their yard-arms almost touched.

In Cadiz harbour several longboats had been manned and equipped to save *Algésiras*. In the night they put out into the darkness and the raging seas. All were lost on their way to the French ship and all aboard them drowned.

With the weather worse and worse, the *Algésiras* swung round until it bumped heavily on the Galera bank. The tide was not yet at its lowest so the crew threw themselves into the task of lightening the back of the ship, jettisoning four 18-pounder guns – two of which had broken loose – as well as all the shifting ballast, shot, and other heavy objects. They opened the water-casks in the aftermost tiers with crowbars and pumped out the water. It was frantic work in appalling conditions with the ship's bottom grinding ominously on the rock. Then the tide rose. To their joy, the ship floated and the carpenters reported no more water coming in than the ship had been making before.

The question now was whether the cable would hold until daybreak. It did. The wind moderated around six and conditions had improved further by eight, although the sea was very heavy. With the light a number of boats reached *Algésiras*. Then de la Bretonnière and Philibert learned how lucky they had been. The *San Francisco de Asís* and the newly rescued *Neptuno* had both dragged their anchors and been driven aground during the night.

At three in the morning *Neptuno* 'parted from our Ankers and not having her other cable bent to bring us up they let her drive ashore', according to William Thorp. 'At this time the confusion on board is inexpressable,' he wrote, 'it being dark, and ignorant what part of the coast whe where cast upon.' They expected the ship to go to pieces at any moment. The Spaniards, whose hopes had been raised and then dashed, were 'naturaly Disappointed' and 'shewed every symptom of Dispair'. Thorp was contemptuous of the indiscipline of the foreign crew who 'run about in wild disorder nor made the least effort to extricate themselves from the Danger that threatened them'.

By Thorp's account it was the British who 'conveyd three ropes on shore, one from the Cat Head, one from the Bowsprit and another from the fore Mast Head, – by the Assistance of which a number of men got safe on shore'. Others, perhaps chiefly Spanish if their accounts are to be credited, were 'employed constructing a raft for more expediciously landing, as well as to convey such as where unwilling to risk themselves by the ropes'. When the raft was finished twenty men ventured on board and arrived safe on shore. But the breakers drove the raft so far on to the rocks that they could not get it off again:

> those on board seeing this sad Disaster, far from giving way to Despair
> immiadietly set about making an other, wich certainly was our last

resource, as whe had not any more spars fit for that purpose, when finished whe launched it over board and 20 men embark on board it who arrived safe one Spanish excepted who was washd off by the surf.

To judge from his account, Thorp left the *Neptuno* on this raft. Having reached the muddy shore, he continued, 'whe then made fast a rope to the raft on shore and there being one already fast from the ship, the People Draggd it of to the ship, when 28 men embarkd on board, All of whom Arrived safe on shore'. The raft was again pulled back to the ship and another twenty-eight people clambered on. This journey was not so fortunate. Four Spaniards were washed off by the surf and perished, and the raft came ashore among rocks, badly damaged. Nevertheless, the men remaining on the ship dragged it back: 'but fate had decreed that all who remained on board should perish the raft laden shoved off from the ship side but ere it gained the shore it upset & every soul perished, no further attempt could be made to save those unfortunate men who remaind on board. All Perishd.'

Thorp and his fellow crewmen from *Minotaur* were marched away to Puerto Santa Maria, 'about 4 miles from St. Martin's Fort where whe where wreckd.' He would not have seen subsequent events on the wreck site and there might have been more survivors than he realised. Cayetano Valdés' official report claimed that 'on the following and succeeding days we worked hard at making rafts, and the people took to these and I understand that only twenty men were drowned; in the end, with the assistance of the fishing boats, I abandoned the ship accompanied by my second in command, who was dangerously wounded, by the rest of the wounded among the crew and by the officers'.

According to Antonio Alcalá Galiano (later a close associate and friend of Valdés), Valdés was still unconscious when *Neptuno* went ashore. He owed his survival to a young midshipman who bravely went back in a boat with some seamen to fetch him when the crew realised that their wounded captain had not been taken off the ship. They took him to the house of a lady friend who nursed him back to health.

By morning *Argonaute* and *Indomptable* were both in difficulty in the harbour mouth. *San Justo* had lost her mizen and mainmast and *Montañés* her mizen, and both were anchored precariously with the dismasted hulk *Santa Ana* in the mouth of the port. Any offensive capacity that the Combined Fleet might have had was at an end. All their ships were now either wrecked or so seriously damaged that they could not be risked again.

Cosmao's sortie was a qualified triumph for the Combined Fleet. They recaptured two important Spanish vessels, but during the night they lost more ships than they had gained during the day. Whether these Spanish ships would have fared any better if they had not sortied is difficult to say, except in the case of *Rayo*, which was clearly risked a second time for reasons of honour rather than pragmatism. The others were driven aground within the bay and this might have happened anyway. On the other hand, the ships might have survived the storm better if they had all retired, like *Principe de Asturias* and *San Leandro*, further into the bay. But the sortie's success was not to be measured in ships. Its true achievement lay in its effect on Admiral Collingwood, who had no idea how few, how battered and how unseaworthy the remaining enemy ships now were. He had been thoroughly unsettled by the boldness of the enemy and feared that at any moment they might come out again in strength to seize back more of their ships.

Sink, Burn, and Destroy

On the night of 23/24 October the reading of the Mégnié barometer at the Royal Observatory just south of Cadiz was among the lowest ever recorded there. The observatory noted pressure, wind strength and direction, and cloud conditions twice a day. The meteorological historian Dennis Wheeler has analysed its records – along with ships' logs – and reconstructed the weather of October 1805.

When low pressure moves into the Gulf of Cadiz it normally drifts rapidly northwards, but in late October 1805 a deep low was trapped there, becoming what is known to weathermen as a 'cut-off low'. This condition produces strong southerly winds and heavy rainfall over southern Spain. Cut-off lows do not normally last long. Few persist at full intensity for a week, like the Trafalgar storm.

During the storm twice the total average October rainfall fell on Cadiz. It rained perpetually from 22 to 25 October with heavy showers continuing for another four days. The observatory's barometer, measuring in Paris feet, dropped two inches the night after the battle and two more inches the following morning. It was more or less steady through Wednesday and Thursday, then dropped another inch and a half on 25 October, reaching its nadir that Friday afternoon.

The winds abated on 27 October but remained strong and occasionally very strong until 30 October. Wheeler judged it highly probable that at its height the gale reached modern 'storm force 10' and even 'violent storm force 11'. The term 'hurricane', employed by Asmus Classen and by the British captains Henry Blackwood and Edward Codrington, was then commonly used to describe all violent winds, not just those of the modern force twelve. But this was undoubtedly a wind to alarm hardened mariners. Charles Tyler wrote to his wife Margaret of how 'a violent gale came on the Tuesday evening, and blew a perfect storm right on shore for four days'. Such a tempest would have been fearsome at any time but to ships in the condition that most of these were in by 23 October, it was terrifying.

Edward Codrington thought this 'the worst hurricane I ever saw'. He described to his brother William how 'the danger of being wrecked on a lee shore' that had dissuaded Cosmao's ships and frigates from pursuing him 'became most alarmingly increased by the hurricane, which came on that night at the most critical moment, and blew all our topsails to atoms'. He could barely believe how 'the foretopsail absolutely blew from the yard after it was snugly clewed up; and for about two hours, all which time we were driving towards the shore in utter darkness, we could not venture to show a rag of canvas'. In *Orion*, and in the undermanned *Bahama* in tow behind her, men peered into the night for land they knew must be within a few miles and tried to detect the roar of breakers over the general noise of the storm. Desperately, *Orion*'s crew cleared away the anchor cables and prepared to cut through the masts.

Then the wind dropped sufficiently for the young topmen to scamper up the humming rigging and edge precariously on to the swaying yard-arms to set the reefed fore and main sails. As they did so, Codrington decided that, to escape, he had to cut the tow-rope and sacrifice the people in *Bahama*. The latter's crew repeatedly fired distress signals but Codrington hardened his heart, wore round, took advantage of the wind veering westward, and fought his way off the shore. He assumed *Bahama* had been lost and had her fate on his conscience when he explained his course of action to Henry Bayntun two days later.

Describing the day's events to his brother William, Codrington added wryly that he thought it

> hard and grievous to be obliged to prepare for a watery grave, and to feed for some hours on bare hope . . . after having so well escaped the chances of the action. It is not fighting, my dear W., which is the severest part of our life, it is the having to contend with the sudden changes of season, the war of elements, the dangers of a lee shore, and so forth, which produce no food for honour or glory beyond the internal satisfaction of doing a duty we know to be most important, although passed by others unknown and unnoticed.

Bahama's prize crew consisted of Fourth Lieutenant John Douglas and four seamen from *Bellerophon*, one of whom was John Markland, aged thirteen and on his first voyage. A few days earlier his late captain, John Cooke, had written that Markland was 'a very fine boy but too mild and delicate to encounter the variety of unpleasant circumstances to which a sailor is exposed'. He was now sampling some of the worst. To these five sailors and the seven marines who accompanied them to guard the 548 fit prisoners, Codrington had considerably added fifteen men from *Téméraire* and six from *Phoebe* who were inured to danger, having previously been part of the prize crew of the *Fougueux*. It was not a strong team but, once again, the threat of imminent death produced a spirit of energetic Anglo-Hispanic co-operation. By luck or by hard work the British and Spanish seamen contrived to miss or get through the shoals off Chipiona and kept going north. *Bahama* had abandoned two anchors off Trafalgar and another two off Cadiz that morning so they were in a truly perilous situation. But the late Dionisio Alcalá Galiano had thoughtfully stored a fifth bower anchor in the hold. Somehow they had it in position in time to drop it before they reached the breakers at the north end of the Arenas Gordas beach. Miraculously, *Bahama* survived the night, even as Edward Codrington quietly reproached himself for her certain destruction.

Until Cosmao's sortie *Sirius* had been towing *Téméraire*. During that emergency she was sent north at speed, leaving the disabled three-decker to fend for herself. 'We have been in constant apprehension of our lives,' wrote Captain Eliab Harvey, 'every sail and yard having been destroyed, and nothing but the lower masts left standing; the rudder-head almost shot off . . . and lower masts all shot through and through in many places.' However, they survived the night after the sortie under sail. *Africa* appeared in the morning 'and said nothing until the evening, when she informed me Admiral Collingwood had sent him to see me into port. I desired him to stay by the ship, but the good Captain Digby thought proper to take care of himself and made off in the night.'

Not far from *Téméraire*, *Agamemnon* was towing *Colossus*. James Morris thought his ship, *Colossus*, might founder. He had cut away her mainmast that afternoon while the sortie was in progress, bringing her total losses to '2 anchors, pinnace, 2 cutters, the fore topmast, main mast and mizen mast, with all the sails, yards, and furniture'. There was nothing to stop her tossing and rolling with horrible instability in the towering seas so he threw the poop carronades overboard to make her less top-heavy. Sir Edward Berry's *Agamemnon* was herself making thirty-six inches of water per hour and her men were pumping for dear life, but he kept *Colossus* doggedly in tow.

The night of 23/24 October had also alarmed the crews of *Spartiate* and *Tonnant*. *Spartiate* had close-reefed her topsails and taken down the topgallant masts and yards in the early part of the night as the storm came on. 'Strong gales, dark misty weather, with hard squalls and rain,' her log reported. The tow-rope broke away from *Tonnant* at ten o'clock, an hour later *Spartiate*'s jib blew loose and then blew away, and soon after 'the fore topmast staysail split, and blew away to pieces'.

Tonnant was blowing out of control towards the coast. She was more or less rudderless, had no main topmast or yard, and no yards for the other topsails. All the masts and spars were badly damaged and liable to break, and the stern of the ship, where the windows had been smashed in the battle along with other serious damage, had been planked up with two little peepholes for light. 'In this state we experienced as heavy a gale as ever I was in,' wrote Benjamin Clement. 'The *Spartiate* parted the tow rope, and to tell you the truth I never thought we should weather the land.' About a dozen of *Tonnant*'s petty officers had recent experience of shipwreck, having survived the loss of the *Magnificent* off Brittany on 24 March 1804. Then they had been rescued by the boats of the fleet. This time they knew they were on their own. Somehow Lieutenant Bennett and his men kept their ship off the coast until the wind began to drop.

Conditions on the remaining prizes were truly appalling. Most of them had badly damaged hulls and were leaking freely. The enemy crew could not be confined because every fit man was needed to work the pumps in relays day and night. In their task of guarding about four hundred unwounded Spaniards while keeping *Monarca* afloat, prize-master Lieutenant Edward Thomas, Midshipman Henry Walker and their eight seamen from *Bellerophon* had been reinforced on Tuesday, with a midshipman and ten marines from *Phoebe*, ten seamen from *Prince*, a midshipman and eleven seamen from *Achille*, and a midshipman and eleven seamen from *Dreadnought*. But before very long this motley crew of fifty-three had raided the Spanish alcohol supplies and were thenceforth 'in a constant state of intoxication'.

They probably needed to be. That night the ship rolled away the mizen and mainmast, and they had had to cut away two anchors, and heave overboard several guns, along with shot and ballast, to lighten the ship. They almost certainly had no leisure to heave the hundred or so corpses overboard. Walker had been calm during the battle, 'but in the prize, when I was in danger of, and had time to reflect upon the approach of death, either from the rising of the Spaniards upon so small a number as we were composed of, or what latterly appeared inevitable from the violence of the storm, I was most certainly afraid'. During the night of Wednesday 23 October, totally exhausted, the nineteen-year-old Mancunian gave up:

> When the ship made three feet water in ten minutes, when our people
> were almost all lying drunk upon deck, when the Spaniards, com-

pletely worn out with fatigue, would no longer work at the only chain pump left serviceable; when I saw the fear of death so strongly depicted on the countenances of all around me, I wrapped myself in a union jack, and lay down upon deck for a short time, quietly awaiting the approach of death.

He was roused from this torpor at midnight by a sudden joint decision from the English and Spanish officers that their only chance lay in reaching Cadiz or, failing that, in running the ship on to some beach. This determination injected new energy into both crews 'and after great exertions on the part of the British and Spanish officers, who had joined together for the mutual preservation of their lives, we got the ship before the wind, determined to run her on shore'.

They survived the night. At daylight on Thursday 24 October the wind moderated and the horizon opened up. The pump was at last winning the battle against the water and although they had missed Cadiz they were able to run the ship on to the sandy beach north of Sanlúcar. Then, close to leeward off Chipiona, they saw something unexpected: a three-decked hulk with no masts flying Spanish colours. There was probably a moment as they hauled to the wind when the Spanish crew cheered. If so, it was brief. Suddenly *Leviathan* and *Donegal* appeared out of the rain, sailing fast. They converged on the three-decker, and after each had fired a single shot the Spanish ship struck without returning fire. Her guns were almost completely masked by fallen wreckage. *Donegal* remained by the three-decker, which turned out to be *Rayo*, while *Leviathan* anchored close to *Monarca*, then lowered her boats to get a cable across.

It is possible that the sight of *Monarca* under sail for the shore was what made up Collingwood's mind for him. He had been a rear admiral for six years and a vice admiral for more than one. He had been Cornwallis's subordinate in rough weather off Brittany and had commanded his own small squadron off Cadiz, but he had never faced a situation remotely like this. He had a huge fleet, half of it consisting of battle-damaged hulks containing almost as many hostile prisoners as healthy British sailors.

His first decision not to anchor had probably been taken out of seamanlike pride and might have been influenced by jealousy of Nelson. As it turned out, it was certainly a mistake and most of the subsequent problems and confusion stemmed from it: the unseaworthy state of many ships could have been improved, the prizes better secured. Given the circumstances, some might still have escaped, but Collingwood's chosen course of action had made it easier for them. 'Command and control' had disappeared in the storm and neither Collingwood nor anybody else knew what was happening. How many prizes were there? How many had escaped? How many ships did the enemy still have to throw against him?

During the afternoon Captain William Rutherford had told him that the *Redoutable* had sunk the previous evening and Collingwood knew that *Santa Ana* and *Neptuno* had escaped. *Santa Ana* was Collingwood's own prize and its loss annoyed him intensely. In his report dated the next day he consoled himself with the idea that since he had completely smashed in her side she must certainly have sunk and that Admiral Álava was dead. He was wrong on both counts.

The prizes had been blown northward, close to Cadiz, and the fit British ships had been forced to follow. Those with enough offing – far enough out to sea – might still take the advice offered in Bayntun's memorandum for a south-west gale and head north for Huelva. But for many ships the problem now, with the wind fully south-west, was that the leeway they made might not allow them to clear the shoals two and a half miles off the Punta del Perro near Chipiona. The writer of Bayntun's memorandum maintained that these were 'falsely represented as very dangerous' when in reality they were nothing like as dangerous as those further south. But they still represented a barrier – probably an impassable barrier with the wind as it was – to any northward progress for the ships that had had to go in very close to the shore.

So Collingwood could not go north without abandoning several ships. He could not go south with the fierce wind against him. He was now stuck and he was only about twenty miles from Cadiz with most of his ships under the gaze of its watchtower. While the storm lasted he had run out of options. The only choice now was between anchoring and staying under sail.

It was an alarming predicament. Having gained so much in battle, all might now be lost to elemental wrath. Only during brief, bright intervals did the murk of the south-westerly gale clear enough for him to see anything, and by now the ships were so scattered that it was difficult to make sense of what he saw.

Collingwood's harassed mind must have been filled with doubts and fears rather than hard realities. The French and Spanish had astonished him by attacking when they should have been well beaten. He could not know that they had suffered so badly overnight that they were unable to attack again. But even without intervention from Cadiz the prizes did not have far to go to escape, and for that purpose the wind had only to shift a little to the west. On the evening of 23 October Collingwood ordered Captains Bayntun and Mackay to take *Leviathan* and *Scout* close in and keep watch.

He passed a fretful, lonely night. He might have consulted with James Clavell, but his trusted lieutenant was unconscious in *Royal Sovereign*. By the morning he had reached a decision, and at eight ten he made a general signal ordering his ships to empty, then destroy the prizes. The first instruction was preparative, and Bayntun seems to have questioned it at eight fifteen with a telegraph message to the flagship. But it was confirmed at nine twelve. The prizes that the fleet had fought hard to keep afloat, not least because they would bring a substantial cash reward, were to be destroyed in case they should fall into the hands of the enemy.

When Collingwood confirmed this order, Bayntun, and Pulteney Malcolm of *Donegal*, closed in on *Monarca* and *Rayo* and began to move the crews out of the prizes; a highly relieved Henry Walker found himself on board *Leviathan*. According to him, the ship transferred from *Monarca* 'all but about 150 prisoners, who were afraid of getting into the boats'. Collingwood signalled Bayntun to take charge of the evacuation and destruction of the ships that had anchored. Malcolm put a prize crew of eighty aboard *Rayo*. Slightly further north Sir William Bolton's *Eurydice* came to an anchor off Sanlúcar and started to unload the French *Berwick*, getting off 189 men, fourteen badly wounded.

About six miles to the south of *Donegal*, *Defence* brought *San Ildefonso* to anchor, took off her prize crew, and then anchored herself half a mile to the south-east. 'We were riding close in shore with two anchors a-head, three cables on each bower, and all our sails were shot to pieces, ditto our rudder and stern, and mainmast, and everything,' the seventeen-year-old midshipman, Charles Reid, wrote to his sister Betty in Edinburgh.

In this lull in the storm it was possible to carry out Collingwood's order, though the mountainous swell made it both difficult and hazardous. *Swiftsure*, *Spartiate*, *Defiance*, *Britannia*, *Conqueror* and *Orion* sent their boats to *Intrépide*, and *Neptune*, *Prince* and *Ajax* began to unload *Santísima Trinidad*. Seamen from *Defiance*, *Revenge* and *Melpomene* rowed over to *Argonauta*, and *Dreadnought* took 149 men from *San Agustín*. *Phoebe* had the French *Swiftsure* in tow and the previous evening she had put her own carpenters on board to help stop up the leaks. She and *Spartiate* now took men from her. The ships were some miles out to sea, south-west of Chipiona. During daylight hours the wind dropped to a mere 'fresh breezes and squally' (force five with fiercer bursts) but the seas were still high.

Between them the three ships took 387 men off *Argonauta*, including *Polyphemus*'s prize crew, but deteriorating weather prevented them from completing the job. Philip Durham, captain of *Defiance*, unloaded his boats at three in the afternoon and even as he did so his topmen were taking in a third reef in the sails. He sent the boats back with hawsers in them 'to take the Argonauta in tow, but, the sea getting so high, found it impracticable'. Instead he sent two boats with Lieutenant Hargrave, three midshipmen and twenty-three seamen to bring the Spanish ship to an anchor, which they did. Men from *Revenge* joined them on board *Argonauta* 'in order to assist at the pumps, for she was much shattered in the hull, between wind and water.'

Intrépide was sinking and there was little chance of saving her. She had been towed by *Ajax*, but had been leaking badly: her crew and the Britons on board had been constantly at the pumps. That night, after the tow parted, this crew also despaired. Auguste Gicquel noticed that the pumping was slowing down and was told that the storeroom doors had been forced. A mixed mob of French and British had piled in to get drunk. As Gicquel arrived, a barrel of *eau-de-vie* had just been broken open and the pool of alcohol was lapping around the base of a candle that had been placed on the floor. Gicquel just had time to snuff the flame out with his foot, but as he plunged them all into darkness he heard menacing voices raised against him. He was expecting a knife at any second when a Frenchman shouted, 'It's Auguste! The one who saved Grévillot', referring to Gicquel's rescue of the sailor who fell overboard in the summer. In the momentary pause Gicquel and the English officer with him appealed to those who could still be reasoned with, then cleared the room and barricaded the doors.

In the morning, boats began to arrive to take off the crew. Lieutenant Charles Anthony of *Britannia* reported Gicquel's conduct so favourably to Northesk that the admiral promised Gicquel his freedom. But a close friend, Sub-lieutenant Poullain, was dying. He was judged too gravely wounded to be moved and begged Gicquel to stay with him in his last agony. Later Gicquel related that, in a fit of sentimental generosity brought on by the news of his impending freedom, he agreed to remain by his friend's side until he died before boarding *Britannia*. The prize-master promised to come back for him, but the wind got up and communication by boat became difficult again. *Britannia* drew further away and, wrote Gicquel, 'My military career disappeared with her.'

When Poullain died there were just three people left on *Intrépide*: an artillery captain and the midshipman from the forecastle with the trembling hand had been reluctant to leave Gicquel on his own. Among the corpses and the blood, the silence was broken only by the noise of the sea and the muffled rumbling of water rising in the hold and spreading through the ship. Night was falling and the ship was sinking. They found a lantern and waved it from the end of a pole. In the dusk the last British boats returned. Gicquel was taken to *Orion* before Charles Anthony came back, as he had promised he would, to set fire to the empty hulk. *Intrépide* blew up at nine thirty, the explosion logged by three English ships and by the Tavira Tower in Cadiz. From the size of the explosion the watchman guessed that a ship-of-the-line had gone.

The destruction of *Santísima Trinidad* was more controversial. She was the biggest and most prestigious prize of all. She was certainly in a bad state, but Midshipman William Badcock, who went aboard from *Neptune*, thought she could have been saved: 'Her top-sides, it is true, were perfectly riddled by our beautiful firing . . . but from the lower part of the sills of the lower-deck ports to the water's edge, few shot of consequence had hurt her between wind and water, and those were all plugged up. She was built of cedar, and would have lasted for ages, a glorious trophy of the battle; but "sink, burn, and destroy," was the order of the day.'

On the other hand, Spanish sources reported that her exhausted crew was losing the battle against the rising water in the hold. Admiral Báltasar de Cisneros reported that 'during the two days that we remained on the ship they suffered from incessant fatigue – the fatigue of keeping under the water and of the many other labours necessitated by the bad condition of the ship being as great as that which they had undergone in serving the guns'. According to Commodore Uriarte, her captain, there were sixty inches of water in the hold at the end of the battle and despite constant pumping, the level had risen to fifteen feet at the time she was abandoned.

The gun-decks were a gruesome sight, as Midshipman William Badcock wrote home to his father: 'she had between 3 and 400 killed and wounded, her Beams where coverd with Blood, Brains, and peices of Flesh, and the after part of her Decks with wounded, some without Legs and some without an Arm; what calamities War brings on . . .'

Moving the men from this huge four-decker presented a daunting challenge in the rough seas. The weather was so bad that no boat could lie alongside. Instead they got under the Spanish ship's stern and men climbed down ropes, probably from the galleries. Under these circumstances the wounded presented a problem: 'We had to tie the poor mangled wretches round their waists, or where we could, and lower them down into a tumbling boat, some without arms, others no legs, and lacerated all over in the most dreadful manner,' recalled Lieutenant John Edwards. *Neptune*'s captain, Thomas Fremantle, acquired a pug dog from the sinking *Santísima Trinidad* and William Badcock was given (or possibly looted) a gilt dirk belonging to Admiral Cisneros' son. Brigadier de Uriarte took home the bullet-scarred painting of the Holy Trinity that had been displayed under the poop. When most of the men had gone, carpenter's crews, including one sent by Collingwood from *Euryalus*, began cutting holes below the waterline. Then, immediately before leaving the ship, they opened the lower deck gunports.

Given that much of this was accomplished in deteriorating weather, during the evening of 24 October, the effort to clear this huge ship was admirable. John Edwards remembered that he left behind 'about thirty-three or four, which I believe it was impossible to remove without instant death'. But British muster books support the assertion of *Ajax*'s lieutenant, who said he left last, that the *Santísima Trinidad* was completely cleared and that he had even rescued the ship's cat: 'They had put off from the starboard quarter when a cat, the only living animal aboard, ran out on the muzzle of one of the lower-deck guns and by a plaintive mew seemed to beg for assistance: the boat returned and took her in.' *Neptune*'s boats took 407 in all, *Prince*'s 350, and *Ajax*'s 207. *Ajax*'s last boat got back after midnight carrying the remaining badly wounded Spaniards and six surgeons. By then the weather was very rough, so this last crossing to save dying men required enormous courage and determination. With the hold flooded and tons of water pouring through the gun-ports at every roll, the largest ship in the world sank 'unwillingly to the bottom' soon after the last boats had left her.

The British fleet and the remaining prizes were now either anchored off Chipiona or under sail in that area. William Cumby in *Bellerophon* had orders to make as much offing as possible with the intention, perhaps, of rounding Cape Trafalgar to make Gibraltar. Edward Berry in *Agamemnon*, who was towing *Colossus*, might have had the same order, and John Stockham in *Thunderer* proceeded as if this was what he had been told. But none could get far enough away from the shore to achieve their object. However, there was one exception to this rule.

Naiad, with *Belleisle* in tow, had persevered in the first attempt to reach Gibraltar. By the morning of 22 October they had come far enough from the coast to be able to see Tarifa at the mouth of the strait thirty miles away. Gradually, during that day, they lost sight of the rest of the fleet. By four in the afternoon only three ships were in sight, but they kept going.

The crew of *Belleisle* spent Tuesday, 22 October, clearing the decks and erecting jury masts to keep the ship under control. By six p.m. they were beating against a tremendous gale. In *Naiad*, some of Captain Thomas Dundas's signal flags blew away while he was attempting to telegraph a message to William Hargood. But Dundas had been ordered to take *Belleisle* in tow and he kept her in tow all through that windy night. They were driven inshore, making more leeway than progress, and *Belleisle* was leaking badly, her men pumping furiously. In the morning of 23 October the wind was lighter. Dundas made all sail and hauled them off the coast again. At noon he took a bearing on Cape Spartel, about twenty-seven miles away in Africa. They were still stuck off Cape Trafalgar, which now looked like a little sand dune dwarfed by the Altos de Meca towering above. But they kept going, and at four, Trafalgar was bearing north-east: they were just about round.

During the afternoon of 23 October the gale returned. They lost sight of all other ships in the driving rain. They did not realise that the other British ships had all sailed north. They had one fright when a ship-of-the-line came into sight, racing up from the south, and they immediately thought of Dumanoir's squadron, but the private signal soon relieved their fears. It was *Donegal* on her way to join the fleet.

At five the tow-rope broke for the first time. Young Paul Nicolas in *Belleisle* became increasingly alarmed: 'The ship laboured excessively, and in spite of the constant exertions of the frigate we drifted fast towards the shore. Several times the tow-rope parted, but notwith-standing the risk of approaching an ungovernable hulk in such a tremendous sea, a line was thrown and repeatedly a hawser was again hauled on board the frigate.' It was not possible to use the boats in the normal way because with the seas as they were the men in them would not have stood a chance. At seven forty the two ships collided. *Naiad*'s jolly-boat was damaged and most of her starboard quarter gallery smashed away.

At some point in the evening Dundas gave up and pulled away from the shore to save his own ship. With the wind and rain now whipping into his cabin, he had problems enough on his hands. Soon after midnight *Naiad*'s larboard topsail sheet blew away and the reefed topsail split. They had to cut away the other sheet to save the yard, but the sail blew overboard. Then the fore topmast staysail blew to bits.

Belleisle drifted fast towards the shore. Nicolas was off duty in his cot and getting used to the prospect of shipwreck:

> The increasing storm had driven us so near the shore that it appeared almost beyond human hope that we should escape the frightful prospect before us. About midnight a midshipman entered the wardroom, where most of our cots were swinging, to say that the captain wished the officers to come on deck, as it was probable that we should be ashore very shortly.

They jumped to their feet. Just at that moment one of the 24-pounders broke away from its lashings: 'The apprehension of our danger had taken such entire possession of our minds, that the crash appeared to announce the approach of our destruction.' While the hands scrambled to secure the gun, which was heavy enough to smash through the side of the ship, the officers clambered on deck. Flashes of lightning lit the scene and thunder rumbled. When the dismasted ship rolled in the trough of the sea the water came in through the ports and crashed over the gangway hammock-netting into the waist. Cannonballs were thrown out of the racks and were rolling wildly about the decks, where exhausted men lay after their turn on the pumps had ended. A few seamen, under Second Lieutenant Thomas Coleman, were struggling in driving rain to set up the jib-boom as a foremast. They eventually hoisted a boat's sail on it to help turn the ship.

Every roll of the sea seemed to Nicolas like the beginning of the breakers on the shore: 'The hours lagged tediously on, and death appeared in each gust of the tempest. In the battle the chances were equal, and it was possible for many to escape; but shipwreck in such a hurricane was certain destruction to all, and the doubtful situation of the ship kept the mind in a perpetual state of terror.' They waited for daylight, hearing each hour sounded by the ship's bell, 'the thoughts of home, kindred, friends, pressed round the heart and aggravated our despair'.

At half past three the lookout saw land. A shout of 'Land on the lee bow! Put the helm up!' brought another burst of frantic confusion. Lieutenant John Owen recalled that 'At this time our fate appeared inevitable: two guns on the maindeck had broken loose, and were with difficulty choked up with the seamen's hammocks; the ship was altogether unmanageable, and gradually drifting towards the surf, the roar of which added to the horrors of the scene.' But with the help of Coleman's sail they wore the ship. When she responded Captain Hargood knew they were safe and congratulated Owen on their survival. The marines were still not sure. 'When we got round, the breakers were distinctly seen about a mile to leeward, throwing the spray to such a terrific height that even in our security we could not behold them without shuddering.' The crew were so exhausted they could hardly feel joy.

With the light *Naiad* found them again near Barbate and took them in tow once more, spread all her canvas, and steered straight for Gibraltar. They were fired on by the Spanish battery at Tarifa, but by eleven were in sight of the Rock. *Naiad* anchored at one thirty, while *Belleisle* was warped in to the mole. The governor had seen them coming. A market boat had brought news of the battle to Gibraltar the previous evening and he had made preparations for the arrival of the British fleet. Instead of a fleet, however, two battered ships arrived, one of which had no masts. It did not stop the garrison celebrating. 'When we arrived near our anchorage,' wrote Nicolas, 'the battery of the Devil's Tongue commenced firing, and a feu-de-joie followed along the lines; each ship manned her yards and cheered as we passed; and our entrance into the mole was very gratifying: crowds of every class came to greet and congratulate us, and to learn particulars of the victory which had been gained.' The officers were all invited to a ball at the governor's house the following night.

Admiral Louis also arrived at Gibraltar with his squadron, on his way back to join the British fleet. As Francis Austen wrote to Mary Gibson:

Having heard of the action as well as that our fleet was in want of assistance to repair their damages and secure their prizes, we proceeded on with a fine, fresh wind at east to run through the Straits; but before we were out of sight of the garrison the wind chopped round to the westward, directly in our teeth, and came on to blow a very heavy gale of wind, which effectually prevented our proceeding. We bore away for this place [Tetouan] and wait a change of wind and weather, not a little anxious for our friends outside, who could have been but ill prepared to encounter such a severe storm as they must have experienced on a lee shore, and probably with crippled masts. Indeed, I hardly expect to hear they have all escaped.

21

The Worst Hurricane I Ever Saw

The savage gales of Tuesday and Wednesday nights were a prelude to the longest phase of continuous bad weather, which began on the evening of Thursday, 24 October, and lasted without a lull for more than twenty-four hours.

The most laconic ship's logs upgraded strong breezes to strong gales during Thursday night. They recorded very squally winds, thunder, lightning, torrential rain and very high seas. For ships that were already battered and whose crews had endured four days and four sleepless nights of harrowing danger, this was the ultimate test.

In such conditions the smallest boats were most vulnerable. The schooner *Pickle* had anchored, but the cutter *Entreprenante* was under sail with the bulk of the British fleet some miles off Chipiona. She was a captured French boat, built for speed, about seventy feet long, with a crew of thirty-five seamen under Lieutenant Robert Young and two midshipmen, a second master and a surgeon.

Young was a thirty-two-year-old Manxman, who had survived the wreck of the old *Colossus* when she went down in 1798 with Sir William Hamilton's collection of antique vases on board. After the battle, Young believed that Nelson had intended to send him home with dispatches, a job that would make him post-captain, and was waiting for the call from Collingwood. In the little cutter were forty Britons and 157 Frenchmen, mostly survivors of the *Achille*, plucked naked from the water four days earlier. Young had given them what linen he had but it wasn't much. Fortunately, although it was wet it wasn't cold. From Thursday's 66° Fahrenheit Friday became steamy as the temperature rose to 70° in the early afternoon.

The final blow came, as south-westerlies do, in a series of intense squalls. In the distance behind them the skies darkened to deep grey or green. Lightning flashed. In the sudden strengthening of the screaming wind, taut rigging hummed, canvas stiffened and *Entreprenante* lost her mainsail. The shreds blew away. Rain pelted down on to the deck, drenching men who were trying to master flying ropes that whipped and writhed like angry snakes. As they got up the trysail and storm jib, the vessel was shipping heavy seas that were breaking on the deck.

What Joseph Conrad called the 'thick, grey, smoky, and sinister tone' of the westerly gale now set in. The horizon contracted, the shores disappeared into the clouds. This was 'thick weather'. Anything at any distance was blurred and indistinct. The dread of rocks and shoals rose in the pits of their stomachs. Suddenly a squall passed, and for a moment visibility improved. There was a brief opportunity to look about and take a quick bearing before the next squall engulfed the cutter in deafening gusts and drenching rain. The wind was variable, for much of the time southerly or even south-easterly, so reducing the danger of being driven ashore, but it was fearfully strong and gusty.

Young hoisted '314' to signal distress and request assistance. He fired a carronade at intervals to draw attention to himself, but for as far as he could see the waters all around were empty. By the afternoon they were almost waterlogged. They heaved five of their ten carronades overboard, with the shot, the remains of the old mainsail, and anything else that would lighten the ship. Then the foresail and storm jib split. Once night fell there was no light from moon or stars, just gleams from leaping phosphorescent foam as waves crashed over them. By night the clouds seemed darker, the seas higher and more dangerous, the wind stronger. For long hours they waited in fear, hearing the crash of breaking seas. But they survived and in the morning found an anchorage in the relative shelter of Sanlúcar Bay where they pumped and bailed and tried to mend their sails.

Bigger ships were also in trouble, notably the two badly damaged former British flagships. *Victory* lost her mainyard late on Friday afternoon; in tearing away it split the main topsail and ripped the mainsail to pieces. As boatswain William Willmot and carpenter William Bunce, with their crews, cleared the wreckage *Polyphemus* pulled away from *Victory*, supposing the hawser had come away. 'We shipped three heavy seas which filled the deck,' wrote William Rivers junior. 'Turned all hands to the pumps. Hoisted the launch lug-sail to a rough spar attached to the cap of the ensign staff [which kept] the ship to and kept her from foundering.' Meanwhile they sounded every hour with the 100-fathom line but found no bottom and stayed in deep water during the night, blowing before the wind.

Just after *Victory*'s mainyard blew away *Royal Sovereign* lost her only remaining mast, the foremast. At five thirty it crashed over the side, taking sails and rigging with it. Ten minutes later the tow-rope broke and the huge hulk was swept away from *Mars*. The crew rigged a jury foremast and fired distress signals. Captain Rotheram took frequent soundings in case they were driving ashore. The ship rolled so steeply that a carronade pitched off the poop into the sea. A great wave smashed into the stern gallery, swept into the cabin and washed the wounded and unconscious Lieutenant James Clavell from his cot and into the wardroom. Clavell would have drowned if Marine Captain Joseph Vallack had not grabbed his senseless body and held on tight. Rotheram admitted in his own notes that his ship came 'very near foundering in the gale from shot holes and loss of all masts'.

Lieutenant William Hennah's *Mars* fared better until after nightfall when she lost her fore topmast. At daylight Hennah discovered that the foremast was so badly damaged that his carpenters had to cut it away. Midshipman James Robinson wrote to his father in Edinburgh, 'Never did ships experience such awful weather as we, without masts (they being shot away) we tossed about at the mercy of the winds and waves and what was worse, the sailor's curse, the land close to us.' In the morning both *Mars* and *Royal Sovereign* were signalling distress, but together they beat back towards the anchored ships off Chipiona and managed to come to an anchor near them when the wind dropped a little, early on Saturday afternoon.

Thomas Capel's frigate *Phoebe* had not been able to evacuate the French *Swiftsure* completely. Her carpenters had plugged most of the holes in her and she had taken off the wounded before losing contact at the height of the storm. She could not get her back in tow but contrived to put aboard a party of men, who brought *Swiftsure* to an anchor on 26 October.

Africa also came close to perdition. Her mainmast snapped just twelve feet above the deck soon after dark on Friday night and carried away the yards of the foresails. The men had three-quarters of an hour in which to begin to clear a path through this confusion before the mizen mast collapsed, smashing two of their boats in its fall. At two thirty in the morning the foremast split in three places. In driving rain and raging winds, with the waves throwing them off their feet, men struggled to clear wreckage and rig jury masts to keep the ship before the wind to stop them broaching to and foundering. This was damage far more serious than ever the French had done. They shifted weight away from the top of the ship by heaving four 18-pounder guns and four of the ten 32-pounder carronades over the side. On Saturday afternoon *Conqueror* saw *Africa*'s distress signals and took the ship in tow.

James Martin and *Neptune*'s other seamen had been working hard to reinforce her masts and spars over the past days: 'Our masts we Strengthaned by Anchor Stocks and our yards by Stunsail Booms, Capstin Bars &c.' They tried to get up a storm rig of courses and staysails but the main staysail blew to pieces the moment they got it up at noon. In the afternoon they reefed the fore and main courses, but the main course blew to shreds at two thirty. They ran before the wind with what was left and saw the coast of southern Portugal about nine miles away towards last light. Having beaten away from this hazard overnight, Thomas Fremantle sighted *Victory* around noon on Saturday and closed in to take her in tow. He succeeded at about four in the afternoon and the two three-deckers limped slowly southwards in strong but less dangerous winds.

Much further south a second knot of British ships was struggling, their last instructions being merely to get as far off the coast as possible. On the evening of 24 October, *Colossus* and *Agamemnon* were almost back where they had started after the battle – on the starboard tack with Trafalgar bearing south-east by east. Crucially, they were a little further out to sea and the Cape was about twenty-one miles away. Captain James Morris of *Colossus* prepared for another rough night by jettisoning the poop carronades. His ship's carpenters had spent the day stopping leaks and tying up the guns even more securely to stop them breaking free as the ship rolled. *Bellerophon* was not far behind and after her *Thunderer* was towing *San Juan Nepomuceno*. They all had a tough time on 25 October, but as the weather eased the next day they made sufficient offing to round Cape Trafalgar. At first light on 27 October William Cumby of *Bellerophon* found himself within sight of *Agamemnon* and *Colossus* and sailed downwind to join them. 'Finding they were steering for Gibraltar,' he reported to Collingwood, 'I thought it expedient, from the small quantity of water remaining on board, and the great sufferings of our numerous wounded, to follow them.' *Thunderer* followed. Collingwood had no idea where she was, but seven days after the battle of Trafalgar, entirely on his own initiative, Lieutenant John Stockham brought the first surviving prize, *San Juan Nepomuceno*, into a British port.

If the height of the storm posed a challenge for the tried and tested seamen in the British ships it was even more alarming to those in Cadiz Bay who had not spent their winters off Brittany and whose acquaintance with their ships and colleagues was slight. Landlubbers, like Infantry Captain Pernot, lying helplessly near the waterline of Julien Cosmao-Kerjulien's ship *Pluton*, were terrified: 'Our anchor did not hold and we dragged. The seas were huge. The jolts the ship had taken during the battle had made her leaky and she was making twenty-six inches of water an hour, and through a surfeit of misfortune, the ship caught fire, so that we did not know from moment to moment whether we were going to run aground or sink or blow up.' *Pluton* was supplied with new anchors from the shore and her leaks were mostly stopped so that after two nights she was safer. Still, Pernot's letter home, dated 5 November, resembled a passage from a Gothic novel:

During these miserable days and nights every minute there was distant gunfire in every direction. I was told that these were the distress signals of dismasted vessels that had been thrown onto the shore. But nobody could help them. People had tried: several launches and boats that had been sent for this purpose had capsized or sunk. The unlucky victims were condemned to perish. Very few men escaped the shipwrecks. The screams of the wounded were appalling. When the tide was low they tried to use the limbs they still possessed to drag themselves across the rocks away from a death that met them further on. It was indescribably ghastly and harrowing, and mostly happening by night.

The reality might not have been so macabre, but the rocks in Cadiz Bay *are* an escape route to shore at low tide and they do become submerged at high tide, so Pernot's account of crawling, wounded, screaming wretches who later drowned is not to be dismissed out of hand.

On 24 October the relatively calm weather allowed many wounded men to be brought ashore. Admiral Álava was taken off *Santa Ana*. But even then the sea was too rough for the badly injured to be moved. Pierre Philibert reported that several Spanish and French boats came out to *Algésiras* to take off the wounded 'but the heavy seas did not allow of us sending off any but the least severely injured'. Laurent Le Tourneur, the three wounded lieutenants and Sub-lieutenant Michel Kerbusso left that day, but Kerbusso died soon after.

Early that morning Lieutenant Voldemar de la Bretonnière of *Algésiras* had been sent a second little stream anchor, this time in a longboat. He ordered his men to double the hawser. They rowed off to lay it out ahead, then tried to haul the ship towards the anchor. But the tide was ebbing and they soon began bumping on the rocks. The crew pawled the capstan, locking it with a bar so the rope would not slip, and shifted their efforts to lightening the ship. They moved the guns in the after batteries forward, smashed up the damaged boats and threw them overboard, jettisoned damaged spars, pumped out all the water, and unloaded the firewood. The effort paid off and at noon they floated clear without serious damage.

A little later a Spanish schooner at last brought the big bower anchor they needed with a cable. Asked to let it out as far ahead as possible, the schooner tried to place it ahead of the stream anchor, but the wind suddenly strengthened, the hawser broke and the anchor dropped uselessly abeam on a rocky bottom. The cable to the principal anchor was now so chafed that only one strand remained. De la Bretonnière could not weigh the anchor, which was fast among the rocks, so he cut the cable and his men heaved on the stream anchor. At high tide the stream anchor was stuck on the edge of the Galera bank. It was the only thing holding them.

De la Bretonnière asked the Spanish pilot whether he was willing to get under way and attempt to reach the anchorage if there was sufficient water over all the reefs for them to get over without touching. He refused, saying it was better to wait where they were until morning. As soon as they had sent him back on shore, the low clouds banked up and the wind stiffened in the south-west.

De la Bretonnière discussed the situation with Philibert and the other surviving officers. They 'foresaw a night even more fearful than the preceding one' and decided to get under way, pilot or no pilot. The crew tripped the stream anchor, used the boats to cast on the proper tack and prayed. It worked: 'The ship at once fetched headway; she steered perfectly under two topgallant sails and her mizen topgallantsail. From that minute we saw that we were saved.' Like true seamen they put down their survival to 'the sailing qualities of the ship' they had come to love.

They passed over the Galera bank and came to an anchor in Cadiz Bay around dawn. 'We let go in 6½ fathom water, sand and mud bottom,' Philibert reported in triumph, but sent an officer at once to

Cosmao's *Pluton* to request a bower anchor as soon as possible: the weather appearing threatening. The horror was not yet over.

At 10 o'clock it came on in squalls, rainy, blowing in gusts; at 11 o'clock, a violent squall made us drag; at once let go a fluke which we had left, to which we clinched a hawser, and fired shots for help. Half an hour after midnight we bumped heavily; our rudder was un-shipped and we lost it as we had no boats and our rudder chains had been severed in the action.

But *Algésiras* survived. At ten in the morning on 25 October a boat from the Carraca let go a best bower anchor well ahead of them, and at last she was safe.

The final French escapee, *Aigle*, was still at large. She was so close to the shore that the British assumed she was aground, but she was not. From Cadiz the Marquis of Solana wrote repeatedly to the commander of the castle at Sancti Petri, urging him to rescue her. But although his outpost was tantalisingly close to where *Aigle* lay at anchor Fermin de Argumosa could not get to her. He wrote harrowing replies, describing the attempts that had been made. On the first night after the battle Antonio Ulloa had led his men into the waves and rescued seventeen swimmers from *Fougueux*. Only two drowned. The following night they had waded into the breakers again; but the sea was lethal for small boats and Argumosa's letters stressed repeatedly how 'absolutely impossible' it was to reach the stricken ship. The sound of distress guns haunted them, but it was not until 24 October that they even recognised *Aigle* and still could not reach her.

Aigle narrowly survived Thursday night, but as the weather deterio-rated on Friday Asmus Classen called a council of the officers. Captain Gourrège was still alive below, but he and the many other wounded needed help. Classen feared that if they stayed where they were any longer they would share the terrible fate of the *Fougueux*, which they had witnessed. But when they had last attempted to move, *Aigle* had proved unmanageable. Since then her hull had taken a severe battering from the violent rollers and they had already thrown over-board the 18-pounder guns, some of the guns from the upper works and about thirty tons of shifting ballast from the lower deck. They decided to risk everything on one last attempt to reach Cadiz. Classen went back on deck.

> The wind had just hauled into the south-west, a strong gale, I instantly took advantage of this to cut the cable and I had the satisfaction of standing on my course under modest canvas and steering by hand, working with a double tiller. I came to an anchor, unpiloted, at the end of a tack at the entrance to the roads, near the Spanish ship *San Justo*.

There, they rode out Friday night, but the illusion of success proved short-lived. As the tide fell, breakers appeared close to starboard of the ship and at dawn 'she grounded hard and unshipped her rudder after several consecutive shocks'. Classen realised that he was too close to the Diamante rocks and could not stay there. He would have to cut his cable but he did not have another. The only chance was to run for the shore. He steered to the south of the Rio Guadelate and deliberately ran the ship on to the soft sand-mud bottom of the shore towards Puerto Real. 'I am in hopes of getting her off,' he reported immediately afterwards, but it was not to be. Nevertheless, with extraordinarily enterprising seamanship he and his colleagues saved the lives of all the crew. Gourrège was brought ashore alive but died soon afterwards of his many wounds, 'sincerely regretted', as a Spanish witness reported, by the many friends he had made in Cadiz.

The night of *Aigle*'s last trial was catastrophic in Cadiz Bay. *Argonaute* and *San Justo* signalled distress, *San Francisco de Asís* broke up onshore and *Indomptable* hit a rock and disappeared so that there was no trace of her in the morning when the Tavira Tower's watchman vainly scanned the bay. Having picked up some of *Bucentaure*'s survivors, *Indomptable* was crowded but just how crowded is uncertain. The figures given by French historian Edouard Desbrière for *Bucentaure*'s losses allow for only sixty-five drowned in *Indomptable*. If this is correct, fewer people might have been in *Indomptable* than the fourteen hundred or more that hysterical witnesses declared. But she probably had about a thousand people on board. According to Captain Pernot, whose regiment provided *Indomptable*'s infantry, only about 150 men survived the shipwreck, and twenty-two out of twenty-four officers died. No account gives more than 180 survivors. *Indomptable*'s captain, Jean-Joseph Hubert, drowned with the rest. Two of *Conqueror*'s men also perished in her.

Out to sea, meanwhile, the British attempt to evacuate and destroy the prizes had stalled owing to the appalling weather. *Monarca* drove from her anchor and was wrecked on Friday at the southern end of the Arenas Gordas north of Sanlúcar with the loss of most or all of the 170 or so Spaniards still on board. 'Thursday night, or Friday morning, the *Monarca* parted, and at daylight was seen drifting into the bight: I fear she is lost, with everyone on board,' Henry Bayntun reported to George Hope on Sunday night. He was himself 'riding very hard'. *Leviathan* had 'carried away the tiller and loosened the upper pintles of the rudder', but Bayntun 'preferred this to keeping the ship under weigh in our crippled state, with a main-yard doubtful even for spreading the top-sail'.

William Rutherford and his crew in *Swiftsure* were fast becoming rescue specialists. They had continued *Dreadnought*'s evacuation work on *San Agustín* and took off 116 men before the weather became impossible. *Ajax* tried to carry on but her pinnace and launch were swamped and lost with all their crew, and only one cutter made it to the Spanish ship, where its eight men remained with *Leviathan*'s prize crew and the three hundred Spaniards still on board. *Ajax* abandoned the evacuation, reporting 'two of the prizes driving past us . . . strong gales and violent squalls, and a great sea running'. *San Agustín* remained afloat until Saturday when it became calmer. Then Bayntun ordered Codrington to complete the evacuation and he anchored *Orion* near her, reporting to Bayntun on Saturday evening that:

The squall & partial shift of wind made me fear that I should pass the prize, or I should have anchored in a more seamanlike situation for executing your orders . . . The Spanish Lieut. of the S Augustin says the ship is tight, makes no water /^{only 8 inches an hour} & has very good pumps, but only one anchor & the cable by which she rides, & no rudder. she has about five hundred people on board. This being the case & the appearance of the weather favourable, I propose giving my over harassed ship's company as much rest as possible tonight & shall be ready to execute your orders in the morning.

The 'appearance' of favourable weather was to be deduced from the barometer, which was rising at last. Codrington's worries now centred around his numerous prisoners and a consequent shortage of water. That afternoon Young had appeared with the *Entreprenante* and had persuaded Codrington to take his '140 naked Frenchmen' (actually 157, according to *Orion*'s muster book). Codrington ordered Young 'to receive the people from the prize which he is unwilling to do being short of water, which I cant give him'. Codrington himself had only fifty tons of water and he soon had almost a thousand people on board. On Monday he emptied *San Agustín* and on Tuesday evening he burned her. One of her junior officers, Joaquín Bocalán, remembered that 'all the dead remained and most of those without legs and arms were left for dead'. Once again, however, the numbers in the British muster books suggest that all the wounded were taken off, and on this occasion the pace of evacuation was leisurely. Captain Cajigal reported that 'our enemies generously saved our lives'.

Codrington passed his time with his officer prisoners Louis Infernet and Auguste Gicquel. 'L'Intrépide's Capt. my present messmate is a tough fellow,' he told Henry Bayntun. 'Says now that he would prefer being a prisoner as he is, having so fought to being any of those van captains who are now in Cadiz & who would not follow his example.' Auguste Gicquel recalled:

On *Orion* I was reunited with Captain Infernet. We spent part of each day together; he was in pretty good humour and drank a lot of 'grogs' in which there were as much spirits as water. When I remarked on this, he replied that it was 'to ruin the enemy'. The English Captain, Codrington, was considerably more educated than he was and wanted to spend long hours chatting with me. He told me of his disappointments in the long cruises and the interminable blockades that England then imposed on her sailors, and where he wasted his life far from his family and what he loved best. There was much talk of duty among them as among us but at least they could cheer themselves with days like that of Trafalgar.

On 27 October Bayntun reported to George Hope of *Defence* on the local situation:

> Since I came here on Thursday forenoon, I have found it necessary to take on me the command of the vessels which anchored, and have endeavoured to forward, in spite of the weather, the signal of the Commander-in-chief – namely, to withdraw men from the prizes and destroy; but such has been the vast rolling sea, and the ships not being near each other, that much less has been done than I most ardently have wished, and many boats have been lost.

He explained that he had ordered *Orion* to anchor next to the rudderless *San Agustín* and *Ajax* to get close to the *Argonauta*, anchored further north and also rudderless, 'to take out the remaining men previous to her being destroyed'.

Argonauta was at anchor with a prize crew from *Defiance*. Led by Lieutenant Henry Hargrave, it included Thomas Townshend of Great Yarmouth, whose wife Jane was in *Defiance*, and Colin Campbell, a master's mate. Since everybody thought the ship was sinking and another gale was coming on, theirs was a grim assignment. The four hundred remaining crew looked to Campbell like '600 Spaniards on board and most of them drunk and her decks full of wounded'. Then the wind got up. 'It came on to blow a very heavy gale of wind that night and continued to blow harder and harder till the night of the 26th [25/26 October] when it blew harder than I ever saw it. We did not expect she would ride the night out with us. The Spaniards were terribly frightened and all turned-to, to pray.' The ship was leaking faster than they could pump and the sea was breaking clean over the ship, bringing in more water. However drunk the Spaniards were they must have joined in, since thirty Englishmen could do little on their own. 'We hove all the main deck guns overboard and let go the sheet anchor under foot in case the best bow anchor should part; about 12 at night the iron littior broke in two and the rudder knocked about so much we thought it would knock her stern post in, but about 3 in the morning it broke adrift altogether which we were very glad of.'

At daybreak they found that the cable to the best bower had indeed broken but the sheet anchor was still holding them. *Monarca*, *Berwick* and *Rayo* had disappeared. *Defiance* was nowhere to be seen and the two boats in which they had come had both sunk during the night. They hoisted a signal of distress and fired guns.

In the afternoon, with the seas still turbulent, *Leviathan* and *Donegal* sent boats to save the British and the few Spaniards they could carry with them. Campbell, along with Townshend, was taken to *Donegal*. 'I was pretty well off there as I fell in with an old shipmate,' he wrote to his father, a month later.

'You see, sir, there is very little hope of any prize from this quarter being saved,' Bayntun reported to Hope, 'nor has there been any idea of it, except as to the Rayo. The Argonaute and St Augustine, having lost their rudders, shall be scuttled the instant we get all the men out; but hitherto that has been a very difficult undertaking, more so at anchor than it would have been under weigh.' On Sunday *Ajax* obeyed Bayntun's order to anchor near *Argonauta*. She completed the evacuation of the Spanish next day, taking out 185 men. Many were wounded and three died on board. Then, on 29 October, *Ajax* sent men to scuttle *Argonauta*.

With what must have been a huge effort *Donegal* took 626 men out of *Rayo* on 24 October. But when the weather closed in there were still nearly three hundred men aboard, including a prize crew of ninety-eight Britons. The three-decker's hull was sound and they hoped to preserve her, but the weather proved too fierce. 'On Friday she drove a great way from the Donegal, but brought up again,' Bayntun reported to Hope. (Much the same had happened to *Berwick*.) But on Sunday morning *Rayo*'s cable parted again. Bayntun 'sent off the Entreprenante to look after her, but there is little hope of the ship being saved'.

He was right. *Rayo* went aground on the Arenas Gordas beach about eight miles above Sanlúcar. *Donegal*'s master, William Dunbar, tied himself to the poop, which had remained above water, and watched as about a hundred men drowned trying to reach land in the boats. Among the victims were twenty-one from *Donegal*, including the ship's carpenter, William Ellis. As soon as the weather moderated, the Spanish sent boats with bread and water for the survivors and eventually lifted them off. Seventy-seven Englishmen were taken prisoner.

At noon on Sunday *Berwick* also broke away from her anchors for a second time. It was widely suspected that the French prisoners deliberately cut the cables, but whatever had happened she was heading straight 'towards the dangerous shoals of St Lucar, then to leeward, where there was hardly a chance of a man being saved'. Captain Malcolm ordered *Donegal* to cut her own cable, made sail and went after her. She overhauled *Berwick*, took off the prize crew under Lieutenant Edward Barnard of *Achille* and 102 Frenchmen.

He dispatched his boats with orders first to save all the wounded Frenchmen before they brought off any of the English, which order was most punctually complied with; the English were next removed, but before the boats could return, the Berwick struck upon the shoals and every soul on board perished, to the number of three hundred.

Meanwhile, Lieutenant Young had taken *Entreprenante* off in search of *Rayo*, as Bayntun had ordered. Instead of *Rayo*, he found *Bahama* anchored off the north end of the Arenas Gordas: 'spoke one of the enemy's hulks, the officers of which informed us the hulk was in great distress – 7½ feet of water in her hold, no pumps, no rudder – and that they had given the ship up to the enemy'. Young located the wreck of the *Rayo*, aground and lost, returned to take the Royal Navy men out of *Bahama*, and made all sail towards the fleet.

On Monday afternoon, under high and scattered clouds and with a moderate breeze, *Donegal* followed Young's directions and found *Bahama*. Pulteney Malcolm took 184 men out of her and carried them to *Royal Sovereign* and *Mars*. Next day, when *Phoebe* approached *Bahama*, Spanish fishing-boats were rescuing the crew. Thomas Capel closed in and sent Lieutenant John Hindmarsh and a party of men to take charge of her. He then sent Lieutenant Dixie with the barge's crew to set fire to the wrecks of *Rayo* and *Monarca*, before taking *Bahama* in tow. They could see that *Berwick* was 'totally lost having parted asunder amidships'. On 1 November, having watched *Monarca* blow up and seen *Rayo* 'in full blaze,' Capel met Malcolm and handed over *Bahama* to *Donegal*. In 'dark rainy weather with thunder & lightning', the three ships rejoined the fleet.

The British crews at Trafalgar were tested first as fighters, then as sailors. Their achievement as fighters was impressive. Their achievement as sailors was extraordinary. The crews had had little sleep for days and to risk their lives in small boats to save men who had been trying to kill them was truly heroic. Most witnesses thought that, by comparison, winning the battle had been easy. It would have been understandable to allow foundering enemy ships to break up on shore with men still in them, but generally this was avoided. Even allowing for confusion and duplication in the British muster books, they provide strong evidence that in the majority of cases all enemy survivors were taken off the prizes. Where ships were lost before evacuation was complete, British seamen were almost always lost with them. At least two thousand people drowned in the Trafalgar storm, of whom rather more than a hundred were British.

Edward Codrington wrote soon afterwards that 'Perhaps the saving the lives of the men on board the prizes, both English and foreigners, previous to their being destroyed or lost, was one of the most trying duties men could possibly be put to; and yet, in spite of the noble exertions made on all sides to effect this object, humanity shudders at the recollection of the numbers who perished.'

22

The Mercy of God

Antonio Alcalá Galiano passed the days when the storm was at its height with his mother in the village of Chiclana. They still knew nothing of the fate of the *Bahama* or of its captain, although they asked everyone they met. Several times Antonio took his telescope to the hermitage at the top of the hill of Santa Ana and stood in the wind and rain looking out across the furious sea. He saw vessels with desperate damage flying signals of distress but not clearly enough to identify them. Finally Señora Galiano could no longer stand the isolation and decided to return to Cadiz.

They made the journey by coach, and after passing Torregorda took the convenient route along the beach that everybody used when the tide was out. But that day it was far from convenient. Huge waves crashed on to the sand, thunderously loud, under a sky dark with menacing black clouds. Wreckage continually blocked their way and the coach had to weave between lengths of cable, pieces of rigging, barrels, spars, even sections of the hulls of ships. Every so often there was a corpse, torn by shot and bloated after days in the water. 'My mother moaned and looked away, expecting each time to recognise the mutilated body of her husband,' wrote Antonio. By now they felt sure he was dead.

Once in Cadiz, they pursued their investigations, but nobody could tell them anything. People gravitated towards the harbour, to find out what was going on and to offer help to the wounded. The magnitude of the defeat was by now clear. A letter sent to Bernardo de Uriarte from Cadiz on 25 October stated plainly that 'Nelson and his Englishmen have gained a complete and decisive victory, and that our Fleet has been, all of it, absolutely destroyed.' By 29 October there were a thousand wounded in the hospitals at Cadiz. Casualties had been especially heavy among the infantry: 'Scarcely a third part remains of the French troops who were embarked on board the Fleet, and it is really heart-rending to see their soldiers wandering about the streets.' Captain Pernot, who had fought on board *Pluton*, confirmed this in a letter home. The expeditionary force that had left France in the spring had been in total over four thousand strong. Now it mustered 756. 'The rest,' Pernot commented bitterly, 'were either killed, or drowned, or amputated and languishing in the hospitals.' In fact, the majority were now prisoners.

During Saturday, 26 October, the barometer at the Royal Observatory outside Cadiz rose six inches, although the wind remained strong and the torrential rain continued. Collingwood signalled the schooner *Pickle* to come within hail and at nine o'clock he gave Lieutenant John Lapenotière orders to return to England with two dispatches containing the first news of the battle. (A bitterly disappointed Robert Young of the *Entreprenante* was sent to Faro two days later with duplicates for the British consul-general in Portugal.) Before *Pickle* could leave, Lapenotière had to unload his cargo of twenty-eight Frenchmen from *Achille*, including a badly wounded officer. When the ship's boat returned at midday, having transferred the Frenchmen to *Revenge*, Lapenotière set sail for home and was out of sight within half an hour.

Collingwood also took advantage of the calmer weather promised by the barometer to send some of the most badly damaged ships to Gibraltar. He ordered *Prince* to tow *Tonnant* there and *Neptune* to take

Victory. His signal found Captain Thomas Fremantle writing his first post-battle letter to his wife Betsy:

> This last Week has been a scene of Anxiety and fatigue beyond any I have ever experienced but I trust in God that I have gained considerable credit . . . I am at present towing the Victory and the Admiral has just made the signal for me to go with her to Gibralter, which is a satisfactory proof to my mind that he is perfectly satisfied with Old Neptune, who behaves as well as I could wish. The loss of Nelson is a death blow to my future prospects here, he knew well how to appreciate Abilities and Zeal, and I am well aware that I shall never cease to lament his loss whilst I live.

In *Neptune*, as in other ships, there was now more time for officers to fraternise with the enemy. 'The Prisoners we have on board say they expected to give us a good licking,' William Badcock wrote to his father. 'They heard we had only 21 ships of the Line and they had 33, their officers told them now the English would pay for all, but I think, they did.'

Fremantle had also been enjoying the society of his prisoners: 'Adml. Villeneuve was with me on board the Neptune over two days,' he wrote. 'I found him a very pleasant and Gentlemanlike man, the poor man was very low!' Fremantle had just put the French admiral on board the *Euryalus*, but he still had Captain Jean-Jacques Magendie, Villeneuve's aides and General Contamine, as well as '450 poor Spaniards from the Santissima Trinidada, with a true Italian priest born at Malta . . . an excellent French cook and a true Spanish pug dog'. The French were full of bravado and of witty flourishes at the expense of their emperor. 'These Frenchmen make me laugh at the gasconade as well as at their accounts of Buonaparte the Palais Royal Paris etc . . .' he told Betsy. 'The French Captain drinks your health regularly every day at dinner. The poor man is married and laments his lot, one of the younger ones is desperately in love with a lady at Cadiz and Frenchmanlike carries her picture in his pocket.'

Fremantle's good cheer was only spoiled by the death of his friend and patron, and a message from the deck with a revised signal from *Euryalus* reminded him of the change for the worse: 'Would you believe that Old Colingwood has now made the Signal for me to go off Cape Espartel instead of Gibralter, the poor man does not know his own mind 5 minutes together.'

Collingwood had learned that certain ships were more badly damaged than he had realised and that those overburdened with prisoners were seriously short of water. In the prevailing conditions it was not possible to take proper care of the enemy wounded. Now that they could be sent ashore Collingwood decided to open a diplomatic channel to the Marquis of Solana. His opening bid was to offer him the wounded Spanish prisoners if the Spanish would bring them in and acknowledge them as prisoners-of-war who would have to be exchanged with equivalent numbers of British prisoners before they could fight against Britain again.

On Monday, a week after the battle, he sent this message to the marquis in the hands of Captain William Prowse, of the frigate *Sirius*, who was already posted outside the port. Flying a flag of truce, *Sirius* dropped a boat at the harbour entrance, then pulled away again. Prowse went slowly into the harbour, taking a good look round Cadiz Bay as he approached. The one-legged frigate captain, who had joined the navy as an able seaman more than thirty years earlier, dined with Solana and stayed overnight with James Duff, the British Consul.

Solana replied next morning, promising the return of those Englishmen who had been captured or driven ashore in the prizes. He reminded Collingwood that a mechanism for the exchange of prisoners had already been agreed with Lord Nelson and put in a bid for the return of all the Spanish and French prisoners, especially of Báltasar de Cisneros, the only Spanish admiral the British held. Two French frigates and the brig *Furet* were loaded with uninjured English prisoners to be exchanged for the Spanish wounded.

As the various frigates returned, Prowse discreetly passed Collingwood a reassuring report on the enemy's remaining strength. He had counted thirteen ships-of-the-line afloat, four frigates, three brigs and a corvette. But of the thirteen ships-of-the-line only two had all their masts and the others were either too badly damaged to sortie or clearly unprepared for immediate service. Francis Austen noted the conclusion of the British officers in his letter to Mary Gibson: 'The greatest part have lost nearly all their masts, and are so completely disabled as to make it impossible they can be again ready for service during the winter.'

At last Collingwood could relax a little. The barometer had fallen back on Sunday but it was now rising steadily again. He sent Captain Hope with *Defence* and *San Ildefonso* off to Gibraltar, followed by *Polyphemus*, towing the French *Swiftsure*. The next day the arrival of Admiral Thomas Louis with four powerful ships and three smaller vessels further reduced the pressure on the new commander-in-chief. It was slightly unfortunate that, unaware of the truce then in force, Louis immediately attempted to capture the *Argonaute*, which was on guard duty outside the mouth of the port. According to *Canopus*'s log: 'On standing in to reconnoitre the position of the enemy's ship it was judged impossible to bring her out with the wind as it was, and that it was not worth the risque of disabling one of the squadron in an attempt to destroy her. She appeared to be warping fast in, and to have a great length of hawser laid out. The batteries fired several shells over us.'

That day Captain Henry Blackwood took *Euryalus* in to deliver a second message from Collingwood to Solana, asking whether each British ship might approach the harbour in turn to discharge its Spanish prisoners, and to discuss the status of Admiral Álava who, having escaped, did not consider himself a prisoner-of-war. Midshipman Hercules Robinson accompanied Blackwood and recalled how the Spanish spectators admired the captain's smart appearance as they walked up the Alameda to the governor's house. He also cherished vivid recollections of the dinner with Solana, which ended with a memorably succulent pineapple and dessert sherry. Robinson and Blackwood slept ashore at Consul James Duff's house.

Some more or less accurate news filtered through from their conversation to the population of Cadiz. They learned that a part at least of the British fleet had weathered the storm, and that the

Santísima Trinidad and *San Ildefonso* had been captured, not sunk. Blackwood and Robinson confirmed that the Combined Fleet had resisted obstinately and that Nelson had been killed. Prowse revealed from personal observation that Captain José de Vargas of the *San Ildefonso* was alive but wounded, but none of the officers who visited had seen much of the other ships. Anxious relatives went to Duff's house to try to find out what had happened to their loved ones, but learned little or nothing. Blackwood was too deeply wounded by the loss of Nelson to spare much sympathy for other people's grief.

Collingwood began to visit his ships to learn about their state. That Wednesday evening Edward Codrington wrote to his wife Jane that '*Euryalus*, with Admiral Collingwood on board, passed under our stern; and shortly afterwards the Admiral sent a boat for me merely to "how d'ye do," and talk over our condition, as being my first communication with him since the action.' It is interesting that Collingwood still had no idea how many prizes had been captured. He told Codrington that 'He makes out eleven French and eleven Spanish who were taken, but three or four got away the first night after, from not being sufficiently secured.'

Codrington reported that *Orion* 'is now getting to rights in her sails and rigging again, and might perhaps be in some order, were it not for the number of prisoners, and the dirt, filth, stench, and confusion they occasion'. In addition to *Orion*'s own crew, now about 530 strong, the ship was packed with 'nearly 100 men of other ships, and 580 prisoners, French and Spanish. In short, we victualled yesterday nearly twelve hundred people.' Collingwood had promised to relieve them of the wounded prisoners next day, 'which is a great comfort: we have about thirty on board, and they not only take up much room and attention, but, poor creatures, the stench is most intolerable'.

Boatload after boatload of wounded men was sent into Cadiz harbour. 'The scenes at the wharfs and in the streets through which the wounded passed were,' wrote an English merchant, who may perhaps be identified as James Duff, 'sufficient to shock every heart not yet hardened to scenes of blood and human suffering.' Whenever careless boatmen or a sudden wave threw a boat against the stone pier 'a horrid cry, which pierced the soul, arose from the mangled wretches on board'. The Spanish gentry in their finest clothes were helping to bring ashore the wounded. This, the Englishman noted, 'had something of the appearance of ostentation', but he helped too, getting them up the steps from the water to the litters waiting above – 'The slightest false step made them shriek out, and I even yet shudder at the remembrance of the sound.' From here they 'were carried away to the hospitals in every shape of human misery, whilst crowds of Spaniards either assisted or looked on with signs of horror. Meanwhile, their companions, who had escaped unhurt, walked up and down with folded arms and downcast eyes, whilst women sat upon heaps of arms, broken furniture, and baggage, with their heads bent between their knees.' He learned that every hospital in Cadiz was already full, and that convents and churches were being commandeered for the remainder. Gabriel Daudignon, first lieutenant of *Bucentaure*, was one of the lucky ones, brought in early from the sinking flagship. His serious splinter wounds in the lower stomach were treated by the surgeon at the Royal Hospital, and after a long course of mineral water he survived.

Captain Pernot was extremely impressed by the performance of the Marquis of Solana, who was to be seen with his most senior officers at the port directing the disembarkation of the wounded. He had assembled the entire transport resources of Cadiz. Stretchers, handbarrows, sedan chairs, gigs, even coaches were ready to transport the wounded to hospital. The journey was made slowly and carefully in consideration for the injured passengers and on either side the people watched this sad procession in tears. This was a perfect stage for Solana's theatrical instincts and he himself carried a stretcher, visited and consoled the victims, offered his help and even his money. 'How many marquises in France,' wrote Pernot, 'would have acted like this brave man whose humanity and generosity tenderise, soothe and elevate the mind?' In the depths of his despair, Pernot paid the warmest tribute to the behaviour of the people of Cadiz and the surrounding area towards the wounded Frenchmen. 'Everywhere our shipwrecked men were given clothes, food and even money by the inhabitants of the places near which they ran aground,' he wrote. 'In sum I doubt whether any maritime *département* of France would have done for the Spanish what these splendid people did for the French.'

Precisely similar encomiums were bestowed by the British. William Dunbar, the master of the *Donegal* who had tied himself to *Rayo*'s poop during her shipwreck, told Edward Codrington afterwards that when he arrived in Cadiz harbour 'a carriage was backed into the water for him to step into from the boat, all sorts of cordials and confectionery were placed in the carriage for him, and clean linen, bed, &c., prepared for him at a lodging on shore'. As his carriage passed along the streets women and priests presented him with delicacies. 'In short, he says, and with very great truth, that had he been wrecked on any part of England he would never have received one-half the attention which he did from these poor Spaniards, whose friends we had just destroyed in such numbers.' Codrington pointed out that, for their part, the English had gone to considerable trouble and put themselves in great danger to save the Spanish survivors of the battle from the jaws of death during the storm so they deserved some gratitude.

William Thorp's account of what had happened to the seamen of *Minotaur* who survived the wreck of the *Neptuno* has the ring of truth about it. After being marched from the wreck site to Puerto Santa Maria 'whe where lodged in Prison and treated kindly by the Spaniards tho our lodging was on the Ground'. They spent three days there and then on Sunday, 27 October, they were again 'marchd 16 miles to a town in the Isle of Loyans Passed a little town called point Royal about nine miles from St Mary's whe where here lodged in prison and served with a Pint of Wine and some bread the next day 28th whe where marched to Cadiz distance about nine miles where whe where again lodged in Prison and received a Quarter Dollar per man.' On 29 October, 'they marched us to the waterside and put us on board two Spanish gun boats & by them carried on board the Hermoine French Frigate, appointed to carry us to the Fleet, to be exchanged, remained on board two nights where our allowance was a Pint of Wine and Bread.' On 1 November they were put on board the *Sirius*, shifted to the *Swiftsure*, and taken to Gibraltar to rejoin *Minotaur*. According to

Thorp 'our loss amounted to four killd by the falling of the Masts Rigging and Drowned'. Thorp, too, maintained that 'no imputation of cruelty or even unkindness can be alleged to the Spaniards those who arrived safe on shore looked upon our Men as their deliverers and there where instances of Grattitude and kindness that would do Honour to any Nation'.

Another seaman, who possibly survived the same wreck, was luckier:

> Now the Spanish prisoners, that had come on shore first, some of them had been and seen their friends, and, as daylight came on, they came down to assist us, which they did, for they brought us some bread, and some figs, and some wine, to refresh us, which we wanted very much, for we had scarcely tasted anything the last twenty-four hours, and the Spaniards behaved very kind to us. As for myself, after I had eaten some bread and fruit, and drank some wine, I tried to get up, but I could not, and one of the Spaniards, seeing the state I was in, was kind enough to get two or three more of his companions, and lifted me up in one of the bullock-carts in which they had brought down the provisions for us, and covered me up with one of their great ponchos, and he tapped me on the shoulder, and said, 'Bono English!' And, being upon the cart, I was out of the wind and rain – for it blew a heavy gale of wind – and I felt myself quite comfortable, only my leg pained me a good deal; but, thanks be to God, I soon fell into a sound sleep, and, as I heard afterwards, the French soldiers came down and marched the rest of my shipmates up to Cadiz, and they put them into the Spanish prison. As for my part, I was taken up to Cadiz, in the bullock-cart, and my kind friend took me to his own house, and had me put to bed, where I found myself when I woke.

In some cases shipwrecked and captured Englishmen had been treated so well by their captors that they were none too happy to be returned to their own ships. Three men from *Donegal* took the opportunity to 'run' at Sanlúcar after the wreck of the *Rayo*. It is possible that they were somehow left behind, but the two Americans among them probably knew that Cadiz was a good place from which to get into an American ship.

Colin Campbell, who had been rescued from *Argonauta* by sailors from *Donegal*, was still in that ship when the French cartel returned his shipmates from *Defiance*; they had survived several days of extreme adventure in the *Aigle* with Asmus Classen. They told him that after Classen ran the ship aground they had been rescued in Spanish boats. There had been 'plenty of mutton for the English officers' and all had been 'treated with the greatest kindness by the Spaniards, had rooms given them to live in and the key to go out and in when they chose. They were quite sorry to come out in the frigate as they had got jack-asses ready to go round to Gibraltar and expected to have a famous cruize.'

The Spanish might justifiably have blamed the French for the disaster that had befallen them. They might have mistreated the British as the enemies who had been killing them. But this, after all, was the 'age of sensibility', with readers of novels under the influence of Lawrence Sterne, Johann Wolfgang von Goethe, Jean-Jacques Rousseau and their many imitators. Writers and artists encouraged people to feel, to be pierced by sentiments of pity and sorrow. Prints with subjects like *The Stormy Night: A Wife waiting the Return of her Husband* or *A Shipwreck'd Sailor Boy telling his Story at a Cottage Door* decorated rooms all over Europe. Here at Cadiz was the real thing on a sublime scale. In the local response there were elements of shock, of mass hysteria, and of thankfulness for the mercy of God who, after such a disaster, had returned so many of the menfolk of Andalucía. A few hard-headed people saw ostentation in the public charity of the rich, but few doubted the sincerity of this extraordinary outpouring of generosity and sympathy.

It was not until 31 October that his wife and son found out what had happened to Dionisio Alcalá Galiano. Antonio's ten-year-old sister went to a girls' school in Cadiz. Every day the teacher asked the girls whether any of those who had relatives in the squadron had had any news of them. When she put the question to the daughters of Lieutenant Roque Guruceta, they replied that they had heard from their father that very day, and when asked which ship he was in they said it was *Bahama*. The Galianos immediately sent a servant to Guruceta's home, and he returned immediately with the dreadful news that confirmed what they had already assumed. 'My doubts and those of my family were removed, leaving us with a grief more lively and bitter,' Antonio wrote.

At the end of the month a messenger arrived at Cadiz with a communication from Napoleon ordering the fleet to remain in port. It had arrived a fortnight too late.

Pickle carried two letters from Collingwood; one, dated 22 October, described the battle, and a second, dated 24 October, described the first part of the storm. The description of the battle was not notable for its accuracy and includes one fictitious incident involving *Téméraire*. Hercules Robinson, who rowed Captain Eliab Harvey from *Téméraire* to *Euryalus* during the night after the battle, said that he was astonishingly loquacious and boastful about his ship's part in the victory and Collingwood seems to have fallen for it.

Collingwood's account of the storm was wilfully reticent on certain key points. The Admiralty then made the dispatches even less forthcoming by suppressing certain of Collingwood's admissions before they were published on 6 November. In the letter that Collingwood addressed to William Marsden, the secretary, on 24 October, he wrote, 'I am under the most serious apprehensions for several of the ships of my squadron – the Belleisle is the only one totally dismasted, but the Victory, Royal Sovereign, Téméraire and Tonnant are in a very decrepid state.' This was omitted so as not to encourage the enemy or worry relatives of people in those ships. For operational reasons they did not publish Collingwood's remark that 'I cannot discover what the destination of the enemy was, but if the Bucentaure is above water when the Gale abates, I will endeavour to do it.'

In a further dispatch of 28 October Collingwood informed the

Admiralty that he had lost his prizes: 'I doubt whether I shall be able to carry a ship of them into Port.' He explained that

if I had anchored such as had good Cables, they (having all their Crews on board) would certainly have cut them and run for Port in the stormy weather; and there were 10 sail and five frigates, ready to come to their assistance in fair weather – so that I hope their Lordships will approve of what I (having only in consideration the destruction of the Enemy's Fleet) have thought a measure of indispensible necessity.

This was also suppressed so as not to detract from the victory. But it highlights two key points in Collingwood's reasoning. The first was that the annihilation of the enemy fleet had been the absolute priority, a view that Nelson would have shared. The second was that, for understandable reasons, Collingwood had overestimated the enemy's resilience. They never did and never could have produced ten ships-of-the-line for a sortie, and after 24 October, Escaño would have been hard pressed to send out one.

It is clear that Collingwood tortured himself over his initial failure to anchor and guard the prizes and the consequent escape of five, and this was what many blamed him for subsequently. Given the wind direction, prizes could only cut their cables and run for Cadiz from a position to the south of the city. Those that cut or broke their cables later on (when they were north-west of Cadiz) ended up on the beach near Sanlúcar, not in the port. Whether *these* prizes had to be destroyed is doubtful. Collingwood could have taken off the enemy crews and waited to see whether the hulks survived the storm at anchor rather than scuttling and burning. But he was undeniably spooked by the bad weather and the sortie. In Collingwood's defence, it can be said that Henry Bayntun was always sceptical about the prospect of saving the ships in his care.

As it turned out, certain commanders – wilfully or otherwise – ignored the instruction to destroy prizes. In his 28 October letter, Collingwood admitted to the First Lord how the gale of 24–5 October had 'completely dispersed the ships, and drove the captured Hulls in all directions'. Since then, Collingwood wrote, he had been 'collecting and destroying them, where they are at anchor upon the coast between Cadiz and six leagues westward of San Lucar, without the prospect of saving one to bring into Port'. He was expecting that if the weather continued to be moderate he would complete the job by the next day. He was unaware that, on that very day, Lieutenant John Stockham's *Thunderer* was bringing the *San Juan* into Gibraltar, having fought her way through the worst of the storm. By 4 November, when he wrote a final dispatch, Collingwood knew that *Bahama*, *San Ildefonso* and *Swiftsure* had been saved, but he still had no idea that *San Juan Nepomuceno* had already been towed to Gibraltar. These two letters were taken to London by Blackwood on 6 November after Collingwood had shifted his flag to *Queen*.

Collingwood's was not the only account of the battle that the Admiralty received. On 4 November Codrington wrote to Lord Garlies, a member of the board, to tell him what he thought of what had happened after the battle. He complained of a lack of communication and control, that ships crowded with passengers and wounded men were kept away from Gibraltar for far too long. His letter began, 'As our admiral is not come in, we know nothing of our destination; but as I feared, so I find, that we are doing every thing in a sort of drivelling way which will not increase the *éclat* of our victory.' It unfolded in a series of complaints.

From the want also of the presence of our admiral, and a unanimity in our proceedings, the ships' companies are beginning to abuse each other. We are all in distress about our poor wives hearing of the action and not knowing if we are dead or alive . . . Poor Morris seems to me much agitated by his fears for his wife under these distressing circumstances . . . Lord Collingwood certainly went into action in the finest style possible, and is as brave a man as ever stepped on board a ship; I can also believe him to be a very good man in his way, but he has none of the dignity an admiral should have, and seems to lose all the great outline of a chief command in his attention to minutiae. What he is now doing God knows . . . At all events, as there is now no longer a Lord Nelson to serve with here, I should wish to get home as soon as possible. *Never* whilst I live shall I cease to regret his loss. *He* made the signal to prepare to anchor; and had Admiral Collingwood *acted upon that hint* we might now have secured almost all our prizes, and the news would, ere this time, have been public at Vienna and in the army of Buonaparte, where it would have made a sensation advantageous to the Austrian cause.

Codrington had returned to Gibraltar without orders, 'before our fevers, which were beginning amongst the Spaniards, increased'. He was anxious about *Leviathan* and *Ajax*, which were still around Cadiz, loaded with prisoners.

On the day he wrote, 4 November, the final act of the drama was taking place. Admiral Dumanoir had sailed his four ships southwards towards the Strait of Gibraltar at the close of the battle. But as the sun set he thought he saw Admiral Louis's ships approaching and changed his mind. He headed north, hoping to make it to Rochefort. His four ships survived the storm with difficulty and the battle-damaged *Formidable* had to jettison twelve of her quarterdeck guns. She was in a poor state by 2 November when Dumanoir's squadron were spotted by two British frigates. They shook them off, but near Ferrol another frigate spotted them, pursued them and found Sir Richard Strachan with the news. Strachan's squadron, guarding Ferrol, had been scattered by the storm but he set off after Dumanoir with what ships he had. After a two-day chase along the Galician coast, his four ships, helped by four frigates, trapped Dumanoir's four off Cape Ortegal and brought them to battle.

It was an uneven contest. 'Our unhappy ship,' wrote Captain Gemähling of the 67th Regiment in the *Duguay-Trouin*, 'totally disabled and making water, was crushed by the fire of two ships of the line and frigates. It was not war as one understands it; it was butchery, a fearful slaughter. Three-quarters of my men lay dead around me; my poor lieutenant, Le Deyeux, lying there, a few feet off, and so many others!' Four more French ships were in British hands.

The wounded Spaniards and Frenchmen who arrived in Cadiz on 30 October were lucky. Most of the British had to wait until they reached in Gibraltar at some point in November. To his further credit the Marquis of Solana offered the British hospital facilities in Cadiz, but Collingwood refused, perhaps to make clear that his casualties were genuinely low.

Indeed, the numbers of wounded were becoming lower as the numbers of dead rose. Some would have died in any circumstances, but the storm did not just drown sailors. By throwing them around and depriving them of facilities ashore it killed many wounded men. In *Victory* Henry Cramwell's splinter wounds developed into gangrene and he died on Saturday. Joseph Gordon's thigh had been amputated successfully but on Sunday he suffered a spasm and died. Midshipman Alexander Palmer had been shot through the thigh by a musket ball. Luckily it missed the bone but he died of tetanus on Monday.

Nelson's Norfolk *protégé*, William Forster, a cousin of the Berrys, died of his wounds just after his arrival at Gibraltar on 30 October. Jack Spratt, the mate from *Defiance* who had boarded the *Aigle* alone and whose leg had been broken by a musket ball, was in poor health:

> Mr. Burnett, Surgeon on board the *Defiance*, came to Captain Durham and asked for a written order to cut off Mr. Spratt's leg, saying that it could not be cured, and that he refused to submit to the operation. The Captain replied that he could not give such an order, but that he would see Mr. Spratt, which he managed to do in spite of his own wounds. Upon the Captain remonstrating with him, Spratt held out the other leg (certainly a very good one) and exclaimed, 'Never! If I lose my leg, where shall I find a match for this?'

William Burnett did his best. During the storm Spratt was 'in great pain from the sudden jerking of our ship as she pitched in the heavy sea'. He could hear as well as feel the broken ends of the bone scraping.

By the time Spratt reached Gibraltar he was in a high fever and delirious. By throwing his legs around he kept dislocating the bone so his surgeon at Gibraltar Hospital, Monsieur Bouvier, put his leg into a box. Spratt felt it itching and thought it must be getting better. When they took off the box and removed the dressing Spratt saw 'hundreds of large red-headed maggots nearly an inch long were sticking into the calf of my precious limb only their tails to be seen'. The maggots, he reckoned, came from the Spanish flies that blackened the hospital, overcrowded as it was with wounded. The ever-cheerful Spratt wrote later that he could 'still see M. Bouvier's expression with his shoulders hunched up to his ears'. The surgeon killed the maggots with a potion and in the end Spratt's leg healed. It ended up nearly three inches shorter than the other, but he considered this better than an artificial limb.

Leviathan was not allowed to go to Gibraltar until 10 November. Bayntun met *Victory* and *Belleisle* on their way back to England on 6 November and unloaded his French prisoners and some Englishmen who had been freed from Cadiz prison, but his ship remained crowded with hundreds of Spaniards. Fever took hold. Thomas Main, the captain of the forecastle, had recovered from his amputation and was 'walking around in good health & spirits' when on 5 November he became feverish. 'It was supposed,' surgeon Shoveller reported, that 'his messmates had given him too much to drink.' He got worse, was taken to Gibraltar Hospital with other feverish wounded, but died five days later.

By the time they reached Gibraltar, the overworked surgeon reported, 'many of our Ships Company were attacked with Bowel Complaints, and in others the slightest injury or scratch became a foul spreading sore'. The spread of disease was exacerbated by desperate overcrowding. *Leviathan* was carrying 463 prisoners and numerous British seamen belonging to other ships as well as her own crew of 618. Ninety of the Spanish prisoners 'were wounded, several with Tourniquets on the different extremities, and which had been applied since the action, four or five days elapsing, consequently most of the Limbs in a state of Mortification, or approaching it'. Shoveller did his best to help them: 'In four of these Cases I amputated – Two Arms, and Two Thighs – the two former did well and were sent on shore at Algesiras, the latter died on the third day of the operation, the stumps becoming mortified.'

It was Shoveller's opinion that the company had been saved from worse ravages from disease by the 'dry system of cleaning – lighted stoves between decks in damp weather – ventilation – and airing the bedding as often as the state of the weather admitted of it'.

The Englishman whose description of conditions at Cadiz harbour was printed in the *Naval Chronicle* walked out afterwards towards the castle of San Sebastian, then southwards along the beach:

As far as the eye could reach, the sandy side of the isthmus bordering on the Atlantic was covered with masts and yards, the wrecks of ships, and here and there the bodies of the dead. Among others I noticed a topmast marked with the name of the Swiftsure, and the broad arrow of England, which only increased my anxiety to know how far the English had suffered, the Spaniards still continuing to affirm that they (the English) had lost their chief admiral, and half their fleet. While surrounded by these wrecks, I mounted on the cross-trees of a mast which had been thrown ashore, and casting my eyes over the ocean, beheld, at a great distance, several masts and portions of wreck floating about. As the sea was now almost calm, with a light swell, the effect produced by these objects had in it something of a sublime melancholy, and touched the soul with a remembrance of the sad vicissitudes of human affairs. The portions of floating wreck were visible from the ramparts, yet not a boat dared to venture out to examine or endeavour to tow them in, such were the apprehensions which still filled their minds of the enemy.

23

We All Cry for Him

Francis Austen may not have shared his sister Jane's literary talents, but they were both acute judges of character. Francis had met Nelson many times and had served under him long enough for the words that he wrote to Mary Gibson on 27 October to carry weight:

> I never heard of his equal, nor do I expect again to see such a man. To the soundest judgment he united prompt decision and speedy execution of his plans; and he possessed in a superior degree the happy talent of making every class of persons pleased with their situation and eager to exert themselves in forwarding the public service.

This latter talent had reduced the fleet to tears when they learned of the death of their leader. Richard Anderson, the master of *Prince*, who had had little acquaintance with the admiral, wrote in his journal to his wife on 1 November:

> We have been so busy & I have had Every thing knock[d] down no place to write – and full of Prisoners oh what a time we have had I never had harder service thank God we are now safe at Gibraltar & are in hopes of being sent Home – we have lost 8 or 9 of the Prizes which will be against our Prize Money but the Greatest loss is the Loss of our Noble Nelson – we all cry for him.

Able Seaman James Martin was one of many sailors to jot down a piece of verse on the death of Nelson:

> What Better End can Best of Heros Claim
> Children yet unborn will lisp the Heros Name
> And Age to Age Record thy Matchless Fame.

Edward Codrington's brief experience of Nelson's leadership had made a similar impression: 'Great and glorious as our victory is,' he wrote to his wife Jane, 'I could almost give up the whole value of it for Nelson's life. In spite of Lady H. he was really a great man, and all who served under him must think so.' Whatever can be said against Nelson's personality, the fact remains that good judges of men would rather have served under him than any other officer.

After an eight-day voyage Lieutenant John Lapenotière arrived at Falmouth on 4 November and travelled overland at top speed. When he reached London, a day and a half later, the capital was enveloped in fog. Lapenotière was shown into the board room of the Admiralty at one a.m. on 6 November, just as Secretary William Marsden was about to turn in for the night. 'Sir, we have gained a great victory, but we have lost Lord Nelson,' the lieutenant reported. Having read the dispatches, Marsden left Lapenotière alone and went off in search of Lord Barham.

The First Lord had retired to rest, as had his domestics, and it was not till after some research that I could discover the room in which he slept. Drawing aside his curtains, with a candle in my hand, I awoke the old peer from a sound slumber; and to the credit of his nerves be it mentioned that he showed no symptoms of alarm or surprise, but calmly asked: 'What news, Mr. M.?' We then discussed, in few words, what was to be done, and I sat up the remainder of the night with such of the clerks as I could collect, in order to make the necessary communications, at an early hour, to the King, Prince of Wales, Duke of York, the Ministers, and other members of the Cabinet, and to the Lord Mayor, who communicated the intelligence to the shipping interest at Lloyd's Coffee House. A notice for the Royal salute was also necessary.

Barham himself wrote to Nelson's wife, Frances, and simultaneously sent a messenger to Emma Hamilton at Merton Place. There, she and Nelson's sister, Susannah Bolton, heard the sound of the Tower guns and speculated that they signalled some victory in Germany. Five minutes later Emma heard the sound of a carriage drawing up.

> I sent to enquire who was arrived. They brought me word, Mr Whitby, from the Admiralty. 'Show him in directly,' I said. He came in, and with a pale countenance and faint voice said, 'We have gained a great Victory' – 'Never mind your victory,' I said, 'My letters – give me my letters' – Capt. Whitby was unable to speak – tears in his eyes and a deathly paleness over his face made me comprehend him. I believe I gave a scream and fell back, and for ten hours after I could neither speak nor shed a rear.

Marsden edited Collingwood's dispatches of 22 and 24 October in time for publication in a *London Gazette Extraordinary* next afternoon. The general response to the news of victory was strangely muted. Lady Elizabeth Hervey reported that as she left the Admiralty 'there was a vast rush of people, but all silent, or a murmur of respect and sorrow . . . A man at the turnpike gate said to Sir Ellis, who was going through, "Sir, have you heard the bad news? We have taken twenty ships from the enemy, but Lord Nelson is killed!"' It was not just Nelson's death that produced the subdued tone. Even after Marsden's efforts, Collingwood's references to heavy losses and a severe gale after the action struck an ominous note. Lady Bessborough observed, 'The scene at the Admiralty was quite affecting – crowds of people, chiefly women, enquiring for husbands, brothers, children.'

Edward Codrington had been furious that Collingwood had made no effort to invite officers to send mail home with the dispatches in

Pickle, and his fears were realised when the first news of the battle that reached his wife came from the newspaper. Jane Codrington's servant rushed in suddenly and told her that 'there had been a grand action and Lord Nelson was dead!' Fortunately, she was in Brighton where the Prince of Wales lived and he was soon able to supply an authoritative list of officers who had been casualties, which did not include her husband. It was worse for Betsy Fremantle, at home in Swanbourne, Buckinghamshire, who had the news from her servants:

> I was much alarmed by <u>Nelly's ghastly</u> appearance immediately after breakfast, who came in to say Dudley had brought from Winslow the account that a most dreadful action had been fought off Cadiz, Nelson & several Captains killed, & twenty ships were taken. I really felt undescribable misery until the arrival of the Post, but was relieved from such a wretched state of anxious suspence by a Letter from Lord Garlies, who congratulated me on Fremantle's safety & the conspicuous share he had in the Victory gained on the 21st off Cadiz.

As a lord of Admiralty, Garlies had soon received the news. He was an old friend of both Codrington and Fremantle and wrote immediately to their wives. Two of the Grenville clan, Lord Temple and Lord George Grenville, rode over from Aylesbury to Swanbourne in their Yeomanry uniforms to wish Betsy 'joy of the good news in the most flattering and friendly manner. How I long for a Letter from Fremantle,' she wrote in her diary. 'I am perfectly bewildered & can think & dream of nothing but the late Victory. Poor Nelson! had he survived, it would have been glorious indeed. Regret at his death is more severely felt than joy at the destruction of the Combined Fleets.'

Blackwood's arrival with the second batch of dispatches from Collingwood brought letters from the fleet. Lieutenant William Hennah had written to Sophia Duff from *Mars* on 27 October, 'I believe that a more unpleasant task, than what is now imposed upon me, can scarcely fall to the lot of a person . . . as being myself the husband of a beloved partner, and the father of children . . .' Her son

Norwich wrote, 'My Dear Mamma, You cannot possibly imagine how unwilling I am to begin this melancholy letter . . .'

Similar letters were being opened in Spain and France. At Cadiz the churches were full of anxious relatives until all the prisoners taken by the British had returned from Gibraltar. A memorial service for those who did not return was held at the Church of the Carmen on 21 November. Official news from Cadiz had arrived on 5 November at Corunna and Ferrol, where seven Spanish ships had been manned and five French ships had been based. According to the captain of a Swedish merchantman interrogated by a British frigate captain, the information 'caused a general consternation, alarm, bustle, and despondency in all ranks of people . . . He saw a list of 22 sail of the line which were missing.'

Admiral Escaño's despatches were published in the *Gazeta de Madrid* that day. While he had put as favourable a gloss as possible on the action, he admitted that 'the loss on board the Fleet generally, must, there is no doubt, have been very great'. That November all the Spanish captains at Trafalgar were promoted and the surviving seamen were offered triple pay for the day. Admiral Gravina died four months later at his house opposite the unfinished cathedral at Cadiz, having refused surgery in a bid to keep his arm.

Napoleon learned the news of Trafalgar on 18 November in Austria. No reference to the battle ever appeared in the French government paper, the *Moniteur*, although a fictitious account of British losses was issued in the *Journal de Paris* of 7 December. This was a slightly enhanced version of a similarly optimistic report published in the *Gazeta de Madrid* on 19 November, naming ten British ships sunk during the battle or afterwards lost in the storm and many more damaged.

The relatives of French officers and men were left for months in ignorance of their fate. This even applied to senior French officers who had performed with great credit. On 21 December the elder son of

Captain Louis Baudouin wrote to ask Decrès whether he knew what had happened to his father. The family had heard nothing since the battle and the loss of Baudouin's ship *Fougueux*: 'My father's silence, and uncertainty about his fate, plunge his unfortunate family into the most cruel pain. His wife, his child and I fear that he fell victim to his courage and bravery.' It took Decrès another month to confirm that they were right.

At the end of January Marguerite Briamant wrote to Decrès from Rochefort:

> I have just been informed by private letters that my husband François Elie Briamant, Enseigne de Vaisseau Entretenu but embarked as acting Lieutenant on board the Redoutable, was shot three times in the fight that this vessel had to maintain against the English ship the Victory, and that he died of his wounds the following day. I am left as the mother of two boys, the elder being eleven years old, and I have no means of supporting the expense of their education.
>
> I beg you sir to order a search to be made in your office, to ascertain if it is possible, whether my husband is in fact dead . . .

The administrative task was complicated by the sheer number of those dead or taken prisoner: 1087 wounded Spaniards and 253 Frenchmen were handed over to the frigates at Cadiz; 210 Spanish officers and 4589 seamen and soldiers were released on parole at Gibraltar during November. A few lucky Frenchmen and one woman, the ever-fortunate Jeanne Caunant, were also freed on parole at Gibraltar, mostly owing to misunderstandings. About three thousand French prisoners captured at Trafalgar were taken to England. Those who landed at Portsmouth were imprisoned at Forton, Portchester and in seven hulks, and those at Plymouth were taken to Millbay Prison and eight hulks. Those who arrived at Chatham were divided between four hulks.

Most French officers ended up living under loose arrest at Crediton or Wincanton and were able to socialise freely and even travel with permission. For the ordinary seamen, the stay in Britain was much less pleasant. Of the French prisoners brought to Britain between 1803 and 1814, 10,341 died in captivity, 17,607 were exchanged and sent home, and 72,000 were still in Britain when the war ended in 1814.

Pierre Villeneuve and Jean-Jacques Magendie were the first prisoners to arrive in England and were sent first to Bishop's Waltham and then to Reading. It was Magendie's third experience of captivity in Britain. At Reading the pair were joined by Louis Infernet and Jean-Jacques Lucas. Codrington wrote to ask his wife Jane to look after Infernet, explaining that 'his wife and family are at Toulon, and he has nothing but his pay, at the age of fifty, after forty years' services'. Infernet was not in immediate need because, Codrington explained, Captain Ben Hallowell 'although not in the action of the 21st, has insisted upon sending him a trunk with two dozen shirts, stockings, a bed, and some cloth to make him a coat, and a draft for £100 as an acknowledgment of the civility he met with from Gantheaume and his officers when their prisoner'.

Magendie and Lucas were given permission to attend Nelson's funeral. After repairs in Gibraltar *Victory* crossed to England with Nelson's body, preserved in a barrel of brandy, and arrived there on 4 December. The government had announced that the next day would be one of national thanksgiving and formal events were held throughout Britain. In Nelson's home county of Norfolk there were balls and suppers at Great Yarmouth, Norwich and Swaffham. The *Norwich Mercury* reported that at King's Lynn 'The roof of the room formed one capacious awning of military banners, ensigns and naval trophies, at the head of which appeared a bust of the Hero of Trafalgar encircled with laurel and underneath the appropriate motto of *"palmam qui meruit ferat"*. One continual blaze of wax tapers lighted up three long tables covered with the choicest delicacies that gold could purchase or art prepare.' Then the toast was proposed: 'To the glorious and immortal memory of our much loved and ever to be lamented hero Lord Viscount Nelson.' At Aylsham a procession was made to church with flags borne by sailors, a naval captain mounted on a charger and a lieutenant with a banner bearing the words 'Immortal Nelson'. After the service the Aylsham volunteers fired into the air, fireworks were ignited and three barrels of beer given to the populace. At Norwich a succession of events culminated in a special County Supper, attended by Sir Edward Berry's wife.

Publishers printed lives of Nelson as fast as they could set the text. One, announcing a fourth edition on 14 December, claimed to have sold more than three thousand copies in the last ten days. Messieurs Colnaghi of Cockspur Street contrived to advertise the first posthumous print of Nelson on the day that news of his death first appeared in *The Times* and within weeks five other portraits were in circulation. The county of Norfolk had its own exclusive picture engraved by Norwich-based Edward Bell from the portrait displayed among the Norfolk worthies in St Andrew's Hall. Thomas Buttersworth, who had published the print of the twenty-six ships-of-the-line that Nelson's forces had taken by 1802, rapidly issued a second edition updating the total of his captures to forty-six. The great printsellers Boydell and Company advertised a reward of five hundred guineas for the best painting of the death of Nelson to be published as a print in the style of *The Death of General Wolfe*. The competition was won by Arthur Devis, who sketched Nelson's corpse on *Victory* after it had been removed from its barrel and placed in a plain coffin.

On 23 December, after a slow journey to London, Nelson's body arrived at Greenwich Hospital to be placed in its final coffin, the one that Captain Ben Hallowell had had made from the mast of *L'Orient* after the battle of the Nile and presented to Nelson years before. It was guarded by a highly emotional Alexander Scott, who was unwilling to be parted from his beloved chief. Fifteen thousand mourners saw the body as it lay in state in the Painted Hall of Greenwich Hospital. Thousands more could not get in.

On 9 January 1806 a huge procession of boats glided upriver with Nelson's coffin in a barge made for Charles II. It rested at the Admiralty overnight, then processed in a specially designed Egyptian-style funeral carriage to St Paul's. The procession was so long that when the head reached the cathedral the rear had still not left Whitehall. The service took place by lamplight and reached an unscripted climax when Sir Isaac Heard ended the list of Nelson's titles with 'the hero, who in the moment of Victory, fell covered with immortal glory'. The forty-eight sailors from *Victory*, who had carried the ship's tattered ensign to the grave, now spontaneously tore away a large piece of it and ripped it into smaller pieces to keep as souvenirs. They laid the remainder on Nelson's coffin.

After the funeral Magendie was sent back to France to set up a mechanism for exchanging prisoners, and Lucas and Infernet were released on parole in April 1806. Villeneuve returned to France shortly afterwards, landing by small boat at Morlaix in Brittany from where he immediately wrote to Decrès requesting instructions and proposing a return via Rennes to Paris. At the Hôtel de la Patrie at Rennes he learned that Lucas and Infernet were to be received by the Emperor at Saint-Cloud. He wrote to Lucas at once to congratulate him, asking him to pass his compliments to Infernet and to be a witness at a court of enquiry at which Villeneuve proposed to name those he blamed for his defeat. But he received no reply to his letter to Decrès. On the morning of 22 April Villeneuve was discovered with six stab wounds to his chest. On a table beside him was a note to his wife. An official investigation produced a verdict of suicide.

It is possible that Villeneuve, finding himself blamed by the Emperor and ostracised by his old friend Decrès, indeed took his own life. Until his arrival in France he might not have been aware of the depth of animosity felt against him. Captain Pernot of the 16th Regiment was not the only Frenchman who felt that, rather than allowing himself to be taken prisoner, Villeneuve should have 'blown his brains out, which was what any man of heart must have done having been the cause of such a great disaster'. But the nature of his wounds suggests that Villeneuve had been dispatched by one of Napoleon's many agents or by someone who shared Pernot's point of view. The supposed 'suicide letter' was never forwarded to his wife.

On 3 May 1806, at Saint-Cloud, Infernet and Lucas were made *commandants* in the Légion d'Honneur.

After much discussion in Parliament about how miserably the award compared with what had been given to John Churchill after Blenheim, George III settled an annual pension of £5000 on Nelson's heirs, with £99,000 to buy a mansion and lands and £10,000 for its modernisation. All of this went to Nelson's pompous and self-seeking brother William. Fifteen thousand pounds was given to each of Nelson's sisters. Emma Hamilton and Nelson's daughter Horatia received nothing, King and country having ignored Nelson's last request.

The Trafalgar prize money, when it was finally paid in the summer of 1807, was also miserable. The prizes and bounty money brought £973 to captains, £65 11s. to lieutenants, £44 4s. 6d. to warrant officers, £10 14s. to petty officers and £1 17s. 6d. to the rest. A much smaller number of men had taken part in Strachan's capture of Dumanoir's squadron, which meant that they received more than five times as much prize money as the Trafalgar veterans, who had driven away Dumanoir's ships in the first place. An extra award of £300,000 voted by Parliament to the officers and men of the fleet at Trafalgar, paid in 1806, had brought the larger sums of £2,389 7s. 6d., £161, £108 12s., £26 6s. and £4 12s. 6d. to the five classes of recipient, but even with this the Trafalgar veterans came off much worse than Strachan's men. Nelson's personal share added £7,303 8s. 2d. to the value of his estate.

One thing the battle of Trafalgar most certainly did not do was end the war and get everybody home, as those in the fleet had hoped it would. Most of the men who fought there remained imprisoned by the Royal Navy for years, while the officers were not much better off. On 16 July 1808 Cuthbert, Lord Collingwood, was off Cadiz once again, surveying the city from his flagship *Queen* with his dog Bounce by his side.

Napoleon had deposed Carlos IV and declared his own brother Joseph Bonaparte King of Spain, but there had been a popular uprising against him in Andalucía. The governor, the Marquis of Solana, was assassinated. Rosily's squadron of French ships had been blockaded in Cadiz harbour ever since Trafalgar. In mid-June, after a short fight, the Spanish, under Juan Ruiz de Apodoca and *Santísima Trinidad*'s former captain Xavier de Uriarte, forced them to surrender, proudly refusing

British aid. A British force was landed at Puerto Santa Maria to support the Spanish against the French, and Collingwood brought his fleet to support the infantry. His old friend Charles Tyler had just joined William Hargood in another squadron blockading Lisbon and Collingwood wrote to him. He had come to take precisely the same view of Napoleon as *Victory*'s numerologist gunner William Rivers:

I think the French will be driven out of Spain and Portugal, but have no expectation of a peace while Buonaparte lives. He is a sort of evil spirit that sows discord wherever he goes. I have no idea of more malignity existing than in him, consequently he answers to my conception of the Devil.

Otherwise his letter was weary with valetudinarian resignation:

When I saw Morris last he was very well, apparently, in his *Colossus* off Toulon but since I left him I have received a letter from him requesting to go to England; he has a rupture, and it is a complaint which, I understand, requires an immediate remedy. I am sorry for it that the flowers of the flock should drop off so soon. I hope he will soon recover.

I am well, thank God, considering all things, but growing old, old and infirm. I have never been in a port since you left me, and I do not suppose I ever shall again . . .

P.S. Mr. Bounce is much obliged to you for your kind remembrances. He is a good dog and a faithful friend to me.

24

The Empire of the Ocean

'Such was the End of this Expedetion the Most Brilliant and Decisetive in the Annals of Naviel Glory,' concluded Able Seaman James Martin, 'wile the Ship was Layen at Giberalter Repairing Damages'.

Brilliant and decisive as Trafalgar was, the battle had no immediate effect on the war. Indeed, its significance was overshadowed by Napoleon's overwhelming victory over the Austrian and Russian armies at Austerlitz on 2 December, which shattered William Pitt's laboriously built coalition. Worn out by work, care, irregular hours and hard drinking, Pitt died on 23 January 1806, believing himself defeated.

'So incomprehensible was its apparent sterility,' wrote the naval historian Sir Julian Corbett of Trafalgar in 1910, 'that to fill the void a legend grew up that it saved England from invasion.' In truth, the chances of invasion in 1805 ended as a result of Calder's indecisive engagement with Villeneuve in July. However, Trafalgar made sure that any renewal of the threat could be taken a good deal less seriously.

The French have always viewed Trafalgar as an unmitigated disaster. Within days of the battle Captain Pernot, commander of the soldiers in *Pluton*, called it 'the most terrible catastrophe ever recorded in the annals of the fleet of any nation'. It was on Trafalgar that the great nineteenth-century French historian and politician Louis Thiers blamed the decline of France's empire and the dominance of Great Britain in his own time: 'We did not win the battle of Trafalgar. We did not remain masters of the seas and we do not have the two hundred million consumers that Britain has. That is the whole secret of our inferiority.'

Trafalgar enabled the British to land troops in the Iberian peninsula in 1808 and support them by sea, an important factor in the eventual fall of Napoleon. The major long-term strategic consequence of the battle was that Britain possessed an unchallenged supremacy on the seas for the best part of a century. This sustained the British Empire and gave Britain the lion's share of world trade, notably with Spain's former provinces in America. Britain had finally won what Lord Rodney had once called 'the empire of the ocean'.

The United States also benefited as her traders took full advantage of the decline of French and Spanish naval power in their hemisphere. Although Britain's use of her naval supremacy rankled with Americans, it underpinned the growing prosperity of the United States well into the nineteenth century.

For the Spanish, Trafalgar was an honourable defeat and a national tragedy. The navy upon which all their hopes of national regeneration had been pinned was more or less destroyed. Honour killed Gravina, Churruca and Galiano, officers drawn into a battle they believed should not have been fought for a cause about which they were at best equivocal. All were treated as national heroes.

Of the four Trafalgar prizes the *San Juan Nepomuceno* remained as a hulk at Gibraltar. *Bahama* and *Swiftsure* became prison hulks in the Medway. *San Ildefonso* became a receiving hulk at Portsmouth. All three were broken up in 1816.

The last survivor of Trafalgar was Gaspar Costela Vasquez whose death in April 1892, at the age of 105, was reported in the Seville *Tribuno*. For many years he had lived in the convalescent hospital of the naval base where 'with great pride he used to recount the exciting affairs of the days of that glorious naval campaign at which he had taken part'. The last surviving French veteran, Louis Cartigny of Hyères, died earlier, in 1892 aged 101. He had fought as a boy in

Redoutable. After some years as a prisoner in England he was attached to the Seamen of the Guard and was present at Napoleon's farewell to his army. In his last years he was proprietor of the Grand Café des Quatre Saisons in the Cours de Strasbourg at Hyères. The last British survivors were Admiral Sir George Sartorius, midshipman of *Tonnant*, who died in 1885 and Colonel James Fynmore, a midshipman in *Africa*, who died two years later.

Other human survivors of the battle met contrasting fates.

Ignacio de Álava took command of the squadron at Cadiz after the death of Gravina in March 1806. In 1810 he was appointed governor of Havana where Hercules Robinson dined with him and heard his story of how one tremendous broadside fired by the *Royal Sovereign* into Álava's *Santa Ana* had killed 350 men – '*Il rompait todos*,' explained Álava in a mixture of French and Spanish. When he returned to Spain in 1812 he was made captain general of Cadiz, then appointed to the Supreme Council of Admiralty. Named Captain General of the Fleet in 1817, he died three months later.

Voldemar de la Bretonnière, who saved the *Algésiras*, was promoted captain in 1811 and married Rose-Françoise Camboul0et, the daughter of the Inspector of the Navy at Martinique, whom he had probably met in the summer of 1805 when she was seventeen. In 1827 he fought in the combined British, French and Russian fleet against the Turks at the battle of Navarino where the British squadron was commanded by Sir Edward Codrington. He became a rear admiral in 1829, retired in 1841, and died in Paris in 1851.

Asmus Classen of *Aigle* left Cadiz soon after the battle. Passing through Bordeaux he was recognised by a Dutchman who had loaned him 1200 francs in 1788 and had assumed that he had died. Now he thought that perhaps Classen could repay him. It is unlikely that he got his money. Classen became an officer in the marines in 1807, went into hospital in 1813 and was forced into a penurious retirement.

Benjamin Clement of *Tonnant* was promoted commander and had numerous successes in small vessels in the Caribbean. He was made post captain in 1811 and in October that year married Ann Mary Prowting. They had two sons and a daughter. He never lost touch with the black seaman Charles Macnamara who had saved him from drowning, and left money to him in his will.

Edward Codrington remained captain of *Orion* until 1808 and continued to serve in the Mediterranean. He took part in the defence of Cadiz in 1810, escorted four Spanish ships-of-the-line to Menorca, then commanded a squadron off the coast of Spain. As captain of the fleet in *Tonnant* he served in the war of 1812, taking part in operations against Washington, Baltimore and New Orleans. Knighted in 1815, he was promoted vice admiral in 1821. As commander-in-chief in the Mediterranean during the Greek war of independence, he led the British squadron against the Turkish and Egyptian fleets at the battle of Navarino in 1827. He was made full admiral in 1837 and died in 1851.

Cuthbert Collingwood was given a pension of £2000 per annum, was created Baron Collingwood and promoted Vice Admiral of the Red. He had a difficult time as commander-in-chief in the Mediterranean and was blamed for failing to prevent Ganteaume relieving Corfu. He had been at sea since 1803 and had been longing to go home even before Trafalgar, but he never saw his family again. Orders to return finally arrived on 3 March 1810 but he died four days later. He was buried near Nelson in St Paul's Cathedral.

After the battle the crew of *Conqueror* found that the head had been shot away from their ship's figurehead. The crew petitioned for it to be replaced with the head of Lord Nelson, which was done. Israel Pellew was captain until 1808. Humphrey Senhouse took part in the debarkation of a British army in Martinique in 1809 and was afterwards promoted commander. After a fierce engagement in 1813 he captured an American privateer and was sent home with dispatches announcing the British success against Castine, Maine. He was made a post captain in October 1814. William Pringle Green of *Conqueror* wrote of Trafalgar soon after: 'In my opinion if the officers had done their duty in every ship, the action would have been over sooner and the whole of the enemy taken or destroyed. So great was the joy of all, the people of England and the remaining Admiral, that all was hushed up.' The precise nature of his complaint remains enigmatic because the next page in his journal has been torn out, but it is evidence that some of the officers in the thick of the fighting were not impressed by the performance of those behind them.

Julien Cosmao-Kerjulien of *Pluton* was promoted rear admiral on 29 May 1806. He outwitted Collingwood to relieve Barcelona in 1809. He married Victoire Bayle and they had two daughters. He was put in charge of the Brest squadron in 1814 and was prefect of Brest during the Hundred Days that led up to the battle of Waterloo in 1815. He retired in 1816 and died in 1825.

Anne Cumby waited at Richmond for her husband William with their baby daughter Jane born on 17 March 1805. The only report she received said that *Bellerophon* had lost several of her officers. When Cumby finally returned to Richmond, Anne gave twenty pounds to the poor. William was promoted commander from 24 December and post-captain on New Year's Day. He attended Nelson's funeral. His letter on behalf of the family of boatswain Thomas Robinson won them an award of eighty pounds from Lloyd's Patriotic Fund. He got forty pounds for Midshipman George Pearson. He did not get a ship until 1807. In 1809 in *Polyphemus* he commanded a squadron off Santo Domingo. He served in Jamaica, America and off France, making a few thousand in prize money, but to Cumby's intense grief Anne died before the war ended. His daughter Jane remembered a visit to the family from the Swede Peter Jansen, who owed his escape from slavery in Oran to Cumby and the crew of *Bellerophon*. On Trafalgar Day 1829, Captains Robert and Hugh Patton and others from *Bellerophon* gathered at Cumby's house to meet Lieutenant John Franklin, just returned from a voyage of exploration in north Canada. Cumby died in 1837.

Denis Decrès retained the post of minister of marine until 1814 and returned to it under Napoleon during the Hundred Days. After Trafalgar he was able to implement his own cautious approach to the recovery of the French navy and proved a gifted administrator. A sustained construction programme raised French naval strength to seventy-three ships-of-the-line and fifty-four frigates, and brief expeditions served to train officers and seamen, but he avoided large-scale confrontation with the British. He was named a duke in 1813 and retired in August 1815. His selection of senior officers continued to be perverse. He died in 1820 of wounds received during an attempted assassination by his *valet de chambre*.

Consul James Duff became a linchpin of the British effort in Spain after the change of alliance at Cadiz in 1808. The next year he entertained Lord Byron when he visited Cadiz. Sir Arthur Wellesley came to value Duff just as highly as Nelson had and Duff was made a baronet after Wellesley's victory at Vitoria. He died unmarried in November 1815.

Pierre Dumanoir, commander of the van division, returned to France in July 1806 but remained in disgrace for five years. Condemned for his actions at Trafalgar by a first enquiry he was eventually exonerated by a council of war. He was put in charge of the squadron at Danzig (Gdansk), was wounded defending the place and captured by the Russians in January 1814, then freed in July. At the Restoration he was elevated to the nobility as a *comte* and appointed to command the division that escorted the French Ambassador to Constantinople. He was deputy for Manche in 1815, promoted vice admiral in January 1819 and died in Paris in 1829.

Fulcran Fournier, who retook *Bucentaure*, transferred to *Aigle* and, still in Cadiz in 1808, attempted to defend the ship when she was attacked in port by the Spanish. After their surrender the French officers were at first kept in the old *Castilla*, then sent to Mallorca where they were attacked and, according to Fournier's account, 'massacred' by the local population. They were transferred to nearby Cabrera, a 'desert rock' on which about nine thousand French prisoners were imprisoned in conditions even worse than in the British prison hulks. From here the British 'rescued' the officers in 1810. Fournier was a prisoner in England until 1814. He remained in the navy until his early death in 1821.

Thomas Fremantle of *Neptune* remained with Collingwood in the Mediterranean until December 1806. He was briefly on the Admiralty board and commanded the yacht *William and Mary* and was promoted rear admiral in 1810. In April 1812 he took charge of the Adriatic squadron, captured Trieste in 1814 and cleared the Adriatic coasts. He was made an Austrian baron. He was commander-in-chief in the

Mediterranean in 1818 but died in Naples on 19 December 1819. Betsy lived on until 1857. Of their numerous children, Thomas became a politician and was created Lord Cottesloe; Admiral Sir Charles Fremantle served in the Crimean war and founded Fremantle in Australia.

Antonio Alcalá Galiano became a passionate orator and conspirator in defence of national liberty and against the Napoleonic invasion. He married for love against his mother's wishes in 1807. A prominent liberal politician in the Cortes at Cadiz, he was one of the architects of the liberal constitution of 1819–20. When King Ferdinando returned with a reactionary government Galiano fled the absolutist terror into exile in London where, in 1828, he became the first professor of Spanish language and literature at the University of London. He returned to Spain in 1834 and occupied various important posts in government. He wrote two volumes of memoirs, *Recuerdos de un Anciano* and *Memorias*, both remarkable for their honesty, as well as important works on literary history. He died on 11 April 1865, following a spirited debate with fellow members of the Spanish government.

Auguste Gicquel of *L'Intrépide* found that Admiral Lord Northesk, who remained afloat, could not persuade the Admiralty to honour his promise to release him and he remained a prisoner on parole in Tiverton for six years. 'I have often remarked the generous hearts of individual Englishmen and at the same time the total unscrupulousness that seems to inform every action of their government,' he commented wryly as his career languished. After his return to France in 1811 he was promoted to lieutenant and twice married. In the *Loire* off Senegal, Gicquel helped to rescue the survivors of the wreck of the *Méduse*, an incident made famous by Théodore Géricault's painting, and blamed by Gicquel on the restored Bourbon régime's appointment of incompetent socialites to the command of ships. He was finally promoted captain in 1827, retired in 1845, wrote his autobiography *Souvenirs d'un marin de la République* in 1848 and died in 1855. His son Albert-Auguste became vice admiral and minister of marine.

Emma Hamilton was rapidly estranged from Nelson's brother William, who refused to honour the codicil to Nelson's will, but she spent much time with Nelson's sisters and their families. She fell deeper and deeper into debt, although Nelson's friends and acquaintances helped her until, one by one, they died. She lived for a while with the singer Elizabeth Billington, but was arrested for debt in 1813. Released a year later, she went to France with Horatia and died in Calais in 1815. Horatia returned to England in the care of Nelson's sisters and their families. At Burnham Market in Norfolk she met a clergyman named Philip Ward, married him in 1822 and had nine children, living first in Norfolk, then in Kent. In 1815 Horatia was given Nelson's last letter to her and finally discovered that he was her father.

William Hargood of *Belleisle* served with Charles Tyler in the blockade of Lisbon in 1808 and, after the surrender of the Russian squadron at Lisbon, in the Adriatic. In 1810, promoted rear admiral, he married Maria Cocks, sister of James Morris's wife, and undertook various jobs at home. He was promoted vice admiral in 1814 and knighted in 1815. He remained a personal friend of the Duke of Clarence and was present at his coronation in 1831 as William IV.

Louis Infernet returned to Toulon as a captain. Commanding the *Annibal*, he took part in Admiral Ganteaume's successful operation to reprovision Corfu, evading interception by Collingwood. Blockaded in Toulon until 1814, he retired as an honorary rear admiral but died the following year.

Jean-Jacques Lucas was freed on parole in April 1806, presented to the Emperor and made a commander of the Légion d'Honneur in whose schools his two daughters were educated. He never became an admiral, having offended Napoleon and Decrès, by defending Villeneuve, and Louis XVIII, by remaining loyal to the Emperor. He retired in 1816 and died in Brest on 6 November 1819. Two of his officers in *Redoutable*, Lieutenant Henri Dupotet and Sub-lieutenant Alexandre Ducrest, did become admirals.

Able Seaman James Martin of *Neptune* continued his career at sea. Some years after Trafalgar when his ship was at Charente close to Rochefort, 'a French man Came on Bord of us he knew me at the first Sight again Sayd he came on Bord to talk with me about the Battle off Trafalgar and with a Large Mug of Cognac Brandy to talk it over but first to give a Tost of his Chosen "Prosperity to England and France and may the two Nations be Long United in Peace".' If this man really did know Martin from Trafalgar he was possibly one of the three men from *Redoutable* that *Neptune* found clinging to wreckage the morning after their ship sank. James and Elizabeth Martin added three more sons to their family, William, John and Robert. James Martin died on 10 April 1855. His 'Book Concerning the Battle of Trafalgar' is still treasured by his family.

Molly Nosworthy presumably heard from her son William about the death of her husband Edward, the gunner's mate in *Neptune*. A year later she was accepted as a nurse at Greenwich Hospital and lived there until her own death in 1826 at the age of sixty.

Gunner William Rivers wrote some 'Lines on a Young Gentleman [his son William] that lost his leg onboard of the Victory in the Glorious action at Trafalgar':

> May every comfort Bless thy future life,
> And smooth thy cares With a fond and tender wife.
> Which of you all Would not have freely died,
> To Save Brave Nelson There Dear Country's Pride.

Benjamin West made portraits of him and his son for his painting of the death of Nelson. He continued as gunner of the *Victory* until his retirement years later. His three daughters all married naval lieutenants. His one-legged son became a Greenwich pensioner.

Charles Tyler returned at the end of 1805 and continued to command *Tonnant* while convalescing from his wound at his home in Pembrokeshire with his wife and children. He was promoted rear admiral in 1808, and escorted the Russian Lisbon squadron to Britain after their surrender. Emma Hamilton wrote to him on behalf of one of Nelson's *protégés*, for whom she had procured an appointment as lieutenant in his ship, and invited Tyler to visit to talk of their days in the Mediterranean, 'happy times never more to be recalled'. Tyler was promoted vice admiral in 1813 and was commander-in-chief at the Cape of Good Hope, to which he was able to take his wife and family.

His son George (now minus one arm) was his flag lieutenant from 1812 to 1815. He handed over this command at St Helena, where he tried to visit Napoleon at Long Wood, but the Emperor claimed to be unwell. On their return the Tylers and their younger children moved to Cottrell House, Glamorgan. He became a full admiral in 1825 and both he and his wife Margaret died in 1835.

Xavier de Uriarte of *Santísima Trinidad* was promoted *jefe de escuadra* in 1806 and succeeded Escaño as major general of the Cadiz squadron. He wrote a magnificent letter of resignation to Joseph Bonaparte and presented himself to the Junta of Seville, who appointed him military governor of the Isla de León, where he helped defend Cadiz during the siege of 1811–12. He became governor of Cartagena in 1816. In 1822 he retired to Puerto Santa María, where he died in 1842 as Captain General of the Fleet.

Cayetano Valdés switched to the army when Napoleon invaded and became lieutenant general, governor and captain general of Cadiz. He opposed Ferdinando VII's absolutism and, having been condemned to death, fled to Britain in 1823. He remained in exile for ten years before he was recalled to Spain by Isobel II, who appointed him Captain General of the Armada. He died in 1835.

On 21 October 1905, on the hundredth anniversary of the battle, a requiem mass was held in the Pantéon de Marinos Illustres (the Pantheon of Illustrious Mariners) at the naval base outside Cadiz, where memorials to Churruca and Galiano stand above Gravina's tomb. By candlelight a choir chanted prayers for the repose of the souls of Federico Gravina, Cosme de Churruca, Dionisio Alcalá Galiano and the other officers and men who died at Trafalgar.

Gravina had spent his last hours in a bedroom of his elegant house opposite the cathedral, whose windows look out to sea towards Trafalgar. Two days before he died he was visited by James Fellowes, a British doctor allowed into Spain in wartime because he was researching the causes of yellow fever. Weak and suffering as he was, Gravina received this visitor from an enemy nation graciously and told him, 'I am a dying man, but I die happy; I am going, I hope and trust, to join Nelson, the greatest hero that the world perhaps has produced!'

These are sentimental words of unconfirmed authenticity but we know that Gravina admired Nelson and he might have spoken in these terms. Great sailors and great leaders had fought first each other and then the elements at Trafalgar, but one thing most of them had in common was an admiration for heroism. Accurate or not, the words serve as a poignant reminder that although the men of Trafalgar may have been separated by the shifting allegiances of a continent at war there were heroes from every nation, illustrious mariners all.

Acknowledgements

At the very beginning of research for this book Susan Morris put us in touch with Peter Warwick and with Colin White and we are most grateful for their generosity in suggesting lines of inquiry. Peter very kindly introduced Tim to Agustín Guimerá who could not have been more generous and helpful when Tim visited Madrid, and whose excellent advice made his trip to Cadiz as enjoyable as it was rewarding. For the generous loan of manuscripts and permission to publish extracts from them we should like to thank Robert Martin, Christine Gunner and Andrew and Shauna MacKenzie. Colin White drew our attention to some new material that has emerged as a result of his Nelson Letters Project, the results of which will be published in July 2005 in his book *Nelson – The New Letters*. Peter Clayton combed the *Norwich Mercury* in Norwich City Library and Jennifer Bryant wrestled with some of the more challenging passages of nineteenth-century Spanish. Stephen Clarke advised on views and descriptions of Merton Place. Guillaume Cousin and Virginie Brac were delightful hosts in Paris. We should like to thank the staff of the libraries and archives that we have contacted or visited. The staff of the reading room of the National Archive have been especially helpful, patient and and understanding and Bruno Pappalardo made some useful suggestions. The staff of Cambridge University Library and of the Caird Library at the National Maritime Museum have also responded cheerfully to a multiplicity of requests. We should also like to thank the staff of the Norfolk Nelson Museum, Bedford Record Office, Essex record office, M. G. Little, archivist of the Royal Marines Museum,

Southsea, and Matthew Sheldon of the Royal Naval Museum Portsmouth; Mariá Dolores Higueras Rodrigues and the staff of the archive of the Museo Naval, Madrid; the staff of the Service Historique de la Marine, Vincennes; Marc Fardet and the staff of the Service Historique de la Marine, Rochefort; Vincent Mollet and the staff of the Service Historique de la Marine, Toulon; Juliet Brightmore and Josine Meijer for picture research; Sandra Oakin for super maps and diagrams; Hazel Orme for a magnificient job as a sympathetic and supportive copy editor; Jane Birkett for proof reading; Rupert Lancaster, Hugo Wilkinson and Kerry Hood.

PHOTOGRAPHIC CREDITS

The Art Archive: 3; Arxiu Mas: 12; Bedfordshire & Luton Archives and Records (Photo: David Stubbs) 20; Bridgeman Art Library: 8 (Crown Estate/Institute of Directors, London), 11 (Bibliothèque Nationale de France), 14 (Private Collection), 18 (Private Collection); British Library: 19; British Museum, 2, 4, 5, 6; Museo Naval, Madrid: 13, 15; © National Maritime Museum: 7, 9, 17, 21, 22, 23; Roger-Viollet/Rex Features: 10; Sotheby's Picture Library: 1; © Tate Gallery: 16.

Notes on Sources

Full publication details of the works mentioned below are provided in the bibliography. The narrative of the battle and storm is based on the British ships' logs (many of which are printed in Sturges Jackson) and the French and Spanish reports (most of which are printed in Desbrière) together with the muster books and various eyewitness accounts. Many of the relevant Spanish documents were published by Pelayo Alcalá Galiano. These sources are listed in the bibliography. Only direct quotations from them are cited in the notes.

The following abbreviations are used in the notes:

BL British Library, London
NA National Archives (formerly Public Record Office), Kew
NMM National Maritime Museum, London
RMM Royal Marines Museum, Southsea
RNM Royal Naval Museum, Portsmouth
SHM Service Historique de la Marine, Château de Vincennes

1 The Miradors of Cadiz

p.2 'a great alabaster ship', Solís, p. 41.

p.2 'the advantage of', Warner, *Collingwood*, p. 133.

p.3 'a selfish old bear', George Elliot, son of Lord Minto and a *protégé* of Nelson, in Kennedy, p. 309.

p.7 'During these five years', Guimerá, 'Commerce and shipping', pp. 22ff.

p.7 'next January it is twenty-seven years', Nelson to James Duff. 4 October 1803, BL Add Mss 34953 ff. 161–2.

p.7 'in their arsenals', NMM MSS CRK4, letters to Nelson from James Duff, 5 August 1803, 2 September 1803 and 12 October 1803.

p.8 'I am clearly of opinion', Nelson to Captain Gore, 13 October 1803, Nicolas, vol. VI, p. 241.

p.8 'too flimsy to go down', Nelson to Captain John Gore 13 October 1804, quoting Cochrane's expression to Consul Hunter in Madrid, ibid., p. 240.

p.9 'tried to justify', Zulueta, p. 299.

p.9 'Mamelukes': these were the Christian slaves who provided the toughest Turkish opposition to Napoleon in Egypt. The name implied that the anti-Bonaparte faction were traitors to Spain's natural alliance and slaves to despotism.

p.9 'The War with this Country', NMM MSS CRK4, Duff to Nelson, 20 February 1805.

p.10 'well loved', Antonio Alcalá Galiano, *Recuerdos*, p. 40.

p.10 'It not being in the interests', Zulueta, p. 301.

p.12 'the British fleet', private collection, 'Book Concerning the Batle of Trafalgar', f. 1.

p.12 'I put a boat', Fremantle, p. 198.

p.12 'a Stainge Sail', private collection, 'Book Concerning the Batle of Trafalgar', f. 2.

p.14 'Gravina had written', Tracy, p. 164.

p.14 'They will follow us', Desbrière, vol. II, p. 22.

p.14 'proud bearing', Lauriston to Napoleon, 21 August 1805, Desbrière, vol. II, p. 114.

p.15 'In short, Sire', ibid.

2 The Plum Pudding in Danger

p.17 Merton Place was added to William Angus's *Seats of the Nobility and Gentry in Great Britain and Wales* in 1804. This essential guide for tourists noted that 'the Apartments are distributed with much Taste and Convenience, and are ornamented with Pictures and Memorials of his Lordship's naval Achievements'.

p.18 'His aspect commanded', Feldborg quoted in Pope, *England Expects*, p. 119.

p.18 'looked up to in', Fremantle to Betsy, 15 August 1805, Fremantle, p. 198; BL Add Ms 34931, S. Sedley to Nelson, 9 September 1805.

p.20 'The movements on the French coast', *Norwich Mercury*, 10 August 1805.

p.21 'has sent away his family', *Norwich Mercury*, 17 August 1805. It also described Madame Jerome Bonaparte's recent visit to the Bank of England!

p.21 'Our prosperity and glory', ibid.

p.22 'the public appearance', Oman, p. 510.

p.22 'when he enters a shop', Pocock, *Horatio Nelson*, p. 309.

p.22 'met Nelson to-day', ibid.

p.23 'The book that Rivers compiled', RNM MSS 1998/41/1.

p.24 'I am now set up', Nelson to Keats, 24 August 1805, Nicolas, vol. VII, p. 16.

p.25 'was the clash of two wills', Crouzet, p. 247.

p.25 'The prize at stake', see Crouzet, pp. 281-6.

p.26 'The bond between', see Duffy, *Soldiers*, p. 23.

p.26 'France is the only power', ibid.

p.26 'It proved all too easy', see Taillemite, *L'Histoire Ignorée*, pp. 280-90.

p.27 'Damn sugar', *Oeuvres du Comte P. L. Roederer*, ed. A. M. Roederer, Paris: Firmin, vol. III, p. 461.

p.27 'the walls of which', Feldborg in Pope, *England Expects*, p. 119.

p.28 'The Name of each ship', BL Egerton MSS 1614, ff. 51-2.

3 Our Incomparable Navy

p.29 'correspondence on all subjects', BL Add MS 34931, Nelson's incoming correspondence September–October 1805.

p.31 'Art critics informed the public', Whitley, vol. II, pp. 62, 89.

p.32 'All the world is following her', ibid., p. 145.

p.32 'offered her two thousand pounds', Fraser, *Beloved Emma*, p. 165.

p.32 'celebrated for her readiness', Whitley, vol. II, p. 146.

p.32 'no Grecian', Fraser, *Beloved Emma*, p. 163.

p.32 'O Knight of Naples', [John Walcot], *The Works of Peter Pindar Esqr.*, vol. III, London: John Walker, 1794, p. 334.

p.33 'I am writing opposite Lady Hamilton', Nicolas, vol. III, p. 144, in Kennedy, p. 152.

p.33 'If I was King of England', BL Add Mss 34989 in Kennedy, p. 152.

p.34 'I cannot forget her appearance', Whitley, vol. II, pp. 107–8.

p.34 'You are to be, recollect', Pocock, *Horatio Nelson*, p. 259.

p.35 'I had luckily got plenty', Tracy (ed.), *Naval Chronicle*, p. 138.

p.35 'where have you been', NMM MSS TYL/1 (Wyndham-Quin, p. 124).

p.35 'a fine steady good officer', Tracy (ed.), *Naval Chronicle*, p. 187.

p.35 'I have heard', ibid., p. 189.

p.36 'courts martial', NA Adm 1/5344 and 5346.

p.36 'an intellectual elite', see Rodger, 'Image and Reality', p. 281.

p.36 'such a very distinguish'd sett', Nelson to the Duke of Clarence, 4 April 1801, BL Add Mss 46356 f. 37.

p.37 'Recent research': the seminal revisionist work is Rodger, *Wooden World*. On changes in the 1790s and early 1800s, see Rodger, 'The inner life of the Navy', 'Shipboard Life in the Georgian Navy', and 'The Naval World of Jack Aubrey' and Lavery, *Nelson's Navy* and *Nelson's Fleet at Trafalgar*.

p.37 'the great "Hot Press"': for more detail on the hot press of 1803, see Lavery, *Nelson's Fleet at Trafalgar*, pp. 8–13.

p.38 'Every merchant ship', Lavery, *Nelson's Navy*, p. 122.

p.38 'Upon getting on board', ibid.

p.39 'well acquainted with his duty,' and following quotation, Burney, *Universal Dictionary of the Marine*, 1815, p. 327, in Lavery, *Nelson's Navy*, p. 129.

p.39 'Among these', NA Adm 101/94/4.

p.40 'in attempting to swim', NA Adm 15818.

p.40 'we got some very excellent', NA Adm 101/94/4.

p.41 'an excellent sailer', Warner, *Life and Letters of Collingwood*, p. 137.

p.41 'a neat stern', Wyndham-Quin, p. 128.

4 Latouche's Monument

p.45 'Indefatigable zeal,' Monaque, pp. 601–2.

p.45 'I had already seen', Gicquel, p. 411.

p.46 'You will have seen', Nelson to William Nelson, 8 August 1804, Nicolas, vol. VI, p. 147.

p.46 'live firing exercises', Monaque, p. 573.

p.47 'We were anchored', Gicquel, p. 411.

p.47 'full manned', Nelson to Melville, 1 July 1804, National Archive of Scotland GD51/2/1082/7. Nelson to Kingsmill 4 August 1804, Nicolas, vol. VI, p. 134 'He is ready, and, by their handling their Ships, apparently well manned;'

p.47 'La Touche has given me the slip,' Nelson to General Villettes, 6 September 1804, and to Ball, 4 October 1804, Nicolas, vol. VI, pp. 190 and 214.

p.47 'He was an officer', Gicquel, pp. 411–12.

p.48 'It is my most ardent wish', Villeneuve to Decrès, 22 January 1805, quoted in Schom, p. 198.

p.49 'request for a list', Taillemite, p. 306.

p.49 'In June 1805', Pelayo Alcalá Galiano, vol. II, p. 557.

p.50 'Despite his fame,' ibid., pp. 696 and 565–8, and González-Ripoll, p. 168.

p.50 'but of the 2220', Pelayo Alcalá Galiano, vol. II, pp. 586–7.

p.51 'The Dons may', Oman, p. 100.

p.51 'In 1783 Spain's merchant fleet', Jean Meyer, 'l'Europe et la mer' in Bérenger *et al.*, p. 173.

p.51 'An epidemic of yellow fever,' Solís, p. 494.

p.52 'in a very healthy place', Desbrière, vol. I, p. 168.

p.52 'not the flimsiest credit', ibid., p. 169

p.53 'I have, in reality,' Terraine, p. 120.

p.54 'Latouche had gathered several such men', Monaque, p. 560; SHM CC[7] dossiers Lucas, Daudignon, Fournier; for Villeneuve's positive view of his flagship's crew, see Desbrière, vol. II, p. 93 (SHM BB[4] 237, f. 88).

p.55 'as big as a drum-major', Fraser, *Enemy*, p. 201.

p.55 'He was of merchant-seaman stock', SHM CC[7] dossier Infernet.

p.56 'slave-hunting bloodhounds', Monaque, p. 546.

p.56 *'levée extraordinaire* in Marseille', Monaque, pp. 565–6.

p.56 'A similar "hot press"', Schom, p. 216.

p.56 'accompanied by only', Nelson to Melville (quoting Capel), 23 November 1804, National Archive of Scotland GD57/2/1082/7.

p.56 'two hundred black prisoners', Monaque, p. 566, SHM CC⁷ dossier Daudignon.

p.57 'A plan was formed', Monaque, p. 567; Desbrière, vol. I, p. 4.

p.57 'the districts were almost depopulated', Monaque, p. 565.

p.58 'This vessel is superb', SHM CC⁷ dossier Gourrège.

p.59 'A penniless fifty-year-old Dutchman', SHM CC⁷ dossier Classen.

p.59 'Rear-Admiral Charles Magon', SHM CC⁷ dossier Magon.

p.60 'no deduction need be made', James, vol. IV, p. 94.

5 As Smooth as the Lake at Stowe

p.61 'is gone inshore', George to Sophia Duff, 31 August 1805, Tracy (ed.), *Naval Chronicle*, p. 190.

p.61 'as the combined fleets', Thomas to Betsy Fremantle, 31 August 1805, Fremantle, p. 198.

p.61 'Alas! I cannot look back', Edward to Jane Codrington, 29 August and 4 September 1805; Bourchier, pp. 46–7.

p.62 Richard Anderson, NMM MSS/80/201.2.

p.62 'Our Admiral is an humble', Thomas to Betsy Fremantle, 6 September 1805, Fremantle, p. 199.

p.62 'We have got into the clutches', Edward to Jane Codrington, 4 September 1805; Bourchier, pp. 46–7.

p.63 'George Duff dined', George to Sophia Duff, 31 August and 7 September 1805, Tracy (ed.), *Naval Chronicle*, p. 190.

p.63 'Finding that the Admiral', Edward to Jane Codrington, 5 September 1805, Bourchier, p. 47.

p.63 'What adds more', Thomas to Betsy Fremantle, 6 September 1805, Fremantle, p. 199.

p.63 'the Grotto being illuminated', diary of Betsy Fremantle, 16 August 1805, Fremantle, p. 187.

p.64 'I wish and hope', Thomas to Betsy Fremantle, 6 September 1805, Fremantle, p. 199.

p.65 'It is, as Mr. Pitt knows,' Oman, p. 519.

p.65 'Ask Lord Barham', Murray, 56, Nicolas, vol. VII, p. 27.

p.65 'Pursuant to instructions', ibid., p. 32.

p.66 'I would go at them at once', ibid., p. 241n.

p.66 'I have no reason to complain', Thomas to Betsy Fremantle, 6 September and 31 August 1805, Fremantle, pp. 199 and 198.

p.66 'Her complement was 738 . . .', Adm 36 15636–40, 16488–9 (*Neptune*); Adm 36 15708 (*Blanche*) Martin family Bible; NMM MSS/88/ 054.7, Edward Nosworthy manuscripts.

p.67 'The very sad sameness', Thomas to Betsy Fremantle, 22 September 1805, Fremantle, p. 205.

p.67 'I do not expect to draw much blood', Edward to Jane Codrington, 20 September 1805; Bourchier, p. 49.

p.68 'The large sum of money', Thomas Fremantle to the Marquess of Buckingham, 28 September 1805, *Mariner's Mirror*, 16 (1930), p. 409.

p.68 '*Neptune's* crew had been paid . . .' NA Adm 51 1515 (*Belleisle*), 1545 (*Neptune*), 1547 (*Tonnant*).

p.68 'The ultimate sanction . . .', NA Adm 1/5370, court-martial of Nathaniel Fish, 18 September 1805.

p.69 'as social a dinner', Edward to Jane Codrington, 20 September 1805; Bourchier, p. 49.

p.69 'You like to be applauded', Pope, *England Expects*, p. 120.

p.70 'really was a very superior man', Pocock, *Horatio Nelson*, p. 308.

p.70 'Epigrammatica Bacchanalia', Wardroper, p. 155.

p.70 'could not eat,' Pope, *England Expects*, p. 120.

6 À la Nelson

p.73 'Having resolved', Terraine, p. 132.

p.74 'As his excessive timidity', Howarth, *Trafalgar*, p. 59.

p.74 'I cannot too highly', Desbrière, vol. II, p. 27.

p.74 'insuperable obstacles', ibid., p. 31.

p.75 'Reports from Tangiers', Pope, *England Expects*, p. 148.

p.75 'it is seamen', Desbrière, vol. II, p. 92.

p.75 'a considerable force', ibid., p. 107.

p.76 'several Frenchmen', *Norwich Mercury*, 12 October 1805.

p.76 'It is very distressing', Desbrière, vol. II, p. 96.

p.77 'a mission to fetch silver', Pelayo Alcalá Galiano, p. 694; González-Ripoll, pp. 167–8.

p.77 'Troops will be re-embarked', Desbrière, vol. II, pp. 101–2.

p.78 'the usual piles of correspondence', BL Add MS 34931; Nicolas, vol. VII, pp. 46–7.

p.79 'if you are in sight of Cadiz', Nicolas, vol. VII, p. 49.

p.79 'was in the habit of reading, Scott, pp. 120–1.

p.80 'There are 39 Sail', BL Add Mss 34931.

p.81 'On the 28th of September', private collection, 'Book Concerning the Batle of Trafalgar', f. 5.

p.82 'Lord Nelson is arrived,' Edward to Jane Codrington, 29 September 1805, Bourchier, p. 51.

p.82 'This is a Great day', NMM MSS/80/201.2.

p.82 'He received me', Edward to Jane Codrington, 29 September 1805, Bourchier, p. 51.

p.82 'He looks better', Fremantle journal, 30 September 1805, *Mariner's Mirror*, 16 (1930), p. 410; Thomas to Betsy Fremantle, 1 October 1805, Fremantle, p. 210.

p.83 'The signal has been made', Bourchier, p. 51.

p.83 'He certainly is the pleasantest', George to Sophia Duff, 28 September 1805, Tracy (ed.), *Naval Chronicle*, p. 191.

p.83 'The juniors and I', Fremantle journal, 30 September 1805, *Mariner's Mirror*, 16 (1930), p. 410.

p.83 'The reception I met with', Tracy (ed.), *Naval Chronicle*, vol. XV, p. 57.

p.84 'When I came to explain', Nelson to Lady Hamilton, 1 October 1805, Nicolas, vol. VII, p. 60.

p.84 'à la Nelson', George to Sophia Duff, 10 October 1805, Tracy (ed.), *Naval Chronicle*, p. 192.

p.84 'We are all busy scraping', ibid.; Thomas to Betsy Fremantle, 1

October 1805, Fremantle, p. 210; NMM MSS/80/201.2; Edward to Jane Codrington, 30 September 1805, Bourchier, p. 52.

p.84 'As Croft, with the greatest', Bourchier, p. 52.

p.84 'We are a fine fleet', Fremantle journal, 30 September 1805, *Mariner's Mirror*, 16 (1930), p. 410.

p.85 'in my impatience', Pope, *England Expects*, p. 168.

p.85 'But at a council of senior officers', Guimerá, 'Gravina', p. 11.

p.85 'On 2 October Gravina was warned', Pelayo Alcalá Galiano, p. 533.

p.85 'He told the Spanish prime minister', Guimerá, 'Gravina', p. 8.

p.85 'Godoy explained to Gravina', ibid., p. 18.

p.86 'informed General Gravina', Desbrière, vol. II, p. 108.

p.86 'our General received', ibid.

p.87 'probably Commodore Enrique Macdonnell': some sources argue that Churruca rather than Macdonnell took part.

p.87 'it were preferable to leave port', Desbrière, vol. II, p. 109.

p.88 'he promised Decrès', ibid., p. 105.

7 Signal Flag Yellow with Blue Fly

p.90 'to ensure that the Officers', Nelson to Castlereagh, 1 October 1805, Nicolas, vol. VII, p. 62.

p.90 'I have no other means', ibid., p. 63n.

p.90 'informed us by signal', Hubback, p. 148.

p.91 'keep from three to four leagues', Nelson to Duff, 4 October 1805, Nicolas, vol. VII, pp. 70–1.

p.91 'as he was on board the *Victory*', George to Sophia Duff, 10 October 1805, Tracy (ed.), *Naval Chronicle*, p. 192.

p.91 'Conceiving from my late observations', Humphrey Senhouse to Nelson, 3 October 1805, BL Add Mss 34931.

p.92 'to see a play', Thomas to Betsy Fremantle, 6 October 1805, Fremantle, p. 211.

p.92 'all sort of fresh provisions', Thomas to Betsy Fremantle, 8 October 1805, Fremantle, p. 212; Edward to Jane Codrington, 4 and 6 October 1805, Bourchier, p. 52.

p.92 'Lord Nelson expects', Thomas to Betsy Fremantle, 11 October 1805, Fremantle, pp. 212–13.

p.94 'Signal Flag Yellow', NMM MSS TUN/61, see Tunstall and Tracy, pp. 250–1.

p.94 'did nothing without my counsel', Collingwood to William Blackett, 2 November 1805, Collingwood, p. 136.

p.95 'I send you my plan', Nicolas, vol. VII, p. 95.

p.95 'I have an order', NMM MSS TYL/1. The note is mistranscribed in Wyndham-Quin (p. 126) so as to make no sense.

p.97 'Instead of eighteen 9-pounder', NA Adm 160/154; WO 55/1832–3 Returns of ships and armament May 1798–October 1805. William James wrote (vol. IV, p. 93) that apart from *Belleisle* 'No other 74-gun ship, however, in the British fleet, to our knowledge, mounted more than 82 guns.' He was wrong. But it was not so much the number as the power of the carronades that was imposing.

p.98 'One shot every four minutes', Monaque, p. 115.

p.99 'fire the city and the Fleet', de Beurnonville to Decrès, 7 October 1805, Desbrière, vol. II, p. 73.

p.99 'do not like us', de Beurnonville to Decrès, 14 and 23 October 1805, ibid., pp. 74 and 81.

p.99 'The English newspapers', Edward to Jane Codrington 6 October 1805, 'I saw to-day papers of the 20th of last month . . . and that he has, in consequence, sent Admiral Duplex [sic, i.e. Decrès] to supersede Villeneuve', Bourchier, p. 53. Nicolas, vol. VII, p. 96 proves that Nelson believed the same report. Both sides had ready if delayed access to each other's newspapers.

p.100 'if Mr. Decrès means to come forth', Nelson to Blackwood, 9 October 1805, Nicolas, vol. VII, p. 96.

p.100 'two unsettling pieces of news', de Beurnonville to Decrès, 20 October 1805, Desbrière, vol. II, p. 78.

p.101 'Here comes Berry', Nicolas, vol. VII, p. 117n.

p.102 'We are, of course, very anxious', Hubback, pp. 148–9.

p.102 'This force of six', Desbrière, vol. II, p. 112.

p.103 'had experienced much unpleasantness', Hyde de Neuville, p. 221.

p.103 'I am informed that', Desbrière, vol. II, p. 111.

p.104 'The secret orders', Escaño to Macdonnell in Desbrière, vol. II, p. 109.

8 Blue Lights

p.106 'The enemy will not confine himself', Desbrière, vol. II, p. 131.

p.107 'I had canvas cartridge-cases', 'Rapport du Capne. De Vau. Lucas', SHM Vincennes CC⁷ dossier Lucas. We have used Fraser's translation (pp. 146–7), except that Fraser added the words 'while at Toulon', which are not in the original. *Redoutable* was never at Toulon during this campaign.

p.108 'The French Ships at Ferrol', John Hunter, Consul General at Madrid, to Duff, 8 September 1803, passed via Richard Strachan to Nelson, NMM MSS CRK4.

p.108 '*Redoutable* carried 643', 'Rapport du Capne. De Vau. Lucas', SHM Vincennes, CC⁷ dossier Lucas (printed in Fraser, *Enemy*, p. 153) and Desbrière, vol. II, p. 236.

p.108 'Regulation Spanish complements': the Spanish manning figures are reprinted in Pelayo Alcalá Galiano: regulation complements p. 606; progressive figures for the ships at Cadiz from 1 May to 24 September, pp. 618–20 and 670–1, and the figures for 19 October, pp. 884–6.

p.108 'French estimates', SHM Vincennes, BB⁴ 237, f. 94. 452.

p.109 'Ships of the line now carried', Jenkins, p. 242.

p.109 'For God's sake ship me', Corbett, pp. 47–8.

p.109 'They had invested heavily in carronades', Rodríguez González, 'Los Españoles en Trafalgar: Navíos, Cañones y Hombres', in Guimerá, A., Ramos, A. and Butrón, G. (coords.), *Coloquio Internacional 'La Bahía de Cádiz y la Europa Atlántica en tiempos de Trafalgar'*, Cadiz, 29 noviembre 2002 (in preparation); see also James, vol. IV, p. 93.

p.110 'But there was no goodbye', Antonio Alcalá Galiano, *Memorias*, p. 96.

p.110 'Say goodbye to them,' Ferrer de Couto, p. 142.

p.112 'What a beautiful day!', Nicolas, vol. VII, p. 129.

p.112 'The *Mars* at this time', NMM MSS JON/7 (Cumby, p. 719).

p.113 'Ancered with Heartfull Satifaction', private collection, 'Book Concerning the Batle of Trafalgar', f. 12.

p.113 'showed their superiority', Henry Walker in Tracy (ed.), *Naval Chronicle*, p. 229.

p.114 'My dearest beloved Emma,' Nicolas, vol. VII, pp. 132–3.

p.115 'the Windsor chairs', 'Memories of the Battle of Trafalgar', *Notes and Queries*, 6th series, vol. IV, p. 504.

p.115 'How would your heart beat', Edward to Jane Codrington, 19 October 1805, Bourchier, p. 57.

p.115 'considerably checked by the apprehension', NMM MSS JON/7 (Cumby, p. 720).

p.117 'All our gay hopes are fled', Edward to Jane Codrington, 20 October 1805, Bourchier, p. 58.

p.117 'Well this Bustles over', NMM MSS/80/201.2.

p.117 'If the Enemy are standing', Memorandum 20 October 1805, Nicolas, vol. VII, p. 136.

p.118 'Night fell', Desbrière, vol. II, p. 424.

p.118 'The night being very dark,' ibid., p. 285.

p.119 'Now the moment was fast advancing', private collection, 'Book Concerning the Batle of Trafalgar', f. 13.

9 A Forest of Masts

p.121 'The first casualty', NA Adm 51/1529; Adm 35/16250.

p.121 'a man at the topmast head', King and Hattendorf, p. 160.

p.121 'Cumby, my boy, turn out', NMM MSS JON/7 (Cumby, pp. 720–1).

p.122 'William Badcock had the first sight', Lovell, p. 44.

p.122 'prehaps the Grandest Sight', private collection, 'Book Concerning the Batle of Trafalgar', f. 14.

p.122 'in a long-tailed navy-blue uniform coat', Robinson, p. 208.

p.123 'all sail was set,' Lovell, pp. 44–5.

p.124 'allowed us the same Rest', private collection, 'Book Concerning the Batle of Trafalgar', f. 15.

p.124 'Though each seemed to exult', Allen, p. 279.

p.124 'perfectly understood', NMM MSS JON/7 (Cumby, p. 721).

p.125 'When the drum beat to quarters': details of *Bellerophon*'s crew at Trafalgar are taken from Captain Rotheram's 1807 description book (NMM MSS LBK/38) in conjunction with the October 1805 muster book (NA Adm 36/16498).

p.126 'his Fire Bucket', 'The Trafalgar General Order Book of HMS Mars', *Mariner's Mirror*, 22 (1936) p. 101.

p.127 'Captain Duff did not trust boys,' ibid.

p.128 'In July that year,' Jackson, p. 12.

p.129 'in large characters', Cumby, p. 722; the description of clearing for action is informed by Goodwin, 'Clearing for action'; Lavery, *Nelson's Navy*, pp. 196–9; 'The Trafalgar General Order Book of HMS Mars', *Mariner's Mirror*, 22 (1936) pp. 87–104; Boudriot, pp. 116–20

p.130 'My sole object', Desbrière, vol. II, p. 138.

p.130 'the leading ship,' Desbrière, vol. II, p. 192.

p.130 'to carry full sail', Gicquel, p. 417.

p.131 '*El general francés*', Ferrer de Couto, pp. 142–3. Ferrer notes that Marliani's account was supplied by José Ruiz de Apodaca, younger brother of Churruca's wife and a *guardia marina* in *San Juan de Nepomuceno*; it should be noted that Marliani's book was written to justify the Spanish navy against the French historian Thiers' accusation that the Spanish were to blame for the defeat.

p.131 'The British Hearts', private collection, 'Book Concerning the Batle of Trafalgar', f. 14.

p.132 'Sailors, they get all the money', Rodger, *Wooden World*, pp. 135–6.

p.132 'when Henry Digby,' see Pope, *England Expects*, p. 175.

p.132 'May God bless you,' Nicolas, vol. VI, p. 497.

p.132 'Santissima Trinidada,' Tracy (ed.), *Naval Chronicle*, p. 229.

p.133 'and was much struck with the preparations', Fraser, *Sailors*, pp. 215–16.

p.133 'were making a sort of verbal will,' King and Hattendorf, pp. 161–2.

p.133 'Should I, my dear parents,' Fraser, *Sailors*, p. 257.

p.134 '<u>My Dearest Sophia</u>,' Tracy (ed.), *Naval Chronicle*, p. 193.

10 Putting a Good Face on It

p.135 'like a haystack', Bevan and Wolryche-Whitmore, p. 109.

p.136 'Both Blackwood and *Victory*'s captain, Thomas Hardy', Clarke and M'Arthur, vol. II, p. 445, in Nicolas, vol. VII, p. 148.

p.136 'had intended to pass her', Lovell, p. 45.

p.136 'Captain Tyler exclaimed,' NA Adm 51/1515; Allen, pp. 279–80.

p.137 'made the signal for the lee division', Sturges Jackson, vol. II, p. 202; see Tracy, p. 183, and Corbett, p. 368n.

p.137 'quite young again', Pope, *England Expects*, p. 221.

p.137 'At daylight saw the Enemy's Combined Fleet. . .' Nicolas, vol. VII, pp. 139–40. We owe this observation about duplication to Colin White who made the point at a Nelson Records seminar at the National Archives.

p.138 'I leave Emma Lady Hamilton,' Nicolas, vol. VII, pp. 140–1.

p.139 'the van was then becalmed', Désiré Clamart in *Achille*, Desbrière, vol. II, p. 286.

p.139 'several ships were doubling', ibid.

p.141 'one of the best', Villeneuve to Decrès, 16 September 1805, Desbrière, vol. II, p. 93 (BB⁴, p. 230, f.276).

p.142 'The *San Justo* not being', Desbrière, vol. II, p. 210.

p.142 'one of the finest', Villeneuve to Decrès, 16 September 1805, Desbrière, vol. II, p. 93.

p.142 'When he saw this', 'Rapport du Capne. De Vau. Lucas', SHM CC⁷ dossier Lucas.

p.143 'Villeneuve thought her a fine ship', Villeneuve to Decrès, 16 September 1805, Desbrière, vol. II, pp. 93.

p.144 'Thanks to overcrowding': see the report in Desbrière, vol. II, p. 410.

p.144 'The sophisticated Spanish *Tratado de Señales* of 1804,' reproduced in Tunstall and Tracy, pp. 240–42.

p.145 'from the very compact line', King and Hattendorf, p. 169.

p.145 'They waited the attack', 'Memoirs of Vice-Admiral . . . Blackwood', *Blackwood's Edinburgh Magazine*, vol. 34 (July 1833) no. 210, p. 8.

p.145 'An enemy of equal spirit', *Macmillan's Magazine*, vol. 81 (April 19146), p. 423.

p.146 'He ordered the gunner's son', NMM MSS WEL/30.

p.146 'I am not certain that our mode', NMM MSS AGC/M/5.

p.146 '10 Sail of Line superior', NMM MSS 80/201.2.

p.146 'behaved notoriously ill', NMM MSS LBK/38.

p.146 'The family of *Britannia*'s,' Lavery, *Nelson's Fleet*, p. 168.

p.147 'called all hands', Fraser, *Sailors*, pp. 216–17.

p.148 'adressed us at our Diffrent Quarters', private collection, 'Book Concerning the Batle of Trafalgar', f. 17.

p.148 'turned the hands up', Smith, 'The *Defiance* at Trafalgar', p. 118; NMM MSS 77/163, Spratt memoir.

p.148 'men, we are now in sight of the enemy', NMM MSS 9735.

p.149 'It was answered by three hearty', Wyndham-Quin, p. 134.

p.149 'No fear of that!' Henry Walker to his mother Mrs R. Walker, 22 November 1805, Sturges Jackson, p. 324.

p.149 'In *Bucentaure* the Imperial Eagle', Desbrière vol. II, pp. 192–3 (BB[4] 237, f. 88).

p.149 'My children, in the name', Ferrer de Couto, p. 142.

p.150 'made the signal to open fire', Desbrière, vol. II, p. 192.

p.150 '*Canonniers, chacun à son poste.*' Details from Boudriot, vol. IV, pp. 123–37.

11 Go Through She Shall, By God

p.153 '"Gentlemen," he said', Nicolas, in Allen, p. 280.

p.154 'the commanding voice', ibid., p. 281.

p.154 'Lie down there,' ibid., p. 141.

p.154 'Then the ranging shots'. This passage is based on the accounts of Nicolas and Owen in Allen, pp. 141–2 and 280–2.

p.155 'our bad habit in the French Navy', Fraser, *Enemy*, p. 213.

p.156 'she gave us a broadside', ibid., p. 214.

p.157 'several men were hiding', Desbrière, vol. II, p. 210 (BB[4] 237 f. 102).

p.157 'looked once out', Fraser, *Sailors*, p. 256.

p.157 'I can assure you it was glorious', ibid.

p.157 'He laid his head', Fraser, *Enemy*, p. 277.

p.158 'On the Spanish side,' Museo Naval, Madrid, MS 1399, ff. 218–20.

p.158 '*Royal Sovereign*'s first raking broadside', James, vol. IV, pp. 35–6. The palpable inaccuracy of James's figure was pointed out by Michael Duffy in a lecture on 'Gunnery at Trafalgar' to be published in A. Guimerá, A. Ramos, and G. Butrón, (coords.), *Coloquio Internacional 'La Bahía de Cádiz y la Europa Atlántica en tiempos de Trafalgar'*, Cadiz, 29 noviembre 2002 (in preparation).

p.158 '*Santa Ana*'s total casualties', Museo Naval, Madrid, MS 2162, f. 48.

p.160 'Prudencio Ruiz Alegria,' Ferrer de Couto, p. 159.

p.161 'We had the enemy's ship', Fraser, *Enemy*, pp. 214–15.

p.162 'Infantry Captain Pernot, whose men', Dillon, pp. 57–8.

p.162 'a three-decker and another', Desbrière, vol. II, pp. 239–40.

p.162 ' "Then," replied the Captain', Tracy (ed.), *Naval Chronicle*, p. 225.

p.162 'when the men heard it', RNM MSS 1992/133.

p.163 'two of the bandsmen', Wyndham-Quin, p. 134.

p.164 'A Spanish soldier named Amor Seco', Ferrer de Couto, pp. 158–9.

p.164 'Although I wish very much', BL MSS Egerton 382, f. 28, translated for Nicolas, vol. VII, p. 290.

p.165 'Eyewitnesses are unreliable.' This is a problem that William James himself highlighted (vol. IV, p. 78): 'How far the published accounts on either side are calculated to guide the historian, has already in part appeared, and will be more fully shown when some of those accounts pass under review. As to the accounts furnished exclusively for this work by individuals present in the battle, much as we, and through us the public, owe to them, they are, in many instances, imperfect, obscure, and even contradictory. Nor can it be wondered at, considering how each officer's attention must have been absorbed in the immediate duties of his station; and how few yards, beyond the side of his own ship, the smoke of so many combatants would permit him to see.'

p.166 'Only one man', Wyndham-Quin, p. 135.

p.167 'Seeing the situation', Benjamin to his father Thomas Clement, 30 November 1805, Clement, p. 479.

p.167 'Pierre Servaux, responsible as Master-at-arms', Fraser, *Enemy*, p. 216.

p.168 'we succeeded in dismasting', Desbrière, vol. II, p. 235.

p.168 'Our flag, however', Fraser, *Enemy*, p. 217.

p.169 'were placed in such situations', Senhouse, p. 424.

p.169 'The mere idea', Conrad, *Mirror of the Sea* (1975 edn), pp. 191–2.

p.169 'Nobly done, Hargood!', Allen, p. 123.

p.169 'There is a topgallant yard gone', King and Hattendorf, p. 172.

12 Take Your Choice

p.171 'She was lying-to under topsails', Lovell, p. 46.

p.172 'to deceive the Enemy', NMM MSS TUN/61.

p.172 'steered for the centre of the van, and thence, hauling to the wind, towards the centre', Cajigal's report, Desbrière, vol. II, p. 400.

p.172 'with the three-deckers', Desbrière, vol. II, p. 404.

p.172 'with our larboard guns', private collection. Westemberg's account is consistent with that of the anonymous author of RNM, 1994/128. In *The Times*, 2 January 1806, Dumanoir wrote, 'The left column of the English, having Admiral Nelson at its head, bore at first on the French vanguard, which I commanded, but finding it too compact, they exchanged some shots with us, and then struck at the centre of our line.' Valdés' diagram illustrating Nelson's approach is in his handwritten report in the Archivo Histórico Municipal de El Puerto de Santa María. Uriarte in Desbrière, vol. II, p. 404; the plans by Magendie and Prigny also show this movement.

p.172 'Is that poor Scott', King and Hattendorf, p. 172.

p.172 'This is too warm work', ibid.

p.173 'I then gave orders to aim', 'Rapport du Capne. De Vau. Lucas', SHM CC[7] dossier Lucas; Fraser, *Enemy*, p. 160.

p.174 'We rejoiced at this,' Desbrière, vol. II, p. 194.

p.175 'A large splinter had scalped', NA Adm 101/125/1.

p.175 *'son courage'*, Fraser, *Enemy*, p. 418.

p.176 'This signal did not appear', Gicquel, p. 418.

p.176 'I cannot help it', King and Hattendorf, p. 173.

p.177 'a round shot and a specially made canister', RNM MSS 1994/128, anonymous account.

p.177 'We were engaging on both sides', RMM MSS 11/12/1; Tracy, *Nelson's Battles*, p. 195.

p.178 'fearing I might', Eliab to Louisa Harvey, 23 October 1805, Sturges Jackson, p. 225.

p.179 'had to use rope rammers', 'Rapport du Capne. De Vau. Lucas', SHM CC⁷ dossier Lucas; Fraser, *Enemy*, pp. 161–2.

p.179 'In the excitement', RMM MSS 11/12/1; Lavery, *Nelson's Fleet*, p. 165.

p.179 'slammed shut the lower deck': on this Lucas's officers and Dr Beatty agree. Lucas says that his guns kept on firing but slowly, and that he gave the order to board in response to a perceived threat from *Victory*. It seems likely that *Victory*'s guns quickly won any artillery duel.

p.179 'at this period', King and Hattendorf, p. 173.

p.180 'Hardy, mind he is provided for', RNM MSS 1998/41/1.

p.182 'sending below most of the men from her poop', NMM MSS JOD/48.

p.182 'all the rigging was cut', Desbrière, vol. II, p. 194.

p.183 'Gicquel claimed that *Intrépide*', Gicquel, p. 418.

p.183 'the Admiral's orders', Hyde de Neuville, p. 219.

p.183 '*Lou capo sur lou* Bucentauro!', Gicquel, p. 418.

p.184 'William Pringle Green reckoned', NMM MSS JOD/48.

13 Incredible Fury on Both Sides

p.187 'We fired our carronades', NMM MSS JON/7 (Cumby, p. 723).

p.190 'Let me lay one minute,' letter from Cumby to Cooke's brother, in Marshall, vol. II ii, p. 969.

p.191 'carried by two men', NMM MSS JON/7 (Cumby, p. 723).

p.191 'seeing what he was about', Fraser, *Enemy*, pp. 207–8, quoting a 'memoir of Sir John Franklin'.

p.192 'Midshipman Robert Patton watched', Cumby, p. 724n.

p.192 'Most providentially', NMM MSS JON/7 (Cumby, pp. 724–5).

p.192 'had got upon our starboard sprit-sail yard-arm', Patton in Cumby, p. 723n.

p.193 'Our quarterdeck, poop', NMM MSS JON/7 (Cumby, pp. 723–4).

p.193 'in the foretop', Traill, pp. 27–8.

p.194 'the well-sustained musketry fire', Desbrière, vol. II, p. 242.

p.194 'were well matched,' Tracy (ed.), *Naval Chronicle*, p. 230.

p.195 'This man has never been paid off.' NMM MSS LBK/38.

p.195 'captains suffered 22 per cent casualties,' Keegan, p. 87.

p.196 'seventeen of her men', Desbrière, vol. II, p. 268 (BB⁴ 237, f. 111).

p.196 'received the full brunt', ibid., p. 274 (BB⁴ 237 f. 136).

p.197 'the Captain judged the moment propitious', ibid.

p.197 'Morris's log reported', NA, ADM 51/1516.

p.198 'approached to place herself', Desbrière, vol. II, pp. 410–11.

p.198 'to luff up into the wind', ibid., p. 411.

p.199 'Many of our men thought it hard', King and Hattendorf, pp. 161–2.

p.199 'Those ships we had thrown into disorder', ibid., p. 162.

p.199 'Our marines with their small arms', ibid.

p.199 'The Frenchman wore under my stern', Robert to Richard Moorsom, 1 November 1805, NMM MSS AGC/M5.

p.200 'what was termed a slaughtering one', King and Hattendorf, p. 165.

p.200 '*Achille's* own officers were falling', Desbrière, vol. II, pp. 286–7 (report of Enseignes de vaisseau Lachasse and Clamart, BB⁴ 237 f. 196).

p.201 'he would act as Lord Nelson had always done', John Greenly to his father, 21 October 1805, RNM MSS 1984/14 (129).

p.201 'the shots were playing their pranks', King and Hattendorf, p. 165.

p.201 'Colin Campbell, in *Defiance*, had reckoned', Colin Campbell to his father, 3 December 1805, Smith 'The *Defiance* at Trafalgar', pp. 116–21.

p.201 'fought his ship as coolly', John Greenly to his father, 21 October 1805, RNM MSS 1984/14 (129).

p.202 'not certain that our mode', Robert to Richard Moorsom, 1 November 1805, NMM MSS AGC/M5.

14 A Mere Matter of Fact

p.204 'They have done for me at last, Hardy', King and Hattendorf, p. 174.

p.204 'I am a dead man', Pocock, *Horatio Nelson*, p. 141.

p.204 'I am killed', Oman, p. 257.

p.204 'Sergeant Robert Guillemard': see Fraser, *Enemy*, pp. 179–81.

p.204 'The marines became exasperated', RMM MSS 11/12/1; Lavery, *Nelson's Fleet*, p. 166.

p.205 'my attention was arrested', Fraser, *Enemy*, pp. 182–3.

p.206 'The upper deck of the Victory', 'Rapport du Capne. De Vau. Lucas', SHM Vincennes CC⁷ dossier Lucas; Fraser, *Enemy*, p. 163.

p.207 'he was spared amidst so many balls', Pope, *England Expects*, p. 261.

p.207 'not wishing that the relics should provide a trophy', Fournier's report, in Desbrière, vol. II, p. 202 (BB⁴ 237 f. 97); see also Magendie's report, Desbrière, vol. II, p. 195 (BB⁴ 237 f. 88).

p.208 'To whom have I the honour', Fraser, *Enemy*, p. 141.

p.208 'The French commander in chief came aboard', James to George Robinson, 12 December 1805, RNM MSS 1992/133.

p.209 'It is impossible to describe the carnage', 'Rapport du Capne. De Vau. Lucas', SHM Vincennes CC⁷ dossier Lucas; Fraser, *Enemy*, p. 164.

p.210 'having the topsail and lower yards shattered', Desbrière, vol. II, p. 232.

p.211 'Henri Dupotet gathered the surgeons', SHM Vincennes CC⁷ dossier Dupotet: 'At this difficult juncture, the ship caught fire and there was no other means of extinguishing it than by ordering the surgeons to abandon the wounded and to call up on deck the men who were passing powder, these being the last of the crew, all others being dead or wounded.'

p.211 'Because, my lord', Helmut von Erffa and Allen Staley, *The Paintings of Benjamin West* (London and New Haven: Yale University Press, 1986), p. 222.

p.212 'Wolfe must not die like a common soldier', ibid.

p.212 'a butcher's shambles', Scott, p. 185.

p.213 'Ah, Mr. Beatty', King and Hattendorf, p. 175.

p.213 'to see many brave seamen mangled', Fraser, *Sailors*, p. 256.

p.214 'the wind from a great shot', Pope, *England Expects*, p. 277.

p.214 'She rolled so much', Fraser, *Sailors*, p. 257.

p.214 'hesitated; then said he hoped', Collingwood to the Duke of Clarence, in Pope, *England Expects*, p. 319.

p.215 'We then gave them three Hearty cheairs', private collection, 'Book Concerning the Batle of Trafalgar', f. 23.

p.215 'This tremendous fabric', Fraser, *Enemy*, pp. 270–1.

p.216 'along on her deck', private collection, 'Book Concerning the Batle of Trafalgar', f. 24.

p.216 'If I were to select the most seamanlike act', Robinson, *Sea Drift*, p. 216.

p.216 'We had now Been Enverloped with Smoak', private collection, 'Book Concerning the Batle of Trafalgar', f. 25.

p.217 'beyond the edge of chaos', Edward A. Smith, *Effects Based Operations, Applying Network Centric Warfare in Peace, Crisis and War*, Command and Control Research Program (US Department of Defense, November 2002), pp. 142–5.

15 The Edge of Chaos

p.221 'was at the time under the break of the poop', Allen, p. 283.

p.223 'The Captain, seeing me actively employed', ibid., p. 144.

p.223 'a mere hulk', ibid., p. 283.

p.223 'No, sir, I am not the fellow', Wyndham-Quin, p. 143; NA Adm 36/16232.

p.224 'Daniel Fitzpatrick, a twenty-eight-year-old', Wyndham-Quin, p. 143; NA Adm 36/16232.

p.224 'According to the account of Manuel Ferrer,' Ferrer de Couto, p. 158.

p.225 'he told me I must try;' Benjamin to his father Thomas Clement, 30 November 1805, Clement, pp. 479–80.

p.227 'Pepe, tell your sister', *Elogio histórico del Brigadier de la Real Armada D. Cosme Damien de Churruca y Elorza* (Madrid, 1806), p. 83.

p.227 'For a while *San Juan* fought on', *Elogio histórico*, pp. 86–9; Ferrer de Couto, pp. 142–5.

p.228 'seized by one of those inexplicable impulses,' Antonio Alcalá Galiano, *Memorias*, pp. 97–8.

p.229 'The wind from one shot', ibid., pp. 102–3.

p.229 'He held a council of officers', Desbrière, vol. II, p. 409; Ferrer de Couto, pp. 155–6.

p.229 'It must be admitted that the Dons', King and Hattendorf, p. 161.

p.230 'we, wearing quicker,' NA Adm 51/1516.

p.230 'As we were the only ship', Edward to Jane Codrington, 30 October 1805, Bourchier, p. 64.

p.230 'and going close under his stern', ibid.

p.230 'and as it was almost a calm', Desbriere, vol. II, p. 268 (BB⁴ 237, f. III).

p.231 'had therefore to undergo', Edward to Jane Codrington, 30 October 1805, Bourchier, p. 65.

p.232 'It had been my unvarying rule' and following quotations, NMM MSS JON/7 (Cumby, pp. 725–6).

p.232 'each viewing the other with glistening arms' and following quotations, NMM MSS/77/163.

p.234 'On *Aigle* Lieutenant Huissier', Desbrière, vol. II, pp. 242–3.

p.235 'with what anxiety every eye turned', Allen, pp. 283–4.

p.235 'and turned the hands up', NA Adm 51/1515.

p.236 'Will no one bring Hardy to me?' and following quotations, King and Hattendorf, p. 176.

16 Death or Victory

p.239 'but a few minets to take a peep', private collection, 'Book Concerning the Batle of Trafalgar', ff. 25–6.

p.240 'but we could not get within three cables', Codrington to Lord Garlies, 28 October 1805, Bourchier, p. 60.

p.241 'one would like to live a little longer', and following quotations, King and Hattendorf, p. 178.

p.243 'According to Jean-Jacques Lucas', 'Rapport du Capne. De Vau. Lucas', SHM Vincennes CC⁷ dossier Lucas; Fraser, *Enemy*, p. 170.

p.243 'according to Midshipman Henry Walker', Tracy (ed.), *Naval Chronicle*, p. 229.

p.245 'Our crew was understrength', Gicquel, p. 416.

p.245 'Though she was supposed to be an eighty', ibid.

p.246 'During the lull that followed Gicquel offered', Gicquel, p. 422.

p.247 'It was seeing Leviathan so harassed', Codrington to Bayntun, 26 October 1805, NMM MSS AGC/C/11.

p.247 'After several fruitless attempts', Edward to Jane Codrington, 31 October 1805, Bourchier, p. 65.

p.247 'and said he hoped, laughing', ibid., Bourchier, p. 66.

p.247 'Auguste Gicquel saw *Orion* coming', Gicquel, pp. 419–20.

p.247 'to get our starboard guns to bear', Edward to Jane Codrington, 31 October 1805, Bourchier, p. 66.

p.248 'François Grévillot was one of the ship's old hands', Gicquel, p. 422.

p.248 'Doctor, I have not been a great sinner', and following quotations, King and Hattendorf, pp. 179–80.

p.249 '*Neptuno* fought on for fifty minutes', NMM MSS 9735; Desbrière, vol. II, p. 399; Sturges Jackson, pp. 275–6.

p.250 'One of those still below was a woman', Fraser, *Enemy*, pp. 223–4. Her name is taken from *Revenge*'s muster book, NA Adm 36/16545.

p.251 'under the direction of Lieutenant Mainwaring', NMM MSS HIS/37.

p.251 'was not very violent', Desbrière, vol. II, p. 288.

p.251 'The hull burst into a cloud', Fraser, *Enemy*, p. 221.

p.252 'floating by the assistance of the ship's quarter billboard', NMM MSS HIS/37.

p.252 'Lieut. Mainwaring and Mr. Anthony', ibid.

p.252 'For the Spanish, the historian Ferrer de Couto', Ferrer de Couto, p. 167.

p.253 'It had got very late in the day', Antonio Alcalá Galiano, *Memorias*, pp. 97–8.

17 The Dangers of a Lee Shore

p.256 'a known sign of an approaching gale': see the memorandum given to the fleet off Cadiz, which was on at least two ships, *Leviathan* (Bedfordshire Record Office X170 7/2) and *Naiad*, NMM MSS HIS/37.

p.256 'This had risen': the page of observations for October 1805 is reproduced in Wheeler, p. 363.

p.256 'Anchor the fleet?', James, vol. IV, pp. 83–4. James seems to have spoken to Hardy, who took a dim view of Collingwood's course of action.

p.257 'at this time our object was to go to Gibraltar', Eliab to Louisa Harvey, 23 October 1805, Sturges Jackson, p. 226. Hercules Robinson, who rowed Harvey across to *Euryalus* in their jolly-boat, said that he was the only Captain Collingwood saw before writing his first dispatch on 22 October, Robinson, *Sea Drift*, p. 217.

p.257 'Eager inquiries were expressed', Allen, p. 285.

p.258 'I found no living person on her deck', ibid., p. 145.

p.258 'were lying beside each other', and following quotations, ibid., p. 285.

p.259 'reeking from the cockpit', ibid., p. 146.

p.259 'as each officer and seaman would meet', King and Hattendorf, pp. 163–4.

p.259 'If you look straight into the wound', 'Memories of the Battle of Trafalgar', *Notes and Queries*, 6th series, vol. IV, p. 504.

p.260 'a very powerful and resolute woman', ibid.

p.260 '*Monarca* had a physician', Muster book of *Leviathan*, Bedfordshire Record Office X170, 2/2.

p.260 'The surgeon and his mate', Lavery, *Nelson's Navy*, p. 215.

p.261 'I thank you, stay where you are;' letter from Henry Bayntun, in Tracy (ed.), *Naval Chronicle*, vol. XV, p. 16–17.

p.261 'severely burnt over his forehead', NA Adm 101/106/1, 'Journal of *Leviathan*, Wm Shoveller, surgeon'.

p.261 'marines lay on the Forecastle', RNM MSS 1998/41/1.

p.262 'a melancholy instance', Senhouse, p. 419.

p.263 'It is impossible to conceive why', Ekins, p. 301.

p.263 'If Lord Nelson had lived', Senhouse, p. 420.

p.264 'observed that the *Euryalus*,' NMM MSS JON/7 (Cumby, p. 726).

p.264 'At 7.36, took aback,' Sturges Jackson, p. 153.

p.265 'now and then tugging at the waistband', BL Add MS 38048 cited in Lavery, *Nelson's Fleet*, pp. 185–6.

p.265 'about four hours too late', James, vol. IV, p. 87.

p.265 'found the decks both above and below', Huskisson, p. 74.

p.266 'in order to give such assistance', Desbrière, vol. II, p. 243.

p.266 'being near the shoals of Trafalgar', Sturges Jackson, p. 254.

p.267 'found she was very leaky', NMM MSS 9735.

p.267 'Our first night's work', Fraser, *Enemy*, p. 272.

p.268 'with a rope to take her in tow', Sturges Jackson, p. 280.

p.268 'According to the notebook of *Naiad*'s master', NMM MSS HIS/37.

p.269 'People who are ignorant', Bedfordshire Record Office, Bayntun papers X170.

p.271 'The Reverend John Greenly', RNM MSS 1984/14 (130); Henry to his mother Mrs R. Walker, 22 November 1805, Sturges Jackson, p. 327.

p.272 'We spent the whole of that night', 'Rapport du Capne. De Vau. Lucas', SHM Vincennes CC⁷ dossier Lucas; Fraser, *Enemy*, p. 170.

p.272 'Commander François Bazin reported', Desbrière, vol. II, p. 236.

p.272 'the scenes of horror on board the ship', Fraser, *Enemy*, p. 298.

18 The Seaman's Last Shift

p.276 'in the morning I ran down', NMM MSS AGC/C/11, Codrington to Bayntun, 26 October 1805.

p.276 'three whole hawsers', Sturges Jackson, p. 308.

p.276 '*Aigle* had "rolled away" all of her masts', Desbrière, vol. II, p. 243.

p.277 'By mid-morning with seventeen other', Fraser, *Enemy*, pp. 298–9; NA Adm 37/18.

p.279 'she should be abandoned to the French', ibid.

p.279 'prevailed upon the officer', ibid.

p.279 'Got all on board except Lieutenant Purchase', Sturges Jackson, p. 255.

p.279 'to rejoin the main body', Desbrière, vol. II, p. 256.

p.279 'great sea and fresh wind', Collingwood's journal, in Sturges Jackson, pp. 204–5.

p.280 'the wind continued to increase', NMM MSS 9735.

p.281 'This desperate situation', Nichelson, p. 104.

p.282 'fired distress signals', Desbrière, vol. II, p. 244.

p.282 'Acting Captain François Bazin estimated later', Desbrière, vol. II, p. 236; *Téméraire*'s losses from Adm 36/15851.

p.282 'from her rolling so violently', Fraser, *Enemy*, p. 299.

p.283 'Few officers of any experience', Lavery, *Nelson's Navy*, p. 189.

p.284 'What added to the horrors of the night', Fraser, *Enemy*, p. 300.

p.284 'drag into his boat', ibid., p. 302.

p.284 'This was the most dreadful scene', ibid., pp. 300–1.

p.285 'When the Boats came alongside', ibid., p. 301; 'Rapport du Capne. De Vau. Lucas' f. 8, SHM Vincennes CC[7] dossier Lucas; Fraser, *Enemy*, p. 171. Ultimately, Lucas reported, all the wounded were sent into Cadiz under a flag of truce, and in the end only thirty-five men from the *Redoutable* were taken to England as prisoners-of-war. NA Adm 36/16549.

p.285 'merely formalised and adopted', Wheeler, p. 366. In Wheeler's judgement 'The terms then employed almost certainly equate to their present-day definitions.'

p.286 'cut away the fore and main courses', Bedfordshire Record Office X170 2/1.

p.286 'committed the body of Captain Duff', NA Adm 51/1493.

p.286 'all adrift, the clewlings', Senhouse, p. 420.

p.286 'the only officer that volunteered', ibid.

p.287 'The circumstances were as urgent', 'The Report of the Recapture and Loss of the Line-of-Battle Ship Bucentaure, by Commander Prigny', BB[4] 237, f. 253, Desbrière, vol. II, p. 199.

p.288 'promised to take the ship', Report of Lieutenant Fulcran Fournier of the *Bucentaure*, BB[4] 237 f. 97, Desbrière, vol. II, p. 202.

p.289 'felt a very severe shock', Desbrière, vol. II, pp. 202–3.

p.289 'We worked all night', ibid., p. 200.

p.290 'the *Bucentaure* and another ship', and following quotations, ibid., p. 257; see also de la Bretonnière's report, BB[4] 237 ff. 241–3.

p.291 'terrorized the Indian seas', Harry Parker, *Naval Battles from the collection of prints formed and owned by Commander Sir Charles Leopold Cust* (London: T. H. Parker, 1911), p. 154.

19 Cosmao's Sortie

p.295 'According to the Spanish account', log of *Principe de Asturias* in Quadrado, p. 153.

p.296 'The rumour was even going round', Antonio Alcalá Galiano, *Memorias*, p. 99.

p.297 'I hurried to see general the marquis of Solana', and following quotations, ibid., p. 100.

p.298 'Night closed in', Quadrado, p. 154.

p.298 'contrary to propaganda', *Gibraltar Chronicle*, 9 November 1805. The report can be read in NMM LBK/38. For its veracity see James, vol. IV, p. 89.

p.299 'the watchman in the Tavira Tower confirmed', Museo Naval, Madrid, MSS MS 2398.

p.299 'In his report Cosmao claimed', Desbrière, vol. II, p. 237 (BB[4] 237 f. 182).

p.300 'Henry Bayntun in *Leviathan* repeated to Collingwood': see her rough log in Bedfordshire Record Office X170 2/1.

p.301 'about three oclock cleared away the best bower', and following quotations, NMM MSS 9735.

p.302 'in a calm, heavy swell, and violent rain', and following quotations, Edward to Jane Codrington, 31 October 1805, Bourchier, p. 66.

p.303 'According to Henry Walker', Tracy (ed.), *Naval Chronicle*, p. 231, where he referred to *Leviathan* as 'the first British ship we had seen for the last thirty hours'.

p.304 'steered amid the breakers', Desbrière, vol. II, p. 244.

p.304 'where whe brought up', NMM MSS 9735.

p.304 'They were not men', Pelayo Alçalá Galiano, p. 589.

p.305 'in a sinking condition', Desbrière, vol. II, p. 238.

p.305 'most fortunately the wind shifted', ibid., p. 259.

p.306 'parted from our Ankers', and following quotations, NMM MSS 9735.

p.307 'on the following and succeeding days', Desbrière, vol. II, p. 400.

p.307 'According to Antonio Alcalá Galiano', Antonio Alcalá Galiano, *Recuerdos*, pp. 37–8.

20 Sink, Burn, and Destroy

p.309 'The meteorological historian Dennis Wheeler': see Wheeler, pp. 380–82. The Trafalgar storm readings are within the lowest 5 per cent of all the readings taken there since 1950.

p.310 'a violent gale came on the Tuesday evening,' Charles to Margaret Tyler, 3 November 1805, NMM MSS TYL/1 (Wyndham-Quin, p. 149).

p.310 'the worst hurricane I ever saw', Codrington to Lord Garlies, 28 October 1805, Bourchier, p. 61.

p.310 'the danger of being wrecked', Codrington to William Bethell, 6 March 1806, Bourchier, p. 76.

p.311 'hard and grievous to be obliged', Codrington to William Bethell, 15 November 1805, Bourchier, p. 73.

p.311 'a very fine boy but too mild', NMM MSS AGC/33/9.

p.312 'We have been in constant apprehension', Eliab to Louisa Harvey, 28 October 1805, Sturges Jackson, pp. 226–7.

p.312 '2 anchors, pinnace, 2 cutters', NA Adm 51/1516.

p.312 'Strong gales, dark misty weather', Sturges Jackson, p. 253.

p.312 'In this state we experienced as heavy a gale', Benjamin to his father Thomas Clement, 30 November 1805, Clement, p. 480.

p.313 'in a constant state of intoxication', Henry to his mother Mrs R. Walker, 22 November 1805, Sturges Jackson, p. 326.

p.313 'but in the prize,' and following quotations, Tracy (ed.), *Naval Chronicle*, p. 231.

p.316 'By the morning he had reached a decision,' Sturges Jackson, p. 206.

p.316 'all but about 150 prisoners', Tracy (ed.), *Naval Chronicle*, p. 231.

p.316 'Sir William Bolton's *Eurydice* came to an anchor', NA Adm 51/1591.

p.317 'We were riding close in shore', Reid, p. 60.

p.317 'to take the Argonauta in tow', Sturges Jackson, p. 256.

p.317 'in order to assist at the pumps', King and Hattendorf, p. 167.

p.318 'Auguste Gicquel noticed', Gicquel, p. 421.

p.319 'Her top-sides, it is true,' Lovell, pp. 50–1.

p.319 'during the two days that we remained', Desbrière, vol. II, pp. 402 and 406.

p.319 'she had between 3 and 400 killed and wounded,' *English Historical Review*, 5 (1890), p. 769.

p.319 'We had to tie the poor mangled wretches', Fraser, *Enemy*, pp. 316–17.

p.320 'They had put off from the starboard quarter', ibid., pp. 314–15.

p.321 'The ship laboured excessively', Allen, p. 288.

p.322 'The increasing storm', and following quotations, ibid., pp. 289–90

p.323 'At this time our fate appeared inevitable', ibid., p. 147.

p.323 'When we got round, the breakers were distinctly seen', ibid., p. 290.

p.324 'When we arrived near our anchorage', ibid., p. 291.

p.324 'Having heard of the action', Hubback, pp. 156–7.

21 The Worst Hurricane I Ever Saw

p.326 'thick, grey, smoky', Conrad, *Mirror of the Sea*, p. 83.

p.327 'We shipped three heavy seas', NMM MSS Wel/30.

p.327 'A great wave smashed into the stern gallery', Collingwood, pp. 142–3.

p.327 'very near foundering', NMM MSS LBK/38.

p.327 'Never did ships experience', James to George Robinson, 12 December 1805, RNM MSS 1992/133.

p.328 'Our masts we Strengthaned by Anchor Stocks', private collection, 'Book Concerning the Batle of Trafalgar', f. 30.

p.329 'Finding they were steering for Gibraltar', Cumby to Collingwood, 27 October 1805, NMM MSS PRY7.

p.329 'Our anchor did not hold', and following quotation, Dillon, p. 59.

p.330 'but the heavy seas did not allow', and following quotations, Desbrière, vol. II, p. 260.

p.332 'From Cadiz the Marquis of Solana wrote repeatedly', Museo Naval, Madrid, MSS MS 1399, ff. 132–44.

p.333 'The wind had just hauled into the south-west', and following quotation, Desbrière, vol. II, p. 244.

p.333 'as a Spanish witness reported', BL Egerton MS 382 f. 41 (Nicolas, vol. VII, p. 291).

p.333 'The figures given by French historian Edouard Desbrière', Desbrière, vol. I, p. 298.

p.334 'hysterical witnesses declared', Egerton, p. 382, f. 41 says she had 300 men from *Bucentaure* on board in addition to her own crew and that 160 were saved; Pernot (Dillon, pp. 59–60) that she had 1400 men on board and 150 were saved.

p.334 'No account gives more', Desbrière, vol. I, p. 298 gives two officers and 178 men; NA Adm 36/16250.

p.334 'Thursday night, or Friday morning', Bayntun to Hope, 27 October 1805 (Collingwood, p. 143). Some Spanish figures mention 103 survivors of *Monarca* who may have been saved from the wreck on the Arenas Gordas (Desbrière, vol. II, p. 430).

p.334 'two of the prizes driving past us', Sturges Jackson, p. 289.

p.335 'The squall & partial shift', NMM MSS AGC/C/11, Codrington to Bayntun, 26 October 1805.

p.335 'according to *Orion*'s muster book', NA Adm 37/18.

p.335 'to receive the people from the prize', NMM MSS AGC/C/11, Codrington to Bayntun, 26 October 1805.

p.335 'all the dead remained', *Revista de Historia Naval*, vol. 52.

p.335 'the numbers in the British muster books', NA Adm 36/15837 *Leviathan*, 36/15955, *Dreadnought*, 36/16538 *Ajax*, 36/16549 *Swiftsure*, and 37/18 *Orion* list 610 men evacuated. The crew of *San Agustín* was 711 so, although there may be some confusion in the British muster books, it is difficult to accommodate the 180 reported killed, no matter about the limbless wounded.

p.335 'our enemies generously', Desbrière, vol. II, p. 401.

p.335 'L'Intrépide's Capt. my present messmate', NMM MSS AGC/C/11, Codrington to Bayntun, 26 October 1805.

p.335 'On *Orion* I was reunited with Captain Infernet', Gicquel, p. 423.

p.336 'Since I came here on Thursday forenoon', and following quotation, Bayntun to Hope, October 1805 (Collingwood, p. 143).

p.336 '600 Spaniards on board and most of them drunk', and following quotations, Colin Campbell to his father, 3 December 1805, Smith, 'The *Defiance* at Trafalgar', pp. 119–20.

p.337 'You see, sir, there is very little hope', and following quotations, Bayntun to Hope, 27 October 1805 (Collingwood, p. 143).

p.338 *'Donegal*'s master, William Dunbar', as Dunbar subsequently told Codrington after transferring to *Orion*, Codrington to William Bethell, 15 November 1805, p. 73.

p.338 'towards the dangerous shoals', and following quotation, NMM MSS LBK/38.

p.338 'spoke one of the enemy's hulks', Sturges Jackson, p. 321.

p.339 'totally lost having parted asunder', ibid., p. 311.

p.339 'dark rainy weather', NA Adm 51/1535.

p.339 'Perhaps the saving the lives', Codrington to William Bethell, 15 November 1805, Bourchier, p. 73.

22 The Mercy of God

p.341 'My mother moaned and looked away', Antonio Alcalá Galiano, *Memorias*, p. 101.

p.343 'Nelson and his Englishmen', BL Egerton MSS 382 f. 28 (Nicolas, vol. VII, p. 290).

p.342 'Scarcely a third part remains', BL Egerton MSS 382 f. 41 (Nicolas, vol. VII, p. 291).

p.342 'The rest,' Pernot commented bitterly', Dillon, p. 60.

p.343 'This last Week has been a scene of Anxiety', Thomas to Betsy Fremantle, 28 October 1805, Fremantle, p. 221

p.343 'The Prisoners we have on board', *English Historical Review*, 5 (1890), p. 769.

p.343 'Adml. Villeneuve was with me on board', and following quotations, Thomas to Betsy Fremantle, 28 October 1805, Fremantle, pp. 221–2.

p.344 'a reassuring report on the enemy's remaining strength', NMM MSS/ 76/001.

p.345 'The greatest part have lost nearly all their masts', Francis Austen to Mary Gibson, 31 October 1805, Hubback, p. 158.

p.345 'On standing in to reconnoitre', Hubback, p. 161.

p.345 'Midshipman Hercules Robinson accompanied Blackwood', Robinson, *Sea Drift*, p. 207.

p.346 'Anxious relatives went to Duff's house', Antonio Alcalá Galiano, *Recuerdos*, p. 40.

p.346 *'Euryalus*, with Admiral Collingwood on board', and following quotation, Edward to Jane Codrington, 31 October 1805, Bourchier, p. 65.

p.346 'is now getting to rights', and following quotations, Edward to Jane Codrington, 30 October 1805, Bourchier, p. 63.

p.346 'The scenes at the wharfs', and following quotations, Tracy (ed.), *Naval Chronicle*, p. 238.

p.347 'Gabriel Daudignon, first lieutenant of *Bucentaure*', SHN CC⁷ dossier Daudignon.

p.347 'How many marquises in France', and following quotations, Dillon, p. 60.

p.348 'a carriage was backed into the water', and following quotations, Codrington to William Bethell, 15 November 1805, Bourchier, p. 73.

p.348 'whe where lodged in Prison', and following quotations, MSS 9735.

p.349 'Now the Spanish prisoners', Fraser, *Enemy*, pp. 339–40, from 'a seaman of the *Spartiate*'.

p.349 'Three men from *Donegal*', NA Adm 36/16502.

p.350 'plenty of mutton', Colin Campbell to his father, 3 December 1805, Smith 'The *Defiance* at Trafalgar', p. 120.

p.351 'My doubts and those of my family', Antonio Alcalá Galiano, *Memorias*, pp. 101–2.

p.351 'Hercules Robinson, who rowed Captain Eliab Harvey', Robinson, *Sea Drift*, p. 217.

p.351 'I am under the most serious apprehensions', and following quotations, NMM MSS/76/001.

p.353 'As our admiral is not come in', and following quotations, Codrington to Lord Garlies, 4 November 1805, Bourchier, p. 70.

p.354 '"Our unhappy ship," wrote Captain Gemähling', Fraser, *Enemy*, p. 234.

p.355 'In *Victory* Henry Cramwell's splinter wounds developed into gangrene', NA Adm 101/125/1.

p.355 'Mr. Burnett, Surgeon on board the *Defiance*', Fraser, *Sailors*, p. 317.

p.355 'in great pain from the sudden jerking', and following quotations, NMM MSS/77/163.

p.356 'walking around in good health & spirits', and following quotations, NA Adm 101/106/1.

p.357 'As far as the eye could reach,' Tracy (ed.), *Naval Chronicle*, p. 238.

23 We All Cry for Him

p.359 'I never heard of his equal', Francis Austen to Mary Gibson, 27 October 1805, Hubback, p. 156.

p.359 'We have been so busy', NMM MS 80/201.

p.360 'What Better End can Best of Heros Claim', private collection, 'Book Concerning the Batle of Trafalgar', f. 39.

p.360 'Great and glorious as our victory is', Edward to Jane Codrington, 4 December 1805, Bourchier, p. 84.

p.360 'Sir, we have gained a great victory', and following quotation, Pope, *England Expects*, p. 37, and Fraser, *Enemy*, p. 352.

p.361 'I sent to enquire who was arrived', Dorothy M. Stuart, *Dearest Bess* (London, 1955) cited in Fraser, *Beloved Emma*, p. 326.

p.361 'there was a vast rush of people', Fraser, *Enemy*, p. 356.

p.361 'The scene at the Admiralty', Pope, *England Expects*, p. 39.

p.362 'there had been a grand action', Bourchier, p. 85

p.362 'I was much alarmed by Nelly's ghastly appearance', and following quotations, Fremantle, p. 216, Betsy's diary for 7 November.

p.362 'I believe that a more unpleasant task', Tracy (ed.), *Naval Chronicle*, vol. XV, p. 274.

p.363 'My Dear Mamma,' Tracy (ed.), *Naval Chronicle*, p. 194.

p.363 'caused a general consternation', Leyland, pp. 367–8.

p.363 'the loss on board the Fleet', *Gazeta de Madrid*, 5 November 1805, in BL MSS Egerton 382, translated for Nicolas, vol. VII, p. 286.

p.364 'My father's silence, and uncertainty about his fate', SHM CC[7] dossier Baudouin.

p.364 'I have just been informed by private letters', SHM CC[7] dossier Briamant.

p.364 '1087 wounded Spaniards and 253 Frenchmen': the figure for the wounded handed to the cartels was given by Fraser, p. 380, without source. That for Gibraltar is an official figure, which was republished from London papers in the *Norwich Mercury* on 8 February 1806. Suspiciously, Abell (p. 45) gives exactly the same figure for French prisoners brought to England. The figure of 3000 is arrived at by adding figures from muster books (a rough rather than a reliable guide because transfers between ships are difficult to trace). A similar number must have been taken by Strachan.

p.365 'his wife and family are at Toulon', and following quotation, Edward to Jane Codrington, 14 November 1805, Bourchier, p. 81.

p.365 'The roof of the room formed one capacious awning', and following quotations, *Norwich Mercury*, 30 November, 7 December, 14 December 1805.

p.366 'Publishers printed lives of Nelson', ibid., 14 December 1805.

p.367 'blown his brains out', Dillon, p. 58.

p.367 'I think the French will be driven out of Spain and Portugal', and following quotation, Collingwood to Tyler, 16 July 1808, NMM TYL/1 (Wyndham-Quin, pp. 166–7).

24 The Empire of the Ocean

p.371 'Such was the End of this Expedetion', private collection, 'Book Concerning the Batle of Trafalgar', ff. 37–8.

p.371 'So incomprehensible was its apparent sterility', Corbett, p. 408.

p.371 'the most terrible catastrophe', Dillon, p. 57.

p.372 'We did not win the battle of Trafalgar', cited in Crouzet, p. 550.

p.372 'with great pride he used to recount', Fraser, *Enemy*, p. 259.

p.373 '*Il rompait todos*', Robinson, *Sea Drift*, p. 206.

p.374 'In my opinion if the officers had done their duty', NMM MSS JOD/48.

p.376 'according to Fournier's account, "massacred"' SHM CC[7] dossier Fournier.

p.377 'I have often remarked the generous hearts', Gicquel, p. 425.

p.378 'a French man Came on Bord of us', private collection, 'Book Concerning the Batle of Trafalgar', f. 41.

p.379 'Lines on a Young Gentleman', RNM MSS 1998/41/1.

p.379 'happy times never more to be recalled', NMM TYL/1 (Wyndham-Quin, p. 168).

p.380 'I am a dying man', *Diary of the first Earl of Malmesbury*, vol. IV, 354, in Fraser, *Enemy*, p. 409.

Bibliography

Bedford, Bedfordshire Record Office

X170 Henry William Bayntun papers

London, British Library

Add Mss 34931 Nelson's incoming correspondence September–October 1805
Egerton 382 Spanish volume on Trafalgar
Egerton 1614 Emma Hamilton's letters from Nelson

London, National Archives

Adm 1/5330–5450
5344 Court Martial of James Morris, 16 April 1798
5346 Court Martial of Charles Tyler, 10 September 1798
5370 Court Martial of Nathaniel Fish, 18 September 1805

Adm 36 Muster Books
15754 *Royal Sovereign*; 15813–4 *Belleisle*; 15818 and 15825 *Colossus*; 15837
Leviathan; 15851 *Téméraire*; 15900 *Victory*; 15942 *Defence*; 15955 *Dreadnought*;
15996 *Britannia*; 16002 *Spartiate*; 16055 *Minotaur*; 16227–8, 16232 *Tonnant*;
16244 *Defiance*; 16250 *Conqueror*; 16262–3 *Mars*; 16274 *Prince*; 15636–40,
16488–9 *Neptune*; 12458, 15590, 16498 *Bellerophon*; 16502 *Donegal*; 16507
Polyphemus; 16520 *Agamemnon*; 16538 *Ajax*; 16545 *Revenge*; 16549 *Swiftsure*;
16607 *Entreprenante*; 16786–7 *Melpomene*; 16964 *Eurydice*; 15708 *Blanche*

Adm 37 Muster Books
18 *Orion*; 52 *Achille*; 99 *Africa*; 192–3 *Thunderer*

Adm 51 Captains' Logs
1493 *Mars*; 1515 *Belleisle*; 1516 *Colossus*; 1518 *Africa*; 1522 *Bellerophon*; 1528 and
1591 *Melpomene*; 1529 *Conqueror*; 1535 *Donegal, Achille, Revenge*; 1544 *Polyphemus*; 1545 *Neptune*; 1547 *Tonnant*

Adm 101 Surgeons' Journals
101/90/1 *Bellerophon* 1803–4; 101/94/4 *Colossus* 1803–4; 101/106/1 *Leviathan*;
101/112/8 *Pickle*; 101/125/1 *Victory*

Adm 160 Naval Ordnance Dept
160/150 proportion tables of ordnance for HM ships
160/154 returns of ordnance on HM ships

FO 72/55: consuls' reports from Spain
WO 55/1832–3: returns of ships and armament May 1798–October 1805

London, National Maritime Museum

MSS/77/163 James Spratt memoir
MSS/80/201.2 Diary of Richard Anderson
MSS/84/058.1 Thomas Huskisson account
MSS/88/054.7 Edward Nosworthy manuscripts
HIS/37 Harry Andrews commonplace book
BNY/2 Henry Bayntun letterbook
CRK/4 Letters to Nelson from James Duff
JOD/48 Journal of William Pringle Green
JON/7 William Cumby letter to his son Anthony
LBK/38 Edward Rotheram commonplace book
NMM PRY/1–11 William Cumby order books and letterbooks
AGC/8/15 Morris to Collingwood, 3 November 1805
AGC/33/9 Letter about John Markland
AGC/C/7 Letter from Thomas Connell in *Dreadnought*

AGC/C/11 Codrington to Bayntun 26 October 1805
AGC/H/18 William Hennah letters
AGC/M/5 Robert Moorsom letters
AGC/M/9 John Mason, quartermaster of *Africa*
AGC/N/11 Paul Harris Nicholas of *Belleisle*
Wel/30 William Rivers notes
TYL/1 Charles Tyler papers
ADM/L/C/167 Lieutenant's log for HMS *Colossus*
MSS 9735 William Thorp account
MSN/1 Diary of Henry Mason, *Prince*
TUN/61 Signal book with Nelson's special signal
MSS/76/001 Collingwood's secret letterbook

Madrid, Museo Naval

MS 1399 Correspondence on Trafalgar
Misc MS 1927 Secret report on the state of the English navy 1793
Misc MS 2162 f. 48 Escaño's list of casualties
Misc MS 2200, doc. 51, f. 119 Churruca's widow's appeal
MS 2238 Combate de Trafalgar, Cartagena Departamento, doc. 73, ff. 254–8
MS 2273 Gravina to Gil y Lemus, 28 July 1805
MS 2398 Copy of diary of Tavira watchtower, Cadiz
MS 10905 Gravina letter

Viso del Marqués, Archivo General de Marina Álvaro de Bazán,

Leg 620/522 summary of Gravina file

Paris, Service Historique de la Marine, Château de Vincennes

BB[4] 230 minutes of the council of war of 8 October 1805
BB[4] 237 'Batailles de Trafalgar et du Cap Ortegal', volume of reports and
other documents including some material that was not published by

Desbrière, such as de la Bretonnière's report on the recapture of *Algésiras*
CC[7] Dossiers on individual officers: Louis Baudouin; François Bazin; Voldemar de la Bretonnière; François Briamant; Désiré Clamart; Asmus Classen; Julien Cosmao; Joseph Daudignon; Louis Deniéport; Alexandre Ducrest; Henri Dupotet; Fulcran Fournier; Auguste Gicquel; Pierre Gourrège; Louis Infernet; Jean-Jacques Lucas; Charles Magon; Louis Tanguy

Portsmouth, Royal Marines Museum

11/12/1 Letters of Lewis Roteley

Portsmouth, Royal Naval Museum

MSS 1983/1064 Boatswain's and carpenters' account book, HMS *Victory*
MSS 1998/41/1 William Rivers papers
MSS 25 Letter and sketch by John Wells, quartermaster in HMS *Britannia*
1963/1 Letter from Able Seaman Benjamin Stevenson, HMS *Victory*
1984/494 Journal kept by Midshipman Richard Roberts, HMS *Victory*
1992/133 Letter from James Robinson, HMS *Mars*
1992/414 Letter from Samuel Rickards, purser HMS *Leviathan*
1994/128 Anonymous account with sketch, HMS *Victory*
1984/14 (129–130) Copies of two letters from Reverend J. Greenly, Chaplain of HMS *Revenge*
1984/14(136) Copy of letter from unknown seaman HMS *Royal Sovereign*
1988/464 Photocopy of letter from Lieutenant C. West of HMS *Minotaur*

Private collections

James Martin, 'Book Concerning the Batle of Trafalgar'
Account by William Westemberg

Abell, F., *Prisoners of War in Britain, 1756–1814*, London: Oxford University Press, 1914
Acerra, Martine and André Zysberg, *L'Essor des Marines de Guerre Européennes 1680–1790*, Paris: Sedes, 1997.
Addis, C. P., *The men who fought with Nelson in HMS Victory at Trafalgar*, Portsmouth: Nelson Society, 1988

Bibliography

Albion, Robert Greenhalgh, *Forests and Sea Power: the Timber Problem of the Royal Navy 1652–1862*, Cambridge, Massachusetts: Harvard Economic Studies XXIX, 1926

Alcalá Galiano, Antonio, *Recuerdos de un anciano*, Madrid, 1878.

Memorias de D. Antonio Alcalá Galiano, 2 vols, Madrid: Enrique Rubiños, 1886

Alcalá Galiano, Pelayo, *El combate de Trafalgar*, 2 vols, Madrid: Ministerio de Marina, 1909–1930

Allen, Joseph (ed.), *Memoirs of the Life and Services of Admiral Sir William Hargood*, Greenwich: Henry Richardson, 1841

Baynham, Henry, *From the Lower Deck*, London: Hutchinson, 1969

Bennett, Geoffrey, *Nelson the Commander*, London: Batsford, 1972 (Penguin Classic, 2002)

The Battle of Trafalgar, Annapolis, Maryland: Naval Institute Press, 1977

Bérenger, Jean *et al.*, *L'Europe à la fin du XVIIIᵉ siècle*, Paris: Sedes, 1985

Bergeron, Louis, *France under Napoleon*, transl. R. R. Palmer, Princeton: Princeton University Press, 1981

Bevan, A. B., and H. B. Wolryche-Whitmore, (eds), *A Sailor of King George: The Journals of Captain Frederick Hoffman*, 1901

Blackwood, 'Memoirs of Vice-Admiral . . . Blackwood', *Blackwood's Edinburgh Magazine*, XXXIV (July 1833), 210, pp. 7–8

Boada y Gonzales Llanos, L., 'Algunos aspectos de la Marinera española en los años previos al del combate de Trafalgar', *Revista de Historia Naval*, XI (1985), pp. 5–21

Boudriot, Jean, *Le Vaisseau de 74 Canons*, 4 vols, Paris: Éditions J. Boudriot, 1986–8

'L'artillerie de Mer Française, part E: Deux Siècles d'Evolutions', *Neptunia*, CIII, pp. 33–8

Bourchier, Lady Jane (ed.), *Memoir of the Life of Admiral Sir Edward Codrington*, 2 vols, London: Longmans, Green, 1873

Paul Butel, 'Aspects généraux de l'économie européenne de 1780 à 1802' in *L'Europe à la fin du XVIIIᵉ siècle*, pp. 151–5

Castle, George, *Nelson Dispatch*, VI, part 8 (October 1998), p. 346

Clement, Benjamin, letter in *Cornhill Magazine*, new series, XXIV (January–June 1895), pp. 478–81

Coleman, Terry, *Nelson*, London: Bloomsbury, 2001

Collingwood, G. L. Newnham (ed.), *Correspondence and Memoirs of Vice-Admiral Lord Collingwood*, 1829

Corbett, Sir Julian, *The Campaign of Trafalgar*, London: Longmans, Green, 1910

Crouzet, François, *De la supériorité de l'Angleterre sur la France*, Paris: Librairie Academique Perrin, 1985

Cruz y Bahamonde, Conde de Maule, Nicolas de la, *De Cadiz y su Comercio (Tomo XIII del Viaje de España, Francia e Italia)*, ed. Manuel Ravina Martin, Cadiz: Universidad de Cadiz, 1997

Cumby, William Pryce, 'The Battle of Trafalgar: an unpublished Narrative', *The Nineteenth Century*, XLVI (November 1899), pp. 718–28

Desbrière, Edouard, *The Trafalgar Campaign*, transl. Constance Eastwick, 2 vols, Oxford: Clarendon Press, 1933

Dillon, William Henry, *A Narrative of my Professional Adventures (1790–1839)* (M. A. Lewis, ed.), London: Navy Records Society, XCVII (1956), pp. 57–60.

Duffy, Michael, *Soldiers, Sugar and Seapower*, Oxford: Clarendon Press, 1987 'Devon and the naval strategy of the French wars, 1689–1815' in *The New Maritime History of Devon*, Michael Duffy et al. (eds), 2 vols, London: Conway Maritime Press, 1992, I, pp. 182–91

Ekins, Sir Charles, *Naval Battles from 1744 to the Peace of 1814*, London: Baldwin, Cradock and Joy, 1824

Ellis, Lady (ed.), *Memoirs and Services of the Late Lieutenant-General Sir S. B. Ellis KCB, Royal Marines, from his own Memoranda*, London: Saunders, Otley, 1866

Elogio histórico del Brigadier de la Real Armada D. Cosme Damien de Churruca y Elorza, Madrid, 1806

Fernández de Castro, C., *El Almirante sin tacha y sin miedo. Vida del Capitán General de la Armada Española Don Federico Gravina y Napoli*, Cádiz: 1956.

Fernandez Duro, C., *La Armada española desde la unión de los reinos de Castilla y Aragón*, edn. facsímil, vol. VIII, Madrid, 1973 pp. 305–65

Ferrer de Couto, José, *Historia del combate naval de Trafalgar, precedida de la del renacimiento de la Marina española durante el siglo XVIII*, Madrid: Wenceslao Ayguals de Izco, 1854

Franco Castañon, Hermenegildo, 'Trafalgar, génesis de una seleccion', *Revista de Historia Naval*, VIII (1985), pp. 55–79

Fraser, Edward, *The Enemy at Trafalgar*, London: Hodder & Stoughton, n.d. [1906]

The Sailors Whom Nelson Led, London: Methuen, n.d. [1913] 'The Journal of Commander Thomas Colby 1797–1815', *Mariner's Mirror*, 13 (1927), pp. 259–71

Fraser, Flora, *Beloved Emma: the Life of Emma, Lady Hamilton*, London: Papermac, 1994

Fremantle, Anne (ed.), *The Wynne Diaries*, vol. III, Oxford: Oxford University Press, 1940

Gardiner, Robert (ed.), *The Campaign of Trafalgar*, London: Chatham Publishing, 1997

Gicquel des Touches, Auguste, 'Souvenirs d'un marin de la république', *Revue des Deux Mondes*, July 1905, 178 ff., August 1905, pp. 407–26

Glover, Richard, *Britain at Bay: Defence against Bonaparte 1803–14*, London: George Allen & Unwin, 1973

Godoy, Manuel de, *Principe de la Paz. Memorias*, vol. II, Madrid: Edición y estudio preliminar de Carlos Seco Serrano, 1956, pp. 41–60.

González-Aller, José Ignacio and Hugo O'Donnell, 'The Spanish Navy in the Eighteenth Century' in S. Howarth (ed.), *Battle of Cape St Vincent 200 Years*, Shelton, Notts: The 1805 Club, 1998, pp. 67–83

González-Ripoll Navarro, M. D., *A las órdenes de las estrellas (La vida del marino Cosme de Churruca y sus expediciones a América)*, Madrid: CSIC, 1995

Goodwin, Peter, 'Clearing for Action', *Battle of Cape St Vincent 200 Years*, Shelton, Notts: The 1805 Club, 1998, 1–7

'Where Nelson Died: an Historical Riddle Resolved by Archeology', *Mariner's Mirror*, LXXXV (1999), pp. 272–87

Nelson's Ships: a History of the Vessels in which he served 1771–1805, London: Conway Maritime Press, 2002

Guimerá, Agustín, 'Commerce and shipping in Spain during the Napoleonic Wars', in S. Howarth (ed.), *Battle of Cape St Vincent 200 Years*, Shelton, Notts: 1805 Club, 1998, pp. 22–37

'Godoy y la Armada', in M. A. Melón, E. La Parra and F. Tomás Perez (eds.), *Manuel Godoy y su tiempo Congreso Internacional 'Manuel Godoy (1767–1851)'*, Castuera-Olivenza-Badjoz, 3–6 Octubre 2001, Badajoz, Editora Regional de Extramadura, vol. 1, pp. 381–403

'Gravina y el liderazgo naval de su tiempo', in Guimerá, A., A. Ramos, and G., Butrón, (coords.), *Trafalgar y el mundo atlántico*, Madrid: Marcial Pons, Editores/Camara de Tenerife

Hamon, Jean Pierre, *Les chirurgiens navigants françaises de la bataille de Trafalgar, 21 octobre 1805*, Nantes: 1982–3

Harbron, John D., *Trafalgar and the Spanish Navy*, London: Conway Maritime Press, 1988

Hattendorf, John B., *et al.* (eds), *British Naval Documents 1204–1960*, Lodnon: Navy Records Society, CXXXI (1993)

Herpin, E., *Mémoires du chevalier de Fréminville (1787–1848)*, Paris: H. Champion, 1913

Hill, Richard, *The Prizes of War: The Naval Prize System in the Napoleonic Wars, 1793–1815*, Stroud: Sutton Publishing, 1998

Howarth, David, *Trafalgar: the Nelson Touch*, London: Collins, 1969

'The Man who lost Trafalgar', *Mariner's Mirror*, LXVV, (November 1971), 4, pp. 361–70

and Stephen Howarth, *Nelson: The Immortal Memory*, London: S. M. Dent & Sons Ltd, 1998

Hubback, J. H. and Edith, C., *Jane Austen's Sailor Brothers*, London: Bodley Head, 1906

Huskisson, Thomas, *Eyewitness to Trafalgar: Thomas Huskisson*, Orwell, Cambs: Ellisons editions [*c.* 1985]

Hyde de Neuville, Jean Guillaume, *Memoirs of Baron Hyde de Neuville, outlaw-exile-ambassador*, transl. F. Jackson, 2 vols., London: Sands & Co., 1914

Jackson, Hilary W., *A County Durham Man at Trafalgar: Cumby of the Bellerophon*, County Durham Local History Society [1998]

James, William, *The Naval History of Great Britain*, 5 vols, London, 1822–4

Jenkins, Ernest Harold, *A History of the French Navy*, London: Macdonald and Jane's, 1973

Keegan, John, *The Price of Admiralty*, London: Hutchinson, 1988

Kennedy, Ludovic, *Nelson and His Captains*, revised edn, London: Collins, 1975

King, Dean and John B. Hattendorf (eds.), *Every Man Will Do His Duty*, London: Conway Maritime Press, 1997

Lavery, Brian, *Nelson's Navy*, London: Conway Maritime Press, 1989
Nelson's Fleet at Trafalgar, London: National Maritime Museum, 2004

Legg, Stuart (ed.), *Trafalgar: an Eye-witness Account of a Great Battle*, London: Hart-Davis, 1966

Lewis, Michael, *A Social History of the Navy 1793–1815*, London: George Allen & Unwin, 1960

Leyland, John (ed.), *Dispatches and Letters Relating to the Blockade of Brest, 1803–1805*, vol. II, London: Navy Records Society (XXI 1902)

Lovell, William Stanhope, *Personal Narrative of Events 1799–1815*, London: William Allen, 1879

Mackenzie, Robert Holden, *The Trafalgar Roll: The Ships and the Officers*, London: George Allen, 1913

Maine, René, *Trafalgar: Napoleon's Naval Waterloo*, transl. R. Eldon and B. W. Robinson, London: Thames & Hudson, 1957

Marliani, Manuel, *Combate de Trafalgar Vindicación de la Armada Española*, Madrid: Impreso de Orden Superior, 1850
A Brief Memoir of the Life and Writings of the late William Marsden, DCL, FRS, privately printed, 1838

Marshall, John, *Royal Naval Biography*, 8 vols, London: 1823–35

Monaque, Remi, *Latouche-Tréville 1745–1804: l'amiral qui défiait Nelson*, Paris: SPM, 2000

Morriss, Roger, *The Royal Dockyards during the Revolutionary and Napoleonic Wars*, Leicester: Leicester University Press, 1983

Murray, Captain A., *Memoir of the Naval Life and Services of Admiral Sir Philip Durham*, London, pub 1846

Nichelson, William, *A Treatise on Practical Navigation and Seamanship*, London: for the author, 1792

Nicolas, Sir Nicholas Harris, *The Dispatches and Letters of Lord Nelson*, 7 vols, 1844–6 (reprinted London: Chatham Publishing, 1997)

Oman, Carola, *Nelson*, London: Hodder & Stoughton, 1947

Pavia, F. P., *Galería biográfica de los generales de marina, jefes y personajes notables que figuraron en la misma corporación desde 1700 a 1868*, Madrid, 1873

Perez Galdos, Benito, *Trafalgar*, 1873

Perrin, W. G., 'Notes on the development of bands in the Royal Navy', *Mariner's Mirror*, IX (1923), pp. 78–83

Phillips, Carla Rahn, ' "The Life Blood of the Navy": Recruiting Sailors in Eighteenth-Century Spain', *Mariner's Mirror*, LXXXVII (2001), pp. 420–45

Pocock, Tom, *Horatio Nelson*, London: Bodley Head, 1988

The Terror before Trafalgar, London: John Murray, 2002

Pope, Dudley, *England Expects: Nelson and the Trafalgar Campaign*, 1959, London: Chatham Publishing, 1998

Life in Nelson's Navy, London: George Allen & Unwin, 1981

Quadrado y De-Roo, F. P., *Elogio histórico del Excelentísimo Señor Don Antonio de Escaño, Teniente General de Marina . . . por Don . . . ministro plenipotenciario, etc., etc.,* Madrid, 1852

Ram, William Andrew, 'Letters of Lt William Andrew Ram, killed at Trafalgar', *Nelson Dispatch*, VI, part 5 (January 1998), pp. 184–7

Reid, Charles, letter in *Mariner's Mirror*, IX (1923), pp. 59–60

Robinson, Hercules, *Sea Drift*, Portsea: T. Hinton, 1858

Rodger, N. A. M., *The Wooden World: an Anatomy of the Georgian Navy*, London: Collins, 1986

'The inner life of the Navy, 1750–1800: change or decay?' in *Guerres et Paix 1600–1815*, Vincennes: Service historique de la marine, 1987

'Shipboard Life in the Georgian Navy, 1750–1800; the Decline of the Old Order?' in Lewis R. Fischer *et al.* (eds.), *The North Sea: Twelve Essays on the Social History of Maritime Labour*, Stavanger: 1992, pp. 29–39

'Devon Men and the Navy, 1688–1815', in Michael Duffy et al. (eds), *The New Maritime History of Devon*, London: Conway Maritime Press, 1992, I, pp. 209–15

'The Naval World of Jack Aubrey', in A. E. Cunningham (ed.), *Patrick O'Brian, Critical Appreciations and a Bibliography*, reprinted in P. O'Brian, *Desolation Island*, London: HarperCollins, 1996, pp. 329–50

'Image and Reality in Eighteenth-Century Naval Tactics', *Mariner's Mirror*, LXXXIX (August 2003), pp. 280–96

Rowbotham, W. B., 'Soldiers' and Seamen's Wives in HM Ships', *Mariner's Mirror*, 47 (1961), pp. 42–8

Schom, Alan, *Trafalgar: Countdown to Battle 1803–5*, London: Michael Joseph, 1990

Scott, Alexander John, *Recollections of the Life of the Rev. A. J. Scott, D.D.*, London, 1842, republished as *Nelson's Spy? The Life of Alexander Scott*, London: Meriden Publications, 2003

Senhouse, Humphrey, letter and memorandum in *Macmillan's Magazine*, LXXXI (April 1900), pp. 415–25

Shannon, David, '"In case I should fall in the noble cause . . ." – the short life of Midshipman Robert Smith', *Nelson Dispatch*, VI, (January 1998), pp. 188–90

Smith, D., *Napoleon's Regiments: Battle Histories of the Regiments of the French Army, 1792–1815*, London: Greenhill Books, 2000

Smith, David Baird, 'The *Defiance* at Trafalgar', *Scottish Historical Review*, XX (1922–3), pp. 116–21

Smith, Edward A., *Effects Based Operations, Applying Network Centric Warfare in Peace, Crisis and War*, Command and Control Research Program, US Department of Defense, November 2002

Solís, Ramón, *El Cádiz de las Cortes*, Madrid: Sílex, 2000

Sturges Jackson, T. (ed.), *Logs of the Great Sea Fights*, London: Navy Records Society, XVIX (1900)

Taillemite, Étienne, *L'Histoire ignorée de la marine française*, Paris: Perrin, 1988

Dictionnaire des marins français, 2nd edn, Paris: Tallandier, 2002

Taylor, A. H., 'The Battle of Trafalgar', *Mariner's Mirror*, 36 (October 1950), pp. 281–321

Terraine, John, *Trafalgar*, London: Sidgwick & Jackson, 1976

Thursfield, H. G. (ed.), *Five Naval Journals 1789–1817*, London: Navy Records Society, XCI (1951)

Tracy, Nicholas, *Nelson's Battles: the Art of Victory in the Age of Sail*, London: Chatham Publishing, 1996

(ed.), *The Naval Chronicle: the Contemporary Record of the Royal Navy at War. Volume III 1804–1806*, London: Chatham Publishing, 1999

Traill, H. D., *The Life of Sir John Franklin, R.N.*, London: John Murray, 1896

Tulard, Jean (ed.), *Dictionnaire Napoléon*, 2 vols, Paris: Fayard, 2nd edn, 1999

Tunstall, Brian and Nicholas Tracy, *Naval Warfare in the Age of Sail: the Evolution of Fighting Tactics 1650–1815*, London: Conway Maritime Press, 1990

Vargas Ponce, J., *Elogio histórico de D. Antonio Escaño*, (1816), ed. J. F. Guillén, Madrid: 1962

Vichot, Jacques, *Répetoire des navires de guerre Français*, Paris: Association des Amis des Musées de la Marine, 1967

Wardroper, John, *Kings, Lords and Wicked Libellers*, London: John Murray, 1973

Warner, Oliver, *Trafalgar*, London: Batsford, 1959
Nelson's Battles, London: Batsford, 1965
The Life and Letters of Vice-Admiral Lord Collingwood, London: Oxford University Press, 1969

Wheeler, Dennis, 'The Weather of the European Atlantic Seaboard during October 1805: an Exercise in Historical Climatology', *Climatic Change*, XLVIII (2001), pp. 361–85.

White, Colin, *The Nelson Companion*, London 1997
The Nelson Encyclopaedia, London: Chatham Publishing, 2002

Whitley, William T., *Artists and their Friends in England, 1700–1799*, 2 vols, London and Boston: Medici Society, 1928

Wyndham-Quin, Colonel, *Sir Charles Tyler, G.C.B. Admiral of the White*, London: Arthur L. Humphreys, 1912

Zimmerman, James Fulton, *The Impressment of American Seamen*, New York: Columbia University Press, 1925

de Zulueta, Julian, 'Trafalgar: the Spanish View', *Mariner's Mirror*, LXVI (1980), pp. 293–318

Index

Figures in italics indicate Plates; those in bold indicate Maps.

Index